MW01068424

EFFECTIVE AUGMENTATIVE AND ALTERNATIVE COMMUNICATION PRACTICES

Effective Augmentative and Alternative Communication Practices provides a user-friendly handbook for any school-based practitioner, whether you are a special education teacher, an augmentative and alternative communication (AAC) consultant, assistive technology consultant, speech-language pathologist, or occupational therapist. This highly practical book translates the AAC research into practice and explains the importance of the use of AAC strategies across settings. The handbook also provides school-based practitioners with resources to be used during the assessment, planning, and instructional process.

M. Alexandra Da Fonte is Assistant Professor of the Practice in the Department of Special Education at Vanderbilt University, USA.

Miriam C. Boesch is Associate Professor in Special Education at the University of North Texas, USA.

EFFECTIVE AUGMENTATIVE AND ALTERNATIVE COMMUNICATION PRACTICES

A Handbook for School-Based Practitioners

M. Alexandra Da Fonte and Miriam C. Boesch

Routledge
Taylor & Francis Group

NEW YORK AND LONDON

First published 2019
by Routledge
711 Third Avenue, New York, NY 10017

and by Routledge
2 Park Square, Milton Park, Abingdon, Oxon, OX14 4RN

Routledge is an imprint of the Taylor & Francis Group, an informa business

Library of Congress Cataloging-in-Publication Data
Names: Da Fonte, M. Alexandra, author. | Boesch, Miriam C., author.
Title: Effective augmentative and alternative communication practices : a handbook for school-based practitioners / M. Alexandra Da Fonte & Miriam C. Boesch.
Description: New York, NY : Routledge, 2018. | Includes bibliographical references and index.
Identifiers: LCCN 2018003726 (print) | LCCN 2018019978 (ebook) | ISBN 9781315200750 (e-book) | ISBN 9781138710177 (hbk) | ISBN 9781138710191 (pbk) | ISBN 9781315200750 (ebk)
Subjects: LCSH: Children with disabilities—Education—Handbooks, manuals, etc. | Communicative disorders in children—Handbooks, manuals, etc.
Classification: LCC LC4015 (ebook) | LCC LC4015 .D25 2018 (print) | DDC 371.9—dc23
LC record available at https://lccn.loc.gov/2018003726

ISBN: 978-1-138-71017-7 (hbk)
ISBN: 978-1-138-71019-1 (pbk)
ISBN: 978-1-315-20075-0 (ebk)

Typeset in Bembo
by Apex CoVantage, LLC

To all the students, families, special education teachers, and services providers who we have worked with throughout the years. This book was inspired by you, and to help those who are currently navigating the process to identify ways to support students with complex communication needs.

CONTENTS

ABOUT THE AUTHORS

Dr. M. Alexandra Da Fonte is an Assistant Professor of the Practice in the Department of Special Education at Vanderbilt University. Dr. Da Fonte has over 25 years of experience working with students with severe disabilities including students with complex communication needs. Her areas of interest include integrating augmentative and alternative communication interventions, working with students with severe disabilities, training pre-service special education teachers to work with students with complex communication needs, teacher preparation, and bridging research-to-practice. Dr. Da Fonte has conducted presentations and training in augmentative and alternative communication at local community partners, and at state, national, and international conferences.

Dr. Miriam C. Boesch is an Associate Professor in Special Education at the University of North Texas. Dr. Boesch has over 15 years of experience working with students with severe disabilities including students with complex communication needs. Her areas of interest include augmentative and alternative communication interventions for individuals with autism, evidence-based strategies for decreasing problem behavior, and pre- and in-service personnel preparation. Dr. Boesch has conducted presentation and trainings in the area of augmentative and alternative communication at the local, national, and international level.

ACKNOWLEDGEMENTS

We would like to acknowledge and offer our most sincere gratitude to all those who helped us accomplish this adventure. A very special thanks to: Gwen Diamond who supported us by providing feedback throughout the process and allowing us to photograph her instructional materials; our research team (in alphabetical order), Olivia Clark, Nathan Dunnavant, Katie McCann, Haley Neil, Shaylin Rawden, and Kayla Richardson who supported us in identifying evidence for each chapter; Christine Douthwaite and Margaret (Mimi) Sanders who allowed us to photograph and use their classrooms and instructional materials as examples.

Alexandra Da Fonte: I am thankful beyond words for my family's patience, support, and encouragement. Thank you both!
Miriam Boesch: I am extremely grateful to my husband Chris. Thank you for your unconditional love and support.

Illustrations

We would like to acknowledge and extend our gratitude to Nathan Dunnavant for his dedication and the creation of all the customized illustrations for this book.

UNIT 1

Students with Complex Communication Needs and the Instructional Team

1

UNDERSTANDING STUDENTS WITH COMPLEX COMMUNICATION NEEDS

Communication is a fundamental skill that is imperative to a child's development. While many children develop their communication, language, and speech in a seamless manner, research suggests that there is an increasing number of children who display *complex communication needs*, also known as CCN (Beukelman & Mirenda, 2013; Black, Vahratian, & Hoffman, 2015; Brady et al., 2016). Balandin (2002) defined CCN as a comprehensive term that encompasses a wide range of physical, sensory, and environmental needs that restricts or limits an individual's independence. This includes an individual's independence in communicating his or her wants and needs across *communication partners*. There are several factors that have been linked to the cause of CCN. These factors may include neurological disorders (e.g., cerebral palsy, traumatic brain injury, or autism), physical structures (e.g., cleft palate), genetic disorders (e.g., Down syndrome), and developmental disabilities (ASHA, 2017a).

Communication disorders are defined as an impairment in the ability to receive, send, process, and comprehend concepts or verbal, nonverbal, and graphic *symbol* systems (ASHA, 1993). Based on these definitions, it can be concluded that students with CCN have difficulties in any one or a combination of the aspects of communication, language, or speech (Jacob, Olisaemeka, & Edozie, 2015). Crichton (2013) explains that students with diverse communication needs may present difficulties, such as making eye contact, interacting with others, or engaging in or repairing a conversation when there is a communication breakdown. Needs in these components of communication can make conversations difficult for the student and the communication partner. Additionally, students who have difficulties with expressive or receptive language may have trouble using correct sentence structure, organizing a sequence of events, or finding the correct words to use (Binger & Light, 2008). These areas of need make it challenging for students to express their wants and needs and understand communicative interactions.

Over the past years, the prevalence of *students* with CCN continues to increase. The National Institute on Deafness and Other Communication Disorders (NIDOCD, 2015) states that nearly 17.9 million people have trouble using their voice. Furthermore, between 6 and 8 million people have some form of a language impairment (NIDOCD, 2015), and, approximately 4 million Americans are unable to meet their communication needs using natural speech (Beukelman & Mirenda, 2013). Moreover, in a national health survey conducted by the National Center for Health Statistics (2012), it was estimated that 55% of students with a communication disorder were receiving intervention services (Black et al., 2015). With the prevalence of communication disorders and services rising, it is expected that services will continue to increase in the classroom for students with CCN. Because of these increasing numbers, it has become even more important for educators to understand the various aspects of communication, how they develop, and how to better instruct and meet the needs of their students.

Understanding the Differences Between Communication, Language, and Speech

Communicative development begins early in a child's life. The early interactions begin with the sharing of affection and attention. It is at this time the child begins to see how his or her behaviors have an impact on the environment (Colonnesi, Stams, Koster, & Noom, 2010; Hoff, 2014). For special education teachers to be effective elicitors of communication in the classroom, it is important that they understand what communication is and how it develops. Da Fonte and Boesch (2016) emphasized that "when special education teachers can recognize, identify, and provide meaning to the form and function of students' communicative attempts, steps can be taken to increase or modify the student's communicative skills to be more effective in a myriad of settings" (p. 51). Communication, language, and speech are closely related, but there are distinct differences between them (see Figure 1.1 for an illustration of this relationship).

Communication

Communication is the process of sharing information among two or more people. The main goal of this process is for social interaction and involves four processes: (1) formulation, (2) transmission, (3) reception, and (4) comprehension (Shannon, 1948; Turnbull & Justice, 2016). *Formulation* is the act of pulling your thoughts together before sharing them with another person (e.g., feeling thirsty and wanting to request a drink of water). *Transmission* is the mechanics of relaying this thought to the person (e.g., saying "I'm thirsty. May I get a drink of water?"). This transmission process supports the last two processes of communication, which are *reception*, the receiving of the message (e.g., hearing the message that the person is thirsty and processing the information), and *comprehension*, the ability to interpret the information (e.g., understanding that the person has a need and is trying to meet it; Brady, Steeples, & Fleming, 2005). See Figure 1.2 for an illustration of this communicative process.

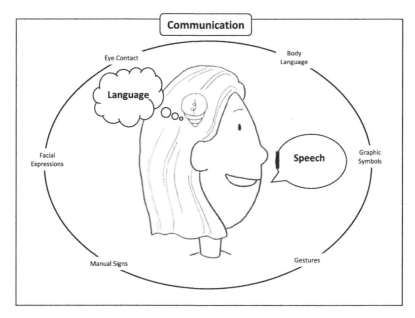

FIGURE 1.1   Relationship between communication, language, and speech.

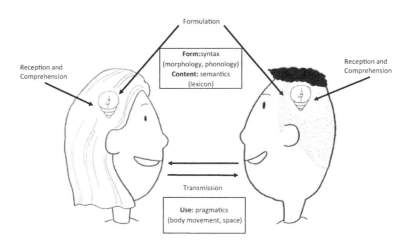

FIGURE 1.2   A model of the communication process.

The goal should be for all students to become independent communicators. Independent communicators have the ability to share their personal ideas using an array of different modalities that they choose for themselves (Beukelman & Mirenda, 2013; King & Fahsl, 2012). The National Academies of Sciences, Engineering, and Medicine (2016) consider language to be a tool that plays a significant role in the communication process. It is crucial to remember that language is not necessary to communicate, as people can also communicate using nonverbal communication. *Nonverbal communication* can be expressed in many forms such as body movement, facial expressions, eye contact, and space or distance as well as features of the environment (Ambady & Rosenthal, 1998; Patrichi, 2013; Wood, 2016).

Language

Language can be defined as a system of conventional spoken or written symbols used by people in a shared culture to communicate (ASHA, 2017c; O'Hare & Bremner, 2016). There are three domains inherent in language, which include (1) content, (2) form, and (3) use (Bloom & Lahey, 1978). De Leo, Lubas, and Mitchell (2012) explain the domains by noting that the *content* of language refers to the words the student uses (vocabulary) and the meaning behind them (*semantics*). That is, how individuals select appropriate vocabulary to compose their message (Landa, 2007). *Form* refers to the words, sentences (syntax), and sounds (morphology and phonology) a student uses to convey the content of their language. Lastly, *use* refers to how language meets the social context, expectations, and demands during interactions. This is also known as *pragmatics*, the social aspect of language. This entails the knowledge of when, where, and to whom the student is communicating. Pragmatics skills are evident in infants well before they develop other language skills (Grosse, Behne, Carpenter, & Tomasello, 2010). Considering all these components, it has been suggested that when a student demonstrates the appropriate use of semantics, syntax, and pragmatics, communication competence is achieved (Landa, 2007; O'Hare & Bremner, 2016).

Consider the example, "I'm thirsty. May I get a drink of water?" According to Landa (2007), the consideration of the words "thirsty," "drink," and "water" is referred to as semantics (content). Within semantics, these words were selected through a vocabulary system, called a *lexicon*, to convey meaning (Turnbull & Justice, 2016). When the student added the /y/ to thirst, they changed the meaning of the word, also referred to as *morphology*. The way the sounds were combined to form syllables and words (i.e., /m/ and /ay/ to create may) is called *phonology*. Morphology and phonology are used to structure sounds, syllables, and words into sentences (Landa, 2007). This structural piece is referred to as *syntax* (form). The facial expression, gestures, who the message was communicated to (communication partner), and eye contact used to relay the message "I'm thirsty. May I get a drink of water?" is called pragmatics (use). When considering pragmatics, you are determining if the student's language is functional and how it is used to meet his or her personal wants and needs, such as effectively conveying their need for water (Landa, 2007; O'Hare & Bremner, 2016).

Speech

Often speech and language are used interchangeably. However, they are not the same. *Speech* is a voluntary neuromuscular behavior and only one of the ways in which language can be expressed (O'Hare & Bremner, 2016; Turnbull & Justice, 2016). In our example, after the student was able to formulate the thought of needing water by using language, he or she was then able to transmit this thought to the listener using speech. While speech can be used to transmit language, students may have the ability to produce typical speech sounds, but have difficulty with language and its various aspects (National Academies of Sciences, Engineering, and Medicine, 2016).

It is important to note that communication is not bound by language and speech. Communication can take place without these aspects. But, language and speech may allow the student to communicate in a more efficient and successful manner in the absence of other modalities (Martin, Onishi, & Vouloumanos, 2011; Turnbull & Justice, 2016).

Typical Communication Development

In order to better support the communication development of students with CCN, it is essential to first understand what typical communication looks like. This knowledge will help determine where the students are in their communication development (assessment), and how you will plan to enhance their communication skills (instruction/intervention). Table 1.1 provides detailed information on the typical stages of communication development.

Communication skills are often divided into two areas, receptive communication skills and expressive communication skills. *Receptive communication* involves the understanding or comprehension of messages and words that are expressed, while *expressive communication* involves the words and messages, both verbal and nonverbal, that people communicate to listeners (Lloyd, Fuller, & Arvidson, 1997). Figure 1.3 provides examples of specific receptive and expressive communication skills.

Receptive Communication Skills

Receptive language skills are closely linked to cognitive development (Owens, 2012). These skills begin to develop at birth and continue to develop throughout life. Receptive language skills are essential in demonstrating communicative competence (ASHA, 2017b; Wisconsin Child Welfare Training System [WCWTS], 2017). According to ASHA (2017b), early in the development of receptive language skills (birth to 5 months of age), children begin to recognize familiar voices, turn their heads to voices, and react to environmental sounds. During the second stage (6 to 11 months of age) children begin to understand the meaning of "no," anticipate events, and understand some routine phrases (e.g., "time to eat"). In stage three (12–24 months of age), children begin to recognize the name of common activities, items, and people, and also begin to understand routine verbs (e.g., "eat"). Later in this stage, children begin to respond to simple requests, follow

TABLE 1.1 Typical Communication Development

Age	Phonology	Syntax and Morphology	Semantics	Pragmatics
Birth	Recognizes different languages in different rhythmic classes (e.g. English vs. Japanese). Makes reflexive sounds.	–	Directs attention to where a sound is being produced and responds to a loud sound by startling.	Starts paying attention to social partners.
2 mo.	Recognizes native language vs. nonnative languages. Makes cooing sounds.	–	Investigates and holds (perhaps with the addition of mouthing) objects for a short period of time.	Will look at people briefly. Can recognize unfamiliar situations and people.
4 mo.	Recognizes different languages in the same rhythmic classes (e.g., English vs. Dutch). Makes vowel sounds, squeals, growls.	–	Identifies the difference between actions that are performed by accident and on purpose.	Looks at faces and will stare. Can understand when own name is said.
6 mo.	Segments words from fluent speech.	–	Understands the meaning of the word "no." Makes efforts to mimic gestures.	Participates in joint attention.
8 mo.	Differentiates native from nonnative stress patterns.	–	Searches in the right place for objects that are out of the individual's range of sight and looks for objects that are partly concealed.	Starts using intentional communication. Has language function pre-verbally in the form of attention seeking, requesting, greeting, transferring, protesting or rejecting, responding or acknowledging, and informing.

Age				
10–12 mo.	Comprehends analytical actions as ways to reach a desired goal.	–	Creates first word. Comprehends five to ten words. Comprehends analytical actions as ways to reach a desired goal.	Will use imperative pointing.
12 mo.	With the exception of some words, most speech is indecipherable.	Half of the verbal pronunciations made are composed of single nouns.	First word spoken.	Can understand people's motive for actions.
16 mo.	A quarter of all words are pronounced clearly.	33% of all spoken words are composed of single nouns. Negation (no) is used.	Utilizes anywhere between 3 and 20 words.	Will take turns while speaking.
20 mo.	Spoken words are processed in increments.	Grammatical morphemes (present progressive "is" followed by a word + -ing) start to be used.	Can say around 50 words. Can use a few adjectives and verbs.	Multiple gestures will be used in combination. Gestures and words will be used together to form meaning.
24 mo.	Questions are asked with ascending intonation. Roughly 65% of total words spoken are pronounced clearly.	Two-word combinations, prepositions "on" and "in," possessive and plural morphemes, and irregular past tense verbs are all used.	Can say around 200 words. Can understand around 500 words.	Will utilize language functions that are imaginative, heuristic, and informative.
28 mo.	Pronounces roughly 70% of all words clearly.	Proficient in the use of present progressive morpheme -ing.	Listens for sentence structure when hearing words for the first time.	Can have brief conversations. Can start talking about a new topic or change the subject. Asks for clarification and clarifies while speaking to others.
32–36 mo.	80% of all words are pronounced clearly.	Uses a single verb about a quarter of the time while speaking. Utilizes a few contractions.	Can say about 500 words. Can understand about 900 words.	

(Continued)

TABLE 1.1 (Continued)

Age	Phonology	Syntax and Morphology	Semantics	Pragmatics
36 mo.	Starts to form shallow phonological awareness abilities.	Utilizes compound sentences with the word "and." Uses approximately 4 or 5 words per sentence.	Utilizes pronouns like "they," "them," and "us."	Conversations become longer in length.
40 mo.	Articulatory skills are continuing to be perfected.	Utilizes adverbs often. Utilizes pronouns regularly.	Can say about 1,000 to 1,500 words. Can understand between 1,500 and 2,000 words Comprehends a few relational terms like "hard–soft."	Starts fixing errors in conversation.
44 mo.	Can say most consonants.	Uses contractions, past tense, and articles appropriately.	Begins to narrow the possible meanings of new words.	Comprehends indirect requests that use pointing.
48 mo.	Reduces phonological processes (e.g., weak-syllable deletion, cluster reduction).	Makes 4–7 word sentences.	Uses reflexive pronouns such as *himself, herself, itself.*	Constructs true narratives.
52 mo.	Very intelligible.	Uses irregular plurals correctly.	Knows how to use "what do, what does, what did" questions.	Begins to make their own indirect request.
56–60 mo.	Knows letters in name. Only has difficulty with sounds that were developed later.	Makes 5–8 word sentences.	Regularly speaks 1,500–2,000 words. Understands 2,500–2,800 words. Uses *this, that, here, there.*	Can begin sequencing events in a narrative.
5–6 yr.	Uses plurals correctly.	Uses morphology to infer meaning of new words.	Begins to learn to read via decoding.	Can use repetition to repair conversations.
7–8 yr.	Can say all American sounds.	Uses noun phrases, adverbs, and conjunctions.	Uses multiword definitions. Improves decoding skills and begins reading unfamiliar words.	Comprehends hints. Makes narratives with all components.

Age				
9–10 yr.	–	Understands verbs like believe and promise.	Starts to read for information.	Remains on topic during conversation even with topic turns.
11–12 yr.	Expresses intent with stress and emphasis.	Comprehends *if* and *though*.	Can make abstract definitions. Reads on an approximate adult level.	Can use and understand abstract topics during conversation.
13–15 yr.	–	Comprehends the use of clausal embedding.	Considers multiple points of view when reading.	Comprehends jokes with ambiguity.
16–18 yr.	Understands vowel-shifting rules.	Uses more words per unit in written language than in spoken language.	Understands around 60,000 word meanings.	Understands the use of sarcasm, double meaning words, metaphors, and multiple perspectives.

Adapted from "*Language Development from Theory to Practice*" (3rd ed.), by K. L., Turnbull and L. M., Justice, 2017, Upper Saddle River, NJ: Pearson, pp. 133–134, 164–165, 202–203, 237–238.

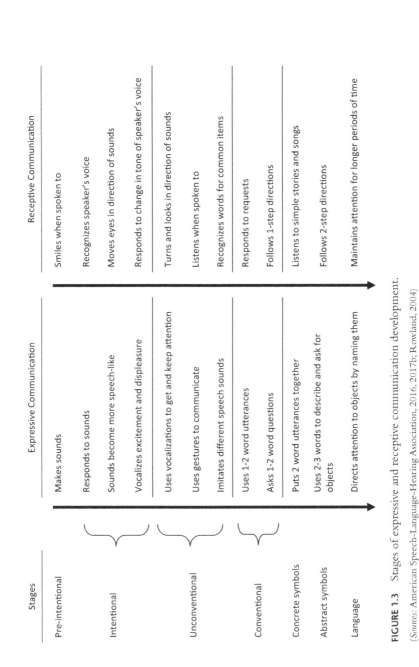

Stages	Expressive Communication	Receptive Communication
Pre-intentional	Makes sounds	Smiles when spoken to
Intentional	Responds to sounds	Recognizes speaker's voice
	Sounds become more speech-like	Moves eyes in direction of sounds
	Vocalizes excitement and displeasure	Responds to change in tone of speaker's voice
Unconventional	Uses vocalizations to get and keep attention	Turns and looks in direction of sounds
	Uses gestures to communicate	Listens when spoken to
	Imitates different speech sounds	Recognizes words for common items
Conventional	Uses 1-2 word utterances	Responds to requests
	Asks 1-2 word questions	Follows 1-step directions
Concrete symbols	Puts 2 word utterances together	Listens to simple stories and songs
Abstract symbols	Uses 2-3 words to describe and ask for objects	Follows 2-step directions
Language	Directs attention to objects by naming them	Maintains attention for longer periods of time

FIGURE 1.3 Stages of expressive and receptive communication development.

(*Sources*: American Speech-Language-Hearing Association, 2016, 2017b; Rowland, 2004)

one-step directions (with and without a gesture), and begin to identify pictures in books, and body parts. By around 24 months of age, children typically are able to understand approximately 300 words, can listen to stories, begin to respond to "wh" questions, and can follow two-step directions. These receptive language skills will continue to develop throughout life as the child's vocabulary and communicative experiences continue to increase.

Expressive Communication Skills

From birth to around 8 months of life, infants who are typically developing are considered *pre-intentional communicators*. Until this point, they do not predict outcomes of their behavior. Therefore, they cannot share the intent of their communication (Adeli, Rahimian, & Tabrizi, 2016; Owens, 2012). This does not mean that infants do not communicate from birth to 8 months, but rather that their communication is characterized by innateness (Bates, Camaioni, & Volterra, 1975). *Intentional communication* (from 9 months of age on) has the motive of affecting a listener (Carter & Iacano, 2002). During the intentional communicative phase, children begin using gestures partnered with eye contact, as well as specific vocalizations (Owens, 2012). These gestures may include showing or giving items to listeners and pointing (Colonnesi et al., 2010). Bates and colleagues (1975) explained that, during this stage, children begin to recognize adults as agents and that their own signals can affect the agent. This suggests that a child begins to understand that specific behaviors influence the world around them. In essence, they begin to have an understanding of cause and effect and begin to develop more sophisticated communicative interactions (e.g., words, phrases, sentences).

Differences in the Communicative Development of Students with Complex Communication Needs

These phases of communication, speech, and language development are true for all communicators, regardless of what point in a person's life they develop (WCWTS, 2017). However, it is important to remember that a person with CCN will most likely develop these skills at a different chronological age than their typically developing peers (Simion, 2014). Light (1997) suggests that, for students with CCN, the process of learning language is, "a difficult one that requires concerted intervention to facilitate" (Light, 1997, p. 158). Students with CCN can have deficits or needs in multiple areas of communication. The New York State Department of Health Information (2013) suggested that students with CCN may need intervention in the following areas: articulation, fluency, language comprehension, language production, morphology, phonology, pragmatics, semantics, syntax, and voice. The goal for students with CCN is to make the move from pre-intentional to *intentional communicators* with appropriate support, while keeping in mind that these stages may just be on a different timeline from their peers who are typically developing (Simion, 2014).

A unique characteristic of students with CCN is that they may or may not have deficits in one or more areas beyond their communication skills. Some potential areas of difficulties can include gross motor, fine motor, sensory integration, or cognitive development, among others. Basil (1992) suggested that students with CCN also often are passive in their communication attempts which can lead to the phenomenon of learned helplessness. She explains that a consequence of learned helplessness may be a lack of motivation to communicate goal-oriented responses. Consequently, understanding the comprehensive needs of students with CCN is critical in order to meet their unique needs in the school setting.

Importance of Understanding Complex Communication Needs in School Settings

At some point in their career, teachers are likely to serve a student with a communication disorder, more specifically, a student with CCN. The goal, as teachers, should be to help students become independent in order for them to lead a productive and enjoyable life. Communication is key in having a successful school experience and it will play an important role in the development of various life and academic skills, including literacy skills. As children learn to read, they also have the opportunity to think about their use of language. Murphy, Justice, Connell, Pentimonti, and Kaderavek (2016) suggested that oral language plays a pivotal role in the development of writing and reading skills, and that writing and reading skills play a pivotal role in language development. See Figure 1.4 for a representation of this relationship. See Chapters 4 and 11 for more information on assessment and instruction of literacy skills.

Not only is communication a skill that is important at school, but it is also a skill that affects students well beyond their school experiences and throughout their lives. Effective communication is a key piece in developing self-determination. Carter, Lane, Pierson, and Stang (2008) explained that the development of effective communication skills is a key factor in students with disabilities obtaining important post-school outcomes (e.g., independent living, secondary education, and employment). Carter and colleagues (2008) also explain that self-determination is a key factor in the post–school success of students with any type of disability, but this is especially true for students with CCN. They define *self-determination* as "the capacity to steer one's own life in personally meaningful ways and valued directions" (Carter et al., 2008; see Chapter 2). If a teacher's, school's, or district's main goal is to prepare students for life after high school, the first goal should be to teach them to communicate effectively. Helping them achieve high level communication skills will support the development of self-determination skills and avoid learned helplessness. Communication is not just a set of skills, but a fundamental human right. The International Communication Project (2014) states that it is "the most fundamental of human capacities." Regardless of level

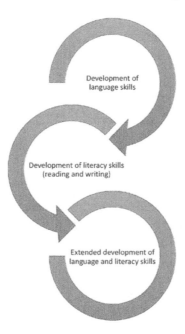

FIGURE 1.4 Relationship between language and reading and writing abilities.

Adapted from "*Language Development from Theory to Practice*" (3rd ed.), by K. L., Turnbull and L. M. Justice, 2017, Upper Saddle River, NJ: Pearson, pp. 229–230.

of speech or disability, all people have the right to make choices and changes to their environment through communication. The *Communication Bill of Rights*, created by the National Joint Committee for the Communication Needs of Persons with Severe Disabilities (1992, 2016), outlines the rights of all students to develop specific appropriate communication skills with the hope that the adoption by all practitioners would create advancements for individuals with communication needs. This Bill of Rights consists of 15 specific rights that all individuals should be afforded in personal, educational, and intervention settings (see Communication Bill of Rights on Figure 1.5). Target areas within the Communication Bill of Rights are addressed that identify potential barriers, such as socialization, learning and sharing knowledge, choice making, judicial and medical access, and respect. In 2016, Brady and colleagues updated the Communication Bill of Rights to highlight the importance of assessment, intervention, community access, and socialization (see Chapter 4 for detailed information on how to evaluate access barriers, and Chapter 7 for information on how to evaluate opportunity barriers). In understanding students with CCN and how to best serve these students' needs, teachers can work together to help students become independent communicators, enabling them to lead high quality and productive lives.

Communication Bill of Rights

FIGURE 1.5 Communication Bill of Rights.

(*Sources:* Brady et al., 2016; Scope's Communication and Inclusion Resource Centre, 2016)

Key Points of Chapter 1

- Communication is a fundamental skill in the development of all children.
- Communication, language, and speech are closely related. However, there are distinct differences between them.
- Students with CCN may have difficulties with one or more aspects of communication, speech, or language.
- It is important to understand how communication typically develops in order to have a better understanding of how development is different for students with CCN.

Understanding

- Understanding CCN is important in school settings because it affects students in day-to-day school activities and in their post-school outcomes.
- When teaching communication skills, the goal should be for students to become independent communicators.

References

Adeli, H., Rahimian, P., & Tabrizi, N. (2016). Communicating with people with profound intellectual disabilities using brain computer interface. *The Journal on Technology and Persons with Disabilities, 4*, 133–144.

Ambady, N., & Rosenthal, R. (1998). Nonverbal communication. In *Encyclopedia of mental health* (Vol. 2, pp. 775–782). San Diego, CA: Academic Press.

American Speech-Language-Hearing Association. (1993). *Definitions of communication disorders and variations.* Retrieved from www.asha.org/policy/RP1993-00208/

American Speech-Language-Hearing Association. (2016). *Typical speech and language development.* Retrieved from www.asha.org/public/speech/development/

American Speech-Language-Hearing Association. (2017a). *Augmentative and alternative communication: Key issues.* Retrieved from www.asha.org/PRPSpecificTopic.aspx?folderid= 8589942773&section=Key_Issues

American Speech-Language-Hearing Association. (2017b). *How does your child hear and talk?* Retrieved March 30, 2017, from www.asha.org/public/speech/development/chart/

American Speech-Language-Hearing Association. (2017c). *What is language? what is speech?* Retrieved August 24, 2017, from www.asha.org/public/speech/development/language_speech/

Balandin, S. (2002). Message from the president. *The ISAAC Bulletin, 67*, 2.

Basil, C. (1992). Social interaction and learned helplessness in severely disabled children. *Augmentative and Alternative Communication, 8*, 188–199. doi:10.1080/07434619212331276183

Bates, E., Camaioni, L., & Volterra, V. (1975). The acquisition of performatives prior to speech. *Merrill-Palmer Quarterly of Behavior and Development, 21*, 205–226. doi:10.1177/002383098302600201

Beukelman, D. R., & Mirenda, P. (2013). *Augmentative and alternative communication: Supporting children and adults with complex communication needs* (4th ed.). Baltimore, MD: Paul H. Brookes.

Binger, C., & Light, J. (2008). The morphology and syntax of individuals who use AAC: Research review and implications for effective practice. *Augmentative and Alternative Communication, 24*, 123–138. doi:10.1080/07434610701830587

Black, L. I., Vahratian, A., & Hoffman, H. J. (2015). *Communication disorders and use of intervention services among children aged 3–17 years: United States, 2012.* (NCHS Data Brief, no. 205). Hyattsville, MD: National Center for Health Statistics. Retrieved from www.cdc.gov/nchs/products/databriefs/db205.htm

Bloom, L., & Lahey, M. (1978). *Language development and language disorders.* New York, NY: Wiley-Blackwell.

Brady, N. C., Bruce, S., Goldman, A., Erickson, K., Mineo, B., Ogletree, B. T., . . . Wilkinson, K. (2016). Communication services and supports for individuals with severe disabilities: Guidance for assessment and intervention. *American Journal of Intellectual and Developmental Disabilities, 121*, 121–138. doi:10.1352/1944-7558-121.2.121

Brady, N. C., Steeples, T., & Fleming, K. (2005). Effects of prelinguistic communication levels on initiation and repair of communication in children with disabilities. *Journal of Speech, Language, and Hearing Research, 48*, 1098–1113. doi:10.1044/1092-4388(2005/076).

Carter, E. W., Lane, K. L., Pierson, M. R., & Stang, K. K. (2008). Promoting self-determination for transition-age youth: Views of high school general and special educators. *Exceptional Children, 75*, 55–70. doi:10.1177/001440290807500103

Carter, M., & Iacono, T. (2002). Professional judgments of the intentionality of communicative acts. *Augmentative and Alternative Communication, 18*, 177–191. doi:10.1080/07434610212331281261

Colonnesi, C., Stams, G. J., Koster, I., & Noom, M. J. (2010). The relation between pointing and language development: A meta-analysis. *Developmental Review, 30*, 352–366. doi:10.1016/j.dr.2010.10.001

Crichton, S. (2013). Understanding, identifying and supporting speech, language and communication needs in children. *Community Practitioner, 86*, 44–47.

Da Fonte, A. M., & Boesch, M. C. (2016). Recommended augmentative and alternative communication competencies for special education teachers. *Journal of International Special Needs Education, 19*, 47–58. doi:10.9782/2159-4341-19.2.47

De Leo, G., Lubas, M., & Mitchell, J. R. (2012, August). Lack of communication even when using alternative and augmentative communication devices: Are we forgetting about the three components of language. [Editorial]. *Autism, 2*, 1–2. doi:10.4172/2165-7890.1000e109

Grosse, G., Behne, T., Carpenter, M., & Tomasello, M. (2010). Infants communicate in order to be understood. *Developmental Psychology, 46*, 1710–1722. doi:10.1037/a0020727

Hoff, E. (2014). *Language development* (5th ed.). Belmont, CA: Wadsworth/Cengage Learning.

International Communication Project. (2014). *The universal declaration of communication rights*. Retrieved from www.internationalcommunicationproject.com

Jacob, U. S., Olisaemeka, A. N., & Edozie, I. S. (2015). Developmental and communication disorders in children with intellectual disability: The place early intervention for effective inclusion. *Journal of Education and Practice, 6*, 42–46.

King, A. M., & Fahsl, A. J. (2012). Supporting social competence in children who use augmentative and alternative communication. *TEACHING Exceptional Children, 45*, 42–49. doi:10.1177/004005991204500106

Landa, R. (2007). Early communication development and intervention for children with autism. *Mental Retardation and Developmental Disabilities Research Reviews, 13*, 16–25. doi:10.1002/mrdd

Light, J. (1997). "Let's go star fishing": Reflections on the contexts of language learning for children who use aided AAC. *Augmentative and Alternative Communication, 13*, 158–171. doi:10.1080/07434619712331277978

Lloyd, L. L., Fuller, D. R., & Arvidson, H. H. (1997). *Augmentative and alternative communication: A handbook of principles and practices*. Needham Heights, MA: Allyn and Bacon.

Martin, A., Onishi, K. H., & Vouloumanos, A. (2011). Understanding the abstract role of speech in communication at 12 months. *Cognition, 123*, 50–60. doi:10.1016/j.cognition.2011.12.003

Murphy, K. A., Justice, L. M., O'Connell, A. A., Pentimonti, J. M., & Kaderavek, J. N. (2016). Understanding risk for reading difficulties in children with language impairment. *Journal of Speech, Language, & Hearing Research, 59*, 1436–1447. doi:10.1044/2016_jslhr-l-15-0110

National Academies of Sciences, Engineering, and Medicine. (2016). *Speech and language disorders in children: Implications for the social security administration's supplemental security income program.* Washington, DC: The National Academies Press. doi:10.17226/21872

National Institute on Deafness and Other Communication Disorders. (2015). *What is voice? What is speech? What is language?* Retrieved from www.nidcd.nih.gov/health/what-is-voice-speech-language

New York State Department of Health, Early Intervention Program. (2013). *Clinical practice guidelines, communication disorders.* Retrieved from www.health.ny.gov/publications/4219.pdf

O'Hare, A., & Bremner, L. (2016). Management of developmental speech and language disorders: Part 1. *Archives of Disease in Childhood, 101,* 272–277. doi:10.1136/archdischild-2014-307394

Owens, R. E. (2012). *Language development an introduction* (8th ed.). Upper Saddle River, NJ: Pearson.

Patrichi, A. (2013). The process of communication in the classroom. *The International Journal of Communication Research, 3,* 342–347.

Rowland, C. (2004). *Communication matrix.* Portland, OR: Oregon Health and Sciences University.

Shannon, C. E. (1948). A mathematical theory of communication. *The Bell System Technical Journal, 27,* 379–423, 623–656. doi:10.1109/9780470544242.ch1

Simion, E. (2014). Augmentative and alternative communication: Support for people with severe speech disorders. *Procedia: Social and Behavioral Sciences, 128,* 77–81. doi:10.1016/j.sbspro.2014.03.121

Turnbull, K. P., & Justice, L. M. (2016). *Language development from theory to practice* (3rd ed.). Upper Saddle River, NJ: Pearson.

Wisconsin Child Welfare Training System. (2017). *Developmental stages of infants and children.* Retrieved from https://wcwpds.wisc.edu/childdevelopment/resources/CompleteDevelopmentDetails.pdf

Wood, J. T. (2016). *Interpersonal communication: Everyday encounters* (8th ed.). Boston, MA: Cengage Learning.

2
UNDERSTANDING COMMUNICATION COMPETENCIES

Communication competence is defined as the ability to comprehend spoken language, follow social rules, and repair communication breakdowns that may occur during a communicative interaction (Chung & Douglas, 2014; Light, 1989). In order to communicate in an effective and socially appropriate manner, individuals must develop communication competence (Trenholm & Jensen, 2008). In essence, a person who has communicative competence understands and demonstrates that he or she knows what, how, when, where, and with whom to communicate in order to meet all purposes of communication.

Students are classified into non-symbolic or symbolic communicators. Non-symbolic communicators are pre-intentional, suggesting that their behaviors are related to the student's awareness of his or her environment, but are initiated without symbolic intent (Adeli, Rahimian, & Tabrizi, 2016; Bates, Camaioni, & Volterra, 1975). Students communicating at the non-symbolic level may laugh, cry, or use gestures, but in a non-referential way (Singh, Iacono, & Gray, 2014). Given that there is no linguistic code attached to the message, *non-symbolic communication* is left up to interpretation by the communication partner (Ogletree, Bruce, Finch, Fahey, & McClean, 2011; Singh et al., 2014). As a result, communication partners often have to guess the intended meaning of the non-symbolic communicator's message (e.g., a student's crying is interpreted as communicating discomfort).

A symbolic communicator refers to a student who understands that communication through intentional symbol exchanges can have an impact on the environment (McLean & Snyder-McLean, 1987). That is, symbolic communicators understand cause and effect (i.e., a change in the environment is caused by an action which they initiated; Light & Drager, 2007) and understand that symbols can represent abstract as well as concrete items and ideas (McLean & Snyder-McLean, 1987). Students communicating at the symbolic level use symbols to represent referents (i.e., ideas or items) both in the presence and in the absence of those referents (Bates et al., 1975). Communication partners can understand the meaning of the message being communicated.

While children who are typically developing acquire language without much difficulty, children with complex communication needs (CCN) may have deficits in each structure of language as well as in specific characteristics innate to communication interactions. The development of communication competence for individuals with CCN is a critical part of attaining a productive and enjoyable life where goals can be achieved in their personal, vocational, and social lives (Calculator, 2009). For students with CCN, communicative independence can be achieved by focusing on the four purposes of communication outlined by Light (1988): (1) communication of needs and wants, (2) information transfer, (3) social closeness, and (4) social etiquette. Research indicates the communication competence of individuals with CCN can be developed through the use of augmentative and alternative communication (AAC) interventions (Light & McNaughton, 2015; Millar, Light, & Schlosser, 2006). The American Speech-Language-Hearing Association (ASHA, 2005), Special Interest Group 12, describes AAC as a specific area of research and practice focused on alleviating the communicative challenges of individuals with severe speech and language impairments. Any mode of communication outside of oral speech falls under the umbrella of AAC. AAC is used to either supplement or replace oral speech in order for the individual to communicate functionally and participate in daily life. AAC includes *unaided communication systems* in which the individual relies on his or her body to convey messages (e.g., facial expressions, gestures, manual signs; refer to Chapter 5 for further information about unaided communication systems), as well as *aided communication systems* (refer to Chapter 6 for further information about aided communication systems) that require specific tools or equipment (e.g., picture symbols, speech-generating devices, written language).

Communication Competencies in Users of Augmentative and Alternative Communication

Historically, the communication competence for individuals who use AAC systems are evaluated using the same definition of communication competence for speech users. However, users of AAC face unique challenges in meeting their communication needs. To better address these challenges, in 1989, Light began to define communication competence specifically for users of AAC (Light, 1989). Light defined communicative competence for people with CCN who require AAC, "as a dynamic, interpersonal construct based on functionality of communication, adequacy of communication, and sufficiency of knowledge, judgement, and skill" (Light & McNaughton, 2014, p. 2). Light (1989) further defined communicative competence to include sufficient knowledge, judgment, and skill in four domains: (1) linguistic, (2) operational, (3) social, and (4) strategic. Figures 2.1 and 2.2 visually depict the skills in each of these competencies.

FIGURE 2.1 A representation of linguistic and operational competence.

(*Sources:* Light, 1989; Light & McNaughton, 2014; MacDonald & Rendle, 1998)

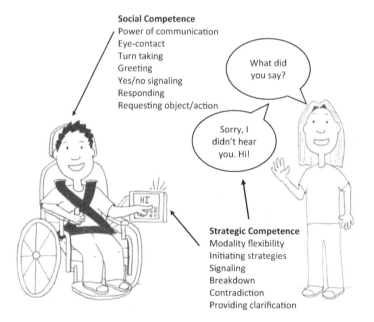

FIGURE 2.2 A representation of social and strategic competence.

(*Sources:* Light, 1989; Light & McNaughton, 2014; MacDonald & Rendle, 1998)

Linguistic Competence

To develop *linguistic competence*, an AAC user must understand the language spoken in their family and community (receptive skills), as well as the language code of their AAC system (expressive skills). Sufficient knowledge, judgment, and skill of the language code of an AAC system requires users to understand what vocabulary the symbols in their system represent (semantics) as well as how to use the *vocabulary* to express their wants, needs, and ideas (syntax; Frankoff & Hatfield, 2011; Light, 1989; Light & McNaughton, 2014).

For users of AAC, the way they receive spoken and written language and express language via aided and unaided AAC systems is very different (Light & McNaughton, 2014). This difference poses a challenge given the user's need to have sufficient knowledge and understanding of both the spoken language and the meaning of the AAC system symbols. To further compound the issue, for some AAC users, the language spoken at home may be different from the language spoken in the community (Light, 1989; Soto & Yu, 2014). Furthermore, the development of linguistic competence for users of AAC is delayed because there is a lack of communication models in the natural environment. This is starkly different from their peers who continuously receive models for the spoken language in their environment. Unfortunately, many who use AAC are not exposed to learning through modeling as they may never have an opportunity to interact with others who use similar AAC systems (Ballin, Balandin, Stancliffe & Togher, 2011). Thus, to develop linguistic competence, it is critical for others to model how to use the AAC system in the person's language in naturalistic settings (Ballin et al., 2011; Beukelman & Mirenda, 2013; Light & McNaughton, 2014). Overall, linguistic competence includes skills in language development and symbolic understanding, both receptive and expressive.

Operational Competence

Operational competence is achieved through sufficient knowledge and technical skills needed to use or operate all modes of a user's AAC system effectively. This includes forming the body movements needed for an unaided system as well as a reliable method for accessing the aided system (Chung & Douglas, 2014; Frankoff & Hatfield, 2011; Light, 1989; Light & McNaughton, 2014). It is important for users to develop operational competence as quickly as possible when beginning AAC intervention (Beukelman & Mirenda, 2013).

Operational competence also involves navigating the system, turning the system on and off, and modifying the language in the system as needed. The user of AAC should be responsible for these operational skills when possible. However, facilitators such as educators, therapists, paraeducators, and caregivers who support the user in the language development should also be knowledgeable in this area (Beukelman & Mirenda, 2013; Chung & Douglas, 2014). The student will need to learn how to access the AAC system. This includes navigating within and between folders of a speech-generating device or communication book. If using an unaided system such as manual signing, operational competence is demonstrated by correctly manipulating the fingers and hands to form identifiable manual signs. Overall, operational competence is comprised of the technical skills necessary to operate the AAC system.

Social Competence

Having *social competence* is evident when an individual is able to use his or her AAC system by having knowledge of when, where, how and to whom he or she should communicate (Frankoff & Hatfield, 2011; Light, 1989; Light & McNaughton, 2014). This also involves the ability to follow pragmatic rules in social environments (Chung & Douglas, 2014). According to Beukelman and Mirenda (2013), social competence "refers to skills of social interaction such as initiating, maintaining, developing, and terminating communication interactions" (p. 12). These discourse strategies, along with interaction functions such as information transfer, and communication of wants and needs are important for users of AAC to develop their social competence (Light, 1989).

Light (1988) also suggested that socio-relational skills play a key role in the development of social competence. These skills include the desire to communicate, responding to communication partners and putting them at ease, having a positive self-image, and actively participating in conversation. Other skills that lead to social competence include the appropriate use of eye contact, greetings, and turn-taking. These socio-relational skills are important for developing interpersonal relationships (Light & McNaughton, 2014). Social competence enables individuals to actively participate in their *environment* and avoid social isolation and negative self-perceptions (King & Fahsl, 2012). Many students with CCN have disabilities that are characterized by deficits in social interactions, such as autism spectrum disorders (Landa, 2007), making social competence both challenging and critical.

Strategic Competence

Achievement of linguistic, social, and operational competence requires the ability to overcome limitations that are present for users of AAC due to their disabilities, environmental barriers, and restrictions of their AAC systems (Beukelman & Mirenda, 2013; Light & McNaughton, 2014). When the user is able to cope with and navigate around these limitations, the user has demonstrated *strategic competence* (Frankoff & Hatfield, 2011; Light, 1989; Light & McNaughton, 2014).

Regardless of which AAC system is used, it is important to note that limitations will exist. Communication breakdowns can happen to anyone regardless if someone is using an AAC system or simply communicating via traditional speech. However, for a user of AAC, the limitations could be greater because of the AAC system itself. For example, if a communication partner is not providing sufficient response time during a conversation, the user could send a message asking the communication partner to slow down and wait for a response. In this scenario, the student may have difficulty navigating the system at an appropriate speed or operating it correctly. Thus, without having strategic competence, the student would not know how to correct the problem. Therefore, adequate strategic competence enables the student to use an alternative mode of communication to indicate that his or her device is not operating correctly and needs help resolving the problem. This scenario shows that when there is a lack of operational competence, it is important for the student to have adequate strategic competence in order to communicate his or her lack of skills. In other words, strategic competence includes the ability to use multiple modes of communication and the ability to provide clarification when necessary. The adaptive strategies used to overcome limitations may not always be required, but they may be temporarily necessary until the student acquires the linguistic, operational, or social competence needed to avoid the limitation all together (Light, 1989).

Identifying the Skills for Independent Communicators

Communication is a fundamental right of all people. Thus, the National Joint Committee for the Communication Needs of Persons with Severe Disabilities (NJC) created the Communication Bill of Rights (Brady et al., 2016). The goal was to highlight the importance of people's right to communicate so that practitioners, including teachers, could improve the instruction of individuals with CCN. When analyzing the importance of communication as a right, it has large implications in the school setting because communication skills are required to actively engage in school activities (Calculator & Black, 2009). The Communication Bill of Rights consists of 15 Rights that were developed to highlight the rights of all people including individuals with severe disabilities. While Light's Communication Competencies are specific to individuals who use AAC, there is an inherent link between these competencies and the Communication Bill of Rights given that many individuals with severe disabilities are also users of AAC. With this perspective, each right can be categorized into one or more of Light's four communication competencies (i.e., linguistic, operational, social, and strategic).

Table 2.1 illustrates the link between the Light's Communication Competencies and the Communication Bill of Rights. Approximately half of the Rights (i.e., 1–4, 6, 7, and 15) interconnect with all four communication competencies, while the other Rights intersect with at least one. This is evident that, when students are trained to communicate with their AAC system using Light's communication competencies as a guide, the students' rights to communicate are also being honored.

Having linguistic competency is essential as it allows students to understand the language used by their community and their AAC systems. Given its importance,

TABLE 2.1 Link Between the Communication Competencies and the Communication Bill of Rights

Rights of the Communication Bill of Rights		Communication Competencies			
		Linguistic	Operational	Social	Strategic
1	Interact socially, maintain social closeness and build relationships	☑	☑	☑	☑
2	Request desired objects, actions, events, and people	☑	☑	☑	☑
3	Refuse or reject undesired objects, actions, events, or choices	☑	☑	☑	☑
4	Express personal preferences and feelings	☑	☑	☑	☑
5	Make choices from meaningful alternatives	☑	☑		☑
6	Make comments and share opinions	☑	☑	☑	☑
7	Ask for and give information, including information about changes in routine and environment	☑	☑	☑	☑
8	Be informed about people and events in one's life	☑		☑	
9	Access interventions and supports that improve communication	☑	☑		
10	Have communication acts acknowledge and responded to even when the desired outcome cannot be realized			☑	
11	Have access to functioning AAC and other AT services and devises at all times		☑		
12	Access environmental contexts, interactions, and opportunities that promote participation as full communication partners with other people, including peers			☑	☑
13	Be treated with dignity and addressed with respect and courtesy			☑	
14	Be addressed directly and not be spoken for or talked about in the third person while present			☑	
15	Have clear, meaningful, and culturally and linguistically appropriate communication	☑	☑	☑	☑

Note. AAC = augmentative and alternative communication; AT = assistive technology. Adapted from "Communication services and supports for individuals with severe disabilities: Guidance for assessment and intervention" by N. C. Brady et al., 2016, *American Journal of Intellectual and Developmental Disabilities, 121*, p. 123. Copyright 2016 by American Association on Intellectual and Developmental Disabilities. Adapted with permission.

it is not surprising that the Communication Bill of Rights includes the right to understand communication. Brady et al. (2016) also emphasized that practitioners should expand their instructional practices to include teaching communication and literacy to individuals who use AAC. In addition to teaching vocabulary (i.e., semantics) to students, it is equally important to teach syntax, phonological awareness, decoding, and other crucial literacy skills. Students who use AAC have the right to participate in literary instruction including shared reading and writing experiences (Barker, Saunders, & Brady, 2012; Berkowitz, 2015). However, research suggests these students have fewer opportunities to participate in these activities as the majority of AAC users receive the bulk of their instruction outside of the general education setting, and most users never develop functional literacy skills (Light & McNaughton, 2014). By having reading and literature competency, individuals with disabilities have a better chance in obtaining future employment, medical care, and quality of life (Barker et al., 2012).

The 15th Right under the Communication Bill of Rights also stipulates that individuals have "the right to have clear, meaningful, and culturally and linguistically appropriate communications" (Brady et al., 2016, p. 123). This Right is important given that a student's language formation stems from exposure to language and cultural activities (Soto & Yu, 2014). However, to address this Right, teachers should have cultural competency to best serve all students including those with complex communication needs. This is particularly important during the AAC assessment and *vocabulary selection* process.

The 11th Right states that individuals have the right to access appropriate AAC and assistive technology and their accompanying services. This is aligned to the operational competency that requires an individual to be able to understand how to operate his or her AAC device. Individuals should have an AAC system that is physically and cognitively appropriate to use at all times. Identifying an appropriate system should involve a transdisciplinary team assessment approach (see Chapter 3 for more details). The team should include a special education teacher, who plays an important role in serving as an advocate and in the identification and assessment of individuals with CCN who need AAC (Binger et al., 2012).

For a student to achieve operational competency in the school setting, it is important for the student to always have access to an AAC system or mode of communication as stipulated in the 11th Communication Bill of Rights. Teachers should facilitate the use of the AAC system across settings and content areas and encourage the student to practice using it to increase fluency. While using the AAC system across settings, use of the system should frequently be modeled by teachers, paraeducators, and peers. This will help the student further acquire operational competency (Douglas, Light, & McNaughton, 2012; King & Fahsl, 2012). Other skills necessary in achieving operational competence include how to power the device on and off, identify when the device needs adjustments, make vocabulary selections and additions, transfer the system across activities, and take responsibility for as many aspects of the system as reasonably possible, to name a few (see DynaVox, 2014).

Communication is a social process; thus, the social competency is highly important to communication. To be socially competent, an individual must know what, when, how, and with whom to communicate. The Communication Bill of Rights includes the 10th and 12th Rights, which specify that individuals have the right to be included in social interactions and to be spoken to with respect. Teachers play an important role in setting the climate of the classroom and school when addressing students. Given that the use of an AAC system does not automatically allow students to master social competency, it is important to teach these skills (DeThorne, Hengst, Fisher, & King, 2014). Therefore, teachers should create opportunities to facilitate and encourage naturally occurring opportunities for students to communicate with a variety of individuals, especially peers, across multiple settings (King & Fahsl, 2012; Therrien, Light, & Pope, 2016). By creating these opportunities, teachers focus on addressing the first right for their students—to develop relationships and social closeness (Brady et al., 2016). Furthermore, teachers and other practitioners are responsible for teaching students how to request, reject, comment, make choices, express feelings, ask questions, and share information, as expressed in Rights 1 through 8 (Brady et al., 2016).

The 10th Right states individuals have the right to have communication attempts recognized and responded to even if the desired result cannot be achieved (Brady et al., 2016). As a result, it is important for teachers to clearly express to students when communication breakdowns have occurred and then assist the students to repair the breakdown by teaching the skills needed to correct the miscommunication (Chung & Douglas, 2014). Teachers should also train students to gain a partner's attention, utilize different modes of communication, manage interactions, and persist in communicating until the message is understood (DynaVox, 2014). Given that strategic competence encompasses all other competencies, it can be the hardest to teach and for the student to master.

The School Setting and Independence

It is important to understand how the communication competencies impact the independence, self-determination and self-advocacy skills of students with CCN. A student who uses AAC and has linguistic, operational, social, and strategic competences has greater independence and control over their own lives. Research shows students with disabilities who have self-determination skills also have better academic (Zheng, Erickson, Kingston, & Noonan, 2014) and post-secondary school outcomes as adults (Shogren, Wehmeyer, Palmer, Rifenbark, & Little, 2015). Martin and Marshall (1995) stated that

> Self-determined individuals know how to choose—they know what they want and how to get it. From an awareness of personal needs, self-determined

individuals choose goals, then doggedly pursue them. This involves assert-
ing an individual's presence, making his or her needs known, evaluating
progress toward meeting goals, adjusting performance, and creating unique
approaches to solve problems.

(p. 147)

Unfortunately, when compared to their peers without disabilities, individuals
with CCN often struggle with post-secondary employment, independent living, recreation, leisure, and socialization (Hamm & Mirenda, 2006). Thus, self-
determination skills can be pivotal to individuals with CCN in their pursuit of a
successful and independent life.

If students who use AAC are to achieve self-determination, it is important for
teachers to focus on teaching self-advocacy and problem solving (Brady et al.,
2016; Zheng et al., 2014). Within the framework of Light's (1989) competencies,
mastery of the linguistic competency allows the student to understand his or
her community's language, thereby increasing independent interactions at work,
recreation and leisure settings, and other areas needed for independent living.
Similarly, operational competence allows the student to become an independent
communicator given the student's ability to use his or her AAC system independently. Depending on the system, this requires the student to independently use
the symbols, navigate the system's folders, add new vocabulary when necessary,
activate use other features, and take ownership of the system.

Social competence is integral to communication and independence as it directly
relates to the student's ability to communicate with others. Students must have the
knowledge and skills to communicate with others if they are to self-advocate for
their wants and needs. Test, Fowler, Wood, Brewer, and Eddy (2005) created a self-
advocacy model in which communication is foundational to being a self-advocate.
The skills associated are assertiveness, negotiation, articulation, body language,
listening, persuasion, and compromise. As with the competencies, strategic competence is also important given a student's need to know when and how to repair
communication breakdowns. These breakdowns are frequently seen in students
who use AAC. Therefore, strategic competence is crucial for building and maintaining relationships, obtaining and retaining employment, and self-advocating
effectively. Wehmeyer (2003) stated that a person does not have to complete a
task independently to have control over the situation. If a person has the ability to
communicate his or her desire to perform a task, he or she has self-determination
regardless if he or she requires assistance or prompting to complete it. Therefore,
self-determination for students with CCN allows them to achieve independence
in their daily lives by communicating their desires and choices.

With the extensive research available outlining the importance of self-
determination for individuals (e.g., Karvonen, Test, Wood, Browder, & Algozzine,
2004; Shogren et al., 2015; Wehmeyer, Palmer, Shogren, Williams-Diehm, &
Soukup, 2013), it is necessary for teams to work together in helping students

TABLE 2.2 Potential Communication Needs Among Students with Special Needs

Disability	Possible Communication Characteristic	Challenges: Comm. Compt.				AAC Considerations
		Linguistic	Social	Operational	Strategic	
Angelman syndrome	Developmental delays in motor functioning and speech development; significant deficits in expressive communication, often are nonverbal; problems with oral–motor functioning; typically social and affectionate, but lack some social appropriateness related to affection.	☑	☑	☑	☑	It is important to begin AAC intervention early; both aided and unaided communication have proven beneficial for this population, as well as low and high-tech devices.
Autism spectrum disorder	Variability in intellectual functioning, social ability, and communication; speech may not develop; echolalia, repetitiveness, monotonous intonations, and idiosyncratic use of words are common if speech develops; receptive and/or expressive language impairments are also common.	☑	☑	☐	☑	It is important to begin early in intervention with AAC; emphasize the pragmatics of communication due to social deficits with ASD; speech-generating devices have been effective with ASD and to teach communication and literacy skills.
Cerebral palsy	Varying difficulties with motor skills, increased or decreased muscle tone, potential involuntary movements; speech intelligibility and language delays or disorders are common.	☑	☑	☑	☑	Due to the variety of motor abilities, use an interdisciplinary team approach for all professionals involved in AAC intervention; interventions should be balanced between motor training, speech therapy, and academic instruction; multimodal communication systems have proven effective.

Condition		Characteristics				Considerations
Deaf-blindness	☑	Varying degrees in both vision and hearing loss that significantly impair the ability to acquire information auditorily or visually; moderate to severe impairments in cognition, daily living skills, and social interactions; individuals with congenital impairments remain in the prelinguistic stage of communication development.	☑	☑	☑	Teams must consider a wide range of AAC options, recognize the timing of dual sensory impairments and the need for systematic instruction; tactile fingerspelling, one or two-handed tactile sign language, adapted sign language, and electronic aids.
Down syndrome	☑	Oral-motor structure, hypotonia, degree of intellectual disability and hearing abilities are common; Expressive and/or receptive language may be affected as well as language delays.	☑	☐	☑	*Note.* These considerations pertain to students with Down syndrome, fetal alcohol syndrome, fragile X syndrome, and intellectual disabilities.
Fetal alcohol syndrome	☑	Speech delays and articulation disorders are common; some hearing loss may be present; delayed language development with difficulties in syntax, semantics, and pragmatics, as well as difficulties in receptive and expressive language.	☑	☐	☑	Availability of inclusive, natural communication opportunities should be considered when selecting vocabulary and instructional techniques used for AAC intervention; most AAC strategies and techniques can be applied to this wide range of students.
Fragile X syndrome	☑	Articulation difficulties, stuttering, auditory-receptive memory and auditory-processing skills are deficient; expressive language may be delayed.	☑	☐	☑	

(Continued)

TABLE 2.2 (Continued)

Disability	Possible Communication Characteristic	Challenges: Linguistic	Comm. Social	Compt. Operational	Strategic	AAC Considerations
Intellectual disability	Limitations in intellectual functioning and adaptive behavior; deficits in language development, more concrete and less spoken language, limited vocabulary, grammatical skills, and receptive language.	☑	☑	☐	☑	
Landau–Kleffner syndrome	Acquired aphasia that results in a significant loss of previous receptive and expressive communication abilities, cannot produce or comprehend language they previously responded to.	☑	☐	☐	☑	Due to the significant loss of language, a multimodal AAC approach works best for these students; some benefit from having a communication partner provide help in related contexts.
Prader–Willi syndrome	Due to hypotonia and lack of oral-motor functioning, speech production, specifically phonemes, are largely affected; articulation varies from mild to unintelligible; often delays in comprehension and production of language.	☑	☐	☑	☑	Due to hypotonia and obesity, positioning and seating will be important for access; a multimodal AAC approach works best; emphasis on expressive and receptive vocabularies.
Rett syndrome	Oral-motor functioning and speech production are impacted after the first year by apraxia; expressive language is impacted by the motor difficulties and receptive language is affected by cognitive impairments; stereotypic hand movements which prevents the use of the hands.	☑	☐	☑	☐	Due to the stereotypic hand movements, alternative access (i.e., head, arms, eyes) to AAC is critical, it is also important to begin AAC intervention early.

Traumatic brain injury	Limitations to communication based on cognitive functioning; language impairments due to damage of language processing in the brain; may acquire aphasia or dysarthria; can have motor impairments that affect communication; communication abilities can change drastically over time.	☑	☑	☑	☑	During early stages of recovery, focusing on consistent and meaningful responses using single switches; during the middle stage, intervention focuses on non-electronic or limited number of displays on an SGD; in the late stages, many use functional speech, but those with more significant impairments may need long-term AAC devices.
Williams syndrome	Delays in language development caused by cognitive abilities; may experience echolalia; usually have exceptionally high expressive language skills accompanied by relatively low receptive language skills; pragmatic skills are a significant difficulty.	☑	☑	☐	☑	Consider focusing on receptive language skills and pragmatics skills during AAC intervention.

Note. Comm. = communication, Compt. = competencies.

(*Sources:* Beukelman & Mirenda, 2013; Calculator, 2013; Glennen & DeCoste, 1997; Lloyd, Fuller, & Arvidson, 1997; Mervis &Velleman, 2011; Richard & Hoge, 1999)

become self-determined and independent communicators. By teaching students who use AAC to master Light's communication competencies, students can become independent communicators and ultimately achieve better post-school outcomes including independent living, social relationships, and employment.

While teaching students the communication competency skills outlined previously, it is noteworthy to mention the development of communication competence for students with CCN is different from their peers without disabilities. Students with CCN have communication impairments that result from specific disabilities. For instance, approximately 38% of individuals with cerebral palsy have articulation and poor speech *intelligibility* (Ashwal et al., 2004). These individuals may also have significant motor impairments that limit their opportunities for typical communication development (Ashwal et al., 2004; Geytenbeek, 2015). Likewise, individuals with intellectual disability may have deficits in expressive and receptive language development. These deficits often limit the active participation of individuals with intellectual disability in day-to-day life (Ogletree et al., 2011). For individuals with autism spectrum disorder, speech can range from typical to echolalic, scripted, or not developed (Johnson & Myers, 2007). Meanwhile, individuals with apraxia of speech have deficits in speech production, which cannot be attributed to a lack of physical ability. Rather, they have difficulties in the motor planning of speech (ASHA, 2017). Table 2.2 illustrates information about the potential communication needs among students with various special needs. Students with CCN require ongoing communication skills training to develop communication competencies. Therefore, teachers, families, and related service providers should work together to identify the most effective means to support the development of these communication competencies to ensure positive communication outcomes for students with CCN.

Key Points of Chapter 2

* Communication competence is required to meet all purposes of communication.
* Linguistic competence is the knowledge of language spoken in an individual's environment, as well as the symbol code of his or her AAC system.
* Operational competence is the ability to effectively use language and the AAC system.
* Social competence is the ability to know what, when, how, and with whom an individual should communicate.
* Strategic competence is the ability to make up for the limitations of an individual's communication system and repair communication breakdowns.
* The Communication Bill of Rights consists of 15 Rights. It can be linked to Light's four communication competencies: linguistic, operational, social, and strategic competencies.
* Communication competency skills play an important role in the students' ability to become independent and self-determined.

References

Adeli, H., Rahimian, P., & Tabrizi, N. (2016). Communicating with people with profound intellectual disabilities using brain computer interface. *The Journal on Technology and Persons with Disabilities, 4*, 134–144.

American Speech-Language-Hearing Association. (2005). *Roles and responsibilities of speech-language pathologists with respect to augmentative and alternative communication: Position statement: ASHA special interest division 12, Augmentative and Alternative Communication (AAC).* Retrieved from www.asha.org/policy/PS2005-00113/

American Speech-Language-Hearing Association. (2017). *Childhood Apraxia of speech.* Retrieved from www.asha.org/public/speech/disorders/ChildhoodApraxia/

Ashwal, S., Russman, B. S., Blasco, P. A., Miller, G., Sandler, A., Shevell, M., & Stevenson, R. (2004). Practice parameter: Diagnostic assessment of the child with cerebral palsy: Report of the quality standards subcommittee of the American Academy of Neurology and the Practice Committee of the Child Neurology Society. *Neurology, 62*, 851–863. doi:10.1212/01.wnl.0000117981.35364.1b

Ballin, L., Balandin, S., Stancliffe, R. J., & Togher, L. (2011). Speech-language pathologists' views on mentoring by people who use speech generating devices. *International Journal of Speech-Language Pathology, 13*, 446–457. doi:10.3109/17549507.2011.522254

Barker, R. M., Saunders, K. J., & Brady, N. C. (2012). Reading instruction for children who use AAC: Considerations in the pursuit of generalizable results. *Augmentative and Alternative Communication, 28*, 160–170. doi:10.3109/07434618.2012.704523

Bates, E., Camaioni, L., & Volterra, V. (1975). The acquisition of performatives prior to speech. *Merrill-Palmer Quarterly of Behavior and Development, 21*, 205–226. doi:10.1177/002383098302600201

Berkowitz, S. (2015). Making words count: Why do some AAC users miss out on literacy instruction? And how can SLPs help get them the reading support they need? *The ASHA Leader, 20*, 52–58. doi:10.1044/leader.FTR2.20072015.52

Beukelman, D. R., & Mirenda, P. (2013). *Augmentative and alternative communication: Supporting children and adults with complex communication needs* (4th ed.). Baltimore, MD: Paul H. Brookes.

Binger, C., Ball, L., Dietz, A., Kent-Walsh, J., Lasker, J., Lund, S., . . . Quach, W. (2012). Personnel roles in the AAC assessment process. *Augmentative and Alternative Communication, 28*, 278–288. doi:10.3109/07434618.2012.716079

Brady, N. C., Bruce, S., Goldman, A., Erickson, K., Mineo, B., Ogletree, B. T., . . . Wilkinson, K. (2016). Communication services and supports for individuals with severe disabilities: Guidance for assessment and intervention. *American Journal of Intellectual and Developmental Disabilities, 121*, 121–138. doi:10.1352/1944-7558-121.2.121

Calculator, S. N. (2009). Augmentative and Alternative Communication (AAC) and inclusive education for students with the most severe disabilities. *International Journal of Inclusive Education, 13*, 93–113. doi:10.1080/13603110701284656

Calculator, S. N. (2013). Parents' reports of patterns of use and exposure to practices associated with AAC acceptance by individuals with Angelman syndrome. *Augmentative and Alternative Communication, 29*, 146–158. doi:10.3109/07434618.2013.784804

Calculator, S. N., & Black, T. (2009). Validation of an inventory of best practice in the provision of augmentative and alternative communication services to students with severe disabilities in general education classrooms. *American Journal of Speech-Language Pathology, 18*, 329–342. doi:10.1044/1058-0360(2009/08-0065)

Chung, Y., & Douglas, K. H. (2014). Communicative competence inventory for students who use augmentative and alternative communication: A team approach. *TEACHING Exceptional Children, 47*, 56–68. doi:10.1177/0040059914534620

DeThorne, L. S., Hengst, J., Fisher, K., & King, A. (2014). Keep your eye on the prize. *Young Exceptional Children, 17*, 39–50. doi:10.1177/1096250613485453

Douglas, S. N., Light, J. C., & McNaughton, D. B. (2012). Teaching paraeducators to support the communication of young children with complex communication needs. *Topics in Early Childhood Special Education, 33*, 91–101. doi:10.1177/0271121412467074

DynaVox Mayer-Johnson. (2014). *The dynamic AAC goal grid 2.* Retrieved from www.mydynavox.com/Content/resources/slp-app/Goals-Goals-Goals/the-dynamic-aac-goals-grid-2-dagg-2.pdf

Frankoff, D. J., & Hatfield, B. (2011). Augmentative and alternative communication in daily clinical practice: Strategies and tools for management of severe communication disorders. *Topics in Stroke Rehabilitation, 18*, 112–119. doi:10.1310/tsr1802–1112

Geytenbeek, J. (2015). *Differentiating between language domains, cognition, and communication in children with cerebral palsy* [Peer commentary on "Language outcomes of children with cerebral palsy aged 5 and 6 years: A population-based study" by C. Mei]. *Developmental Medicine and Child Neurology, 58.* doi:10.1111/dmcn.12990

Glennen, S. L., & DeCoste, D. C. (1997). *Handbook of Augmentative and Alternative Communication.* San Diego, CA: Cengage Learning.

Hamm, B., & Mirenda, P. (2006). Post-school quality of life for individuals with developmental disabilities who use AAC. *Augmentative and Alternative Communication, 22*, 134–147. doi:10.1080/07434610500395493

Johnson, C. P., & Myers, S. M. (2007). Identification and evaluation of children with autism spectrum disorders. *Pediatrics, 120*, 1183–1215. doi:10.1542/peds.2007–2361

Karvonen, M., Test, D. W., Wood, W. M., Browder, D., & Algozzine, B. (2004). Putting self-determination into practice. *Exceptional Children, 71*, 23–41. doi:10.1177/001440290407100102

King, A. M., & Fahsl, A. J. (2012). Supporting social competence in children who use augmentative and alternative communication. *TEACHING Exceptional Children, 45*, 42–49. doi:10.1177/004005991204500106

Landa, R. (2007). Early communication development and intervention for children with autism. *Mental Retardation and Developmental Disabilities Research Reviews, 13*, 16–25. doi:10.1002/mrdd

Light, J. (1988). Interaction involving individuals using augmentative and alternative communication systems: State of the art and future directions. *Augmentative and Alternative Communication, 4*, 66–82. doi:10.1080/07434618812331274657

Light, J. (1989). Toward a definition of communicative competence for individuals using augmentative and alternative communication systems. *Augmentative and Alternative Communication, 5*, 137–144. doi:10.1080/07434618912331275126

Light, J., & Drager, K. (2007). AAC technologies for young children with complex communication needs: State of the science and future research directions. *Augmentative and Alternative Communication, 23*, 204–216. doi:10.1080/07434610701553635

Light, J., & McNaughton, D. (2014). Communicative competence for individuals who require augmentative and alternative communication: A new definition for a new era of communication? *Augmentative and Alternative Communication, 30*, 1–18. doi:10.3109/07434618.2014.885080

Light, J., & McNaughton, D. (2015). Designing AAC research and intervention to improve outcomes for individuals with complex communication needs. *Augmentative and Alternative Communication, 31*, 85–96. doi:10.3109/07434618.201

Lloyd, L. L., Fuller, D. R., & Arvidson, H. H. (1997). *Augmentative and alternative communication: A handbook of principles and practices.* Boston, MA: Allyn and Bacon.

MacDonald, A., & Rendle, C. (1998). Laying the foundations of communicative competence for very young children. In A. Wilson (ed.), *Augmentative communication in practice: An introduction*. Edinburgh, Scotland: University of Edinburgh CALL Centre.

Martin, J. E., & Marshall, L. H. (1995). ChoiceMaker: A comprehensive self-determination transition program. *Intervention in School and Clinic, 30*, 147–157. doi:10.1177/105345129503000304

McLean, J., & Snyder-McLean, L. (1987). Form and function of communicative behavior among persons with severe developmental disabilities. *Australia and New Zealand Journal of Developmental Disabilities, 13*, 83–98. doi:10.3109/13668258709023350

Mervis, C. B., & Velleman, S. L. (2011). Children with Williams syndrome: Language, cognitive, and behavioral characteristics and their implications for intervention. *Perspectives on Language Learning and Education, 18*, 98–107. doi:10.1044/llel8.3.98

Millar, D. C., Light, J. C., & Schlosser, R. W. (2006). The impact of augmentative and alternative communication intervention on the speech production of individuals with developmental disabilities: A research review. *Journal of Speech, Language, and Hearing Research, 49*, 248–264. doi:10.1044/1092–4388(2006–2021).

Ogletree, B. T., Bruce, S. M., Finch, A., Fahey, R., & McLean, L. (2011). Recommended communication-based interventions for individuals with severe intellectual disabilities. *Communication Disorders Quarterly, 32*, 164–175. doi:10.1177/1525740109348791

Richard, G. J., & Hoge, D. R. (1999). *The source for syndromes*. East Moline, IL: LinguiSystems, Inc.

Shogren, K. A., Wehmeyer, M. L., Palmer, S. B., Rifenbark, G. G., & Little, T. D. (2015). Relationships between self-determination and postschool outcomes for youth with disabilities. *The Journal of Special Education, 48*, 256–267. doi:10.1177/0022466913489733

Singh, J., Iacono, T., & Gray, K. M. (2014). An investigation of the intentional communication and symbolic play skills of children with Down syndrome and cerebral palsy in Malaysia. *Journal of Early Intervention, 36*, 71–89. doi:10.1177/1053815114562044

Soto, G., & Yu, B. (2014). Considerations for the provision of services to bilingual children who use augmentative and alternative communication. *Augmentative and Alternative Communication, 30*, 83–92. doi:10.3109/07434618.2013.878751

Test, D. W., Fowler, C. H., Wood, W. M., Brewer, D. M., & Eddy, S. (2005). A conceptual framework of self-advocacy for students with disabilities. *Remedial and Special Education, 26*, 43–54. doi:10.1177/07419325050260010601

Therrien, M. C. S., Light, J., & Pope, L. (2016). Systematic review of the effects of interventions to promote peer interactions for children who use aided AAC. *Augmentative and Alternative Communication, 32*, 81–93. doi:10.3109/07434618.2016.1146331

Trenholm, S., & Jensen A. (2008). *Interpersonal communication*. New York, NY: Oxford University Press.

Wehmeyer, M. L. (2003). *Theory in self-determination: Foundations for educational practice*. Springfield, IL: Charles C Thomas.

Wehmeyer, M. L., Palmer, S. B., Shogren, K., Williams-Diehm, K., & Soukup, J. H. (2013). Establishing a causal relationship between intervention to promote self-determination and enhanced student self-determination. *The Journal of Special Education, 46*, 195–210. doi:10.1177/0022466910392377

Zheng, C., Erickson, A. G., Kingston, N. M., & Noonan, P. M. (2014). The relationship among self-determination, self-concept, and academic achievement for students with learning disabilities. *Journal of Learning Disabilities, 47*, 462–474. doi:10.1177/0022219412469688

3

THE INSTRUCTIONAL TEAM

Effective augmentative and alternative communication (AAC) assessment and instruction occur when all stakeholders (e.g., family, related service providers, special education teacher, student) are well trained, informed, and have shared goals (Ball, Standing, & Hazelrigg, 2010; Binger et al., 2012; Calculator & Black, 2009). This is a challenging task for families as, too often, they do not have the knowledge and skills needed to advocate for and support their child (Burke, 2013). Families need to seek knowledge so they can feel empowered (Burke, 2013; Chung & Douglas, 2014), and so they can better advocate for and support their child's needs (García, Madrid, & Galante, 2017; Saito & Turnbull, 2007). When evaluating and planning for instruction for students with complex communication needs (CCN), it is important to collaborate with the appropriate service providers. In doing so, families and professionals can ensure that accurate information is gathered about the student's present level of performance in regard to the student's overall abilities (e.g., behavior, communication, hearing, motor, visual). This is also critical as the Individuals with Disabilities Educational Improvement Act (IDEA; PL 108–446) of 2004 indicates that families and the student's educational team jointly develop *individualized educational programs* (IEPs) that consider and include assistive technology (AT) and AAC systems and services. In fact, teams are required to do the following:

(1) *Assessment.* A comprehensive assessment of the student. Including the identification of the student's strengths and areas of needs in the student's natural settings.
(2) *System provision.* Identification and provision of an AT or AAC systems that meets the student's needs by purchasing or leasing.
(3) *System customization.* Selecting, tailoring, or adapting the AT or AAC system to meet the needs of the student.

(4) *Training.* Designing and provision of training and assistance needed to support the student, the family, professionals, and employers.

As such, instruction for students with CCN requires a team structure where all team members are actively involved and committed to the student's plan (Ball et al., 2010; Dietz, Quach, Lund, & McKelvey, 2012; Rombouts, Maes, & Zink, 2017). Beyond this commitment, all team members, including professionals and family members, will need to develop, demonstrate, and embrace team skills that can facilitate communication and collaboration among all team members (Baxter, Enderby, Evans, & Judge, 2012). Baxter and colleagues (2012) suggested that a potential barrier to successful assessment and instruction of students with CCN is the lack of collaboration between school professionals and family members. They emphasized the importance of all professional team members (e.g., special education teachers, speech-language pathologists, and other school personnel) to have the training needed to be able to actively and successfully support students with CCN in various settings.

Collaboration is key for effective instruction of students with CCN (Bailey, Parette, Stoner, Angell, & Carroll, 2006; Ganz, 2014; Rombouts et al., 2017). Yet, it is a challenging task. Collaboration is more than just working together or having a conversation with a colleague about a student or situation (Hamilton-Jones & Vail, 2013; Robinson & Buly, 2007). Collaboration involves professionals and family members coming together to work on identifying the most effective means to complete and implement a task (e.g., assessment, instruction). In other words, it is a partnership between two or more team members who set goals or outcomes for the student and share responsibility, accountability, and resources in order to accomplish these goals (Friend & Cook, 2017). Effective and successful collaboration occurs when professionals voluntarily participate and have mutual goals (Hamilton-Jones & Vail, 2013) and are willing to make the effort to support and train or be trained, as needed, to support the student effectively (Dietz et al., 2012; Robinson & Buly, 2007).

Unified plans of support (UPS) have been suggested to be a means to create and enhance collaboration among disciplines (Hunt, Doering, Hirose-Hatae, Maier, & Goetz, 2001; Hunt, Soto, Maier, Liboiron, & Bae, 2004; Hunt, Soto, Maier, Muller, & Goetz, 2002; Mehr, 2017; Mortier, Hunt, Leroy, Van de Putte, & Van Hove, 2010). The focus should be on identifying and creating individualized support plans for the students (e.g., instructional educational programs) as a team that outline the most appropriate and effective instruction to accomplish shared goals. To achieve this, team members should be thoughtfully selected to ensure that the student's specific needs are being met (Calculator & Black, 2009; Chung & Douglas, 2014), and team structure, roles, and responsibilities should be identified early to successfully meet these within the team (Chung & Douglas, 2014; Dietz et al., 2012). See Figure 3.1 for an example of an augmentative and alternative communication (AAC) and assistive technology (AT) collaboration checklist.

AAC/AT Team Collaboration Checklist

Student: _____   Date: _____

Team members: _____

_____

Instructions. Identify the person responsible for each task listed below and check the appropriate box to indicate if the task is in progress (IP) or if it has been completed (C).

Note. *IP* indicates that a person has been identified to complete each specific task for the team. *C* indicates that a person was identified to complete the task and he or she has met the plan set by the team.

		Task	Person responsible	IP	C
Student	1	Complete self-interest assessment *(for high school and transition age students)*		☐	☐
	2	Feedback on ongoing goals for the student		☐	☐
	3	Feedback on AAC/AT system		☐	☐

		Task	Person responsible	IP	C
Team	1	Complete and submit referral documentation		☐	☐
	2	Schedule and conduct assessment		☐	☐
	3	Review and discuss assessment		☐	☐
	4	Identify AAC/AT system		☐	☐
	5	Identify and review funding possibilities		☐	☐
	6	Identify and set ongoing student goals		☐	☐
	7	Identify and set ongoing team goals		☐	☐
	8	Identify progress monitoring tool and frequency		☐	☐
	9	Schedule progress monitoring review		☐	☐
	10	Schedule ongoing team meetings		☐	☐
	11	Identify training needs *(content and people)*		☐	☐

FIGURE 3.1   AAC/AT team collaboration checklist.

(*Sources:* Hunt et al., 2001; Hunt et al., 2004; Hunt et al., 2002; Soto, Müller, Hunt, & Goetz, 2001a, 2001b; Soto & Zangari, 2009)

Team Structure

Having a clear understanding of the different team structures will help outline the roles and responsibilities of each team member, as well as ensure service provision. Three main team structures have been discussed in the literature (Batorowicz & Shepherd, 2011; Glennen & DeCoste, 1997; Hartgerink et al., 2014; Nancarrow et al., 2013): (1) multidisciplinary, (2) interdisciplinary, and (3) transdisciplinary teams.

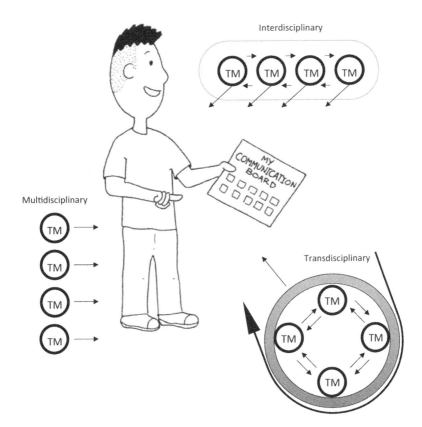

FIGURE 3.2   Team structures.

Note. TM = team members

Adapted from "Handbook of Augmentative and Alternative Communication," by S. L. Glennen and D. C. DeCoste, 1997, San Diego, CA: Singular Publishing (p. 24).

A *multidisciplinary team* consists of different specialists from multiple disciplines or areas of expertise who provide services to the student in isolation from each other. Instructional goals, under this team structure, are set and worked on by each discipline (Graybill et al., 2006). That is, goals are not reinforced across disciplines (Hartgerink et al., 2014). Batorowicz and Shepherd (2011) described this team structure as a team where each team member works independently, in separate settings, and only come together to summarize findings.

As with the multidisciplinary team, in an *interdisciplinary team* structure, specialists from multiple disciplines perform only tasks that are specific to their respective disciplines or area of expertise. The main difference is that, in an interdisciplinary team, team members share information (i.e., goals being set) with other members in an attempt to unify their plans and outcomes (Batorowicz & Shepherd, 2011;

Glennen & DeCoste, 1997; Graybill et al., 2006). The main purpose of unifying this information is to reinforce the skills or set goals across disciplines during the instruction. Typically, in an interdisciplinary team, there will be more active communication among team members throughout the assessment, goal setting, and instructional phases (Nancarrow et al., 2013).

Lastly, the *transdisciplinary team* follows the same overall team structure as the interdisciplinary team. However, the main difference is that, in a transdisciplinary team, the focus is on holistic goals for the individual, instead of being discipline specific (Nancarrow et al., 2013). This team structure is the most collaborative (Batorowicz & Shepherd, 2011; Glennen & DeCoste, 1997; King et al., 2009). However, it is the most difficult to achieve due to the high communicative demands required from each team member (Batorowicz & Shepherd, 2011; King et al., 2009). Just as in the interdisciplinary team, transdisciplinary team members will be involved and will maintain ongoing communication throughout the assessment and instructional process (Lamontagne, Routhier, & Auger, 2013). However, in this team structure, training across disciplines or expertise areas is needed to ensure effective reinforcement and instruction of the holistic goals being set for the student (Batorowicz & Shepherd, 2011). Although the transdisciplinary team structure may be the most ideal when serving students with CCN, the selection of the team structure often times is not determined by the team members. Instead, this is set by the school or the district, as it is dependent on the resources available (Batorowicz & Shepherd, 2011; Mirenda, 2014). See Figure 3.2 for a visual representation of the team structure.

Team Development

When identifying and developing a team for a student with CCN there are three main levels of collaboration with a school system that should be considered. These levels of collaboration include the following: (1) the school system level, (2) the practitioner or team level, and (3) the student and family level. At the school system level, collaboration for AT and AAC services will only occur if the system has an infrastructure that supports administrative initiatives. These initiatives include the following: (1) the development, support, and maintenance of collaboration among and across teams; (2) allocation of time and resources needed to support teamwork; and (3) allocation of funds for professional development training in AT and AAC (Ball et al., 2010; Hunt et al., 2004; Hunt et al., 2002; Mavrou, 2011).

At the practitioner or team level, effective collaboration will occur when teams outline clear roles and responsibilities for each team member and determine the most effective team structure. Additionally, teams should have (1) common and clear goals for the student and the team; (2) effective and functional plans; (3) acknowledgement and acceptance of opinion across team members; (4) strong lines of communication among team members; and (5) high proficiency in interpersonal skills (Beukelman, Hanson, Hiatt, Fager, & Bilyeu, 2005; Beukelman & Mirenda, 2013; Cooper-Duffy & Eaker, 2017). This is the level that most likely will be working and interacting directly with the student and family. To better support collaboration and communication among team members, teams will need to allocate time to work as a team, be open and available to dialog and brainstorm, serve as a resource by sharing expertise area with team members and families, and provide and obtain training as needed (Goldbart & Marshall, 2004; Hunt et al., 2002; Talladay, 2013; Woolfson, 2004). The student and family level is the primary purpose of the team. Therefore, collaboration between professionals and the school system with the families requires strong interpersonal and communication skills. Sensitivity towards the family, the student, and their needs is crucial to effectively plan and implement instructional programs. The goal of the team should be to build a strong rapport and relationship with the family. As families feel understood and supported by the school system, a family's openness and willingness to consider AT and AAC services for their child will increase (Angelo, 2000; Angelo, Jones, & Kokoska, 1995; Angelo, Kokoska, & Jones, 1996; Mandak, O'Neill, Light, & Fosco, 2017). This willingness will help the team set common goals that will better support the student.

Determining team members may seem "a given." However, teams should be crafted with caution to ensure that the needs of the student are being met. Tuckman (1965) outlined four stages of team formation:

(1) *Forming.* Forming is establishing the team; that is, coming together as a group. In forming, members are recruited and form a team using a shared model.
(2) *Storming.* Storming involves resolving any conflicts or tensions among the team: that is, communicating to ensure that same goals are shared. In storming, the individual members act as resources to other team members with the purpose of developing trust. In this phase, team members understand there will be differences of opinions and views, yet all team members work towards the same set of goals (Beukelman, Burke, Ball, & Horn, 2002; Beukelman et al., 2005; Burke, Beukelman, Ball, & Horn, 2002; Lamontagne et al., 2013).
(3) *Norming.* Norming is when the team is cohesive and ready to successfully implement their roles and responsibilities. Team members collaborate to ensure the success and effectiveness of the team as a whole.
(4) *Performing.* In performing, the team is ready to act and makes decisions to meet the set goals (i.e., implementation of the set plans). To achieve this, each team members will need to be given the responsibility of a task that will support the team's views, goals, and plans. This will support accountability across team members and successful implementation of the set plans.

See Figure 3.3 for an example form to effectively develop teams for students with CCN.

Team Development and Accountability Form

Student: _____ Lead person: _____ Date: _____

Instructions. Complete the form by selecting, stating, and describing all components. In the *Forming* section, select all individuals that should be part of the student's team. Under *Storming*, describe the purpose of the team and role of each member and state the team expectations across all members. In the *Norming* section, outline and prioritize tasks and the person who is responsible or who will serve as the lead person on this task. Under *Performing*, indicate the means of reporting (data collection) to ensure the accountability of all team members as well as how to provide a progress report for each task.

STEP 1. Forming	
☐ Family/guardian	☐ Student
☐ Special education teacher	☐ General education teacher
☐ Speech language pathologist	☐ Occupational therapist
☐ Physical therapist	☐ Behavior therapist/consultant
☐ AAC consultant	☐ AT Consultant
☐ Teacher of the Deaf and hard of hearing	☐ Interpreter
☐ Teacher of English language learners	☐ Teacher of the visually impaired
☐ Paraeducators	☐ Others _____

STEP 2. Storming
Team goal/purpose
Expectation

STEP 3. Norming	
Task	Lead person
1	
2	
3	
4	

FIGURE 3.3 Team development and accountability form.

Team Members

Effective AAC services for students with CCN in the school setting is going to be dependent upon the team (Kent-Walsh, Stark, & Binger, 2008; DeFelice, Scheer-Cohen, & Hughes, 2014). For this reason, the AAC team should be composed of various stakeholders who will help enhance the communication skills of students with CCN (Beukelman et al., 2002; Burke et al., 2002; Beukelman et al., 2005; Binger et al., 2012). Team members should include the following:

(1) *The student with CCN.* The student is the most important team member. The user of AAC should be allowed to indicate his or her needs, choices, and feedback on the system under consideration and used.
(2) An *AAC advocate and facilitator.* These should include the most frequent communication partners (e.g., family, teachers) and a person who will take the lead role as an advocate for the individual, will monitor the system, and plan for its implementation.
(3) An *AAC finder.* That is, the person who refers or identifies the need for AAC.
(4) *Educators and related service providers.* These team members will provide daily services to support the use of the AAC system in activities and routines as well as facilitate the user's independence.
(5) The *AAC specialist.* This is the person who will design the instructional program. This team member can provide direct or consult services.
(6) In some instances, an *AAC expert.* Often times, this is a university faculty member who conducts consultation services and/or training, provides legal and policy guidance, and conducts research in the area (Ball et al., 2010; Beukelman & Mirenda, 2013).

The special education teacher and speech-language pathologist (SLP) play a crucial role in the team of students with CCN (Ball et al., 2010; Soto et al., 2001a, 2001b). Although it may seem that these responsibilities lie exclusively in the SLP's role, this is not the case. It is true that there is an overall agreement that SLPs receive more training than special education teachers do in this area (Costigan & Light, 2010; Da Fonte & Boesch, 2016). However, unfortunately, the training for SLPs have decreased over the past years (Ballin, Balandin, Togher, & Stancliffe, 2009; Binger et al., 2012; Kent-Walsh et al., 2008; Ratcliff, Koul, & Lloyd, 2008), and there has been increased recognition for special education teachers to have AAC training (see the Council for Exceptional Children Special Educator Professional Preparation Standard for more details) to ensure effective services for all students (Da Fonte & Boesch, 2016).

SLPs are responsible for conducting the formal assessment, will most likely be involved in obtaining funding for the speech–generating device (SGD), and will need to provide AAC instruction. SLPs will also need to have knowledge of the system to ensure its maintenance. They will also, most likely, provide AAC training to the student, families, and other important stakeholders (e.g., educators, related service provides; Ball et al., 2010; Kent-Walsh et al., 2008; Mandak & Light, 2017). On the other hand, special education teachers will be involved with designing and implementing the AAC instruction, identifying and adapting the curriculum needed to support the use of the AAC system, and developing peer support and social opportunities to increase communicative interactions. Similar to SLPs,

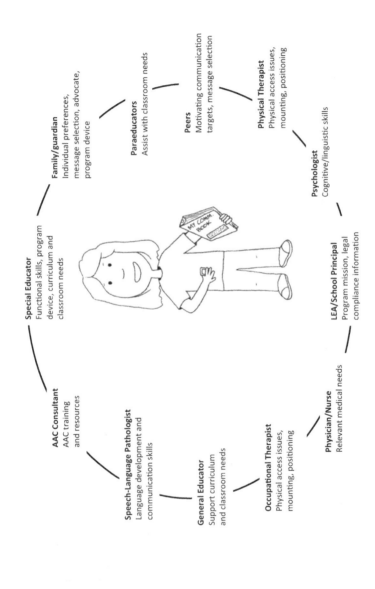

FIGURE 3.4 Roles and responsibilities of team members.

(*Sources*: Beukelman & Mirenda, 2013; Glennen & DeCoste, 1997; Hunt et al., 2002; Saito & Turnbull, 2007; Soto et al., 2001a)

special education teachers will also need to have the knowledge and skills necessary to implement and evaluate the use of the AAC system (see Units 3 and 4), and ensure the maintenance of the AAC system (Soto et al., 2001a; Soto et al., 2001b).

Besides the SLP and the special education teacher, all members of the team will need to understand their explicit role and responsibilities throughout the assessment and intervention process (Ball et al., 2010; Binger et al., 2012). They need to ensure that they are also providing effective social and communication opportunities (Light & McNaughton, 2012). Moreover, they will need to allocate the time and resources necessary to work as a team, be committed to collaborating with team members, provide training, and monitor the student's progress (Hunt et al., 2002). See Figure 3.4 for a summary of potential team members and their roles and responsibilities as team members.

The Challenges

Collaboration and teamwork is important when serving students with CCN. However, challenges will occur even in the most successful team (e.g., Dietz et al., 2012; Friend & Cook, 2017). Some of the most common challenges when working with students with CCN can be divided into three main categories: (1) the school system, (2) the team, and (3) the AAC communication system.

Challenge 1—The School System

The school system, at times, may exhibit challenges that are difficult to overcome. Most commonly, these challenges may be due to the increasing number of students being referred to special education services, the increasing number of students with CCN, personnel shortages, and limited numbers of professionals specialized in a given discipline (e.g., assistive technology, AAC; Da Fonte & Boesch, 2016; Light & McNaughton, 2012). With the rise in students who are being referred for special education services there is also a larger influx of students who present CCN or who use AAC (Iacono, 2014; Light & McNaughton, 2012). This may be due in part to the increase in prevalence of certain disabilities (e.g., autism spectrum disorder, cerebral palsy, etc.) that have a high comorbidity rate with CCN (see Chapter 1; National Center for Education Statistics, 2016). Additionally, Light and McNaughton (2012) highlight that the increased number of students who use AAC are also displaying increased diversity in cultural and linguistic backgrounds.

Not only have the number of students with CCN increased, but the use of AAC systems and strategies have risen among students with more complex needs and with students who could use extra support with learning various communication skills (Costantino & Bonati, 2014; Light & Drager, 2007). The increased complexity of individuals who utilize AAC places increased demands on school districts that may already be limited in their resources or may be facing financial restrictions that will impact the funding available for such services (ASHA, 2017b; Dowden et al., 2006; Sutherland, Gillon, & Yoder, 2005). Funding for AAC is a complex issue that affects most developed countries (Baxter et al., 2012). When discussing funding of AAC, the question of educational and medical necessity arises (ASHA, 2017b). According to IDEA 2004, schools must provide access to needed assistive technology, but they are not solely responsible for the financial aspect (IDEA, 2004). Funding for AAC services and devices can come from medical insurance, government programs, companies who create AAC devices, or the public school system. Within the public school system, funding for AAC devices and services may fall under the category of special education, related services, or assistive technology according to IDEA (2004). Additionally, with the increased rate of students needing AAC services and devices, funds will need to be stretched accordingly, making this a significant challenge for school systems (Binger et al., 2012; McNaughton & Light, 2015). This may result in turning to cheaper and more easily attained options (Light & McNaughton, 2012) which, at times, may not be the most effective or appropriate means for that student (Mirenda, 2014).

Challenge 2—The Team

The team can be exposed to various challenges. Most often, the challenges faced are based on the limited time to meet, plan, and implement instructional programs (Calculator & Black, 2009; Dowden et al., 2006; Stoner, Angell, & Bailey, 2010), overall AAC service provision (Mukhopadhyay & Nwaogu, 2009; Sutherland et al., 2005), and differences in philosophies or goals being set (Lamontagne et al., 2013). These challenges can get intensified when teams only meet yearly. This has a major impact on the program implementation and, as a result, the student's success (Chung & Stoner, 2016). Hence, the goal should be for teams to take the time to communicate, collaborate, and schedule ongoing communicative interactions to be more goal-directed (Alant, Champion, & Peabody, 2013; Lamontagne et al., 2013).

The lack of knowledge, skills, and level of experience among team members will present a significant barrier in the collaboration process (Chung & Stoner, 2016; Dowden et al., 2006). Knowledge of AAC systems and assessment is needed by all members in order to collaborate effectively (Alant et al., 2013) and be able to adequately implement the plans (Da Fonte & Boesch, 2016; Kent-Walsh et al., 2008). Members will need to support the team by providing training (Chung & Stoner, 2016), supporting positive and engaging attitudes (Batorowicz & Shepherd, 2011; Friend & Cook, 2017), and decreasing the opportunity barriers the student may be exposed to (Beukelman & Mirenda, 2013; Soto et al., 2001a).

Beyond knowledge, team members must have mutually shared goal(s) and an understanding of the overall purpose of the team (i.e., success of the student). Members should also understand how individual components and processes contribute to the overall goal of the team (Friend & Cook, 2017). Team members should share responsibility, be accountable, and be part of the decision-making process. In other words, the team should be composed of individuals who share goals and philosophies with positive attitudes and approaches to have the most positive effect for students. (Chung & Stoner, 2016; Friend & Cook, 2017).

The Family as a Team Member

Family involvement in the team is essential (DeFelice et al., 2014). Allowing families to be active members of the team will help increase the family's readiness for AAC supports (Alant et al., 2013; Anderson, Balandin, & Stancliffe, 2016). A family's involvement in the team will also help professionals to better understand the family's perspective (McNaughton et al., 2008). In this regard, professionals among the team need to consider using a family-centered approach to support and involve families in their child's plan (Mandak & Light, 2017). That is, show respect and acknowledge the important and unique role the family plays in the team and the decision-making process, ensuring that the family has a voice in making decisions that best fit their child and family lifestyle (Bailey et al., 2006; DeFelice et al., 2014). Additionally, having families as active team members will provide an opportunity for professionals in the team to help and support by providing potential plans for enhancing communication opportunities in a variety of settings and across communication partners (McNaughton et al., 2008).

Even though families are key members, too often, family members feel they do not have the knowledge and skills needed to have an active role within the team (Anderson et al., 2016). Having the necessary knowledge and skills is critical as parents play an active role in keeping the AAC systems up-to-date and in working on the communicative goals in the home setting (Anderson et al., 2016). Some possible ways to help alleviate the lack of knowledge and skills are the following:

(1) Including families in the diagnostic and assessment process. This includes explaining knowledge and key concepts related to AAC (DeFelice et al., 2014).
(2) Explaining the student's current levels of performance and the justification for selection of strategies or interventions (DeFelice et al., 2014).
(3) Creating an effective means of communication between the families and the school (Bailey et al., 2006; DeFelice et al., 2014).
(4) Understanding the family's background (García et al., 2017).
(5) Acknowledging the family's perspective on their child's disability (Bailey et al., 2006).
(6) Acknowledging and respecting the family's goals for their child (Chung & Douglas, 2014).
(7) Teaching the skills, interventions, and strategies that will be targeted to family and other adults before they assist the child in learning. Individuals who are teaching should not be learning the skill alongside the child (DeFelice et al., 2014).

(8) Understanding the support the family is able to provide their child, the needs of the family, and the demands the family faces when it relates to caring for their child with disabilities (Bailey et al., 2006; Mandak & Light, 2017).

Furthermore, family acceptance of the need for AAC will also have an impact on the team (Baxter et al., 2012; Sutherland et al., 2005). Therefore, families will need to be educated on the "myths and realities" of AAC to be able to have a cohesive goal for the student (Anderson et al., 2016; Romski & Sevcik, 2005; see Key Points of the chapter for resources that address the myths and realities of AAC). The task of educating family members is the team's responsibility. Other team members will need to provide families with the knowledge and skills needed to actively and effectively participate as team members (McNaughton et al., 2008) and offer the family the opportunity to participate in any professional development activities provided to the school staff. In fact, families have reported the need and desire for training, specifically related to AAC (Bailey et al., 2006; Chung & Stoner, 2016; McNaughton et al., 2008). Yet, not a lot of training provided considers or is focused on meeting the needs of families (García et al., 2017). Figure 3.5 provides a checklist for family members to use to help them identify their training needs. This will allow all team members to better understand the goals being set, the outcomes being projected, and for families to better advocate for their child (Chung & Stoner, 2016; DeFelice et al., 2014; Edwards & Da Fonte, 2012). Figures 3.6 and 3.7 offer an example form to be used by the team to identify training needs across team members. The form in Figure 3.6 is to be completed to identify trainers within the school system and Figure 3.7 for trainers from outside agencies.

Multicultural Considerations

There is a strong likelihood that teams will work with students with CCN from various linguistic and cultural backgrounds. Four major areas of difficulty have been reported in the literature when working with students with CCN from diverse backgrounds. These include (1) assessment, (2) support, (3) which language to use for intervention, and (4) how to collaborate with families who speak another language (Soto & Yu, 2014).

In order to properly assess communication abilities in more than one language, an accurate assessment must be used and the professional assessing must have an understanding of bilingual development of students with CCN (De Lamo & Jin, 2011; Soto & Yu, 2014). This suggests that, during assessment, professionals should consider accepting the correct answer in either language and consider observing the individual across settings with family, peers, and other adults (De Lamo & Jin, 2011; Soto & Yu, 2014).

Families have indicated that they feel there is a lack of support and available options for AAC devices and systems that support more than one language

Families as a Team Member: Knowledge and Skills Checklist

Name of the student: _____ Date: _____

Parent's name: _____ Teacher's name: _____

Instructions. Check the appropriate box to indicate your request. Note. *Knowledge* refers to the family's understanding of the content indicated in each question. *Skills* refer to your ability to implement or address this component within the home or community setting. *Requested* is for when you are requesting training to increase your knowledge and skills in this area. *Suggested* refers to when a professional suggests that your family receive training to increase your knowledge and skills in this area.		Yes, I have knowledge	Yes, I have the s kills	Training	
				Requested	Suggested
Do you know how to identify your child's needs?	Academic needs	☐	☐	☐	☐
	Behavior needs	☐	☐	☐	☐
	Communication needs	☐	☐	☐	☐
	Daily living needs	☐	☐	☐	☐
	Motor needs	☐	☐	☐	☐
Do you know how to prioritize and feel confident in identifying and setting goals for your child?	Academic skills	☐	☐	☐	☐
	Behavior skills	☐	☐	☐	☐
	Communication skills	☐	☐	☐	☐
	Daily living skills	☐	☐	☐	☐
	Motor skills	☐	☐	☐	☐
Are you aware of the various related services potentially available to your child?	Alternative communication	☐	☐	☐	☐
	Assistive technology	☐	☐	☐	☐
	Augmentative communication	☐	☐	☐	☐
	Behavioral supports	☐	☐	☐	☐
	Occupational therapy	☐	☐	☐	☐
	Physical therapy	☐	☐	☐	☐
	Speech language pathology	☐	☐	☐	☐
	Other _____	☐	☐	☐	☐
Do you know how to implement instructional plans and strategies in your everyday activities?	Community	☐	☐	☐	☐
	Home	☐	☐	☐	☐
Do you feel confident in monitoring the progress of the goals identified for your child?		☐	☐	☐	☐

FIGURE 3.5 Families as a team member knowledge and skills checklist.

(Kulkarni & Parmar, 2017). Companies and professionals will need to work together to identify potential solutions and resources for families and students with CCN in order to improve students' communication skills. Interestingly, research has suggested that families prefer to use *low-technology* options or natural speech in the home, as it better accommodates the first language than most AAC devices (Kulkarni & Parmar, 2017). Strong collaboration between families and professionals is key for effective instruction both with the home language and the language used in school (Cheatham & Hart Barnett, 2017). The need for translators will

AAC/AT Training and Professional Development Form (within the school system)

Student name: _____   Date: _____

Team members: _____

_____

Instructions. Indicate information related to the team training needs and select if the task is in progress (IP) or if it has been completed (C).

Note. *IP* indicates that a person has been identified to complete each specific task for the team. *C* indicates that a person was identified to complete the task and he or she has met the plan set by the team.

TASKS AND STEPS				
STEP 1. Identify Training Needs				
Team members to be trained	**Topic/Content**	**Person responsible for the training**	IP	C
☐ Family/guardian ☐ Special education teacher	1		☐	☐
☐ General education teacher ☐ Speech language pathologist	2		☐	☐
☐ Occupational therapist ☐ Physical therapist	3		☐	☐
☐ Behavior therapist/consultant ☐ AAC consultant	4		☐	☐
☐ AT consultant ☐ Paraeducators ☐ Others _____				
STEP 2. Schedule and Provide Training				
Trainer	**Location**	**Date**	**Time**	IP C
1				☐ ☐
2				☐ ☐
3				☐ ☐
4				☐ ☐
STEP 3. Schedule Follow-up Training Meeting				
Person responsible	**Location**	**Date**	**Time**	IP C
1				☐ ☐
2				☐ ☐
3				☐ ☐
4				☐ ☐

FIGURE 3.6   AAC/AT training and professional development form (within the school system).

(*Sources:* Hunt et al., 2001; Hunt et al., 2004; Hunt et al., 2002; Soto et al., 2001a, 2001b; Soto & Zangari, 2009)

AAC/AT Training and Professional Development Form: Outside Agencies

Student name: _____   Date: _____

Team members: _____

_____

Instructions. Indicate information related to the team training needs and select if the task is in progress (IP) or it has been completed (C).

Note. *IP* indicates that a person has been identified to complete each specific task for the team. *C* indicates that a person was identified to complete the task and he or she has met the plan set by the team.

TASKS AND STEPS			
STEP 1. Identify Training Needs and Potential Outside Agency			
Team members to be trained	**Outside agency**	IP	C
☐ Family/guardian	☐ Company representative	☐	☐
☐ Special education teacher	☐ Consultants		
☐ General education teacher	☐ Educational service centers	☐	☐
☐ Speech language pathologist	☐ Local expert		
☐ Occupational therapist	☐ Outreach community centers	☐	☐
☐ Physical therapist	☐ University faculty expert		
☐ Behavioral therapist/consultant	☐ Others _____	☐	☐
☐ AAC consultant			
☐ AT consultant			
☐ Paraeducators			
☐ Others _____			

STEP 2. Content and Agency				
Topic/Content	**Trainer**	**Agency**	IP	C
1			☐	☐
2			☐	☐
3			☐	☐
4			☐	☐

STEP 3. Schedule and Provide Training					
Trainer	**Location**	**Date**	**Time**	IP	C
1				☐	☐
2				☐	☐
3				☐	☐
4				☐	☐

STEP 4. Schedule Follow-up Training Meeting					
Person responsible	**Location**	**Date**	**Time**	IP	C
1				☐	☐
2				☐	☐
3				☐	☐
4				☐	☐

FIGURE 3.7 AAC/AT training and professional development form: outside agencies.

(*Sources:* Hunt et al., 2001; Hunt et al., 2004; Hunt et al., 2002; Soto et al., 2001a, 2001b; Soto & Zangari, 2009)

need to be identified early, so build a strong relationship between school and family. Furthermore, developing the home language is important to ensure that the individual can still participate in his or her rich family social context (Kohnert, 2013). Lastly, successful instructional implementation and effective collaboration is only going to occur when professionals understand and respect the family's cultural perspective on disability (Kulkarni & Parmar, 2017). By collaborating with families and respecting their cultural and linguistic background, professionals can ensure more effective intervention and reduce AAC system abandonment (Kulkarni & Parmar, 2017; Soto & Yu, 2014).

Challenge 3—The Augmentative and Alternative Communication System

The AAC system may present a significant impact on the student's outcomes, which too often results in AAC abandonment (Arroyo, Goldfarb, & Sands, 2012; Sutherland et al., 2005). One of the main reasons for such abandonment is the lack of knowledge and skills from team members (Stoner et al., 2010). Abandonment of the AAC system has also often related to the lack of ongoing support in the use of the system by the student's various communication partners (e.g., families, professionals, staff), not specifically from the user him or herself (Ballin et al., 2009; Anderson et al., 2016; DeFelice et al., 2014; Stoner, 2010). This may be due to the lack of frequent use of the AAC system by the student or the lack of effective use among families and professionals (DeFelice et al., 2014). This lack of effective use most likely is heavily lying on the shortage of trained professionals in the field (Ballin et al., 2009; Mukhopadhyay & Nwaogu, 2009). As a result, students are less exposed to these systems and they become less available (Mukhopadhyay & Nwaogu, 2009).

To effectively meet the student's needs, support needs to be enhanced, attitudes of communication partners must be changed, communication partners need to be educated, and an AAC system that specifically meets the student's communicative needs must be considered (Helling & Minga, 2014; Torrison, Jung, Baker, Beliveau, & Cook, 2007). These changes in the everyday life of students with CCN will help alleviate the opportunity barriers being imposed on the user of AAC (Mirenda, 2014; Soto et al., 2001a; Torrison et al., 2007; see Chapter 7 for more details on opportunity barriers).

Overcoming the Challenges

Challenges will exist in any team. Team members should aim to take a proactive role in how to overcome the challenges. Evidence exists that the most common challenges faced by teams are lack of communication (e.g., Alant et al., 2013; Lamontagne et al., 2013), lack of time to meet (e.g., Bailey et al., 2006; Chung & Stoner, 2016; Mirenda, 2014), and lack of training (e.g., Mirenda, 2014). These challenges can be overcome by team members being committed to communicating, improving interpersonal skills, working as team to advocate for shared planning time, and seeking ways to provide and be part of internal and external training (Friend & Cook, 2017).

One major challenge teams may face is the impact that self-efficacy has in the successful inclusion of the AAC system and AAC services for students with CCN (Robinson & Solomon-Rice, 2009; Ruppar, Dymond, & Gaffney, 2011). "Although legal requirements and administrative support provide the necessary conditions to initiate AAC support within schools and districts, the frontline professionals are responsible for service delivery and follow up" (Robinson & Solomon-Rice, 2009, p. 295). A potential solution to this challenge is scheduling regular in-person meetings and outlining clear roles and expectations for each team member. These are critical in the success of the team (Binger et al., 2012). Clear accountability and performance evaluations are also important when supporting communication, collaboration, and teamwork among all members (Ganz, 2014).

The size of a team often has an impact the overall function of the team. Beukelman and Mirenda (2013) indicated that team size should be maintained at approximately four to six members. They also suggested that, when having large teams, one should consider identifying a core team within the larger team to help promote and maintain ongoing collaboration among all team members. In this case, the core team should consist of key members who can identify and address the student's needs. The goal should be for all team members to actively engage in collaboration and communication opportunities to support more effective teamwork. To encourage and sustain collaborative teams, it is critical to have support from the school system's administration (Robinson & Solomon-Rice, 2009) and families (Burke, 2013; Ganz, 2014). Stronger collaborative cultures are directly influenced by administrators and their stances on the importance of teamwork (Friend & Cook, 2017). School cultures that encourage collaboration show a correlation with improved student outcomes (Friend & Cook, 2017). The remediation and ways to absolve conflicts in collaboration are also heavily influenced by administration (Friend & Cook, 2017).

Collaboration with families not only provides the opportunity to provide the services to the students, but also to assist and support the family (García et al., 2017). Edwards and Da Fonte (2012) suggested a 5-Point Plan to support and enhance the collaboration efforts between schools and families. These five strategies are grounded in the "12 principles of effective help-giving delineated" by Dunst and Trivette (1994, p. 167). The 5-Point Plan suggests that teachers:

(1) "Be positive, proactive and solution oriented.
(2) Respect families' roles and cultural backgrounds in their children's lives.
(3) Communicate consistently, listen to families' concerns, and work together.
(4) Consider simple, natural supports that meet the individual needs of the student.
(5) Empower families with knowledge and opportunities for involvement in the context of student's global needs" (Edwards & Da Fonte, 2012, p. 8).

Collaborative Problem-Solving Form

Student's name: _____   Date: _____

Lead person: _____   Challenge reported by: _____

Team members (present): _____

_____

Instructions. Five questions are outlined to support teams in problem-solving challenges they are facing. Answer each question in detail and identify the team member responsible to implement the solution or the team member who will take the lead in this challenge.

Q1. What is the situation?

Q2. What are potential solutions to address the situation?
1
2
3

Q3. Are these feasible to implement?		
1 ☐ Yes ☐ No	2 ☐ Yes ☐ No	3 ☐ Yes ☐ No
Pros. *Cons.*	*Pros.* *Cons.*	*Pros.* *Cons.*

Q4. What are we going to do?	
Task	Person responsible
1	
Suggestions and consideration for implementation.	
2	
Suggestions and consideration for implementation	

FIGURE 3.8   Collaborative problem–solving form.

(*Sources:* Friend & Cook, 2017; Salisbury et al., 1997)

3	
Suggestions and consideration for implementation	

Q5. When can we reconvene?		
Date: _____	Time: _____	Location: _____

Data, Progress, Outcome	
Solution 1	
Solution 2	
Solution 3	
Additional notes.	

FIGURE 3.8   (Continued)

These strategies can help alleviate barriers among families and other team members. The goal for these strategies is to help set the stage for a more supportive and welcoming team. Having a "buy-in" from families is key in this process and families must have the knowledge and skills needed to be able to advocate for their child.

Salisbury, Evans, and Palombaro (1997) suggested that teams should consider a collaborative problem-solving (CPS) approach when challenges arise. This approach outlines five steps to identify the situation and potential solutions in order support the continuum of effective services. These steps include the following: (1) identifying the issue; that is, outline the challenges faced and converse about them amongst team members; (2) generating all possible solutions; possible solutions are identified, outlined, and described by the team; (3) screening solutions for feasibility; the team will need to determine the likelihood of each solution as well as the positives or negatives associated; (4) choosing a solution to be implemented; the team chooses a solution and the data collection method, and then decides which team member(s) is responsible for the direct implementation; and (5) evaluating the solution after its implementation; discuss and evaluate the progress of changes, and determine if other situations have arisen. See Figure 3.8 for an example form to outline the challenge faced and potential solutions.

With the current emphasis on improving the effectiveness of teacher instruction and student learning, effective collaboration is critical (Lingo, Barton-Arwood, & Jolivette, 2011). Furthermore, with the increasing number of students with CCN and the demands for assistive technology and AAC services, a key to instructional and service provision success will be dependent on professional development and staff training on AT and AAC (Da Fonte & Boesch, 2016; Dietz et al., 2012).

Key Points of Chapter 3

- Collaboration is fundamental to the successful implementation of AAC.
- Teams should be developed to meet the needs of the student.
- All team members should have the knowledge and skills needed to actively participate in the system identification, assessment, goal setting, and implementation.
- There are three team structures: multidisciplinary, interdisciplinary, and transdisciplinary. Transdisciplinary teams are the most desirable and effective, but time constraints in the school system often make this structure a difficult one.
- Families and team members need to be provided with ongoing training.
- Team challenges should be productively overcome by identifying the problem, possible solutions, and following up on the implementation of the solution.
- Consider using collaborative problem solving (CPS) when challenges arise.
- Consider using the 5-Point Plan to support families and enhance the collaboration opportunities.

Additional Resources

- AAC Myths Revealed (Tobii Dynavox): www.dynavoxtech.com/implementation-toolkit/learning-paths/list/?id=7
- Augmentative and Alternative Communication (ASHA): www.asha.org/PRPSpecificTopic.aspx?folderid=8589942773&section=Key_Issues
- Myths (PrAACtical AAC): http://praacticalaac.org/tag/myths

References

Alant, E., Champion, A., & Peabody, E. (2013). Exploring interagency collaboration in AAC intervention. *Communication Disorders Quarterly, 34,* 172–183. doi:10.1177/1525740112455432

American Speech-Language-Hearing Association. (2017b). *Funding for services.* Retrieved from www.asha.org/NJC/Funding-for-Services/

Anderson, K. L., Balandin, S., & Stancliffe, R. J. (2016). "It's got to be more than that." Parents and speech-language pathologists discuss training content for families with a new speech generating device. *Disability and Rehabilitation: Assistive Technology, 11,* 375–384. doi:10.3109/17483107.2014.967314

Angelo, D. H. (2000). Impact of augmentative and alternative communication devices on families. *Augmentative and Alternative Communication, 16,* 37–47. doi:10.1080/07434610012331278894

Angelo, D. H., Jones, S., & Kokoska, S. (1995). A family perspective on augmentative and alternative communication: Families of young children. *Augmentative and Alternative Communication, 11*, 193–201. doi:10.1080/07434619512331277319

Angelo, D. H., Kokoska, S., & Jones, S. (1996). A family perspective on augmentative and alternative communication: Families of adolescents and young adults. *Augmentative and Alternative Communication, 12*, 13–20. doi:10.1080/07434619612331277438

Arroyo, C. G., Goldfarb, R., & Sands, E. (2012). Caregiver training in an AAC intervention for severe aphasia. *Journal of Speech-Language Pathology and Applied Behavior Analysis, 5*, 59–64.

Bailey, R. L., Parette, H. P., Stoner, J. B., Angell, M. E., & Carroll, K. (2006). Family members' perceptions of augmentative and alternative communication device use. *Language, Speech, and Hearing Services in Schools, 37*, 50–60. doi:0161–1461/06/3701–0050

Ball, L. J., Standing, K., & Hazelrigg, D. (2010). AAC considerations during transition to adult life. In D. B. McNaughton & D. R. Beukelman (Eds.), *Transition strategies for adolescents and young adults who use AAC* (pp. 201–216). Baltimore, MD: Paul H. Brookes.

Ballin, L., Balandin, S., Togher, L., & Stancliffe, R. J. (2009). Learning to use Augmentative and Alternative Communication (AAC): Is there a mentoring role for adults experienced in using AAC? *Journal of Intellectual and Developmental Disability, 34*, 89–91. doi:10.1080/13668250802676038

Batorowicz, B., & Shepherd, T. A. (2011). Teamwork in AAC: Examining clinical perceptions. *Augmentative and Alternative Communication, 27*, 16–25. doi:10.3109/07434618.2010.546809

Baxter, S., Enderby, P., Evans, P., & Judge, S. (2012). Barriers and facilitators to the use of high-technology augmentative and alternative communication devices: A systematic review and qualitative synthesis. *International Journal of Language and Communication Disorders, 47*, 115–129. doi:10.1111/j.1460–6984.2011.00090.x

Beukelman, D. R., Burke, R., Ball, L., & Horn, C. A. (2002). Augmentative and alternative communication technology learning part 2: Preprofessional students. *Augmentative and Alternative Communication, 18*, 250–254. doi:10.1080/07434610212331281331

Beukelman, D. R., Hanson, E., Hiatt, E., Fager, S., & Bilyeu, D. (2005). AAC technology learning part 3: Regular AAC team members. *Augmentative and Alternative Communication, 21*, 187–194. doi:10.1080/07434610400006638

Beukelman, D. R., & Mirenda, P. (2013). *Augmentative and alternative communication: Supporting children and adults with complex communication needs* (4th ed.). Baltimore, MD: Paul H. Brookes.

Binger, C., Ball, L., Dietz, A., Kent-Walsh, J., Lasker, J., Lund, S.,. . Quach, W. (2012). Personnel roles in the AAC assessment process. *Augmentative and Alternative Communication, 28*, 278–288. doi:10.3109/07434618.2012.716079

Burke, M. M. (2013). Improving parental involvement. *Journal of Disability Policy Studies, 23*, 225–234. doi:10.1177/1044207311424910

Burke, R., Beukelman, D., Ball, L., & Horn, C. (2002). Augmentative and alternative communication technology learning part 1: Augmentative and alternative communication intervention specialists. *Augmentative and Alternative Communication, 18*, 242–249. doi:10.1080/07434610212331281321

Calculator, S. N., & Black, T. (2009). Validation of an inventory of best practices in the provision of augmentative and alternative communication services to students with severe disabilities in general education classrooms. *American Journal of Speech-Language Pathology, 18*, 329–342. doi:10.1044/1058–0360(2009/08–0065)

Cheatham, G. A., & Hart Barnett, J. E. (2017). Overcoming common misunderstandings about students with disabilities who are English language learners. *Intervention in School and Clinic, 53*, 58–63. doi:10.1177/1053451216644819

Chung, Y-C., & Douglas, K. H. (2014). Communicative competence inventory for students who use augmentative and alternative communication: A team approach. *TEACHING Exceptional Children, 47*, 56–68. doi:10.1177/0040059914534620

Chung, Y-C., & Stoner, J. B. (2016). A meta-synthesis of team members' voices: What we need and what we do to support students who use AAC. *Augmentative and Alternative Communication, 32*, 175–186. doi:10.1080/07434618.2016.1213766

Cooper-Duffy, K., & Eaker, K. (2017). Effective team practices: Interprofessional contributions to communication issues with a parent's perspective. *American Journal of Speech-Language Pathology, 26*, 181–192. doi:10.1044/2016_ajslp-15–0069

Costantino, M. A., & Bonati, M. (2014). A scoping review of interventions to supplement spoken communication for children with limited speech or language skills. *PLoS ONE, 9*, 1–15. doi:10.1371/journal.pone.0090744

Costigan, F. A., & Light, J. (2010). A review of preservice training in augmentative and alternative communication for speech-language pathologists, special education teachers, and occupational therapists. *Assistive Technology, 22*, 200–212. doi:10.1080/10400435.2010.492774

Da Fonte, M. A., & Boesch, M. C. (2016). Recommended augmentative and alternative communication competencies for special education teachers. *Journal of International Special Needs Education, 1*, 47–58. doi:10.9782/2159–4341–19.2.47

De Lamo White, C., & Jin, L. (2011). Evaluation of speech and language assessment approaches with bilingual children. *International Journal of Language and Communication Disorders, 46*, 613–627. doi:10.1111/j.1460–6984.2011.00049.x

DeFelice, H., Scheer-Cohen, A. R., & Hughes, D. M. (2014). Communicate and collaborate! Strategies for facilitating AAC use at home and school. *Perspectives on Augmentative and Alternative Communication, 23*, 157–162. doi:10.1044/aac23.3.157

Dietz, A., Quach, W., Lund, S., & McKelvey, M. (2012). AAC assessment and clinical-decision making: The impact of experience. *Augmentative and Alternative Communication, 28*, 148–159. doi:10.3109/07434618.2012.704521

Dowden, P., Alarcon, N., Vollan, T., Cumley, G. D., Kuehn, C. M., & Amtmann, D. (2006). Survey of SLP caseloads in Washington state schools: Implications and strategies for action. *Language Speech and Hearing Services in Schools, 37*, 104–117.

Dunst, C. J., Trivette, C. M., & Deal, A. G. (1994). Enabling and empowering families. In C. J. Dunst, C. M. Trivette, & A. G. Deal (Eds.), *Supporting and strengthening families, Vol. 1. Methods, strategies and practices* (pp. 2–11). Cambridge, MA: Brookline Books.

Edwards, C. C., & Da Fonte, M. A. (2012). The 5-point plan: Fostering successful partnerships with families of students with disabilities. *TEACHING Exceptional Children, 44*, 6–13. doi:10.1177/004005991204400301

Friend, M., & Cook, L. (2017). *Interactions: Collaboration skills for school professionals* (8th ed.). Boston, MA: Pearson.

Ganz, J. B. (2014). Aided augmentative communication for individuals with autism spectrum disorders. *Autism and Child Psychopathology Series*, 43–51. doi:10.1007/978-1-4939-0814-1_4

García, M. P., Madrid, D., & Galante, R. (2017). Children and Augmentative or Alternative Communication System (AACs). A perceptive vision of the role played by families and professionals. *Anales De Psicología, 33*, 334–341. doi:10.6018/analesps.33.2.267631

Glennen, S., & DeCoste, D. C. (1997). *The handbook of augmentative and alternative communication.* Australia: Thomson/Delmar Learning.

Goldbart, J., & Marshall, J. (2004). "Pushes and pulls" on the parents of children who use AAC. *Augmentative and Alternative Communication, 20,* 194–208. doi:10.1080/0743461040010960

Graybill, J. K., Dooling, S., Shandas, V., Withey, J., Greve, A., & Simon, G. L. (2006). A rough guide to interdisciplinarity: Graduate student perspectives. *Bioscience, 56,* 757–763. doi:10.1641/0006-3568(2006)56[757:ARGTIG]2.0.CO;2

Hamilton-Jones, B. M., & Vail, C. O. (2013). Preparing special educators for collaboration in the classroom: Pre-service teachers' beliefs and perspectives. *International Journal of Special Education, 29,* 76–86.

Hartgerink, J. M., Cramm, J. M., Bakker, T. J. E. M., van Eijsden, A. M., Mackenbach, J. P., & Nieboer, A. P. (2014) The importance of multidisciplinary teamwork and team climate for relational coordination among teams delivering care to older patients. *Journal of Advanced Nursing, 70,* 791–799. doi:10.1111/jan.12233

Helling, C. R., & Minga, J. (2014). Developing an effective framework for the augmentative and alternative communication evaluation process. *Perspectives on Alternative and Augmentative Communication, 23,* 91–98. doi:10.1044/aac23.2.91

Hunt, P., Doering, K., Hirose-Hatae, A., Maier, J., & Goetz, L. (2001). Across-program collaboration to support students with and without disabilities in a general education classroom. *Research and Practice for Persons with Severe Disabilities, 26,* 240–256. doi:10.2511/rpsd.26.4.240

Hunt, P., Soto, G., Maier, J., Liboiron, N., & Bae, S. (2004). Collaborative teaming to support preschoolers with severe disabilities who are placed in general education early childhood programs. *Topics in Early Childhood Special Education, 24,* 123–142. doi:10.1177/02711214040240030101

Hunt, P., Soto, G., Maier, J., Müller, E., & Goetz, L. (2002). Collaborative teaming to support students with augmentative and alternative communication needs in general education classrooms. *Augmentative and Alternative Communication, 18,* 20–35. doi:10.1080/aac.18.1.20.35

Iacono, T. (2014). What it means to have complex communication needs. *Research and Practice in Intellectual and Developmental Disabilities, 1,* 82–85. doi:10.1080/23297018.2014.908814

Individuals with Disabilities Education Act (IDEA), 20 U.S.C. § 300.105 (2004).

Individuals with Disabilities Education Act, 20 U.S.C. § 1400 (2004).

Kent-Walsh, J., Stark, C., & Binger, C. (2008). Tales from school trenches: AAC service-delivery and professional expertise. *Seminars in Speech and Language, 29,* 146–154. doi:10.1055/s-2008-1079128

King, G., Strachan, D., Tucker, M., Duwyn, B., Desserud, S., & Shillington, M. (2009). The application of a transdisciplinary model for early intervention services. *Infants and Young Children, 22,* 211–223. doi:10.1097/iyc.0b013e3181abe1c3

Kohnert, K. (2013). *Language disorders in bilingual children and adults* (2nd ed.). San Diego, CA: Plural Publishing.

Kulkarni, S. S., & Parmar, J. (2017). Culturally and linguistically diverse student and family perspectives of AAC. *Augmentative and Alternative Communication, 33,* 170–180. doi:10.1080/07434618.2017.1346706

Lamontagne, M., Routhier, F., & Auger, C. (2013). Team consensus concerning important outcomes for augmentative and alternative communication assistive technologies: A pilot study. *Augmentative and Alternative Communication, 29,* 182–189. doi:10.3109/07434618.2013.784927

Light, J., & Drager, K. (2007). AAC technologies for young children with complex communication needs: State of the science and future research directions. *Augmentative and Alternative Communication, 23,* 204–216. doi:10.1080/07434610701553635

Light, J., & McNaughton, D. (2012). The changing face of augmentative and alternative communication: Past, present, and future challenges. *Augmentative and Alternative Communication, 28*, 197–204. doi:10.3109/07434618.2012.737024

Lingo, A. S., Barton-Arwood, S. M., & Jolivette, K. (2011). Teachers working together. *TEACHING Exceptional Children, 43*, 6–13. doi:10.1177/004005991104300301

Mandak, K., & Light, J. (2017). Family-centered services for children with ASD and limited speech: The experiences of parents and speech language pathologists. *Journal of Autism and Developmental Disorders.* doi:10.1007/s10803–017–3241-y

Mandak, K., O'Neill, T., Light, J., & Fosco, G. M. (2017). Bridging the gap from values to actions: A family systems framework for family-centered AAC services. *Augmentative and Alternative Communication, 33*, 32–41. doi:10.1080/07434618.2016.1271453

Mavrou, K. (2011). Assistive technology as an emerging policy and practice: Processes, challenges, and future directions. *Technology and Disability, 23*, 41–52. doi:10.3233/TAD-2011–0311

McNaughton, D., & Light, J. (2015). What we write about when we write about AAC: The past 30 years of research and future directions. *Augmentative and Alternative Communication, 31*, 261–270. doi:10.3109/07434618.2015.1099736

McNaughton, D., Rackensperger, T., Benedek-Wood, E., Krezman, C., Williams, M. B., & Light, J. (2008). A child needs to be given a chance to succeed: Parents of individuals who use AAC describe the benefits and challenges of learning AAC technologies. *Augmentative and Alternative Communication, 24*, 43–55. doi:10.1080/07434610701421007

Mehr, D. L. (2017). Supporting the communication needs of students with severe disabilities in inclusive settings: Practices and perspectives. In *Culminating projects in special education.* St. Cloud, MN: St. Cloud State University.

Mirenda, P. (2014). Revisiting the mosaic of supports required for including people with severe intellectual or developmental disabilities in their communities. *Augmentative and Alternative Communication, 30*, 19–27. doi:10.3109/07434618.2013.875590

Mortier, K., Hunt, P., Leroy, M., Van de Putte, I., & Van Hove, G. (2010). Communities of practice in inclusive education. *Educational Studies, 36*, 345–355. doi:10.1080/03055690903424816

Mukhopadhyay, S., & Nwaogu, P. (2009). Barriers to teaching non-speaking learners with intellectual disabilities and their impact on the provision of augmentative and alternative communication. *International Journal of Disability, Development and Education, 56*, 349–362. doi:10.1080/10349120903306590

Nancarrow, S., Booth, A., Ariss, S., Smith, T., Enderby, P., & Roots, A. (2013). Ten principles of good interdisciplinary team work. *Human Resources for Health, 11.* doi:10.1186/1478-4491-11-19

National Center for Education Statistics. (2016). *Children and youth with disabilities.* Retrieved May 14, 2018, from https://nces.ed.gov/programs/coe/indicator_cgg.asp

Ratcliff, A., Koul, R., & Lloyd, L. L. (2008). Preparation in augmentative and alternative communication: An update for speech-language pathology training. *American Journal of Speech-Language Pathology, 17*, 48–59. doi:10.1044/1058–0360(2008/005)

Robinson, L., & Buly, M. R. (2007). Breaking the language barrier: Promoting collaboration between general and special educators. *Teacher Education Quarterly, 34*, 83–94.

Robinson, N. B., & Solomon-Rice, P. (2009). Supporting collaborative teams and families in AAC. In G. Soto & C. Zangari (Eds.), *Practically speaking: Language, literacy, and academic development for students with AAC needs* (pp. 289–309). Baltimore, MD: Paul H. Brookes.

Rombouts, E., Maes, B., & Zink, I. (2017). The behavioural process underlying augmentative and alternative communication usage in direct support staff. *Journal of Intellectual and Developmental Disability, 42,* 101–113. doi:10.3109/13668250.2016.1219023

Romski, M., & Sevcik, R. A. (2005). Augmentative communication and early intervention, myths and realities. *Infants and Young Children, 18,* 147–185. doi:10.1097/00001163-200507000-00002

Ruppar, A. L., Dymond, S. K., & Gaffney, J. S. (2011). Teachers' perspectives on literacy instruction for students with severe disabilities who use augmentative and alternative communication. *Research and Practice for Persons with Severe Disabilities, 36,* 100–111. doi:10.2511/027494811800824435

Saito, Y., & Turnbull, A. (2007). Augmentative and alternative practice in the pursuit of family quality of life: A review of the literature. *Research and Practice for Persons with Severe Disabilities, 32,* 50–65. doi:10.2511/rpsd.32.1.50

Salisbury, C. U., Evans, I. M., & Palombaro, M. M. (1997). Collaborative problem-solving to promote the inclusion of young children with significant disabilities in primary grades. *Exceptional Children, 63,* 195–209. doi:10.1177/001440299706300204

Soto, G., Müller, E., Hunt, P., & Goetz, L. (2001a). Critical issues in the inclusion of students who use augmentative and alternative communication: An educational team perspective. *Augmentative and Alternative Communication, 17,* 62–72. doi:10.1080/aac.17.2.62.72

Soto, G., Müller, E., Hunt, P., & Goetz, L. (2001b). Professional skills for serving students who use AAC in general education classrooms. *Language Speech and Hearing Services in Schools, 32,* 51. doi:10.1044/0161–1461(2001/005)

Soto, G., & Yu, B. (2014). Considerations for the provision of services to bilingual children who use augmentative and alternative communication. *Augmentative and Alternative Communication, 30,* 83–92. doi:10.3109/07434618.2013.878751

Soto, G., & Zangari, C. (2009). *Practically speaking: Language, literacy, and academic development for students with AAC needs.* Baltimore, MD: Paul H. Brookes.

Stoner, J. B., Angell, M. E., & Bailey, R. L. (2010). Implementing augmentative and alternative communication in inclusive educational settings: A case study. *Augmentative and Alternative Communication, 26,* 122–135. doi:10.3109/07434618.2010.481092

Sutherland, D. E., Gillon, G. G., & Yoder, D. E. (2005). AAC use and service provision: A survey of New Zealand speech-language therapists. *Augmentative and Alternative Communication, 21,* 295–307. doi:10.1080/07434610500103483

Talladay, K. (2013). *Perceived expectations of roles in training and maintenance of augmentative and alternative communication devices.* (Unpublished master's thesis). Eastern Michigan University, Ypsilanti, MI.

Torrison, C., Jung, E., Baker, K., Beliveau, C., & Cook, A. (2007). The impact of staff training in Augmentative Alternative Communication (AAC) on the communication abilities of adults with developmental disabilities. *Developmental Disabilities Bulletin, 35,* 103–130. doi:10.7939/R33775V5J

Tuckman, B. W. (1965). Developmental sequence in small groups. *Psychological Bulletin, 63,* 384–399. doi:10.1037/h0022100

Woolfson, L. (2004). Family well-being and disabled children: A psychosocial model of disability-related child behavior problems. *British Journal of Health Psychology, 9,* 1–13. doi:10.1348/135910704322778687

4

IDENTIFYING THE BARRIERS IN THE ENVIRONMENT

A main consideration in the evaluation process of a student with complex communication needs (CCN) is the impact the student's environment may have in communicative interactions (Crisp, Draucker, & Cirgin Ellett, 2014). The environment is where the student will be exposed to experiences and will be expected to engage and participate. This chapter outlines and describes the Participation Model originally developed by Rosenberg and Beukelman (1987) and later revised by Beukelman and Mirenda (1988). Figure 4.1 outlines the Participation Model in which the student with CCN is the center of the model. The goal in this model is to consider individualized elements of the student's environment. More specifically, the student's access and opportunities barriers are evaluated to plan for student's outcomes.

The Participation Model "provides a systematic process for conducting augmentative and alternative communication (AAC) assessments and designing interventions based on the functional participation requirements of peers without disabilities of the same chronological age as the person with CCN" (Beukelman & Mirenda, 2013, p. 108). The Participation Model is based on the premise that, when students are given access to appropriate communication strategies and opportunities, they can be successful (Rosenberg & Beukelman, 1987). The model can serve as an assessment tool to help guide participation patterns of students with CCN. The Participation Model consists of two main types of potential barriers that may impact or inhibit the student's participation in a specific activity, task, or area. The two types are access and opportunity barriers. Figure 4.2 provides an outline of the various opportunity and access barriers. The diagram on the left indicates the types of opportunity barriers imposed on the student with CCN (discussed in this chapter), and the diagram on the right outlines access barriers (see Chapter 5 for more information about and descriptions of access

The Participation Model

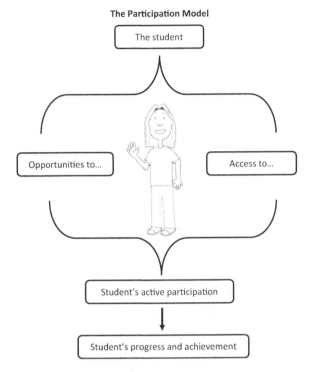

FIGURE 4.1   The participation model.

Adapted from "*The participation model*," Rosenberg & Beukelman, 1987, In C. A. Coston (Ed.), *Proceedings of the national planners conference on assistive device service delivery*, p. 159–161, Washington, DC: Association for the Advancement of Rehabilitation Technology.

barriers). The purpose of this chapter is to focus solely on opportunity barriers and highlight potential environmental considerations for successful interaction with students with CCN. The five opportunity barriers suggested by the Participation Model are addressed within two main categories, advocacy and abilities.

Opportunity Barriers

Opportunity barriers are barriers that are imposed on a student with CCN by other people in his or her environment (Beukelman & Mirenda, 2013; Ostergren & Guzzino, 2014; Torrison, Jung, Baker, Beliveau, & Cook, 2007). There are five main opportunity barriers that merge from the Participation Model: (1) policy, (2) practice, (3) attitude, (4) knowledge, and (5) skill. Often, barriers within the environment are due to a lack of understanding or knowledge of how to effectively interact, evaluate, and implement AAC practices (Light & McNaughton,

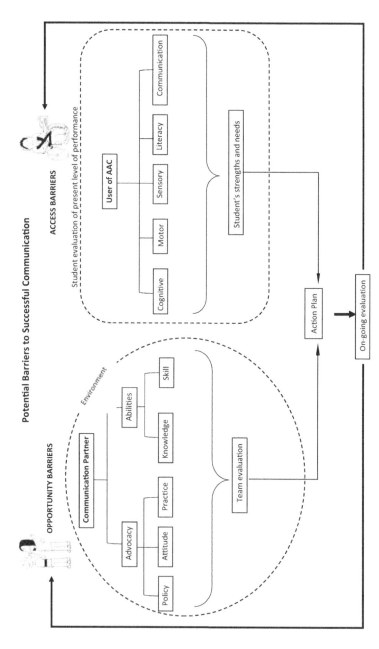

FIGURE 4.2 Potential barriers to successful communication.

2014).The root cause of these opportunity barriers is attributable to two general categories, advocacy and abilities.

The Advocacy Category

The advocacy category of opportunity barriers is an overarching term that encompasses barriers that are based on the communication partner's lack of understanding or the ability to advocate for the student with CCN.There are three main barriers included within this category: (1) lack of advocacy with regard to policy changes, (2) implementing general and instructional practices to support students with CCN, and (3) changing the attitudes of communication partners (or potential communication partners). Barriers under this category are related to lack of understanding on how policies, attitudes, and practices may impact the effectiveness of social and learning opportunities for the student with CCN.This includes the use of the communication system within various settings and across communication opportunities and partners.

Policy Barriers

Policy barriers refer to policies or regulations which may impact the student with CCN with regard to services and the communication system being provided: that is, policies that are the offset of legislative, standards, regulations, or school-based decisions that may inhibit students' access to communication in their classrooms (Beukelman & Mirenda, 2013; Light & McNaughton, 2014). Lack of funding for AAC services, systems, and training can be considered policy barriers as these directly impact students with CCN (McNaughton & Light, 2015;Torrison et al., 2007).

In the past 20 years, federal policies and regulation have been created to better support individuals with special needs, including students with CCN.The goal of these policies and regulations is to have documentation of the individual's needs and the supports needed. For example, the Individuals with Disabilities Education Act (IDEA) and the 2004 amendments indicate that the student's communication and assistive technology needs should be reported in Individualized Educational Program (IEPs) and Individualized Family Service Plans (IFSPs). Additionally, the Rehabilitation Act Amendments of 1992 indicates that assistive technology equipment should be considered and documented on the service plan for vocational rehabilitation for individuals with special needs (Ratcliff, Koul, & Lloyd, 2008). To accomplish the support needed, the Assistive Technology Act (2004) requires national funding to be allocated to states with the purpose to provide assistive technology to individuals with special needs (including students with CCN). While these policies and regulations are in place to help these students, there is still a lack of funding (Torrison et al., 2007) which consequently imposes a barrier for students with CCN.

Practice Barrier

Practice barriers refer to procedures within schools, work settings, or the community that may not be set or documented as a policy within that specific setting, yet are accepted practices (Beukelman & Mirenda, 2013; Light & McNaughton, 2014). An example of practice barriers is not allowing the student with CCN to take the AAC systems from the school or day program to their home setting (Torrison et al., 2007) or not having access to the AAC system while participating in school activities or routines (Huisman, 2014). Another challenge often faced is how professionals providing AAC services (e.g., special education teachers and speech-language pathologists) disagree on the AAC intervention (Finke & Quinn, 2012). Disagreement and differing implementation of AAC practices will impose barriers on the student as practices may not be effective (Thistle & Wilkinson, 2015). Staffing ratios and limited training on strategies when working with students with limited functional communication can also impose practice barriers to the student with CCN (Ballin, Balandin, Toger, & Stancliffe, 2009; Paterson, 2017; Torrison et al., 2007).

Attitude Barriers

Attitude barriers are attitudes, beliefs, and negative feelings from the communication partner that are imposed on the student. In some capacity, these attitudes impact the student's ability to fully participate in his or her environment (Beukelman & Mirenda, 2013; Light & McNaughton, 2014; Torrison et al., 2007). Too often, students with CCN are faced with low expectations in their performance due to their communication skills (Torrison et al., 2007). These students often have limited opportunities to actively engage and interact with peers (Therrien & Light, 2016) and are presented with limited participation opportunities (Anderson, Balandin, & Clendon, 2011). The attitudes of individuals within the environment can have a strong influence on the student's increased or decreased opportunities to participate (Quinton, 2014). Attitude barriers can be imposed on the student with CCN by peers, teachers, family members, professionals, or individuals in society in general (Lund & Light, 2007). Unfortunately, ineffective interaction may be perceived as appropriate practices which, in turn, may change the interactions or attitudes among others within the setting (Beck, Thompson, Kosuwan, & Prochnow, 2010). In fact, Iacono and Cameron (2009) found that, often, families of AAC users put forth a negative attitude towards the use of AAC, which can have an impact on the successful use of the AAC system. This suggests that effective and successful use of an AAC system will often be dependent on the supports available to the user, the views on the system and the user among communication partners, and the attitudes of family members on the user and the communication system (Baxter, Enderby, Judge, & Evans, 2012; Helling & Minga, 2014).

The Ability Category

The ability category describes two additional opportunity barriers, knowledge and skills. Knowledge and skill barriers occur due to the communication partner's lack of understanding of ways to interact, communicate, integrate, and support students with CCN. Barriers under the ability category are often related to the communication partner's lack of training. That is, communication partners do not have the ability to effectively engage, interact, and support students with CCN. Unfortunately, these barriers are too often observed across settings, as many practitioners have insufficient knowledge and skills to implement effective AAC practices (Costigan & Light, 2010; Da Fonte & Boesch, 2016; Light & McNaughton, 2012; Srinivasan, Matthews, & Lloyd, 2011). Families have reported that the obstruction of the successful use of an AAC system is often due to the lack of trained professionals to implement AAC assessment and interventions which, in turn, leads to inappropriate intervention practices (Mikolay, 2015).

Knowledge Barriers

Knowledge barriers refer to the communication partner's lack of familiarity or understanding of overall AAC assessment, intervention, and strategies. Knowledge barriers can also be related to the lack of understanding of how to effectively provide the student with CCN opportunities to interact with other communication partners and activities. Often, these barriers can arise from the communication partners having insufficient understanding regarding students with CCN and AAC, resulting in decreased participation opportunities for students with CCN (Torrison et al., 2007). Other common implications of knowledge barriers include insufficient professional help, negative responses from other individuals towards students with CCN (e.g., school, community, and families), communication partners dominating conversations when communicating with students with CCN, communication partners not allowing enough time for students with CCN to put together messages, communication partners not acknowledging the communicative attempt, and insubstantial financial support (Collier, Mcghie-Richmond, & Self, 2010; Crisp et al., 2014; Mandak, O'Neill, Light, & Fosco, 2017). Unfortunately, these barriers can lead to helplessness and social isolation, which can increase the risk for discrimination, victimization, and mental distress for students with CCN (Collier et al., 2010).

Skill Barriers

Skill barriers can be defined as the communication partners inability to implement AAC strategies or the lack of ability to interact and support students with CCN. Professionals who lack knowledge and skills of AAC may impact the communication skills and successful use of an AAC system (Baxter et al., 2012). Professional training with regard to AAC has increased, yet speech-language pathologists (SLP) and special education teachers still have reported a lack of experience, time, and preparedness to deliver effective AAC services (Costigan & Light, 2010; Dean, 2013; Helling & Minga, 2014). Skill barriers are not just caused by professionals, but can also result from other communication partners (King & Fahsl, 2012). The communication partner's skills will have an impact on communicative interactions. These have the potential to decrease or restrict the opportunities for the student with CCN to participate (Binger, Kent-Walsh, Ewing, & Taylor, 2010; Hagan & Thompson, 2013), increase ineffective communication interactions where the communication partners dominate the conversations (Collier et al., 2010), and decrease the use or integration of the communication system (Baxter et al., 2012; Belani, 2013). This, in turn, increases AAC system abandonment (Kent-Walsh, Murza, Malani, & Binger, 2015).

Identifying Opportunity Barriers and Creating an Action Plan

Students with CCN who depend on AAC systems face opportunity barriers in their environment. Teachers and professionals need to better understand how to determine and evaluate opportunity barriers within the student's environment. A starting point in this process is determining if the student with CCN is facing any opportunity barriers and determining an action plan. Figure 4.3 provides a *Team Assessment Consideration of Opportunity Barriers Checklist*. The purpose of this

Team Assessment Consideration of Opportunity Barriers Checklist

Student's name: _____ Date of completion: _____ Date for plan implementation: _____

Name: _____ Role: _____

Instructions. Complete the questions for each barrier domain by checking *Yes* or *No* in the response section. Begin with Q1 in each subdomain. If you mark *No* for three or more responses under each subdomain, there is a barrier in that domain. Any barrier identified should be addressed in the *Action Plan*. Include any additional anecdotal data in the *Notes* section.

Advocacy Opportunity Barriers			Response	
			Yes	No
Policy	Q1	Does the student have limited use of the AAC system within a health-care center?	☐	☐
	Q2	Does the student have access to use of the AAC system within the school?	☐	☐
	Q3	Does the student with CCN have social opportunities within the school?	☐	☐
	Q4	Does school district have a district-wide system selection?	☐	☐

FIGURE 4.3 Opportunity barriers evaluation form.

Adapted from Beukelman, D. R., & Mirenda, P. M. (2013). *Augmentative and alternative communication: Supporting children and adults with complex communication needs* (4th ed.). Baltimore, MD: Paul H. Brookes.

Note. IEP = Individualized education plan.

			Yes	No
Practice	Q1	Does school have access to professional practices	☐	☐
	Q2	Does the student have access to use of the system after school hours?	☐	☐
		☐Weekdays ☐Weekends		
	Q3	Does the student have access to use of the system during school breaks?	☐	☐
	Q4	Does the student have access to use of the system as a loan?	☐	☐
Attitude	Q1	Do the IEP team members or peers have reduced expectations?	☐	☐
	Q2	Do the IEP team members or peers have limited engagement with student with CCN?	☐	☐
	Q3	Do the IEP team members or peers have limited participation opportunities for the student with CCN?	☐	☐
	Q4	Do the IEP team members feel unqualified to interact with students with CCN?	☐	☐
	Q5	Do the IEP team members feel unqualified to implement AAC strategies?	☐	☐

Notes.

Action Plan

Abilities Opportunity Barriers			**Response**	
			Yes	No
Knowledge	Q1	Do the IEP team members understand data collection methods?	☐	☐
	Q2	Do the IEP team members understand options for intervention?	☐	☐
	Q3	Do the IEP team members understand instructional strategies?	☐	☐
	Q4	Do the IEP team members understand aided communication strategies?	☐	☐
		☐Low technology options ☐High technology options		
Skill	Q1	Do the IEP team members implement data collection?	☐	☐
	Q2	Do the IEP team members implement options for intervention?	☐	☐
	Q3	Do the IEP team members implement instructional strategies?	☐	☐
	Q4	Do the IEP team members implement unaided communication systems?	☐	☐
	Q5	Do the team members implement aided communication systems?	☐	☐
		☐Low technology systems ☐High technology systems	☐	☐

Notes.

Action Plan

FIGURE 4.3 (Continued)

Opportunity Barrier Data Collection Form

Name: ____________________ Date: __________ Time: __________

Activity/Task: ____________________ Observer: ____________________

Instructions: This form addresses five domains. In the left column, under *Environment or Setting*, list the specific environment in which you are observing the student. Place a checkmark for each subdomain there is barrier in the student's environment. In the *Results* section, write the total number of barriers *per domain* and *sub-domain*. If the observer indicates 2 or more checkmarks in the subdomains, a barrier has been identified for that domain. Write any additional notes in the *Anecdotal Notes* section.

			Opportunity Barriers																		
		Domains	Policy				Practice	Attitude				Knowledge					Skill				
		Sub-Domains	Federal	State	District	School	Unwritten policy	Expectations	Inclusion	Adult interaction	Peer interaction	Comm. dev. and comp.	AAC assessment	AAC systems	AAC inst. strategies	Collaboration	Comm. dev. and comp.	AAC assessment	AAC systems	AAC inst. strategies	Collaboration
Environment or Setting																					
1		S																			
		P																			
2		S																			
		P																			
3		S																			
		P																			
4		S																			
		P																			
5		S																			
		P																			

FIGURE 4.4 Opportunity barrier data collection form.

(*Sources:* Beukelman & Mirenda, 1988, 2013; Rosenberg & Beukelman, 1987)

Note. Comm. = communication; Comp. = competencies; Dev. = development

Results															
Total (per sub-domain)															
Total (per domain)															

Supports needed.

Anecdotal data.

FIGURE 4.4 (Continued)

checklist is for teams to identify opportunity barriers and create an action plan to effectively support the student. The *Team Assessment Consideration of Opportunity Barriers Checklist* is divided into the two categories of opportunity barriers, advocacy and abilities. Each member of the IEP team (e.g., family, special education teacher, speech–language pathologist, general education teacher, occupational therapist, physical therapist, administrator) should individually complete the *Team Assessment Consideration of Opportunity Barriers Checklist* for the student. The goal is for each team member to answer the questions provided on the checklist to the best of his or her knowledge, and then discuss with all team members to more accurately determine if barriers exist. Any notes or additional comments can be recorded for further discussion during the team meeting. During the meeting, the team should devise a possible plan of action for decreasing or eliminating these barriers in the student's environment.

Beukelman and Mirenda (2013) also suggest the use of the Activity Participation Inventory (API; see Beukelman & Mirenda, 2013 for more details and an example form). The API should be completed during the student's routine activities, including activities at home and school. Another possible way to assess the student's environment to determine if any opportunity barriers are being imposed on the student is by collecting data in particular environments or settings. Figure 4.4 offers an *Opportunity Barrier Data Collection Form*. The intent of this form is to be used during direct observations of the student across environments and communication partners. This form allows for comparison of the opportunities being provided to the student with CCN to other peers. The *Opportunity Barrier Data Collection Form* will also allow teams to determine the potential type of opportunity barriers being imposed, if any. This additional information can help guide teams in the creation of action plans to decrease opportunity barriers for the student.

Advocacy: Action Plan

To eliminate policy barriers within the student's environment, a first step is for careful evaluation and examination of policies being imposed (Light & McNaughton, 2014). Policy changes are challenging as they are perceived beyond our immediate means. To effectively support students with CCN, changes in policies are crucial to successful implementation of AAC practices (Paterson, 2017). However, these changes may be long term, as careful evaluation and consideration must take place prior to any revisions. Paterson (2017) suggest that taking advantage of social media to make policy changes for students with CCN may be a first step. The fact that social media can serve as an outlet to raise awareness of the needs of students with CCN and how policies may impact their opportunities and outcomes may play an important role in effective service delivery options. On the other hand, practice barriers may be barriers that can be changed in a shorter timeframe. Practices barriers can be decreased by providing appropriate and evidence-based instructional strategies (Dean, 2013). Collaboration, communication, and effective interaction models are also key in this process (Torrison et al., 2007). To decrease practice barriers, the system (e.g., classroom setting, school, school district) will need to evaluate their practices (i.e., unwritten rules) and make changes based on individual cases and overall evidence-based practices.

A set of overarching common beliefs and goals in the classroom, school, and school district is what will set the stage in how students with CCN are perceived. This will help decrease the attitude barriers. Similarly, the use of people first language (PFL) should be implemented to remind school personnel, and families, of the importance of acknowledging the person first and the condition second. Using PFL will support high expectations for the student with CCN and remind everyone that individualization is essential. The use of people's first language could be critical in decreasing attitude barriers, as the use of certain labels to identify or describe a student can be overgeneralized, inaccurate, and stereotypical (Snow, 2010). At the same time, lack of training and acknowledgement of individual differences can create attitude and opportunity barriers between the adults working with students with exceptionalities (Snow, 2010). Modeling of effective PFL and overall interactions will encourage positive attitudes and expand social acceptance of students with CCN and their communication systems (Light & McNaughton, 2014; Therrien & Light, 2016; Torrison et al., 2007). To provide these modeling opportunities for school personnel and peers, explicit activities and tasks will need to be identified and embedded throughout the day for students with CCN to increase their opportunities to communicate. Figure 4.5 outlines the three opportunity barriers within the category of advocacy and provides potential solutions for teams to consider.

Abilities: Action Plan

The main action plan for knowledge and skill barriers is the need for effective training (Baxter et al., 2012; Costigan & Light, 2010; Da Fonte & Boesch, 2016; Dean, 2013; Desai, Chow, Mumford, Hotze, & Chau, 2014; Mandak et al., 2017). Torrison and colleagues (2007) found that school personnel were often unaware of the process of AAC intervention. Educating and providing the necessary knowledge and skills to school personnel on how to accurately and effectively communicate with students with CCN is a crucial factor in eliminating knowledge and skill barriers. Barriers imposed on students with CCN in the abilities category are not just caused by professionals, but can also result from other communication partners, such as families and peers (King & Fahsl, 2012). Service providers have the responsibility to educate the peers and family on AAC systems and service. The family needs knowledge and skills to successfully communicate with their child (Mandak et al., 2017) and promote the communication skills while reinforcing the use of the AAC system (Kent-Walsh, Binger, & Hasham, 2010).

Advocacy Barriers and Potential Solutions

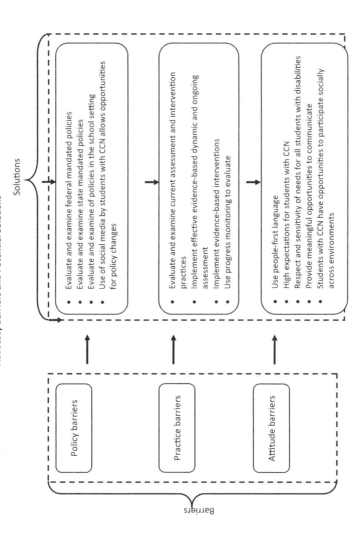

Solutions

- Evaluate and examine federal mandated policies
- Evaluate and examine state mandated policies
- Evaluate and examine of policies in the school setting
- Use of social media by students with CCN allows opportunities for policy changes

- Evaluate and examine current assessment and intervention practices
- Implement effective evidence-based dynamic and ongoing assessment
- Implement evidence-based interventions
- Use progress monitoring to evaluate

- Use people-first language
- High expectations for students with CCN
- Respect and sensitivity of needs for all students with disabilities
- Provide meaningful opportunities to communicate
- Students with CCN have opportunities to participate socially across environments

Policy barriers

Practice barriers

Attitude barriers

Barriers

FIGURE 4.5   Advocacy barriers and potential solutions.

(*Sources:* Dean, 2013; Light & McNaughton, 2014; Paterson, 2017)

A key component in the success of family implementation is not only for families to have knowledge and skills, but also that the family's opinions and perspectives are considered when selecting an AAC system (Mandak et al., 2017). Similarly, training will also need to extend to peers who will be interacting both academically and socially with the student (Lindsay, 2010; Stoner et al., 2010). Figure 4.6 outlines the two opportunity barriers within the category of abilities and provides potential solutions for teams to consider with regard to the various training needs. This figure also highlights the importance of training all communication partners on the same skills.

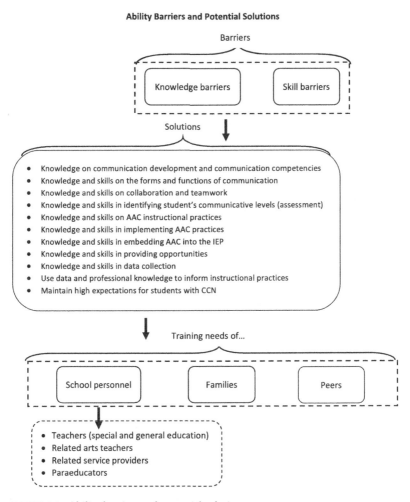

FIGURE 4.6   Ability barriers and potential solutions.

(*Sources:* Da Fonte & Boesch, 2016; Council for Exceptional Children, 2015)

Identifying opportunity barriers is a challenging task, yet it is critical to effectively serve students with CCN. Teams need to come together, collaborate, self-reflect, and evaluate their practices to determine if opportunity barriers are being imposed to the student with CCN. This should not be a judgment of the team or its members. The goal of this self-evaluation opportunity should be to enhance the team's practices, and to reflect on how to better support students. Lastly, opportunity barriers under the ability category may continuously exist, due to the vast technology advances and the ongoing evaluation of instructional practices. Thus, it is the responsibility of each team member to seek ongoing training to support each student in the most effective manner.

Key Points of Chapter 4

- Opportunity barriers are imposed by others on the student with CCN.
- There are two main categories of opportunity barriers, advocacy and abilities.
- The advocacy category includes barriers related to policy, practices, and attitudes.
- The abilities category includes barriers related to the knowledge and skills of the communication partner(s).
- Teams must identify opportunity barriers and create effective action plans to eliminate or decrease these barriers for students with CCN.
- Ongoing training is essential to decrease and eliminate opportunity barriers.
- Training should be provided to all communication partners (i.e., families, peers, professionals, staff).

Additional Resources

AAC-RERC
http://aac-rerc.psu.edu/index-1023.php.html
AAC Scotland—CALL
www.aacscotland.org.uk/Online-Learning-Modules/
Assistive Technology Internet Modules
www.atinternetmodules.org
Indiana Resource Center for Autism—Indiana University Bloomington
www.iidc.indiana.edu/pages/aac-training-and-technology
International Society for Augmentative and Alternative Communication (ISAAC)
www.isaac-online.org/english/home/
Manchester Metropolitan University—Augmentative and Alternative Communication (AAC)
https://aacmanmet.wordpress.com/aac-module-2/
Pennsylvania Department of Education—Power AAC

www.pattan.net/category/Educational%20Initiatives/Assistive%20Technol
    ogy/page/POWER_AAC.html
United States Society for Augmentative and Alternative Communication
    (USAAC)
www.ussaac.org

References

Anderson, K., Balandin, S., & Clendon, S. (2011). "He cares about me and I care about
    him." Children's experiences of friendship with peers who use AAC. *Augmentative and
    Alternative Communication, 27*, 77–90. doi:10.3109/07434618.2011.577449
Assistive Technology Act, 29 U.S.C. § 3001 (2004).
Ballin, L., Balandin, S., Toger, L., & Stancliffe, R. J. (2009). Learning to use Augmentative
    and Alternative Communication (AAC): Is there a mentoring role for adults expe-
    rienced in using AAC? *Journal of Intellectual and Developmental Disability, 34*, 89–91.
    doi:10.1080/13668250802676038
Baxter, S., Enderby, P., Judge, S., & Evans, P. (2012). Barriers and facilitators to the use of
    high-technology augmentative and alternative communication devices: A systematic
    review and qualitative synthesis. *International Journal of Language and Communication Dis-
    orders, 47*, 115–129. doi:10.1111/j.1460–6984.2011.00090.x
Beck, A. R., Thompson, J. R., Kosuwan, K., & Prochnow, J. M. (2010). The development
    and utilization of a scale to measure adolescents' attitudes towards peers who use
    Augmentative and Alternative (AAC) devices. *Journal of Speech, Language, and Hearing
    Research, 53*, 572–587. doi:10.1044/1092–4388(2009/07–0140)
Belani, H. (2013). Augmentative requirements engineering for trustworthy and usa-
    ble ICT- based services. *Human Factors in Computing and Informatics*, 815–818.
    doi:10.1007/978-3-642-39062-3_59
Beukelman, D. R., & Mirenda, P. (1988). Communication options for persons who cannot
    speak: Assessment and evaluation. In C. A. Costen (Ed.), *Proceedings of the national planners
    conference on assistive device service delivery* (pp. 151–165). Washington, DC: Association for
    the Advancement of Rehabilitation Technology.
Beukelman, D. R., & Mirenda, P. (2013). *Augmentative and alternative communication: Support-
    ing children and adults with complex communication needs* (4th ed.). Baltimore, MD: Paul
    H. Brookes.
Binger, C., Kent-Walsh, J., Ewing, C., & Taylor, S. (2010). Teaching educational assistants
    to facilitate the multisymbol message productions of young students who require aug-
    mentative and alternative communication. *American Journal of Speech-Language Pathology,
    19*, 108–120. doi:10.1044/1058–0360(2009/09–0015)
Collier, B., Mcghie-Richmond, D., & Self, H. (2010). Exploring communication assistants
    as an option for increasing communication access to communities for people who use
    augmentative communication. *Augmentative and Alternative Communication, 26*, 48–59.
    doi:10.3109/07434610903561498
Costigan, F. A., & Light, J. (2010). Effect of seated position on upper-extremity access to
    augmentative communication for children with cerebral palsy: Preliminary investiga-
    tion. *American Journal of Occupational Therapy, 64*, 596–604. doi:10.5014/ajot.2010.09013
Council for Exceptional Children. (2015). *CEC professional standards*. Retrieved from
    www.cec.sped.org/Standards

Crisp, C., Draucker, C. B., & Cirgin Ellett, M. L. (2014). Barriers and facilitators to children's use of speech-generating devices: A descriptive qualitative study of mothers' perspectives. *Journal for Specialists in Pediatric Nursing, 19,* 229–237. doi:10.111/jspn.12074

Da Fonte, M. A., & Boesch, M. C. (2016). Recommended augmentative and alternative communication competencies for special education teachers. *Journal of International Special Needs Education, 19,* 47–58. doi:10.9782/2159–4341–19.2.47

Dean, A. K. (2013). *Speech language pathologists' epistemological beliefs related to augmentative and alternative communication service provisions.* (Unpublished master's thesis). Wichita State University, Kansas.

Desai, T., Chow, K., Mumford, L., Hotze, F., & Chau, T. (2014). Implementing an iPad-based alternative communication device for a student with cerebral palsy and autism in the classroom via an access technology delivery protocol. *Computers and Education, 79,* 148–158. doi:10.1016/j.compedu.2014.07.009

Finke, E. H., & Quinn, E. (2012). Perceptions of communication style and influences on intervention practices for young children with AAC needs. *Augmentative and Alternative Communication, 28,* 117–126. doi:10.3109/07424618.2012.677959

Hagan, L., & Thompson, H. (2013). It's good to talk: Developing the communication skills of an adult with an intellectual disability through augmentative and alternative communication. *British Journal of Learning Disabilities, 42,* 68–75. doi:10.1111/bld.12041

Helling, C. R., & Minga, J. (2014). Developing an effective framework for the augmentative and alternative communication evaluation process. *Perspectives on Augmentative and Alternative Communication, 23,* 91–98. doi:10.1044/aac23.2.91

Huisman, A. J. (2014). *Barriers to accessing Augmentative and Alternative Communication (AAC): Pogo Boards as a potential solution.* (Unpublished honors program thesis). University of Northern Iowa, Iowa.

Iacono, T., & Cameron, M. (2009). Australian speech-language pathologists' perceptions and experiences of augmentative and alternative communication in early childhood intervention. *Augmentative and Alternative Communication, 25,* 236–249. doi:10.3109/07434610903322151

Kent-Walsh, J., Binger, C., & Hasham, Z. (2010). Effects of parent instruction on the symbolic communication of children using augmentative and alternative communication during storybook reading. *American Journal of Speech-Language Pathology, 19,* 97–107. doi:10.1044/1058–0360(2010/09–0014)

Kent-Walsh, J., Murza, K. A., Malani, M. D., & Binger, C. (2015). Effects of communication partner instruction on the communication of individuals using AAC: A meta-analysis. *Augmentative and Alternative Communication, 31,* 271–284. doi:10.3109/07434618.2015.1052153

King, A. M., & Fahsl, A. J. (2012). Supporting social competence in children who use augmentative and alternative communication. *TEACHING Exceptional Children, 45,* 42–49. doi:10.1177/004005991204500106

Light, J., & McNaughton, D. (2012). The changing face of augmentative and alternative communication: Past, present, and future challenges. *Augmentative and Alternative Communication, 28,* 197–204. doi:10.3109/07434618.2012.737024

Light, J., & McNaughton, D. (2014). Communicative competence for individuals who require augmentative and alternative communication: A new definition for a new era of communication. *Augmentative and Alternative Communication, 30,* 1–18. doi:10.3109/07434618.2014.885080

Lindsay, S. (2010). Perceptions of health care workers prescribing augmentative and alternative communication devices to children. *Disability and Rehabilitation: Assistive Technology, 5,* 209–222. doi:10.3109/17483101003718195

Lund, S. K., & Light, J. (2007). Long-term outcomes for individuals who use augmentative and alternative communication: Part II—communicative interaction. *Augmentative and Alternative Communication, 23*, 1–15. doi:10.1080/07434610600720442

Mandak, K., O'Neill, T., Light, J., & Fosco, G. M. (2017). Bridging the gap from values to actions: A family systems framework for family-centered AAC services. *Augmentative and Alternative Communication, 33*, 32–41. doi:10.1080/07434618.2016.1271453

McNaughton, D., & Light, J. (2015). What we write about when we write about AAC: The past 30 years of research and future directions. *Augmentative and Alternative Communication, 31*, 261–270. doi:10.3109/07434618.2015.1099736

Mikolay, R. M. (2015). *The challenges and perceptions of raising a child who uses AAC: A review of the literature.* (Unpublished honors research project). University of Akron, Ohio.

Ostergren, J. A., & Guzzino, S. (2014). Group therapy. In J. A. Ostergren (Ed.), *Speech language pathology assistants: A resource manual* (pp. 317–337). San Diego, CA: Plural Publishing.

Paterson, H. L. (2017). The use of social media by adults with acquired conditions who use AAC: Current gaps and considerations in research. *Augmentative and Alternative Communication, 33*, 23–31. doi:10.1080/07434618.2016.1275789

Quinton, M. C. (2014). Self-employment as a solution for attitudinal barriers: A case study. *Work, 28*, 127–130. doi:10.3233/WOR-141861

Ratcliff, A., Koul, R., & Lloyd, L. L. (2008). Preparation in augmentative and alternative communication: An update for speech-language pathology training. *American Journal of Speech-Language Pathology, 17*, 48–59. doi:10.1044/1058–0360(2008/005)

Rosenberg, S., & Beukelman, D. (1987). The participation model. In C. A. Coston (Ed.) *Proceedings of the national planners conference on assistive device service delivery* (pp. 159–161). Washington DC: RESNA, The Association for the Advancement of Rehabilitation Technology.

Snow, K. (2010). *To ensure inclusion, freedom, and respect for all, it's time to embrace people first language.* Retrieved from Disability is Natural E-Newsletter www.acdd.org/wp-content/uploads/ 2011/01/People_First_Language.pdf

Srinivasan, S., Matthews, S. N., & Lloyd, L. L. (2011). Insights into communication intervention and AAC in South India: A mixed-methods study. *Communication Disorders Quarterly, 32*, 232–246. doi:10.1177/1525740109354775

Stoner, J. B., Angell, M. E., & Bailey, R. L. (2010). Implementing augmentative and alternative communication in inclusive educational settings: A case study. *Augmentative and Alternative Communication, 26*, 122–135. doi:10.3109/07434618.2010.481092

Therrien, M. C., & Light, J. (2016). Using the iPad to facilitate interaction between preschool children who use AAC and their peers. *Augmentative and Alternative Communication, 32*, 163–174. doi:10.1080/07434618.2016.1205133

Thistle, J. J., & Wilkinson, K. M. (2015). Building evidence-based practice in AAC display design for young children: Current practices and future decisions. *Augmentative and Alternative Communication, 31*, 124–136. doi:10.3109/07434618.2015.1035798

Torrison, C., Jung, E., Baker, K., Beliveau, C., & Cook, A. (2007). The impact of staff training in Augmentative Alternative Communication (AAC) on the communication abilities of adults with developmental disabilities. *Developmental Disabilities Bulletin, 35*, 103–130.

UNIT 2

Assessment

The Student and The
Communication System

5

IDENTIFYING THE STUDENT'S PRESENT LEVEL OF PERFORMANCE

When considering students with complex communication needs (CCN), assessment is a multifaceted process that consists of gathering information on several components. Assessment should yield information specific to (1) the user of augmentative and alternative communication (AAC; Chapters 1, 2, 5, 6, 10, 11, and 12), (2) the AAC system (Chapters 7, 8, and 9), (3) the communication partners (Chapters 3 and 4), and (4) the environments (Chapters 4 and 12). The culmination of this assessment process allows the special education teachers and the IEP team to create an appropriate instructional plan and, subsequently, evaluate the effectiveness of the current instructional plan (Beukelman & Mirenda, 2013). Given the complexity of assessing students with CCN, who often have multiple disabilities, it is best to determine the goal for conducting the assessment prior to embarking on a full-scale assessment process. Otherwise, the assessment process may get overwhelming for the AAC team, the student, and the family.

The assessment is a multifaceted process in which information is gathered about a student's present level of performance and academic achievement to serve multiple goals. Therefore, it is recommended that the assessment process is comprehensive in order to create a robust profile of the student's abilities and needs. To capture a complete view of the student's abilities via data, the assessment process should be conducted by practitioners who have knowledge and skills in AAC and by using a variety of methods. Special education teachers play an important role in this assessment process.

Access Barriers

Chapter 4 provided an overview of the participation model and focused on opportunity barriers. This current chapter addresses the other component of the

AAC Present Level of Performance Assessment and Intervention Process

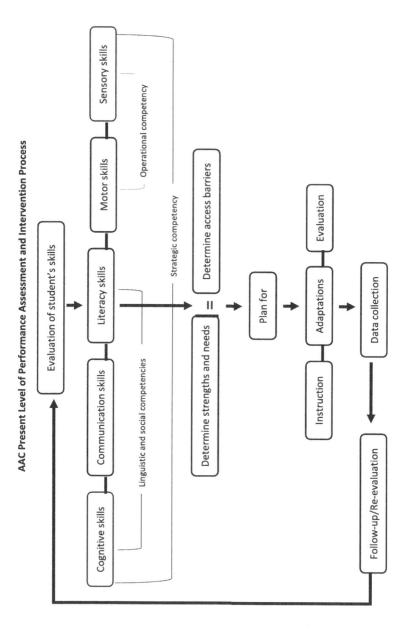

FIGURE 5.1   AAC present level of performance assessment and intervention process.

(*Sources:* Beukelman & Mirenda, 1988, 2013; Rosenberg & Beukelman, 1987)

participation model, which consists of access barriers. *Access barriers* refer to the conditions which result in communication difficulties by the user of AAC, due to a disability, and from the inherent features of the AAC system (Beukelman & Mirenda, 2013; Calculator, 1999; Torrison, Jung, Baker, Beliveau, & Cook, 2007). Access barriers take into account the student's cognitive abilities, communicative skills, literacy competency, motoric capabilities, and sensory responses (Beukelman & Mirenda, 2013; Torrison et al., 2007). Given the complexity of assessing all of these areas, it is important for special education teachers to collaborate with other school-service providers (e.g., occupational therapist, physical therapist, psychologist, speech-language pathologist). This allows the team to clearly identify the student's present level of performance and any potential access barriers the student may be facing.

When determining the present level of performance, the AAC Present Level of Performance Assessment and Intervention Process (see Figure 5.1) can be used as a guide in adequately planning the evaluation of a student's overall present level of performance. In this model, access barriers can be identified by assessing the areas of cognition, communication, literacy, motor, and sensory skills.

One of the first steps in the assessment process is to gather baseline data. The baseline data is important in understanding the student's abilities and areas of need. Figure 5.2 provides an example tool of an *Access Barrier Evaluation Form* that identifies the following five core domains: (1) cognitive abilities, (2) communicative skills, (3) literacy skills, (4) motoric abilities, and (5) sensory skills. Given the complexity of literacy skills, Chapter 6 focuses solely on the assessment of literacy skills for users of AAC. With the exception of literacy, the other four domains on this form are described in the next sections. Teachers may use the form to describe the observed activity or task and check for access barriers in specific subcomponents within the cognitive and communication domains. The motor, sensory, and the remainder of the cognitive subcomponents in Figure 5.2 should be completed by a psychologist, occupational therapist, physical therapist, and hearing specialist with input from the special education teacher to identify the access barriers.

Cognitive Skills

A key component of any communication and language assessment is to evaluate the student's *cognitive skills*. This includes evaluating a student's awareness, communicative intent, memory, symbolic representation, and world knowledge as these areas directly impact how a student learns to use an AAC system (Beukelman & Mirenda, 2013; Rowland & Schweigert, 2003). However, special education teachers will primarily focus on identifying the student's symbolic representation and world knowledge abilities. The other areas are outside of the teacher's scope of expertise, although he or she can provide assistance to the related service providers who are responsible for evaluating the other areas.

Access Barriers Evaluation Form

Name: _____   Date: _____   Time: _____

Activity/Task: _____   Observer: _____

Instructions: This form addresses five domains. Each domain should be completed by the appropriate specialist listed under the domain. In the left column, under *Activities/Task*, list the specific task the student will be completing. In the *S* (student) row, place a checkmark for each access barrier that applies to the student during the specific task. In the *P* (peer) row, place a checkmark for each access barrier that applies to the peer during the same task. In the *Results* section, write the total number of barriers per *domain and sub-domain*. Then, place a checkmark for each specialist whose support will be necessary, along with notes about the supports required based on the barriers faced by the student.

Domains		Cognitive					Communication				Literacy			Motor				Sensory				
Specialist		Psychologist			SPED Teacher		SLP and SPED Teacher				SPED Teacher			Physical Therapist				Audiologist, OT, Other				
Sub-Domains		Awareness	Intent	Memory	Symbolic rep.	World knowl.	Linguistic	Operational	Social	Strategic	Reading	Writing	Spelling	Fine	Gross	Mobility	Position	Auditory	Gustatory	Olfactory	Visual	Tactile
Activities/Tasks																						
1	S																					
	P																					
2	S																					
	P																					
3	S																					
	P																					
4	S																					
	P																					
5	S																					
	P																					

FIGURE 5.2 Access barriers evaluation form.

(*Sources:* Beukelman & Mirenda, 1988, 2013; Blackstein–Adler, 2003; Rosenberg & Beukelman, 1987)

Note. knowl. = knowledge; p = peer; rep. = representation; s = target student; SLP = speech-language pathologist; SPED = special education

Results							
Total (per sub-domain)							
Total (per domain)							

Supports needed by...

☐ AAC consultant/specialist   ☐ Physical therapist

☐ Audiologist   ☐ Psychologist

☐ English language learner specialist   ☐ Speech language pathologist

☐ Occupational therapist   ☐ Teacher of students with visual impairment

☐ Orientation and mobility   ☐ Teacher of the students with hearing impairment

Anecdotal Notes.

FIGURE 5.2 (Continued)

Language involves a shared symbol system (e.g., sign language, writing, Braille, picture symbols) of understanding between the messenger and the message receiver (Ondondo, 2015). Students who use AAC may have differing levels of linguistic understanding (i.e., non-symbolic or symbolic). While some elements of non-symbolic and symbolic understanding may be assessed by school psychologists or speech-language pathologists, classroom teachers can also help determine if a student is functioning at the non-symbolic or *symbolic communication* level. Teachers may use a screening questionnaire such as the one illustrated in Figure 5.3 given the frequency with which they observe the student's communicative behaviors across settings and communication partners. This screening tool allows for a simple method of evaluating the student's communicative skills and determining if a student is communicating at the non-symbolic or symbolic level. Once this screening is completed, teachers should proceed to completing Figures 5.7 or 5.8 based on the screening results. Both of the evaluation forms are described in the communication skills domain within the context of Light's communication competencies.

To assess symbolic representation, teachers may use commercially available tools as well as classroom observations to determine the student's ability to recognize and understand the communicative value of symbolic representations (Dietz, Quach, Lund, & McKelvey, 2012) such as objects, tangible symbols, photographs, line drawings, or written words (see Figure 5.4 for an example of the various types of symbolic representations). Assessing symbolic representation also includes determining the student's ability to identify symbols of varying iconicity levels. *Iconicity* refers to how closely a symbol (e.g., line drawings, manual sign, photograph) is related to the message being communicated (Markham & Justice, 2004). There are three levels of iconicity: (1) transparent, (2) translucent, and (3) opaque. Figure 5.5 illustrates the various levels of iconicity of a symbol.

(1) *Transparent.* A *transparent* symbol is when the meaning of the symbol can be guessed with ease even when the referent for the symbol is absent.
(2) *Translucent.* A *translucent* symbol is when the meaning of a symbol can be identified once the relationship between symbol and referent is explained.
(3) *Opaque.* An *opaque* symbol means there is no clear relationship between the symbol and its referent even when the meaning of the symbol is known (see Lloyd, Fuller, and Arvidson, 1997, for additional information on iconicity).

Refer to Chapters 8 and 9 for specific assessment information pertaining to aided low and high technology.

Furthermore, it is important to evaluate a student's world knowledge as it directly impacts the student's ability to learn symbols, including vocabulary. Concept development is potentially one of the most important parts of learning to use an AAC device (Murray & Goldbart, 2009). When there is a lack of experience and world knowledge, it can limit the student's understanding of the symbols

Non-symbolic and Symbolic Communicators Screening Questionnaire

Student name: Completed by: Date:

_____   _____   _____

The purpose of this screening questionnaire is to provide a general outline of the student's non-symbolic and symbolic communicative behaviors. It is highly recommended that a comprehensive assessment be conducted in collaboration with other teams members, including the speech-language pathologist, to determine a more accurate level of the student's communicative performance.

Instructions: Respond to the following questions by selecting *yes* or *no* based on the student's ability. If any responses to questions 1-4 are *yes* and all responses to questions 5-10 are *no*, the student is most likely functioning at the non-symbolic communication level. If all responses to questions 1-4 are *yes*, and some or all of the responses to questions 5-10 are *yes*, the student is functioning at the symbolic level.

General Questions		Response	
		YES	NO
Q1.	Can the student's communication attempt be understood by familiar communication partners?	☐	☐
Q2.	Does the student use one or more of the following *forms* of communication: gestures, body language, facial expressions to express wants and needs?	☐	☐
Q3.	Does the student accept and reject when presented with an item or person?	☐	☐
Q4.	Does the student express excitement when interacting with a familiar communication partner by smiling, looking, gazing, or reaching?	☐	☐
Q5.	Does the student use one or more of the following *forms* of communication: pointing, showing, giving?	☐	☐
Q6.	Does the student demonstrate understanding that a symbol (e.g., object, photograph, or line drawing) represents words?	☐	☐
Q7.	Can the student follow commands from daily routine tasks or activities?	☐	☐
Q8.	Does the students recognize and label symbols, objects, photographs, or line drawings?	☐	☐
Q9.	Is the student able to actively participate in a communicative interaction by following the conversation, taking turns, and/or sharing information?	☐	☐
Q10.	Can the student engage in communicate interactions on various topics with his/her communication partner?	☐	☐

FIGURE 5.3   Non-symbolic and symbolic communicators screening questionnaire.

(*Sources:* DynaVox Mayer-Johnson, 2014; Rowland, 2004)

involved in the AAC system. A lack of world knowledge may impact the student's semantic development if he or she does not have the concept knowledge to go along with the symbol used in the AAC device (Murray & Goldbart, 2009). Similarly, a student's ability to learn graphic symbols is affected by his or her world knowledge as previous exposure to graphic symbols can affect his or her ability to use the symbols (Dada & Alant, 2009). A survey study by Chompoobutr, Potibal, Boriboon, and Phantachat (2013) found that students with different cultural and educational backgrounds and experiences understand graphic symbols differently. Furthermore, world knowledge is critical for reading comprehension (Light, McNaughton, Weyer, & Karg, 2008; Soto & Hartmann, 2006) and motivation to communicate (Chompoobutr et al., 2013). Because world knowledge impacts the use of AAC systems in multiple ways, it is important to refer to the assessment data to determine the most appropriate organization and layout of the AAC

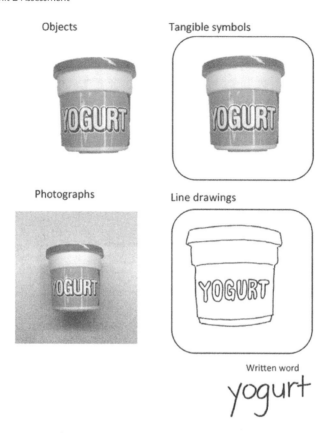

FIGURE 5.4 Examples of symbolic representations.

system. If the AAC system is not organized in a manner that relates to the student's life experiences, retrieving information from the AAC system will be difficult. Because of this, it is important to use relevant, high-context images (Beukelman, Hux, Dietz, McKelvey, & Weissling, 2015). Overall, the assessment process should include a careful evaluation of the student's world knowledge so that teachers, SLPs, and other related service providers can plan for and use effective strategies to address the limited world knowledge that many people with disabilities have.

Communication Skills

When assessing a student's communication skills, it is crucial to understand what forms of communication the student may already have and what is the function of the communication interaction. Often times, the form of communication is more obvious, while the function of the communicative attempt tends to be more complex (King & Fahsl, 2012). Different *forms of communication* for individuals

ICONICITY

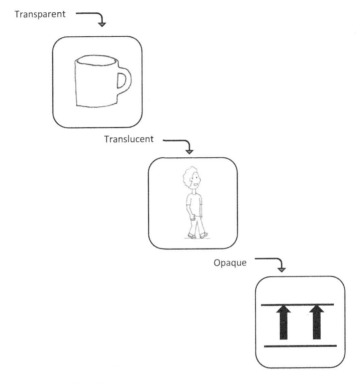

Transparent

Translucent

Opaque

FIGURE 5.5   Examples of iconicity

who are in the prelinguistic stage can include gestures, pointing, and vocalizations (Brady, Marquis, Fleming, & McLean, 2004). Other forms of communication include a range of potential communicative acts, such as gestures, eye gaze, facial movements, challenging behavior, laughing, smiling, crying, whining, and physical manipulation (Carvey & Bernhardt, 2009; McClean & Snyder-McClean, 1987; Sigafoos et al., 2000). The *functions of communication*, including prelinguistic behaviors, can include behavioral guidelines, social interaction, joint attention, rejecting or requesting objects or actions, imitating, requesting information, and sharing emotions (Carvey & Bernhardt, 2009; Didden et al., 2009; Sigafoos et al., 2000). It can be a challenge to determine the function of these prelinguistic behaviors (Didden et al., 2009). Thus, one potentially helpful tool designed to assess the function is the Checklist of Communicative Functions and Means (Wetherby, 1995).

For challenging behaviors, a functional behavior assessment (FBA) is helpful in identifying the function of these communicative behaviors. An FBA consists of observing and collecting data on the behavior(s) in different antecedent and consequent environments and activities and with different communicative partners so

Symbolic Representation Screening Questionnaire and Informal Observation

Student name: _____ Completed by: _____ Date: _____

This screening questionnaire provides a general outline of the student's symbolic representation. It is highly recommended that a comprehensive assessment (e.g., TASP – Test of Aided Communication Symbol Performance) be conducted in collaboration with other teams members to determine a more accurate level of the student's symbolic representation.

Note: Transparent refers to a symbol that can be guessed with ease even when the referent for that symbol is absent. *Translucent* refers a symbol that can be perceived once the relationship between symbol and referent after a symbol has been taught. *Opaque* refers to a symbol with no clear relationship between the symbol and its referent even when the meaning of the symbol is known (e.g., verbs, adjectives).

Symbolic Representation Questions	YES	NO
Instructions: Complete the following questions by selecting *yes* or *no* based on the student's ability. If *yes* is selected for Q1 and Q2, the student is able to identify *objects* as symbolic representation. If *yes* is selected for Q1-Q4, the student is able to identify *photographs* as symbolic representation. If *yes* is selected for Q1-Q6, the student is able to use *line drawings* as a symbolic representation.		
Q1. Does the student understand that *objectives* have a meaning?	☐	☐
Q2. Does the student use *objects* to request?	☐	☐
Q3. Does the student understand that *photographs* have a meaning?	☐	☐
Q4. Does the student use *photographs* to request?	☐	☐
Q5. Does the student understand that *line drawings* have a meaning?	☐	☐
Q6. Does the student use *line drawings* to request?	☐	☐

Iconicity Questions	Transparent	Translucent	Opaque
Instructions: Complete the following questions by adding a checkmark based on the student's ability to understand and use symbolic representation based on the levels of iconicity (Q7 and Q8 for photographs; Q9 and Q10 for line drawings).			
Q7. What type of *photographs* does the student understand consistently?	☐	☐	☐
Q8. What type of *photographs* does the student use consistently to communicate?	☐	☐	☐
Q9. What type of *line drawings* does the student understand consistently?	☐	☐	☐
Q10. What type of *line drawings* does the student use consistently to communicate?	☐	☐	☐

Additional Comments or Notes

FIGURE 5.6 Symbolic representation screening questionnaire.

that the behavior can be analyzed for its function (Heath, Ganz, Parker, Burke, & Ninci, 2015; Iwata, Dorsey, Slifer, Bauman, & Richman, 1994). In addition to documenting when these behaviors occur (i.e., antecedent and consequence), with whom, and under what circumstances, teachers, parents, and other service providers can use tools such as the Functional Assessment Screening Tool (Iwata & DeLeon, 2005), Questions About Behavioral Function (Matson & Vollmer, 1995), Motivation Assessment Scale (Durand & Crimmins, 1992), and others. Understanding the form and function of the communicative interaction is a crucial step in supporting the development of communicative competence (Bradshaw, 2013).

Another key component of the AAC assessment process should be for teams to determine the communicative competency level of the student. This entails determining the student's ability within Light, Arnold, and Clark's (2003) four communication competencies: (1) linguistic, (2) operational, (3) social, and (4) strategic (see Light & McNaughton, 2014 for a complete description on these communicative competencies). Although it is important to determine the student's level of performance for each communication competency during the AAC assessment process, it should be noted that each competency is interrelated, and requires "integration of knowledge, judgment, and skills" (Light et al., 2003, p. 13) across all domains.

Linguistic Competence

Linguistic competence refers to the student's knowledge of language, symbols, or linguistic code (DeVeney, Hoffman, & Cress, 2012; Light, 1989; Light & McNaughton, 2014). Students who use AAC should work towards becoming fluent in the native language at home, in various social circles, and within the greater communities (Light et al., 2003; Light & McNaughton, 2014; Soto & Yu, 2014). As such, assessing a student's linguistic competence is a complex task. It requires the evaluation of a combination of multiple processing systems used in communication (e.g., auditory, visual). To simplify this assessment, teachers and related service providers should divide this process into two main areas: (1) evaluating the student's linguistic communication (i.e., content, form, and use) and (2) assessing the student's motor, visual, and auditory skills (Brady et al., 2016; Light, 1989; Light et al., 2003). Although, these two main areas of assessment should be considered for both non-symbolic and symbolic communicators, the specific skills assessed will vary.

Students who are non-symbolic communicators should be evaluated based on their current modes of communication (e.g., eye gaze, vocalizations). For example, a student may grab, cry, or yell in an attempt to communicate a request, rejection, or seek attention. To isolate the function of these communication forms, the teacher and service providers should observe the communication behaviors of the student during typical daily activities. During these observations, it is necessary to consider the communicative behavior, the environment, and the response of the communication partner. Because non-symbolic communicative behaviors are left to the interpretation of the communicative partner, the partner plays a key role in the communicative attempt.

With non-symbolic communicators, it is important to create a student's communicative repertoire where the communication partner can provide meaning to the student's communicative attempts. Most non-symbolic communicators have a limited understanding that pictures or words represent ideas. Instead, they rely on gestures, facial expressions, and vocalizations to meet their needs, which require caregivers to interpret the meaning of these non-symbolic interactions (Hostyn,

Non-symbolic Communication Behaviors Evaluation Form

Student's name:_____   Activity:_____

Observer's name:_____   Date/Time of observation:_____

Instructions: For each competency, check *yes* for the skills your student does independently or *no* for the skills your student does not do independently. Under *anecdotal notes*, add any additional relevant information that may occur during the observation.

	Skills	Yes	No	Anecdotal Notes
Linguistic	Behavior changes (cries)	☐	☐	
	Screams or yells	☐	☐	
	Vocalizes	☐	☐	
	Protests	☐	☐	
	Refuses or rejects	☐	☐	
	Accepts offered items	☐	☐	
	Requests objects	☐	☐	
Operational	Uses joint attention (partner-object)	☐	☐	
	Uses auditory attention	☐	☐	
	Uses physical attention	☐	☐	
	Eye tracks	☐	☐	
	Explores the system	☐	☐	
Social	Smiles	☐	☐	
	Makes facial expressions	☐	☐	
	Responds and request attention	☐	☐	
	Makes eye contact	☐	☐	
	Shows affection	☐	☐	
	Grabs or reaches	☐	☐	
	Uses proximity (joint attention)	☐	☐	
	Uses gestures	☐	☐	
	Takes turns (object-based)	☐	☐	
Strategic	Recognizes that his/her communicative behavior has an impact on the communication partner (cause-effect)	☐	☐	
	Recognizes communication breakdown and responds in a functional manner	☐	☐	

FIGURE 5.7   Non-symbolic communicative behaviors evaluation form.

(*Sources:* DynaVox Mayer-Johnson, 2014; Rowland, 2004)

Daelman, Janssen, & Maes, 2010; Singh, Iacono, & Gray, 2014). A checklist, such as the one shown in Figure 5.7, the *Non-Symbolic Communicative Behaviors Evaluation Form*, can be useful identifying the student's communication level. This checklist contains behaviors that are indicative of someone who is functioning at the non-symbolic level. However, further assessment using the *Symbolic Communicative Behaviors Form* (Figure 5.8) is warranted if the student demonstrates the majority

Symbolic Communication Behaviors Evaluation Form

Student's name:_____   Activity:_____

Observer's name:_____   Date/time of observation:_____

Instructions: For each competency, check *yes* for the skills your student does independently or *no* for the skills your student does not do independently. Under *anecdotal notes*, add any information that is relevant during the observation.

Linguistic Competency					
Skills	Yes	No	Skills	Yes	No
Uses words	☐	☐	Labels objects, people, and/or places with concrete symbols	☐	☐
Uses phrases	☐	☐	Labels actions, feelings, and/or concepts with abstract symbols	☐	☐
Uses sentences	☐	☐	Uses concrete/abstract symbols to state phrases	☐	☐
Uses *yes* and *no*	☐	☐	Uses concrete/abstract symbols to state sentences	☐	☐
Makes choices	☐	☐	Asks questions	☐	☐
Anecdotal notes					

Operational Competency					
Skills	Yes	No	Skills	Yes	No
Transports AAC system	☐	☐	Adjusts volume and screen	☐	☐
Locates preferred vocabulary related to a task or activity	☐	☐	Turns system on/off	☐	☐
Navigates AAC system w/support	☐	☐	Asks for assistance	☐	☐
Navigates AAC system independently	☐	☐	Participates in adding vocabulary to system	☐	☐
Anecdotal notes					

FIGURE 5.8 Symbolic communication behaviors evaluation form.

(*Sources:* DynaVox Mayer-Johnson, 2014; Fenson et al., 2007; Rowland, 2004)

of these skills. A student who is a symbolic communicator will display these skills plus more advanced skills.

For symbolic communicators, an evaluation targeting *receptive* and *expressive language* is key. In this process, the teacher will need to work jointly with the speech-language pathologist so that a formal evaluation can be conducted. Symbolic communicators may have different levels of linguistic understanding when

Social Competency					
Skills	Yes	No	Skills	Yes	No
Makes eye contact	☐	☐	Uses *please* and *thank you*	☐	☐
Requests action	☐	☐	Uses humor	☐	☐
Requests object	☐	☐	Takes turns	☐	☐
Asks questions	☐	☐	Initiates and terminates conversations	☐	☐
Shares personal and novel information	☐	☐	Maintains topic	☐	☐
Greets	☐	☐	Requests information	☐	☐
Anecdotal notes					

Strategic Competency					
Skills	Yes	No	Skills	Yes	No
Gains partner's attention	☐	☐	Uses various communication modalities	☐	☐
Initiates with familiar and unfamiliar communication partners	☐	☐	Requests the AAC system	☐	☐
Ends a conversation	☐	☐	Repairs communication breakdowns	☐	☐
Changes topics	☐	☐	Adapts interaction to communication partner	☐	☐
Anecdotal notes					

FIGURE 5.8 (Continued)

learning to engage in symbolic communication during daily communication exchanges (Robinson & Soto, 2013). At the same time, teachers should consider evaluating the student's understanding of symbolic representations (Mims, Browder, Baker, Lee, & Spooner, 2009). This process often begins with students labeling objects with a picture or symbol, using a variety of symbols to state phrases, and then creating independent sentences (Light & McNaughton, 2014). Observations of a student's linguistic abilities should include monitoring his or her ability to use words, phrases, and sentences, and the ability to use concrete and abstract symbols in order to label objects, actions, and to state phrases or sentences (Brady et al., 2016; Rowland, 2011). See Figure 5.8 for an example of a *Symbolic Communicative Behaviors Evaluation Form*.

Operational Competence

Operational competence refers to the technical skills necessary to use an AAC system or techniques (Light, 1989; Light & McNaughton, 2014). To assess the student's ability to manage specific AAC systems, the teacher will need to collaborate with the occupational and physical therapist in providing them with information about the student's performance in various educational situations and settings. These two professionals will have a key role in this process as they are the ones who can outline and determine the student's strengths and areas of need with regard to his or her fine motor skills (e.g., used to activate the icons on the SGD or turning it on and off) and gross motor skills (e.g., used to take the SGD or communication book to various environments). Understanding the student's present level of performance in operating an AAC system is critical in ensuring the student is successful as it may require specific physical, visual, and cognitive skills to operate low- and high-technology AAC systems (Beukelman & Mirenda, 2013).

Specifically, assessing a student's operational competence consists of observing a student's ability to transport the AAC system, navigate the AAC system, adjust the volume and screen, turn the system on and off, ask for assistance, and participate in adding vocabulary to the system. Furthermore, observations targeting motor control (e.g., pointing) should be conducted to help inform the best access methods for the target individual (e.g., pointing to activate an SGD). Typically, the occupational therapist will be a key person in identifying the student's strengths and areas of need to ensure the access method of the AAC system is appropriate and effective for the student (Beukelman & Mirenda, 2013; Binger et al., 2012; Brady et al., 2016).

Social Competence

Social competence considers pragmatic adjustments made by the student such as the ability to relate to interpersonal dynamics (e.g., actively participating in a communicative interaction) and pragmatic discourse strategies (e.g., initiating a conversation; Chung & Douglas, 2014; Light et al., 2003; Light, Parsons, & Drager, 2002). It involves using language for different purposes, changing language according to the needs of a listener or situation, and following the unspoken rules of conversations (ASHA, 2017; Shane et al., 2012). To develop these social skills, Light and McNaughton (2014) break down social competence into two necessary sets of skills: (1) sociolinguistic and (2) socio-relational. *Sociolinguistic skills* include pragmatic aspects of communicative functions such as requesting an object, asking for attention, protesting, requesting information, or confirming (Johnston, Reichle, Feeley, & Jones, 2012; King & Fahsl, 2012; Light & McNaughton, 2014; Teachman & Gibson, 2013). This skillset also includes discourse strategies such as turn-taking, initiation, and the ability to terminate conversations when appropriate (Light & McNaughton, 2014). For students without CCN, many of these pragmatic skills are learned through natural interactions. Unfortunately, students with CCN may not inherently develop these skills due to a variety of barriers. Thus, understanding the impact of CCN on these skills is critical in determining the appropriate level of support needed to establish social competence (Raghavendra, Olsson, Sampson, Mcinerney, & Connell, 2012). *Socio-relational competence* refers to the ability to communicate by participating in interactions, showing an interest in partners, or promoting oneself in a positive light (Light et al., 2003; Light & McNaughton, 2014). Unfortunately, students with CCN may not inherently develop these skills due to a variety of barriers (Raghavendra et al., 2012).

Special education teachers should identify which social skills are evident in students communicating at the non-symbolic level. Skills that may be present include smiling, making eye contact, grabbing or reaching for desired items or people, and using proximity to demonstrate joint attention. These individuals may also engage in object-based turn-taking during play activities and use gestures such as pointing to items of interest, or they may request or respond to attention.

Symbolic communicators should be assessed on their ability to request for an action or object using a picture symbol, to use please and thank you when appropriate in a social situation, to demonstrate an interest in others by initiating a conversation, and to participate in interactions actively by maintaining the topic of conversation, taking conversational turns, and requesting information from the communication partner. Similarly, social competence is evident in a symbolic communicator when the student is able to use humor and share personal and novel information. All these skills are necessary to effectively communicate and participate in a communicative interaction. To encourage these communicative skills, teachers and SLPs focus on increasing the student's attempts to share information rather than the information exchange itself.

Strategic Competence

Strategic competence refers to how the individual can communicate despite barriers that occur due to the environment or the student's limited speech. Some skills that demonstrate strategic competence include the ability to gain a partner's attention, to initiate and end a conversation, to use a variety of communication modalities, and to repair communication breakdowns. Given the likelihood of communication breakdowns for a student with CCN, it is important for the student to gain strategic competence (Chung & Douglas, 2014; Raghavendra et al., 2012; Teachman & Gibson, 2013). The teacher may assess these prerequisite skills by building and assessing other domains. For example, the student may build interaction skills to prepare for strategic competence by using humor to build positive rapport with other students. Building a good rapport with students using humor can help repair communication breakdowns or teach students how to initiate communication. In this way, the teacher may assess prerequisite skills by looking at the other domains (Light & McNaughton, 2014).

For a student who is functioning at the non-symbolic level, the primary areas of assessment include determining if the student recognizes his or her communicative impact on the communication partner. In other words, does the student understand cause and effect? Also, does the student recognize when a communication breakdown occurs and respond in a functional manner? On the other hand, students who use symbolic communication should be assessed on their ability to gain the communicative partner's attention, initiate communication with familiar and unfamiliar people, change conversation topics when appropriate, end a conversation, use various communication modalities appropriate for the situation, or repair communication breakdowns.

Motoric Abilities

Identifying the student's strengths and needs to develop a holistic profile extends beyond the cognitive, language, and communication domains. It is also equally important to evaluate the motor abilities of the student to better inform the decision-making process about the appropriate AAC system, AAC placement, AAC access method, and student positioning. However, these evaluations should be conducted by service providers such as occupational therapists, physical therapists, or even adapted physical education teachers in collaboration with the special education teacher. Occupational therapists can functionally evaluate *gross motor* (e.g., reaching, grasping, passing) and *fine motor skills* (e.g., pointing, gripping, writing, pinching) in order to inform the decision-making process. Along with occupational therapists, physical therapists can also provide meaningful insight through systematic assessment related to mobility (e.g., walking, pushing, side-strength) and positioning (e.g., functional seating to increase engagement or line of vision, use of standers or sidelyers to promote muscle growth and development). The AAC team must identify and address any motor difficulties in order to provide support and modifications to the environment in order to ensure that there are no negative effects on the student's performance with the AAC system in the classroom (Piek, Hands, & Licari, 2012).

Students with CCN may also have motor difficulties which affect their range of seating and positioning. Positioning can influence a student's ability to functionally access the AAC system. If a student is seated in a safe and supported position, it allows the student the opportunity to access his or her device in a variety of positions (Lund, Quach, Weissling, McKelvey, & Dietz, 2017). Beukelman and Mirenda (2013) suggest two areas for consideration when assessing motor abilities. First, the student should have a method to respond to the evaluation team during the assessment. Second, the student should have an alternative method to respond on a long-term basis. Without a reliable and efficient selection method, it is difficult for the student to respond to questions. Thus, it will likely lead the assessment team to draw inaccurate conclusions about the student's abilities. According to Lund and colleagues (2017), direct selection technique is the most reliable way for

Classroom Support Form:
Positioning, Seating, and Mobility

Student name: _____   Completed by: _____   Date: _____

The purpose of this form is to provide general guidelines for the classroom teacher and support staff on how to position, seat, or move a particular student. It is highly recommended that a comprehensive assessment be conducted by the specialized team member, including an occupational therapist and a physical therapist to determine the best strategies to be used with the student.

Note. This form should be completed by the physical and/or occupational therapist.

SEATING	
Chair	
Do's	**Don'ts**
Wheelchair	
Do's	**Don'ts**
POSITIONING	
Standers	
Do's	**Don'ts**
Laying	
Do's	**Don'ts**

FIGURE 5.9   Classroom support form: Positioning, seating, and mobility.

(*Sources:* Brady et al., 2016; Whitmore et al., 2014)

students with motor difficulties to provide answers, although it may be strenuous for the student.

Scanning is an alternative selection technique which requires minimal motor ability. However, it is not as reliable as direct selection during the assessment process. Scanning has a greater cognitive load due to its reliance on other core areas including cognitive, motor, and sensory (Beukelman & Mirenda, 2013). The accuracy of the student's selection with scanning can also be impacted by the type

MOBILITY	
Range of Motion	
Do's	Don'ts
Strength and Tone	
Do's	Don'ts
Voluntary Control	
Do's	Don'ts
SPECIFIC ENVIRONMENTAL ARRANGEMENTS	
SENSORY CONSIDERATIONS	
Additional Comments/Notes	

FIGURE 5.9 (Continued)

of scanning technique the student uses. (McCarthy et al., 2006). Thus, it may be difficult to determine the cause of the errors made by the student. Nonetheless, it is important to evaluate both direct and scanning selection methods to determine which long-term access method is best for the student. The student's hand and arm mobility are most important when assessing which method is appropriate, followed by head and foot control (Beukelman & Mirenda, 2013; Whitmore, Romski, & Sevcik, 2014). Figure 5.9, the *Classroom Support Form: Positioning, Seating, and Mobility*, is an example of a motor guidelines form that can be used to provide general guidelines to the classroom teacher and support staff on how to position, seat, or move a particular student. However, this form should be completed by the physical and/or occupational therapist. The *Classroom Support Form* addresses seating guidelines for chairs and wheelchairs, positioning guidelines for sidelyers, and mobility guidelines for range of motion, strength and tone, and voluntary control. It also allows the physical and/or occupational therapist to suggest specific environmental arrangements necessary for the student, and any sensory considerations that may impact the student's effective use of his or her AAC system.

Sensory Responses

Students with CCN may have additional impairments pertaining to vision and hearing. Understanding these sensory responses supplements assessment information gathered about the student's cognitive, communicative, and literacy levels to ensure the appropriate AAC system is recommended. Sensory response information also helps the teacher create an instructional environment that is aligned to the student's abilities and needs. Obtaining information related to these types of sensory responses requires *consultation* with the appropriate specialists, such as vision and hearing specialists.

Symbol-based AAC systems often require a significant amount of visual functioning (Clarke, Price, & Griffiths, 2016). Thus, a vision assessment is necessary to evaluate a student's visual abilities such as sharpness of vision, the motor functioning of the eyes, the student's sensitivity to light and color, the size of the student's visual field, how stable the student's vision is, and other visual functions (Higginbotham, Shane, Russell, & Caves, 2007). All of these considerations must be addressed by a vision specialist during the AAC assessment process before an appropriate AAC system can be selected for the student. These factors pertaining to visual abilities will impact what type of symbols are used, how big the symbols should be, where the device is placed, and what the spacing is like within the device. (Beukelman & Mirenda, 2013). Furthermore, a vision assessment may identify a student's need for an AAC system that uses enlarged print, a solid-color background, high-contrast items, tactile supports, or information presented in multiple formats. Visual abilities may also determine if the student will need to use objects instead of pictures or if an SGD would be appropriate to enhance the student's access to a speech model rather than a low-technology grid of symbols (Ray, 2015).

Assessing a student's hearing is important for the functionality of the output of an SGD. This is considerably more important for those with visual impairments, and who may need to rely solely on auditory scanning. As with more specialized assessments, the assessment team will need to collaborate with an audiologist during the hearing assessment process (Lund et al., 2017). In addition to using universal screening tools and monitoring the student's developmental hearing milestones, the audiologist may use more specialized assessments if a hearing impairment is suspected (Harlor & Bower, 2009). The audiologist may use a variety of testing methods such as conventional screening audiometry, comprehensive audiological evaluations, evoked otoacoustic emissions, play audiometry, pure-tone audiometry, tympanometry, brainstem auditory evoked response, and others (Hain, 2012; Harlor & Bower, 2009; Swanepoel, Mngemane, Molemong, Mkwanozi, & Tutshini, 2010).

Key Points

- Assessment should yield information specific to the user of AAC, the AAC system, the communication partners, and the student's environments.
- Access barriers must be identified and assessed in order for AAC device selection and intervention to be successful.
- The areas to be assessed should include access barriers, cognitive skills, communication skills, operational competence, strategic competence, motoric abilities, and sensory response.
- Communication competencies have four main areas to be assessed. These include (1) linguistic, (2) social, (3) operational, and (4) strategic skills.
- Assessment for students with CCN should be conducted as a team and should be considered as an ongoing process that involves parents, teachers, and specialists in order to make purposeful instructional decisions.
- Teachers can partner with service providers to develop a holistic profile describing students' needs.

References

American Speech-Language-Hearing Association. (2017). *Augmentative and Alternative Communication (AAC)*. Retrieved from www.asha.org/public/speech/disorders/AAC/

Beukelman, D. R., Hux, K., Dietz, A., McKelvey, M., & Weissling, K. (2015). Using visual scene displays as communication support options for people with chronic, severe aphasia: A summary of AAC research and future research directions. *Augmentative and Alternative Communication, 31*, 234–245. doi:10.3109/07434618.2015.1052152

Beukelman, D. R., & Mirenda, P. (1988). Communication options for persons who cannot speak: Assessment and evaluation. In C. A. Costen (Ed.), *Proceedings of the national planners conference on assistive device service delivery* (pp. 151–165). Washington, DC: Association for the Advancement of Rehabilitation Technology.

Beukelman, D. R., & Mirenda, P. (2013). *Augmentative and alternative communication: Supporting children and adults with complex communication needs* (4th ed.). Baltimore, MD: Paul H. Brookes.

Binger, C., Ball, L., Dietz, A., Kent-Walsh, J., Lasker, J., Lund, S., & Quach, W. (2012). Personnel roles in the AAC assessment process. *Augmentative and Alternative Communication, 28*, 278–288. doi:10.3109/07434618.2012.716079

Blackstien-Adler, S. (2003). *Training school teams to use the participation model: Evaluation of a training-the-trainer model.* (Unpublished master's thesis). Ontario Institute for the Study of Education, University of Toronto.

Bradshaw, J. (2013). The use of augmentative and alternative communication apps for the iPad, iPod and iPhone: An overview of recent developments. *Tizard Learning Disability Review, 18*, 31–37. doi:10.1108/13595471311295996

Brady, N. C., Bruce, S., Goldman, A., Erickson, K., Mineo, B., Ogletree, B. T., & Wilkinson, K. (2016). Communication services and supports for individuals with severe disabilities: Guidance for assessment and intervention. *American Journal on Intellectual and Developmental Disabilities, 121*, 121–138. doi:10.1352/1944-7558-121.2.121

Brady, N. C., Marquis, J., Fleming, K., & McLean, L. (2004). Prelinguistic predictors of language growth in children with developmental disabilities. *Journal of Speech Language and Hearing Research, 47*, 663. doi:10.1044/1092-4388(2004/051)

Calculator, S. N. (1999). AAC outcomes for children and youths with severe disabilities: When seeing is believing. *Augmentative and Alternative Communication, 15*, 4–12. doi:10.1080/07434619912331278525

Carvey, J. S., & Bernhardt, B. M. (2009). Communicative acts of a child with Rubinstein-Taybi syndrome during early communicative development. *Child Language Teaching and Therapy, 25*, 172–190. doi:10.1177/0265659009102976

Chompoobutr, S., Potibal, P., Boriboon, M., & Phantachat, W. (2013). Perception and multimeaning analysis of graphic symbols for Thai picture-based communication system. *Disability and Rehabilitation: Assistive Technology, 8*, 102–107. doi:10.3109/17483107.2012.737531

Chung, Y., & Douglas, K. H. (2014). Communicative competence inventory for students who use augmentative and alternative communication: A team approach. *TEACHING Exceptional Children, 47*, 56–68. doi:10.3109/07434618.2014.885080

Clarke, M., Price, K., & Griffiths, T. (2016). Augmentative and alternative communication for children with cerebral palsy. *Pediatrics and Child Health, 26*, 373–377. doi:10.1016/j.paed.2016.04.012

Dada, S., & Alant, E. (2009). The effect of aided language stimulation on vocabulary acquisition in children with little or no functional speech. *American Journal of Speech-Language Pathology, 18*, 50–64. doi:10.1044/1058-0360(2008/07-0018)

DeVeney, S. L., Hoffman, L., & Cress, C. J. (2012). Communication-Based Assessment of Developmental Age for Young Children with Developmental Disabilities. *Journal of Speech Language and Hearing Research, 55*, 695–709. doi:10.1044/1092-4388(2011/10-0148)

Didden, R., Korzilius, H., Smeets, E., Green, V. A., Lang, R., Lancioni, G. E., & Curfs, L. M. (2009). Communication in individuals with Rett Syndrome: An assessment of forms and functions. *Journal of Developmental and Physical Disabilities, 22*, 105–118. doi:10.1007/s10882-009-9168-2

Dietz, A., Quach, W., Lund, S. K., & McKelvey, M. (2012). AAC assessment and clinical-decision making: The impact of experience. *Augmentative and Alternative Communication, 28*, 148–159. doi:10.3109/07434618.2012.704521

Durand, V. M., & Crimmins, D. (1992). *Motivation assessment scale*. Retrieved from https://cchmc.cloud-cme.com/assets/cchmc/Presentations/7681/KB%20Clinical%20Tool_Motivation%20Assessment%20Scale.pdf

DynaVox Mayer-Johnson. (2014). *The dynamic AAC goal grid 2*. Retrieved from www.mydynavox.com/Content/resources/slp-app/Goals-Goals-Goals/the-dynamic-aac-goals-grid-2-dagg-2.pdf

Fenson, L., Marchman, V. A., Thal, D. J., Dale, P. S., Reznick, J. S., & Bates, E. (2007). *MacArthur-bates communicative development inventories: User's guide and technical manual* (2nd ed.). Baltimore, MD: Paul H. Brookes.

Hain, T. C. (2012, October). *Hearing testing*. American Hearing Research Foundation. Retrieved from www.american-hearing.org/disorders/hearing-testing/#whatis

Harlor, A. D. B., & Bower, C. (2009). Hearing assessment in infants and children: Recommendations beyond neonatal screening. *PEDIATRICS, 124*, 1252–1263. doi:10.1542/peds.2009-1997

Heath, A. K., Ganz, J. B., Parker, R., Burke, M., & Ninci, J. (2015). A meta-analytic review of functional communication training across mode of communication, age, and disability. *Review Journal of Autism and Developmental Disorders, 2*, 155–166. doi:10.1007/s40489-014-0044-3

Higginbotham, D. J., Shane, H., Russell, S., & Caves, K. (2007). Access to AAC: Present, past, and future. *Augmentative and Alternative Communication, 23*, 243–257. doi:10.1080/07434610701571058

Hostyn, I., Daelman, M., Janssen, M. J., & Maes, B. (2010). Describing dialogue between persons with profound intellectual and multiple disabilities and direct support staff using the scale for dialogical meaning making. *Journal of Intellectual Disability Research, 54*, 679–690. doi:10.1111/j.1365-2788.2010.01292.x

Iwata, B., & DeLeon, I. (2005). *The functional analysis screening tool.* Gainesville, FL: The Florida Center on Self-Injury, University of Florida.

Iwata, B. A., Dorsey, M. F., Slifer, K. J., Bauman, K. E., & Richman, G. S. (1994). Toward a functional analysis of self-injury. *Journal of Applied Behavior Analysis, 27*, 197–209. doi:10.1901/jaba.1994.27-197 (Reprinted from *Analysis and Intervention in Developmental Disabilities, 2*, 3–20, 1982).

Johnston, S. S., Reichle, J., Feeley, K. M., & Jones, E. A. (2012). *AAC strategies for individuals with moderate to severe disabilities.* Baltimore, MD: Paul H. Brookes.

King, A. M., & Fahsl, A. J. (2012). Supporting social competence in children who use Augmentative and alternative communication. *TEACHING Exceptional Children, 45*, 42–49. doi:10.1177/004005991204500106

Light, J. C. (1989). Toward a definition of communicative competence for individuals using augmentative and alternative communication systems. *Augmentative and Alternative Communication, 5*, 137–144. doi:10.1080/07434618912331275126

Light, J. C., Arnold, K. B., & Clark, E. A. (2003). Finding a place in the "social circle of life". In J. C. Light, D. R. Beukelman, & J. Reichle (Eds.), *Communicative competence for individuals who use AAC: From research to effective practice* (pp. 361–397). Baltimore, MD: Paul H. Brookes.

Light, J. C., & McNaughton, D. (2014). Communicative competence for individuals who require augmentative and alternative communication: A new definition for a new era of communication? *Augmentative and Alternative Communication, 30*, 1–18. doi:10.3109/07434618.2014.885080

Light, J. C., McNaughton, D., Weyer, M., & Karg, L. (2008). Evidence-based literacy instruction for individuals who require augmentative and alternative communication: A case study of a student with multiple disabilities. *Seminars in Speech and Language, 29*, 120–132. doi:10.1055/s-2008-1079126

Light, J. C., Parsons, A. R., & Drager, K. D. R. (2002). "There's more to life than cookies": Developing interactions for social closeness with beginning communicators who require augmentative and alternative communication. In J. Reichle, D. Beukelman, & J. Light (Eds.), *Exemplary practices for beginning communicators: Implications for AAC* (pp. 187–218). Baltimore, MD: Paul H. Brookes.

Lloyd, L. L., Fuller, D. R., & Arvidson, H. H. (1997). *Augmentative and alternative communication: A handbook of principles and practices.* Boston, MA: Allyn and Bacon.

Lund, S. K., Quach, W., Weissling, K., McKelvey, M., & Dietz, A. (2017). Assessment with children who need Augmentative and Alternative Communication (AAC): Clinical decisions of AAC specialists. *Language Speech and Hearing Services in Schools*, *48*, 56. doi:10.1044/2016_lshss-15–0086

Markham, P. T., & Justice, E. M. (2004). Sign language iconicity and its influence on the ability to describe the function of objects. *Journal of Communication Disorders*, *37*, 535–546. doi:10.1016/j.jcomdis.2004.03.008

Matson, J. L., & Vollmer, T. R. (1995). *Questions About Behavioral Function (QABF)*. Retrieved from www.liberty.k12.ga.us/ourpages/auto/2016/2/1/43422828/Doc_%205%20QABF%20Questions%20About%20Behavioral%20Functions.pdf

McCarthy, J., McCarthy, J., Light, J., Drager, K., McNaughton, D., Grodzicki, L., . . . Parkin, E. (2006). Re-designing scanning to reduce learning demands: The performance of typically developing 2-year-olds. *Augmentative and Alternative Communication*, *22*, 269–283. doi:10.1080/00498250600718621

McClean, J., & Snyder-McClean, L. (1987). Form and function of communicative behavior among persons with severe developmental disabilities. *Australia and New Zealand Journal of Developmental Disabilities*, *13*, 83–98. doi:10.3109/13668258709023350

Mims, P. J., Browder, D. M., Baker, J. N., Lee, A., & Spooner, F. (2009). Increasing comprehension of students with significant intellectual disabilities and visual impairments during shared stories. *Education and Training in Developmental Disabilities*, *44*, 409–420.

Murray, J., & Goldbart, J. (2009). Cognitive and language acquisition in typical and aided language learning: A review of recent evidence from an aided communication perspective. *Child Language Teaching and Therapy*, *25*, 31–58. doi:10.1177/0265659008098660

Ondondo, E. A. (2015). Acquired language disorders as barriers to effective communication. *Theory and Practice in Language Studies*, *5*, 1324. doi:10.17507/tpls.0507.02

Piek, J. P., Hands, B., & Licari, M. K. (2012). Assessment of motor functioning in the preschool period. *Neuropsychology Review*, *22*, 402–413. doi:10.1007/s11065-012-9211-4

Raghavendra, P., Olsson, C., Sampson, J., Mcinerney, R., & Connell, T. (2012). School participation and social networks of children with complex communication needs, physical disabilities, and typically developing peers. *Augmentative and Alternative Communication*, *28*, 33–43. doi:10.3109/07434618.2011.653604

Ray, J. (2015). Real-life challenges in using augmentative and alternative communication by persons with amyotrophic lateral sclerosis. *Communication Disorders Quarterly*, *36*, 187–192. doi:10.1177/1525740114545359

Robinson, N. B., & Soto, G. (2013). *AAC in the schools: Best practices for intervention*. Verona, WI: Attainment Company.

Rosenberg, S., & Beukelman, D. R. (1987). The participation model. In C. A. Coston (Ed.), *Proceedings of the national planners conference on assistive device service delivery* (pp. 159–161). Washington, DC: Association for the Advancement of Rehabilitation Technology.

Rowland, C. (2004). *Communication Matrix*. Unpublished manuscript, Institute on Development and Disability, Oregon Health & Science University, Portland, OR.

Rowland, C. (2011). Using the communication matrix to assess expressive skills in early communication. *Communication Disorders Quarterly*, *32*, 190–201. doi:10.1177/1525740110394651

Rowland, C., & Schweigert, P. (2003) Cognitive skills and AAC. In J. Light, D. Beukelman, & J. Reichle (Eds.), *Communicative competence for individuals who use AAC* (pp. 241–275). Baltimore, MD: Paul H. Brookes.

Shane, H. C., Laubscher, E. H., Schlosser, R. W., Flynn, S., Sorce, J. F., & Abramson, J. (2012). Applying technology to visually support language and communication in individuals with autism spectrum disorder. *Journal of Autism and Developmental Disorders*, *42*, 1228–1235. doi:10.1007/s10803–011–1304-z

Sigafoos, J., Woodyatt, G., Keen, D., Tait, K., Tucker, M., Roberts-Pennell, D., & Pitten-dreigh, N. (2000). Identifying potential communicative acts in children with developmental and physical disabilities. *Communication Disorders Quarterly, 21*, 77–86. doi:10.1177/152574010002100202

Singh, S. J., Iacono, T., & Gray, K. M. (2014). An investigation of the intentional communication and symbolic play skills of children with down syndrome and cerebral palsy in Malaysia. *Journal of Early Intervention, 36*, 71–89. doi:10.1177/1053815114562044

Soto, G., & Hartmann, E. (2006). Analysis of narratives produced by four children who use augmentative and alternative communication. *Journal of Communication Disorders, 39*, 456–480. doi:10.1016/j.jcomdis.2006.04.005

Soto, G., & Yu, B. (2014). Considerations for the provision of services to bilingual children who use augmentative and alternative communication. *Augmentative and Alternative Communication, 30*, 83–92. doi:10.3109/07434618.2013.878751

Swanepoel, D. W., Mngemane, S., Molemong, S., Mkwanozi, H., & Tutshini, S. (2010). Hearing assessment—Reliability, accuracy, and efficiency of automated audiometry. *Telemedicine and e-Health, 16*, 557–563. doi:10.1089/tmj.2009.0143

Teachman, G., & Gibson, B. E. (2013). "Communicative competence" in the field of augmentative and alternative communication: A review and critique. *International Journal of Language & Communication Disorders, 49*, 1–14. doi:10.1111/1460–6984.12055

Torrison, C., Jung, E., Baker, K., Beliveau, C., & Cook, A. (2007). The impact of staff training in Augmentative Alternative Communication (AAC) on the communication abilities of adults with developmental disabilities. *Developmental Disabilities Bulletin, 35*, 103–130. doi:10.7939/R33775V5J

Wetherby, A. M. (1995). *Checklist of communicative functions and means.* Retrieved from https://connectability.ca/Garage/wp-content/uploads/files/communicativeFunctionsChecklist.pdf

Whitmore, A. S., Romski, M. A., & Sevcik, R. A. (2014). Early augmented language intervention for children with developmental delays: Potential secondary motor outcomes. *Augmentative and Alternative Communication, 30*, 200–212. doi:10.3109/07434618.2014.940466

6

IDENTIFYING THE STUDENT'S LITERACY SKILLS

Literacy (i.e., reading and writing) is considered one of the most fundamental skill that students learn in school (Bailey, Angell, & Stoner, 2011; Erickson & Clendon, 2009). This chapter will focus on how to assess literacy skills pertaining to reading, writing, and spelling of students with complex communication needs (CCN) and will outline key considerations in the instructional process. The development of literacy skills for students with CCN is critical, as students who develop functional literacy skills have greater functional, academic, and employment outcomes (Light & McNaughton, 2013). Erickson and Clendon (2009) emphasized the importance of literacy for individuals who need augmentative and alternative communication (AAC) strategies. They stated that:

> Literacy is the most important functional skill we can address. Literacy will provide these individuals with the voice they require to direct their own lives. It will provide these individuals with a means of establishing and maintaining relationships. Literacy is an essential life skill that is far more important than rehearsing partial participation in the activities of daily living.
>
> *(p. 200)*

Despite the importance of literacy, most students with CCN who use AAC supports leave the school system without having functional literacy skills (Foley & Wolter, 2010).

Reading Development

Literacy development is influenced by the student's linguistic competence, as it is linked to the student's understanding of print concepts, letter-sound correspondence, vocabulary, fluency, and comprehension (Light & McNaughton, 2013; Light, McNaughton, Weyer, & Karg, 2008; Mims, Browder, Baker, Lee, & Spooner, 2009;

Myers, 2007). According to Chall (1983, p. 10–24), children go through six stages of reading.

Stage 0. Stage 0 is pre-reading (birth–6 years)
Stage 1. Stage 1 (6–7 years) is initial reading or decoding
Stage 2. Stage 2 (7–8 years) is confirmation, fluency, and ungluing from print
Stage 3. Stage 3 (9–13 years) is reading for learning the new
Stage 4. Stage 4 (14–18 years) is multiple viewpoints
Stage 5. Stage 5 (18+ years) is construction and reconstruction—a world view

Figure 6.1 provides an illustration of Chall's reading development process.

When compared with students without disabilities, many students with language disorders, learning disabilities, significant hearing impairments, as well as students from low socioeconomic status, tend to fall behind in reading during stage 3 (Chall, Jacobs, & Baldwin, 2009). This occurs given that, in stage 3, students begin to learn new knowledge through reading. When students are already disadvantaged in other areas, these difficulties exacerbate their ability to read and decode, and, therefore, it manifests in further difficulties in learning through reading (Chall et al., 2009).

The National Reading Panel (National Institute of Child Health and Human Development—NICHHD, 2000) describes five areas for reading instruction: (1) phonemic awareness, (2) *phonics*, (3) fluency, (4) vocabulary, and (5) text comprehension. The trajectory for acquiring these literacy skills is typically different for students with CCN when compared to their peers (Fallon & Katz, 2008). One reason for this difference is attributed to the impairments the students with CCN may be facing, as it may have a direct impact on how they learn literacy skills (Smith, 2005). Yet, the extent to which their disability impacts their literacy skills is unclear due to the many variables associated with each affected area (Smith, 2005). In other words, reading and writing draws upon a person's sensory, perceptual, motor, cognitive, and spoken language skills (Light & McNaughton, 2009). Thus, when a student has a disability in one or more of these areas, his or her ability to acquire reading and writing skills is affected (Smith, 2005). To further complicate these difficulties, students with CCN can also be impacted by several external factors including context, instruction, opportunities, and nature of orthography (Light & McNaughton, 2013; Smith, 2005).

Bailey et al. (2011) indicated that for students with typical development, preliteracy skills begin to develop very early through experiences that include story time and other literacy activities. This exposure allows them to gain knowledge about the connection between words and print. It also helps develop their speech with continued practice of phonological and phonemic awareness activities Bailey et al., 2011). For children with disabilities, they are not always exposed to similar literacy-rich environments as children without disabilities (McDonnell et al., 2014). Thus, when students with CCN have less exposure to print and limited opportunities to fully engage in literacy activities (Bailey et al., 2011) due to intrinsic factors, it is not surprising to see a gap between the literacy skills

Stages of Reading Development

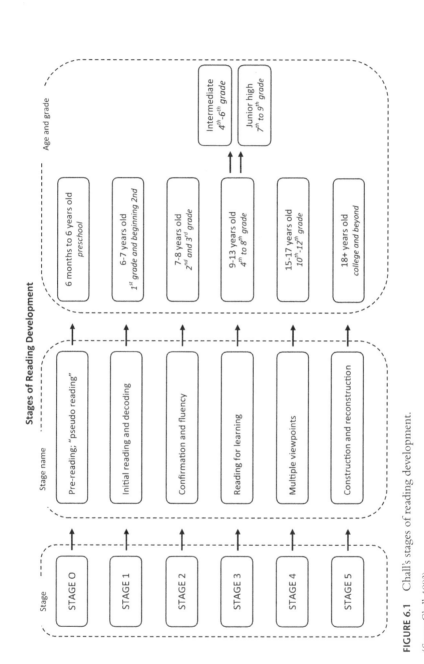

FIGURE 6.1 Chall's stages of reading development.

(*Source*: Chall, 1983)

of students with CCN and students without disabilities. Figure 6.2 provides an overview of the potential intrinsic and extrinsic factors.

In general, assessing the literacy abilities of students with CCN is complex due to the nature of the intrinsic and extrinsic factors affecting literacy. As a result, Smith and Blischak (1997, pp. 421–422) proposed five assessment principles:

(1) Literacy achievement represents an integration of many factors, both intrinsic and extrinsic to the individual.
(2) Assessment should be time-efficient and guide intervention.
(3) Assessment must be goal-driven and reflect the varied functions of literacy for individuals using AAC.
(4) Assessment should, where appropriate, reflect the developmental nature of literacy attainment.
(5) Assessment should consider the adaptations required by AAC users and the extent to which those adaptations may change task demands.

There are many reasons why students with CCN have difficulty gaining reading and writing skills. These difficulties impact the students' ability to learn how to use more advanced AAC strategies and systems (Fallon, Light, McNaughton, Drager, & Hammer, 2004). Thus, it is important for teams to conduct a comprehensive literacy assessment that evaluates all domains: that is, (1) reading, (2)

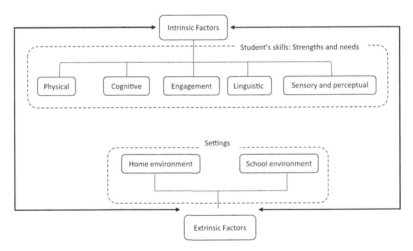

FIGURE 6.2 Challenges for students with complex communication needs: intrinsic and extrinsic factors.

(*Sources:* Smith, 2005; Light & McNaughton, 2013)

spelling, and (3) writing. This will support the implementation of accurate and effective individualized literacy instructional programs that are conceptualized based on the needs of the student.

Reading Assessment

It is important for teams to assess students with CCN to establish a comprehensive literacy skills profile. This profile allows teams to develop and implement appropriate instructional programs. The assessment areas described in this reading section pertain to phonological and phonemic awareness skills that are applicable to students with CCN and augmentative and alternative communication (AAC) needs. Specific skills include letter–sound correspondence, sound blending, phoneme segmentation, and decoding. However, the team should conduct an assessment that evaluates all skills deemed important for the student with CCN. Other phonological and phonemic awareness skills may include but are not limited to rhymes (e.g., detection, production, and oddity), syllables (e.g., blending, segmentation, deletion-compound, and deletion-multisyllabic), and other phoneme skills (e.g., counting, deletion, substitution, and reversal; Pufpaff, 2009).

Assessment Tools

There are several commercially available reading assessment programs developed to adhere to national best practices. Many of the assessment tools require the student to respond through spoken language. However, this method of responding may not be appropriate for students who have difficulty using speech. Therefore, the assessment procedures should incorporate alternative methods of responding such as touching or pointing to picture symbols or using eye gaze to select the correct response (see Chapter 7–8 for more details on unaided and aided means of communication). The following assessment tools can be used to evaluate literacy skills applicable to students with AAC needs: the *Accessible Literacy Learning* (ALL) *Reading Program*, the *Brigance® Comprehensive Inventory of Basic Skills* II and III, and the *Early Literacy Skills Builder* (ELSB).

The *Accessible Literacy Learning* (ALL) *Reading Program* (Light & McNaughton, 2015; www.TobiiDynavox.com) is different from other assessment tools in that ALL was created specifically to assess and teach basic but fundamental reading skills to students with CCN and AAC needs. The benefit of using the assessment component is that it does not require the student to respond verbally. Instead, the student uses alternative methods such as eye gaze, touching/pointing, and, if using the software version of the assessment, the student can use a mouse, switch, or another access apparatus. The purpose of the ALL is to assess literacy skills, specifically sound blending, phoneme segmentation, letter–sound correspondence, single word decoding, sight word recognition, and shared reading (Tobii Dynavox, 2015). The software can be used with Tobii Dynavox speech-generating devices, on computers and tablets with Windows 7 or later, and on Apple tablets with iOS 7.0 or later. Figure 6.3 shows an example of the ALL software program.

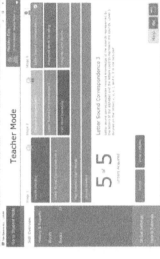

FIGURE 6.3 ALL: *Accessible Literacy Learning* for ALL learners. Tobii-Dynavox©. (Reprinted with permission)

The *Brigance® Comprehensive Inventory of Basic Skills* II and III (CIBS II and III) and the *Inventory of Early Development* III (IED III; Curriculum Associates, 2010; www.curriculumassociates.com) are widely used for assessing a number of domains from reading to math in individuals with varying ability levels. The section on reading and English Language Arts in the CIBS focuses on readiness, speech, listening vocabulary and comprehension, word recognition, oral reading, and reading vocabulary and comprehension. For the IED, there are two types, the criterion-referenced and the norm-referenced. The criterion-referenced version is for birth to developmental age 7, while the norm-referenced version is for birth to chronological age 7. The IED III has a subtest on literacy which includes a phonological awareness assessment component. While all of these assessment areas yield different information pertaining to literacy abilities, it is not necessary to complete every assessment battery for students with severe disabilities and CCN.

The *Early Literacy Skills Builder* (ELSB; Browder, Gibbs, Ahlgrim-Delzell, Courtade, & Lee, 2016; www.attainmentcompany.com) is another a curriculum with a complete set of materials that can be used as an assessment tool as well as an instructional program. The goal of the ELSB is to promote the development of reading for students with autism, multiple, and severe disabilities at the elementary and secondary level. The ELSB is a seven-level curriculum that focuses on literacy skills ranging from sight words to syllable and phoneme segmentation, letter-sound correspondence, sound blending, comprehension and more. The ELSB can be combined with the *Early Literacy Communication*, which it includes pre-made communication overlays. The overlays can be used independently or can be used with some low-technology speech-generating devices (e.g., GoTalk from Attainment Company©).

Phonological and Phonemic Awareness

Students who have *phonological awareness* can recognize and use words, syllables and other larger units of speech (Pufpaff, 2009). *Phonemic awareness* is the ability to recognize and use individual units of speech sounds or phonemes (NICHHD, 2000; Pufpaff, 2009). Students with phonological and phonemic awareness can comprehend the sound structure of language. To assess these areas, the team will need to look at the student's abilities in a variety of areas pertaining to words and phonemes.

Letter–Sound Correspondence

The ability to know that a sound is represented by a letter and that a letter represents a sound is referred to as *letter–sound correspondence* (Light et al., 2008). It is a foundational skill necessary for literacy instruction and should be assessed. Assessing letter–sound correspondence is typically done by asking the student to say the sound as the teacher points to a specific letter. However, this may not

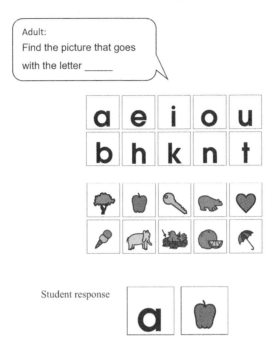

FIGURE 6.4   Letter correspondence.

be possible for some students with CCN who have difficulty using speech. An alternative method of assessing this skill is to allow the student to point, touch, or look at the letter that matches the sound. If the data show that the student does not possess letter–sound correspondence, it should be one of the starting points of instruction for the student. See Figure 6.4 for an example of an assessment task on letter–sound correspondence.

Sound Blending

The ability to blend phonemes or sounds to create words is referred to as *sound blending* (Light & McNaughton, 2013). Sound blending is necessary for reading given that it is used to decode words the student has not yet mastered. In Figure 6.5, assessment of sound blending is done by asking the student to listen to a word spelled out orally by the adult and then having the student identify the picture that represents the spelled word. The goal is to determine if the student is able to put the sounds together to create a word. Assuming the student is unable to say the spelled word, this assessment trial only requires the student to point or touch the picture that corresponds with the phonemes /s/ /i/ /t/.

FIGURE 6.5 Example of sound blending.

(*Sources:* Light & McNaughton, 2013) Tobii-Dynavox ©2017 Boardmaker. All rights reserved. (Used with permission.)

Phoneme Segmentation

With *phoneme segmentation*, the student is able to look at a written word and segment or break the word into its different sounds (Light & McNaughton, 2013; Light et al., 2008). Because words consist of initial, medial, and final sound segments, it is appropriate to assess the student's ability in these three areas. It is recommended that assessment of phoneme segmentation start with the initial position and then move to medial and final positions (Smith, 2005). There are different variations for assessing phoneme segmentation. Some methods are simple while others assess more complex skills. One assessment method described by Smith (2005) is illustrated in Figure 6.6: beginning sound assessment. The adult is conducting three phoneme segmentation assessment trials for the beginning sound. The adult presents two picture cards, says the name of each image on the picture cards, and then asks the student if both images start with the same sound. For trial 1, both images begin with the phoneme /c/, so the response is yes. For trial 2, the correct response is also yes given that the initial phoneme is /m/. In the last trial, the beginning phonemes do not match. In Figure 6.7, the adult presents three picture cards and gives the spoken model for each (i.e., *"bug," "bus," "up"*) and asks the student if these words start with the same sound. If the student's response is "no" in whichever manner the student can express this, then the adult asks, "Which one does not start with the same sound as the others?" If the student points to *"up,"* then the response is counted as correct. Another assessment method with slightly more task complexity is the adult saying a sound and then

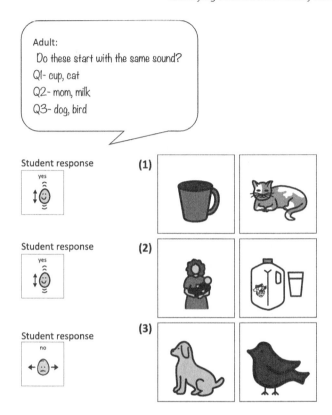

FIGURE 6.6   Example of beginning sound assessment.

(*Sources:* Light & McNaughton, 2013; Smith, 2005) Tobii-Dynavox ©2017 Boardmaker. All rights reserved. (Used with permission.)

instructing the student to match the sound with the picture card of a word that starts with that same sound. With this method, Light and McNaughton (2013) recommend that the adult present an array of four picture cards for the student to choose from. In all of these assessment trials, the student can respond through a variety of ways that do not consist of speaking the response.

Decoding

A student with decoding skills is able to use letter–sound correspondence and *phoneme blending* to decode words. In other words, the student is able to decode the written word *"pen"* because he or she knows that the individual sounds that correspond to the letters *p, e,* and *n.* Therefore, the student uses that knowledge to blend the sounds together and come up with *p-e-n* when he or she sees the printed word. Identifying the student's ability to decode is important given that decoding is a precursor to reading fluency and reading for knowledge acquisition

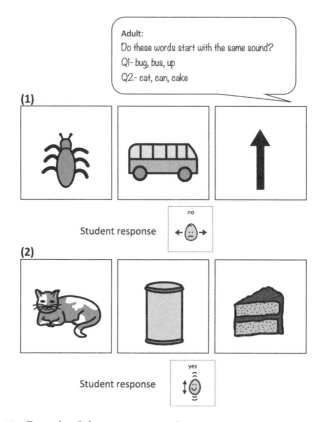

FIGURE 6.7   Example of phoneme segmentation.

(*Sources:* Beukelman & Mirenda, 2013; Light & McNaughton, 2013; Smith, 2005) Tobii-Dynavox ©2017 Boardmaker. All rights reserved. (Used with permission.)

(Dynia, Brock, Logan, Justice, & Kaderavek, 2016). Assessing decoding skills in students with CCN can be done using several strategies. In Figure 6.8, the student is asked to look at a target word (*"bug"*—trial 1; *"car"*—trial 2), think about the sounds that make up the word, and then select the corresponding picture for each target word. An assessment variation of the same decoding skill is demonstrated in Figure 6.9.

Given that decoding skills correspond to text comprehension and reading fluency, assessment in this area is also important for students with CCN. Text comprehension refers to a person's ability to read text and obtain meaning from it (Beukelman & Mirenda, 2013). For students with CCN, their ability to demonstrate comprehension of the text is limited if the assessment procedures require oral responses. However, an alternative strategy is to have students point to pictures to respond to *wh-* questions (Browder et al., 2009; Shurr & Taber-Doughty, 2012). Depending on the student's abilities, the text or passages may be read to

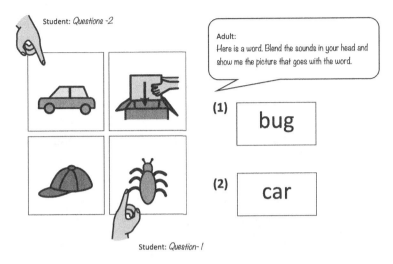

FIGURE 6.8 Example of word decoding.

(*Sources:* Beukelman & Mirenda, 2013; Light & McNaughton, 2013) Tobii-Dynavox ©2017 Board-maker. All rights reserved. (Used with permission.)

the student and then asked to answer a variety of *wh-* questions. Assessment may also include having the student silently read passages at various levels of difficulty and then answer *wh-* questions.

Reading *fluency* is the ability to decode words accurately and at a rate and expression level that is appropriate for the developmental age and have a vocabulary base of sight words (see Chapter 12; Bradford, Shippen, Alberto, Houchins, & Flores, 2006). Yet, fluency is difficult to assess in students with CCN because most assessments require students to read aloud (Browder et al., 2009). While reading fluency is important for students with CCN, it is not critical that they demonstrate reading fluency through speech. Instead, it might be best to evaluate fluency by looking at the student's ability to read and comprehend text with minimal effort (Kuhn, Schwanenflugel, & Meisinger, 2010). Similarly, speed and accuracy are other components of fluency in need of consideration (Kuhn et al., 2010). Students who use AAC are already at a disadvantage due to the extra steps needed to access and compose messages on an AAC system. Thus, students who can accurately recognize words on their AAC system in a relatively quick amount of time are more likely to also construct messages faster and more accurately than students who have to put more effort into decoding vocabulary. Overall, the goal of identifying the student's fluency skills is to determine the student's present level of performance in order to formulate an appropriate intervention plan. Students who have greater fluency are able to gain knowledge because of their reading skills and use that knowledge to communicate more effectively. Effective and efficient communication is critical in meeting the student's communication needs.

FIGURE 6.9 Example of single word decoding.

(*Sources:* Beukelman & Mirenda, 2013; Light & McNaughton, 2013) Tobii-Dynavox ©2017 Boardmaker. All rights reserved. (Used with permission.)

Writing Development

The ability to write is a critical skill for all students, especially for students who have little to no spoken language. Students with CCN are already at a disadvantage because they cannot rely on their spoken language to communicate. Instead, they are reliant on other methods. Students who have strong literacy skills, including, reading, writing, and spelling, are able to communicate at a level that far exceeds individuals who communicate with non-literacy-based AAC systems. Writing allows students with CCN to generate messages without being confined to the symbols on their AAC system (Millar, Light, & McNaughton, 2004). It is not uncommon for communication systems to primarily consist of vocabulary that are noun-based. To compound the issue, the vocabulary is often set up for the student to request items and activities, but not to communicate abstract concepts, ideas, and other things that most people communicate (Trembath, Balandin, & Togher, 2007). Therefore, written language development should be a goal for students of all ages, from the early years and into adulthood. Foley and Staples (2003) stressed that learning spoken and written language is possible even in adulthood for individuals with disabilities, particularly those on the autism spectrum.

Writing assessment

Developing emergent writing skills is a process that extends from drawing to conventional writing (Foley, Koppenhaver, & Williams, 2009; Sulzby, 1990). Foley and colleagues discussed six writing stages based on Sulzby's (1990) emergent literacy development framework: (1) drawing, (2) scribble, (3) nonphonetic letter strings, (4) invented spelling, (5) conventional copying, and (6) conventional writing. Given that students with CCN do not always develop these skills in a linear trajectory (Foley et al., 2009), assessing writing skills consists of multiple areas that are also applicable to reading skills.

Skills such as phonological and phonemic awareness skills are as important for the development of emergent writing skills as they are for reading development (Beukelman & Mirenda, 2013; Foley et al., 2009; Millar et al., 2004). Although these reading skills were discussed in a previous section, the assessment information yielded regarding phonological and phonemic awareness skills is also relevant when creating a comprehensive profile of the student's emergent writing skills. The following section only discusses assessing skills that are relevant for the emerging writer. For a more comprehensive assessment overview of more advanced writers with AAC needs, refer to Foley and colleagues (2009).

There are six areas described by Foley and colleagues (2009) that should be assessed to capture baseline measures of emergent writing under the umbrella of directed writing. These include the following:

(1) *Name writing.* The student is asked to write his or her name. Although this type of assessment is short and does not generate a lot of information, it can be evaluated for spelling, orientation, and letter formation. If the student types his or her name, orientation and letter formation cannot be evaluated.
(2) *Word generation.* The student is asked to write as many words as the student is able to in short amount of time (e.g., 10 minutes). For students with CCN, it might be best to use a visual prompt such a picture or photograph to give the student direction.
(3) *Developmental spelling.* The student is given a short spelling test using target words that are at the student's developmental level. The student's spelled words are then examined to determine where on the continuum the student is spelling (i.e., arbitrary to the conventional writing level).

(4) *Non-word spelling.* The student is asked to spell a few non-words to evaluate their phonological awareness, including letter–sound correspondence. Non-words should be short, about three letters.

(5) *Transitional spellings.* The student is asked to spell regular target words. This type of assessment is aligned to a spelling assessment described by Beukelman and Mirenda (2013; spontaneous spelling) and Masterson and Apel (2000; dictation spelling).

(6) *Sentence dictation.* The student is asked to write sentences that are orally produced by the adult. This assessment is the most advanced of the emergent writing tests because it requires the student to have a variety of skills needed for conventional writing.

Spelling

As part of the writing process, the ability to spell words is critical in the development of literacy skills. Foley and colleagues (2009) described several adapted spelling assessments. Beukelman and Mirenda (2013) discussed three complimentary assessment areas pertaining to spelling that are applicable to students with CCN:

(1) *Spontaneous spelling.* This type is described as words spelled out letter-by-letter by the student. Masterson and Apel (2000) referred to this type of spelling as *dictation.* Students who demonstrate spontaneous spelling are able to generate any message within their skillset on an AAC system. To assess spontaneous spelling, the adult simply says the target word and asks the student to spell it out. Students can demonstrate their ability through any means (e.g., typing, writing, pointing to letters; refer to Figure 6.10 for an example of spontaneous spelling using preprinted letters).

(2) *First-letter-of-word spelling.* This type of spelling assessment entails the student spelling the first few letters of a word. With this method, almost any word can be generated using the *word prediction* and spell check features of many high-technology AAC systems. Even individuals without CCN benefit from the approximation of spelled words given that mobile technologies offer word prediction and spell check. Assessing this type of spelling includes asking the student to identify the first letter of a word after (1) showing the student an image depicting the target word, or (2) by asking the student to identify the first letter of the target word after the adult says it.

(3) *Recognition spelling.* This type of spelling consists of the student's ability to recognize the correct spelling of a word (Masterson & Apel, 2000). Assessment is done by presenting two or more variations of the target word, with only one of the choices being correct. The student is asked to select the correctly spelled word. Assessing recognition spelling is only needed if the student fails to demonstrate spontaneous spelling or first-letter-of-word spelling.

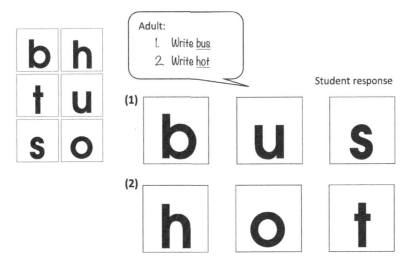

FIGURE 6.10   Example of writing.

Masterson and Apel (2000) identified three types of spelling assessments: (1) dictation, (2) connected writing, and (3) recognition. Dictation consists of the student spelling a word after the adult orally states the word. Depending on the assessment method used, scoring procedures can vary. Simply documenting a spelled word as correct or incorrect may not be sufficient to capture the student's skills in this domain (Smith, 2005). Treiman and Bourasse (2000) developed a scale from 0–11 in which points were assigned based on letter use and correct letter blending. If the student is unable to write via pencil and paper, other output writing strategies should be used. For example, the student may need to type the word on a device or use preprinted letters to spell the word. Alternatively, a student may benefit from hearing the spoken word as well as seeing a picture that captures the essence of the word.

Connected writing is an advanced writing skill. Assessing this type of writing requires that the student write about a picture or story the student looked at, listened to, or read (Masterson & Apel, 2000). To evaluate the text, it can be done similarly to the procedures used with single word spelling. Students with CCN have difficulty independently generating this type of text as it does not reflect how they communicate (Smith, 2005). Nonetheless, it is an important area to assess and develop as connected writing allows students to maximize their communicative competence when using AAC strategies. In terms of the recognition assessment described by Masterson and Apel (2000), the procedures mirror those described by Beukelman and Mirenda (2013).

Completing a comprehensive assessment of literacy skills, which includes reading, writing, and spelling, is vital for students with CCN. The results of this assessment can yield information that will support effective instructional programs. By acquiring literacy skills, students with CCN will be able to gain skills in other areas, become more social in electronic formats, and become more independent and self-advocate.

Key Points of Chapter

- Literacy skills are important for students with CCN.
- Literacy skills affect communication skills, academic skills, functional skills, and future employment.
- Phonological and phonemic awareness skills are critical skills for reading, writing, and spelling.
- Writing and spelling use several foundational skills as those used in reading.
- Students with CCN should be assessed and receive instruction in all areas of reading and writing.

Resources

The *Accessible Literacy Learning Reading Program*
www.TobiiDynavox.com
The Brigance® Special Education Assessments
www.curriculumassociates.com
The *Early Literacy Skills Builder*
www.attainmentcompany.com
National Reading Panel
www.nichd.nih.gov/research/supported/nrp

References

Bailey, R. L., Angell, M. E., & Stoner, J. B. (2011). Improving literacy skills in students with complex communication needs who use augmentative/alternative communication systems. *Education and Training in Autism and Developmental Disabilities, 46*, 352–368.

Beukelman, D. R., & Mirenda, P. (2013). *Augmentative and alternative communication: Supporting children and adults with complex communication needs* (4th ed.). Baltimore, MD: Paul H. Brookes.

Bradford, S., Shippen, M. E., Alberto, P., Houchins, D. E., & Flores, M. (2006). Using systematic instruction to teach decoding skills to middle school students with moderate intellectual disabilities. *Education and Training in Developmental Disabilities, 414*, 333–343.

Browder, D., Gibbs, S., Ahlgrim-Delzell, L., Courtade, G. R., Marz, M., & Flowers, C. (2009). Literacy for students with severe developmental disabilities: What should we teach and what should we hope to achieve? *Remedial and Special Education, 30*, 269–282. doi: 10.1177/0741932508315054

Browder, D., Gibbs, S., Ahlgrim-Delzell, L., Courtade, G., & Lee, A. (2016). *Early Literacy Skills Builder (ELSB)*. Verona, WI: Attainment.

Chall, J. S., (1983). *Stages of reading development.* New York, NY: McGraw Hill.

Chall, J. S., Jacobs, V. A., & Baldwin, L. E. (2009). *The reading crisis: Why poor children fall behind.* Cambridge, MA: Harvard University Press.

Curriculum Associates. (2010). *The brigance comprehensive inventory of basic skills II and III.* North Billerica, MA: Author.

Dynia, J. M., Brock, M. E., Logan, J. A. R., Justice, L. M., & Kaderavek, J. N. (2016). Comparing children with ASD and their peers' growth in print knowledge. *Journal of Autism and Developmental Disorders, 46,* 2490–2500. doi:10.1007/s10803-016-2790-9

Erickson, K. A., & Clendon, S. A. (2009). Addressing the literacy demands of the curriculum for beginning readers and writers. In G. Soto & C. Zangari (Eds.), *Practically speaking: Language, literacy, and academic development for students with AAC needs* (pp. 195–216). Baltimore, MD: Paul H. Brookes.

Fallon, K. A., & Katz, L. A. (2008). Augmentative and alternative communication and literacy teams: Facing the challenges, forging ahead. *Seminar in Speech and Language, 29,* 112–119. doi:10.1055/s-2008–1079125

Fallon, K., Light, J., McNaughton, D., Drager, K., & Hammer, C. (2004). The effects of direct instruction on the single-word reading skills of children who require augmentative and alternative communication. *Journal of Speech, Language, and Hearing Research, 47,* 1424–1439.

Foley, B. E., Koppenhaver, D. A., & Williams, A. R. (2009). Writing assessment for students with AAC needs. In G. Soto & C. Zangari (Eds.), *Practically speaking: Language, literacy, and academic development for students with AAC needs* (pp. 93–123). Baltimore, MD: Paul H. Brookes.

Foley, B. E., & Staples, A. H. (2003). Developing Augmentative and Alternative Communication (AAC) and literacy interventions in a supported employment setting. *Topics in Language Disorders, 23,* 325–343.

Foley, B., & Wolter, J. A. (2010). Literacy intervention for transition-aged youth: What is and what could be. In D. McNaughton & D. Beukelman (Eds.), *Language, literacy, and AAC issues for transition-age youth* (pp. 35–68). Baltimore, MD: Paul H. Brookes.

Kuhn, M. R., Schwanenflugel, P. J., & Meisinger, E. B. (2010). Aligning theory and assessment of reading fluency: Automaticity, prosody, and definitions of fluency. *Reading Research Quarterly, 45*(2), 230–251. doi:10.1598/rrq.45.2.4

Light, J. C., & McNaughton, D. B. (2009). Addressing the literacy demands of the curriculum for conventional and more advanced readers and writers who require AAC. In C. Zangari & G. Soto (Eds.), *Practically speaking: Language, literacy, and academic development for students with AAC needs* (pp. 217–246). Baltimore, MD: Paul H. Brookes.

Light, J. C., & McNaughton, D. B. (2013). Literacy intervention for individuals with complex communication needs. In D. Beukelman & P. Mirenda (Eds.), *Augmentative and alternative communication: Supporting children and adults with complex communication needs* (pp. 309–351). Baltimore, MD: Paul H. Brookes.

Light, J. C., & McNaughton, D. B. (2015). *The Accessible Literacy Learning (ALL) reading program.* Pittsburgh, PA: TobiiDynavox.

Light, J. C., McNaughton, D. B., Weyer, M., & Karg, L. (2008). Evidence-based literacy instruction for individuals who require augmentative and alternative communication: A case study of a student with multiple disabilities. *Seminars in Speech and Language, 29,* 120–132. doi:10/1055/s-2008–1079126

Masterson, J., & Apel, K. (2000). Spelling assessment: Charting a path to optimal intervention. *Topics in Language Disorders, 20,* 50–65.

McDonnell, A. P., Hawken, L. S., Johnston, S. S., Kidder, J. E., Lynes, M. J., & McDonnell, J. J. (2014). Emergent literacy practices and support for children with disabilities: A national survey. *Education and Treatment of Children, 37*, 495–530. doi:10.1353/etc.2014.0024

Millar, D. C., Light, J. C., & McNaughton, D. B. (2004). The effect of direct instruction and writer's workshop on the early writing skills of children who use augmentative and alternative communication. *Augmentative and Alternative Communication, 20*, 164–178. doi:10.1080/07434610410001699690

Mims, P. J., Browder, D. M., Baker, J. N., Lee, A., & Spooner, F. (2009). Increasing comprehension of students with significant intellectual disabilities and visual impairments during shared stories. *Education and Training in Developmental Disabilities, 44*, 409–420.

Myers, C. (2007). Towards a model of literacy learning for young augmented speakers. *Forum on Public Policy, 2007*, 1–28.

National Institute of Child Health and Human Development. (2000). *Report of the national reading panel: Teaching children to read: An evidence-based assessment of the scientific research literature on reading and its implications for reading instruction—Reports of the subgroups* (NIH Publication No. 00–4754). Washington, DC: U.S. Government Printing Office.

PufPaff, L. A. (2009). A developmental continuum of phonological sensitivity skills. *Psychology in the Schools, 1*, 1–13. doi:10.1002/pits

Shurr, J., & Taber-Doughty, T. (2012). Increasing comprehension for middle school students with moderate intellectual disability on age-appropriate texts. *Education and Training in Autism and Developmental Disabilities, 47*, 359–372.

Smith, M. (2005). *Literacy and augmentative and alternative communication.* San Diego, CA: Elsevier.

Smith, M. M., & Blischak, D. M. (1997). Literacy. In L. L. Lloyd, D. R. Fuller, & H. H. Arvidson (Eds.), *Augmentative and alternative communication: A handbook of principles and practices* (pp. 414–444). Needham Heights, MA: Allyn and Bacon.

Sulzby, E. (1990). Assessment of emergent writing and children's language while writing. In L. M. Morrow & J. K. Smith (Eds.), *Assessment for instruction in early literacy* (pp. 83–109). Upper Saddle River, NJ: Prentice Hall.

Tobii Dynavox. (2015). *Accessible Literacy Learning (ALL) user's manual.* Pittsburgh, PA: Author. Retrieved from http://tdvox.web-downloads.s3.amazonaws.com/ALL/documents/TobiiDynavox_ALL_UsersManual_v1-1_en-US_WEB.pdf

Treiman, R., & Bourasse, D. (2000). Children's written and oral spelling. *Applied Psycholinguistics, 21*, 183–204.

Trembath, D., Balandin, S., & Togher, L. (2007). Vocabulary selection for Australian children who use augmentative and alternative communication. *Journal of Intellectual and Developmental Disability, 32*, 291–301. doi:10.1080/13668250701689298

7

DEFINING AND IDENTIFYING UNAIDED COMMUNICATION SYSTEMS

When identifying a system that is best suited for a student with complex communication needs (CCN), one should consider both unaided and aided communication systems (Lund, Quach, Weissling, McKelvey, & Dietz, 2017; Sigafoos & Drasgow, 2001). This chapter will solely discuss unaided communication systems. It will also highlight the importance of identifying and implementing an unaided system as part of the student's communication modalities (see Chapters 8 and 9 for details on aided communication systems).

Unaided communication systems refer to a communication modality that does not require any external equipment. That is, it relies solely on what individuals are able to do independently with their own bodies to indicate their communicative purpose or intentionality (Drager, Light, & McNaughton, 2010). Because unaided communication systems rely solely on the individual's abilities, the main advantage is that the student with CCN will always have the unaided communication system available (Drager et al., 2010).

Unfortunately, there are several disadvantages of unaided communication systems. For example, earlier evidence suggested that an advantage of unaided communications systems is that they did not require higher level of cognitive skills (e.g., Lloyd, Quist, & Windsor, 1990). However, more recent literature supports the notion that unaided communication systems may be more cognitively demanding that other communication systems (Beukelman & Mirenda, 2013; Lorah, Parnell, Whitby, & Hantula, 2014). The main reason for unaided communication systems having a higher cognitive demand from the student is the diverse topography of responses when using unaided communication. Research has demonstrated some additional disadvantages in unaided communication systems, including the following: (1) the dependence on the communication partner's knowledge of the communication system (Brady et al., 2016; Lorah et al., 2014); (2) the knowledge and skills needed from the communication partner to understand of the student with CCN's communicative intent (Reichle, Drager, Caron, & Parker-McGowan, 2016; Sigafoos & Drasgow, 2001); (3) the reliance on the individual's body and movements, especially when considering the student's motor skills, which may impact the clarity of the message being communicated (Lorah et al., 2014); and (4) strong imitative skills are needed for the acquisition and use of an unaided communication system (Lorah et al., 2014; Mirenda, 2003). To ensure that students with CCN have the opportunity to learn an effective means of unaided communication, it is critical to understand the various types of unaided communication systems and their demands on the student. Having a clear understanding of the type and level of skills needed by each unaided communication system will allow practitioners to more effectively identify the most appropriate unaided system for the student, based on the student's overall skills.

Types of Unaided Communication Systems

There many ways for an individual to communicate using an unaided communication system. These means can be categorized into four main types of unaided communication systems: (1) vocalizations, (2) gestures, (3) eye gaze, and (4) manual signs.

Vocalizations

Vocalizations can be defined as any voluntary sound production or speech produced by an individual. Some examples include moaning and yelling (Beukelman & Mirenda, 2013). Vocalizations can be observed early in the child's life and become more sophisticated as the child develops, turning into words (Lederberg & Everhart, 1998; Sigafoos, Didden, & O'Reilly, 2003). One important advantage of vocalization is that, due to the sound production attached to it, it is easier to gain the communication partner's attention. Unfortunately, the disadvantage of vocalizations is closely linked to the advantages. That is, the student can only use vocalizations to communicate, not words. If this is the case, vocalizations may require translation from a familiar communication partner as unfamiliar communication partners may miss the student's communication attempt or respond in an undesirable way. The literature supports the notion that students who may benefit from the use of vocalizations as a means to communicate include students who are young or who may be beginning communicators (e.g., Branson & Demchak, 2009). Evidence also suggests that students with Williams syndrome may use vocalization as a means to communicate over other forms of unaided communication systems (e.g., Hoff, 2013; Singer Harris, Bellugi, Bates, Jones, & Rossen, 1997).

Gestures

Gestures are another type of unaided communication. *Gestures* refer to hand and body movements, facial expressions, and body language that are intentionally conducted with the purpose of communicating something to the communication partner (Lee, Jeong, & Kim, 2013; Quinn & Rowland, 2017). An important unique characteristic of gestures is that they are culturally bound (Brady et al., 2016; Soto & Yu, 2014; Wray, Saunders, McGuire, Cousins, & Norbury, 2017). Gestures have specific culture connotations that must be considered when working with individuals of diverse cultural backgrounds (Soto & Yu, 2014).

Gestures as a communication means need to be intentional in nature. Evens so, often people use unintentional gestures during a communicative interaction. These unintentional gestures do occur, but do not have a set form or an intended function during the message delivery. Intentional gestures on the other hand, can be *deictic*. That is, gestures that are non-symbolic, but are used to refer to an object or people who may be present during the communicative interaction (Özçalışkan, Adamson, & Dimitrova, 2016). Gestures that are used to refer to an object, person, or event within a specific context, are known as *conventional gestures* (Johnston & Coseby, 2012; Wray et al., 2017). A unique characteristic of conventional gestures is that they hold a specific meaning based on the student's culture (Wray et al., 2017). On the other hand, *iconic gestures* are gestures that represent the object or action that is being communicated and can be understood across cultures (Wilkinson, 2013). Both conventional and iconic gestures are considered *representational gestures* as they represent in some form (e.g., shape, action, reference) what is being communicated (Wray et al., 2017). Figure 7.1 provides examples of deictic, iconic, and conventional gestures.

There is an overall agreement that gestures may be beneficial as a means of communication for students with CCN. For example, it has been reported that students with Down syndrome can develop gestures at similar rates as peers who are typically developing in the area of requesting and social routines (e.g., Chan & Iacono, 2001). In addition, students with Angelman syndrome most frequently utilize gestures for communication purposes according to parent reports (Calculator, 2013; Quinn & Rowland, 2017). Even with these successes, evidence exists that suggests that students with intellectual or developmental disabilities may experience difficulty using gestures (e.g., Johnston & Coseby, 2012), and that students with autism have demonstrated more difficulties with the use of gestures, especially for social purposes (e.g., Mitchell et al., 2006).

Eye Gaze

Eye gaze, also known as eye pointing or eye tracking, is another type of unaided communication. *Eye gaze* refers to the individual's ability to use his or her eye gaze

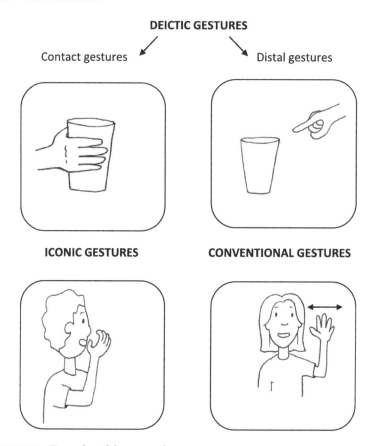

FIGURE 7.1 Examples of the types of gestures.

intentionally to point by looking at an object long enough to indicate communicative intent (Beukelman & Mirenda, 2013; Sargent, Clarke, Price, Griffiths, & Swettenham, 2013). Sargent and colleagues (2013) indicated that eye gaze is

> an interpersonal phenomenon that integrates the actions of both people with communication disabilities and their communication partners in establishing intended meanings. Its use can involve a constellation of linked behaviors; whether these are considered intentionally communicative often depends on the conversational context.
>
> *(p. 479)*

Eye gaze is often a good consideration of an unaided means of communication for students who may present motor difficulties and do not have the possibility

FIGURE 7.2 Examples of eye gaze.

to make a selection with their hands or arms (Sargent et al., 2013). Several skills are needed to effectively use eye gaze as a means of communication. This includes the ability to (1) focus, shift, and control gaze; (2) intentionally communicate; and (3) express preferences (Clarke, 2014). A challenge with eye gaze is that eye gaze is not as an isolated means of communication, as pointing or vocalizing can be (Clarke, 2014). Yet, it can be an effective means of communication for those students who have significant motor needs, such as students with cerebral palsy (Sargent et al., 2013). Figure 7.2 provides an example of eye gaze. This figure displays a student using eye gaze to select music from various possibilities on an eye gaze board.

Manual Signs

Manual signs are one of the most frequently used means of unaided communication (Grove & Woll, 2017). In fact, manual signs have been reported as the most commonly used augmentative and alternative communication (AAC) strategy for students with CCN before 1990 (Beukelman & Mirenda, 2013). *Manual sign* refers to the use of hand shapes to communicate (Beukelman & Mirenda, 2013; Hourcade, Pilotte, West, & Parette, 2004), and includes the use of American Sign Language (ASL), manually coded language, and tactile signs (Grove & Woll, 2017). The key to successful communication when using manual signs is that the communication partner has knowledge of manual signs in order understand the communicative attempt. The *motor complexity* of manual signs is one of the most common disadvantages. Some students may use adapted or unique signs in order to communicate, creating communication breakdowns between the communication partners (Johnston & Coseby, 2012). This is critical when considering manual signs for a student, as only 10–30% of ASL are identifiable by typical adults (Beukelman & Mirenda, 2013). ASL is used extensively in the Deaf community. However, the use of ASL by the Deaf community and of other students with various needs may drastically differ (Grove & Woll, 2017). For example, ASL used by the Deaf community focuses on language and structure, whereas the non-Deaf community focuses on key word signing or using signing in addition to speech (Grove & Woll, 2017).

Manual signs were previously the most researched AAC communication system for students with CCN (Schlosser & Raghavendra, 2004). However, research in the area of unaided communication has decreased in recent years. Even so, an ongoing debate on the use of manual signs with students with autism continues (Ganz et al., 2012; Mirenda, 2003; Sigafoos, O'Reilly, Lancioni, & Sutherland, 2014; Wendt, 2009). Some evidence suggests that students with autism may present challenges in learning to use manual signs due to the fine motor difficulties (Ganz et al., 2012). Others have indicated that students with autism may benefit from the use of manual signs (Bonvillian & Nelson, 1976; Carr, Binkoff, Kologinsky, & Eddy, 1978; Falcomata, Wacker, Ringdahl, Vinquist, & Dutt, 2013). Whereas others suggest that students with autism should learn through total communication approaches that combine both manual signs and speech (Gevarter et al., 2013; Remington & Clarke, 1983; Yoder & Layton, 1988). It has also been recommended that a preference assessment be conducted when teaching students with autism to communicate using manual signs, as students with autism may only use manual signs to communicate preferred items and activities (Sigafoos et al., 2014).

To successfully determine what system is most suitable for a student with CCN, a dynamic assessment should be conducted. A dynamic assessment is a type of assessment that includes assessing a skill and ability to learn new knowledge in a specific context and the individual's performance in relation to the observer, the activity, or the setting (Brady et al., 2016; Lund et al., 2017). Figure 7.3 outlines all the components to consider when conducting a dynamic assessment, and the process for such assessment. One main goal in this process is to determine the student's skills and areas of needs (see Chapter 5 for a detailed description), but also to identify both access and opportunity barriers (see Chapter 4 and Chapter 5 for details) and evaluate the quality of interactions between the student with CCN and his or her communication partners (Brady et al., 2016).

Dynamic Assessment Process in Augmentative and Alternative Communication

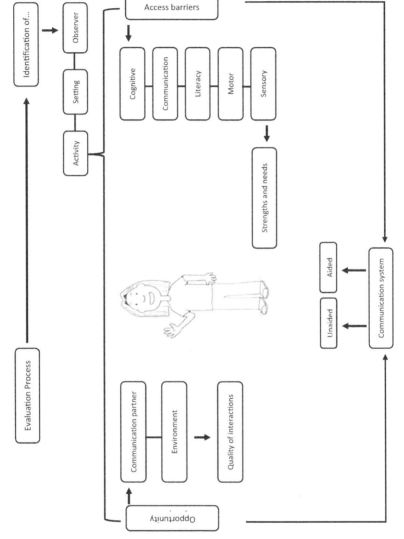

FIGURE 7.3 Dynamic assessment process in augmentative and alternative communication.

Unaided Communication Feature Matching

Beyond the dynamic assessment process, one way to identify the most suitable means of communication is considering a feature-matching process (see Chapters 8 and 9 for information on feature matching in aided communication systems). Each of these unaided communication systems should be systematically evaluated across various settings and communication partners to ensure that the student with CCN is effectively using these to communicate. To gather this information, teams will need to identify tools that are effective and appropriate to assess the student, or create systematic and objective data collection forms that can be used to gather such information. One example is conducting feature matching. *Feature matching* refers to the process of matching the features of the communication system to the student's strengths and needs based upon a systematic and dynamic assessment and ongoing data collection (Costello, Shane, & Caron, 2013). To more effectively and accurately select a communicative system for a student with CCN, other elements should be considered beyond the assessment. This includes the following: (1) the student, (2) the student's medical history and needs, (3) the student's motor, cognitive, social, and sensory skills, (4) the student's cultural background, and (5) the family dynamic and support needs (Glennen & Decoste, 1997; Lund et al., 2017; Stowers, Altheide, & Shea, 1987). See Chapter 5 for more details on specific assessment domains, potential assessment tools, and additional assessment considerations.

The feature-matching process should be person-centered. That is, the student's strengths and areas of needs should be the basis for systematically identifying the most suitable communication system for the student. Figure 7.4 provides an example of an unaided feature-matching tool. The purpose of the *Unaided Feature Matching Screening Form* is to identify and outline the student's motor control and communication abilities. This form helps determine whether an unaided communication system is suitable for the student. For example, under the *Communication* heading, the observer indicates how the student currently communicates (e.g., facial expressions, gestures, vocalizations). Likewise, the observer selects what the student is able to do independently under the heading of *Motor Control*. The goal is to identify what the student is able to do consistently and to determine if further evaluation is needed to determine if the student can use an unaided communication system successfully.

Another example of a potential screening tool is suggested on Figure 7.5. The purpose of the *Gesture Screening Form* is to help determine the type of gestures the student is using to communicate. This screening outlines the student's independent use of deictic, conventional, and iconic gestures. This form helps identify whether the student is able to perform these gestures across a variety of social settings. Further data will need to be collected to determine the consistency and effectiveness of use.

Unaided Feature Matching Screening Form

Student's name: _____   Observer's name: _____   Date: _____

This screening questionnaire provides general guidelines to assess the student's motor and communicative behaviors. It is highly recommended that a comprehensive assessment be conducted in collaboration with other teams members to determine a more accurate level of the student's ability to use unaided forms of communication.

Instructions. Complete the questions for each of the domain by checking Yes or No is the *Response* section. Begin with Q1. Record the total number of Yes and No is the *Results* section. Record any additional notes in the *Anecdotal Data* section.

Motor Control		
Instructions. Complete the questions addressed under *Motor Control* by checking Yes or No in the *Response* section. For Q6, select Right or Left in the boxes provided. If the student does not have hand control (Q1) or body control (Q2), do not move forward with this screener and continue to the *Aided Feature Matching Evaluation Form*, as your student will not benefit from unaided communication.		

			Response	
			YES	NO
Q1	Does the student have hand control?		☐	☐
Q2	Does the student have body control?		☐	☐
Q3	Does the student have hand movement control?		☐	☐
Q4	Does the student have body movement control?		☐	☐
Q5	Does the student point?		☐	☐
Q6	Which hand does the student use?		☐	☐
	☐ Left	☐ Right		

Communication		
Instructions. Complete the questions addressed under *Communication* by checking Yes or No is the *Response* section. For Q5, list the vocalizations the student uses, if any, in the space provided. For Q6, select whether the student has a reliable way to communicate "Yes" or "No" in the boxes. Describe how the student communicates "Yes" or "No" in the space provided below on Q6. If the student cannot perform the skills addressed in Q1-Q3, unaided communication is inappropriate for this student and you should continue to the *Aided Feature Matching Evaluation Form*.		

		Response	
		YES	NO
Q1	Does the student use facial expressions?	☐	☐
Q2	Does the student use body language?	☐	☐
Q3	Does the student use hand gestures?	☐	☐
Q4	Does the student use manual signs?	☐	☐
Q5	Does the student use vocalizations?	☐	☐
	Which one(s)_____		
	To communicate _____		
Q6	Does the student express ☐ Yes ☐ No	☐	☐
	How _____		

Results			
Motor control		Communication	
NO	YES	NO	YES
/6	/6	/6	/6

System Recommendation	Type of System
☐ Unaided system	☐ Vocalizations
☐ Aided system	☐ Gestures
	☐ Eye gaze
	☐ Manual signs

Anecdotal data.

FIGURE 7.4   Unaided feature-matching checklist.

(*Source:* AAC TechConnect, 2010)

GESTURES SCREENING FORM

Student's name: _____   Activity: _____

Observer's name: _____   Date/time of observation: _____

Instructions. For each gesture type and classification, check *yes* for the skills the student is able to complete independently or *no* for the skills the student cannot complete independently.

Deictic Gestures	Yes	No
Student extends his/her arms to show you an object he/she is holding	☐	☐
Student reaches out to give you an object he/she is holding	☐	☐
Student extends his/her arm and opens and closes his/her hand to request an object	☐	☐
Student points to draw your attention to an object	☐	☐
Student performs gestures to call attention to a wide variety of objects	☐	☐
Student performs gesture in close proximity to the object or communication partner	☐	☐
Student performs gesture when the object or communication partner is at a distance	☐	☐
Student makes eye contact with communication partner while performing the gesture	☐	☐
Conventional Gestures	**Yes**	**No**
Student waves *hi/bye* on his/her own when someone leaves	☐	☐
Student shakes his/her head to indicate *no*	☐	☐
Student nods his/her head to indicate *yes*	☐	☐
Student puts finger to his/her lips to indicate *be quiet*	☐	☐
Student performs gesture in a variety of social settings	☐	☐
Student makes eye contact with communication partner while performing the gesture	☐	☐
Iconic Gestures	**Yes**	**No**
Student uses his/her hands to convey the shape of an object	☐	☐
Student uses his/her hands to convey an action related to an object	☐	☐
Student performs these gestures in a variety of settings	☐	☐
Student makes eye contact with communication partner while performing the gesture	☐	☐

FIGURE 7.5   Gestures assessment.

(*Sources:* Crais, Douglas, & Campbell, 2004; Özçalışkan et al., 2016)

Beyond these initial screening forms, to ensure that the student is and continues to communicate using the most effective means, it is important to collect ongoing data on the student's communicative forms and functions. That is, data should be collected when the student is attempting to communicate with his or her various communication partners (e.g., peers, special education teacher, general education teacher, family members, related service providers) and across different communicative settings. It is also important to continuously record the student's progress in using the unaided form of communication across various communication functions. Figure 7.6 offers an example of a data collection system designed to evaluate the type of unaided communication system currently used by the student (i.e., eye gaze, gestures, manual sign, vocalizations) and the function of his or her communicative attempt (e.g., to accept, reject, request,

Unaided Communication Data Collection Form

Student's name: _____   Observer's name: _____   Date: _____

Evaluation of: ☐ Communication partner   ☐ Setting _____   ☐ Activity _____

Instructions. Under *evaluation,* indicate when or where the evaluation will be completed. Under *communication forms,* select the communication modality being used and indicate the specific form of communication. If there are multiple types under the same category, it is highly suggested that each communication form be evaluated independently. Under *communication functions,* indicate the purpose of the student's communicative attempt. Under *data trials,* indicate if the student attempted to communicate independently over five different trials. Under the *anecdotal notes,* include any additional information gathered during the observation.

Communication forms

☐ Eye gaze   ☐ Gestures   ☐ Manual signs   ☐ Vocalizations

Communication functions	Data trials					Communication functions	Data trials				
	1	2	3	4	5		1	2	3	4	5
Accepts	☐	☐	☐	☐	☐	Accepts	☐	☐	☐	☐	☐
Rejects	☐	☐	☐	☐	☐	Rejects	☐	☐	☐	☐	☐
Gives	☐	☐	☐	☐	☐	Gives	☐	☐	☐	☐	☐
Requests action	☐	☐	☐	☐	☐	Requests action	☐	☐	☐	☐	☐
Requests object	☐	☐	☐	☐	☐	Requests object	☐	☐	☐	☐	☐
Protests	☐	☐	☐	☐	☐	Protests	☐	☐	☐	☐	☐
Shows	☐	☐	☐	☐	☐	Shows	☐	☐	☐	☐	☐
Comments	☐	☐	☐	☐	☐	Comments	☐	☐	☐	☐	☐
Imitates	☐	☐	☐	☐	☐	Imitates	☐	☐	☐	☐	☐
Makes choice	☐	☐	☐	☐	☐	Makes choice	☐	☐	☐	☐	☐
Initiates	☐	☐	☐	☐	☐	Initiates	☐	☐	☐	☐	☐
Other	☐	☐	☐	☐	☐	Other	☐	☐	☐	☐	☐

Anecdotal data

FIGURE 7.6 Example of unaided communication data collection form.

comment). The *Unaided Communication Data Collection Form* can also help determine consistency in the use of unaided communication modalities across settings and communication partners.

The goal in the identification of unaided communication systems is to make certain that the student is being taught to use the most effective means of communication based on his or her skills. A key component when selecting a system for a student is to ensure that regardless of the system being used, unaided or aided, it is essential that the student has a means to respond to "yes and no" questions no matter the situation he or she is in (e.g., if the student is sick and does not have his or her system; Glennen & Decoste, 1997). Another important consideration for the instruction of any communicative system is that generalization and maintenance of the student's use of the system is built into the instructional program from the very beginning (Schlosser & Lee, 2000).

Because the expectations are changing for students with CCN, the hope is for these students to become active participants in educational, vocational, and social settings (Williams et al., 2008). To do so, these students will need to have access to a wide range of communication means, including not just aided systems, but also unaided communication systems (Light & McNaughton, 2014). Consequently, the focus in this complex process should adhere to the individualization of the system, which inherently meets the student's communicative needs.

Key Points of Chapter 7

- Unaided communication does not require an outside system.
- Unaided communication relies heavily on the ability of the communication partner to understand the communicative intent.
- Unaided communication systems include the following: vocalization, gestures, eye gaze, and manual signs.
- The main advantage of unaided communication system is that it is always with the student.
- The main disadvantages of unaided communication systems are the dependence on the communication partner's knowledge of the communication system and the strong imitative skills needed from the user.
- Data collection is essential in determining the unaided communication means being used by the student across settings and communication partners.
- Data should be collected not only on the means of communication, but also on the communication functions being used by the student.
- It is essential for students with CCN to have an unaided means to respond to yes and no questions.

References

AAC TechConnect. (2010). *The person: Skills and features to consider for assistive technology.* Retrieved from https://atspedresources.wikispaces.com/file/view/Person%20AT%20 consideration.pdf/596117582/Person%20AT%20consideration.pdf

Beukelman, D. R., & Mirenda, P. M. (2013). *Augmentative and alternative communication: Supporting children and adults with complex communication needs* (4th ed.). Baltimore, MD: Paul H. Brookes.

Bonvillian, J. D., & Nelson, K. E. (1976). Sign language acquisition in a mute autistic boy. *Journal of Speech and Hearing Disorders, 4,* 339. doi:10.1044/jshd.4103.339

Brady, N. C., Bruce, S., Goldman, A., Erickson, K., Mineo, B., Ogletree, B. T., . . . Wilkinson, K. (2016). Communication services and supports for individuals with severe disabilities: Guidance for assessment and intervention. *American Journal on Intellectual and Developmental Disabilities, 121,* 121–138. doi:10.1352/1944-7558-121.2.121

Branson, D., & Demchak, M. (2009). The use of augmentative and alternative communication methods with infants and toddlers with disabilities: A research review. *Augmentative and Alternative Communication, 25,* 274–286. doi:10.3109/07434610903384529

Calculator, S. N. (2013). Parents' reports of patterns of use and exposure to practices associated with AAC acceptance by individuals with Angelman syndrome. *Augmentative and Alternative Communication, 29,* 146–158. doi:10.3109/07434618.2013.784804

Carr, E. G., Binkoff, J. A., Kologinsky, E., & Eddy, M. (1978). Acquisition of sign language by autistic children. I: Expressive labelling. *Journal of Applied Behavior Analysis, 11,* 489–501. doi:10.1901/jaba.1978.11–489

Chan, J., & Iacono, T. (2001). Gesture and word production in children with down syndrome. *Augmentative and Alternative Communication, 17,* 73–87. doi:10.1080/714043370

Clarke, M. T. (2014). Eye-pointing, joint attention, interpersonal interaction and language development in children provided with AAC. In *Research Symposium of International Society for Augmentative and Alternative Communication, 16.* International Society for Augmentative and Alternative Communication (ISAAC).

Costello, J. M., Shane, H. C., & Caron, J. (2013). *AAC, mobile devices, and apps: Growing pains with evidence based practice.* Retrieved from www.childrenshospital.org/clinicalservices/ Site2016/mainpageS2016P20.html,1-8.

Crais, E., Douglas, D. D., & Campbell, C. C. (2004). The intersection of the development of gestures and intentionality. *Journal of Speech, Language, and Hearing Research, 47,* 678–694. doi:1092–4388/04/4703–0678

Drager, K., Light, J., & McNaughton, D. (2010). Effects of AAC interventions on communication and language for young children with complex communication needs. *Journal of Pediatric Rehabilitation Medicine: An Interdisciplinary Approach, 3,* 303–310. doi:10.3233/ PRM-2010–0141

Falcomata, T. S., Wacker, D. P., Ringdahl, J. E., Vinquist, K., & Dutt, A. (2013). An evaluation of generalization of mands during functional communication training. *Journal of Applied Behavior Analysis, 46,* 444–454. doi:10.1002/jaba.37

Ganz, J. B., Earles-Vollrath, T. L., Heath, A. K., Parker, R. I., Rispoli, M. J., & Duran, J. B. (2012). A meta-analysis of single case research studies on aided augmentative and alternative communication systems with individuals with autism spectrum disorder. *Journal of Autism and Developmental Disorders, 42,* 60–74. doi:10.1007/s10803-011-1212-2

Gevarter, C., O'Reilly, M. F., Rojeski, L., Sammarco, N., Lang, R., Lancioni, G. E., & Sigafoos, J. (2013). Comparisons of intervention components within augmentative and alternative communication systems for individuals with developmental disabilities: A review of the literature. *Research in Developmental Disabilities, 34,* 4404–4414. doi:10.1016/j.ridd.2013.09.018

Glennen, S. L., & DeCoste, D. C. (1997). *Handbook of Augmentative and Alternative Communication.* San Diego, CA: Cengage Learning.

Grove, N., & Woll, B. (2017). Assessing language skills in adult key word signers with intellectual disabilities: Insights from sign linguistics. *Research in Developmental Disabilities, 62,* 174–183. doi:10.1016/j.ridd.2017.01.017

Hoff, E. (2013). *Language development* (5th ed.). Belmont, CA: Wadsworth/Cengage Learning.

Hourcade, J., Pilotte, T. E., West, E., & Parette, P. (2004). A history of augmentative and alternative communication for individuals with severe and profound disabilities. *Focus on Autism and Other Developmental Disabilities, 19,* 235–244. doi:10.1177/1088357604 0190040501

Johnston, S. S., & Coseby, J. (2012). Building blocks of a beginning communication system: Communicative modes. In J. Reichle, K. M. Feeley, and S. S. Johnston (Eds.), *AAC strategies for individuals with moderate to severe disabilities* (pp. 311–345). Baltimore, MD: Paul H. Brookes.

Lederberg, A. R., & Everhart, V. S. (1998). Communication between deaf children and their hearing mothers. *Journal of Speech Language and Hearing Research, 41,* 887. doi:10.1044/jslhr.4104.887

Lee, Y., Jeong, S-W., & Kim, L-S. (2013). AAC intervention using a VOCA for deaf children with multiple disabilities who received cochlear implantation. *International Journal of Pediatric Otorhinolaryngology, 77,* 2008–2013. doi:10.1016/j.ijporl.2013.09.023

Light, J., & McNaughton, D. (2014). Communicative competence for individuals who require augmentative and alternative communication: A new definition for a new era of communication? *Augmentative and Alternative Communication, 30,* 1–18. doi:10.3109 /07434618.2014.885080

Lloyd, L., Quist, R., & Windsor, J. (1990). A proposed augmentative and alternative communication model. *Augmentative and Alternative Communication, 6,* 172–183. doi:10.108 0/07434619012331275444

Lorah, E. R., Parnell, A., Whitby, P. S., & Hantula, D. (2014). A systematic review of tablet computers and portable media players as speech generating devices for individuals with autism spectrum disorder. *Journal of Autism and Developmental Disorders, 45,* 3792–3804. doi:10.1007/s10803-014-2314-4

Lund, S. K., Quach, W., Weissling, K., McKelvey, M., & Dietz, A. (2017). Assessment with children who need Augmentative and Alternative Communication (AAC): Clinical decisions of AAC specialists. *Language Speech and Hearing Services in Schools, 48,* 56. doi:10.1044/2016_lshss-15–0086

Mirenda, P. (2003). Toward functional augmentative and alternative communication for students with autism: Manual signs, graphic symbols, and voice output communication aids. *Language, Speech, and Hearing Services in Schools, 34,* 203–216. doi:10.1044/ 0161–1461(2003/017)

Mitchell, S., Brian, J., Zwaigenbaum, L., Roberts, W., Szatmari, P., Smith, I., & Bryson, S. (2006). Early language and communication development of infants later diagnosed with autism spectrum disorder. *Journal of Developmental and Behavioral Pediatrics, 27*(Supplement 2), S69–S78. doi:10.1097/00004703–200604002–00004

Özçalışkan, Ş., Adamson, L. B., & Dimitrova, N. (2016). Early deictic but not other gestures predict later vocabulary in both typical development and autism. *Autism, 20*, 754–763. doi:10.1177/1362361315605921

Quinn, E. D., & Rowland, C. (2017). Exploring expressive communication skills in a cross-sectional sample of children and young adults with Angelman syndrome. *American Journal of Speech-Language Pathology, 26*, 369. doi:10.1044/2016_ajslp-15–0075

Reichle, J., Drager, K., Caron, J., & Parker-McGowan, Q. (2016). Playing the long game: Considering the future of augmentative and alternative communication research and service. *Seminars in Speech and Language, 37*, 259–273. doi:10.1055/s-0036–1587706

Remington, B., & Clarke, S. (1983). Acquisition of expressive signing by autistic children: An evaluation of the relative effects of simultaneous communication and sign-alone training. *Journal of Applied Behavior Analysis, 16*, 315–327. doi:10.1901/jaba.1983.16–315

Sargent, J., Clarke, M., Price, K., Griffiths, T., & Swettenham, J. (2013). Use of eye-pointing by children with cerebral palsy: What are we looking at? *International Journal of Language and Communication Disorders, 48*, 477–485. doi:10.1111/1460–6984.12026

Schlosser, R. W., & Lee, D. (2000). Promoting generalization and maintenance in augmentative and alternative communication: A meta-analysis of 20 years of effectiveness research. *Augmentative and Alternative Communication, 16*, 208–226. doi:10.1080/07434 610012331279074

Schlosser, R. W., & Raghavendra, P. (2004). Evidence-based practice in augmentative and alternative communication. *Augmentative and Alternative Communication, 20*, 1–21. doi:1 0.1080/07434610310001621083

Sigafoos, J., Didden, R., & O'Reilly, M. (2003). Effects of speech output on maintenance of requesting and frequency of vocalizations in three children with developmental disabilities. *Augmentative and Alternative Communication, 19*, 37–47. doi:10.1080/0743461032000056487

Sigafoos, J., & Drasgow, E. (2001). Conditional use of aided and unaided AAC: A review and clinical case demonstration. *Focus on Autism and Other Developmental Disabilities, 16*, 152–161. doi:10.1177/108835760101600303

Sigafoos, J., O'Reilly, M. F., Lancioni, G. E., & Sutherland, D. (2014). Augmentative and alternative communication for individuals with autism spectrum disorder and intellectual disability. *Current Developmental Disorders Report, 1*, 51–57. doi:10.1007/s40474–013–0007-x

Singer Harris, N. G., Bellugi, U., Bates, E., Jones, W., & Rossen, M. (1997). Contrasting profiles of language development in children with Williams and Down syndromes. *Developmental Neuropsychology, 13*, 345–370. doi:10.1080/87565649709540683

Soto, G., & Yu, B. (2014). Considerations for the provision of services to bilingual children who use augmentative and alternative communication. *Augmentative and Alternative Communication, 30*, 83–92. doi:10.3109/07434618.2013.878751

Stowers, S., Altheide, M. R., & Shea, V. (1987). Motor assessment for unaided and aided augmentative communication. *Physical and Occupational Therapy in Pediatrics, 7*, 61–78. doi:10.1080/J006v07n02_06

Wendt, O. (2009). Research on the use of graphic symbols and manual signs. In P. Mirenda & T. Iacono (Eds.), *Autism spectrum disorders and AAC* (pp. 83–139). Baltimore, MD: Paul H. Brookes.

Wilkinson, R. (2013). Gestural depiction in acquired language disorders: On the form and use of iconic gestures in aphasic talk-in-interaction. *Augmentative and Alternative Communication, 29,* 68–82. doi:10.3109/07434618.2013.767558

Wray, C., Saunders, N., McGuire, R., Cousins, G., & Norbury, C. F. (2017). Gesture production in language impairment: It's quality, not quantity, that matters. *Journal of Speech Language and Hearing Research, 60,* 969. doi:10.1044/2016_jslhr-l-16–0141

Yoder, P., & Layton, T. (1988). Speech following sign language training in autistic children with minimal verbal language. *Journal of Autism & Developmental Disorders, 18,* 217–229. doi:10.1007/bf02211948

8

DEFINING AND IDENTIFYING LOW-TECHNOLOGY AIDED COMMUNICATION SYSTEMS

Students with complex communication needs (CCN) have strengths and needs that may not be well served with unaided forms of communication. Thus, it is equally important to determine if aided communication systems are suitable for students with CCN. Aided communication systems require the use of materials beyond a person's body or voice. These aided systems can vary greatly from the use of paper and pencil techniques to highly sophisticated, electronic *speech-generating devices* (SGDs), computers, and mobile technologies (Thistle & Wilkinson, 2013). Aided communication is selection-based, meaning that the student is required to point, grab, or touch a symbol(s) to convey a message (Albis & Reed, 2012; Williams & Grove, 1989). Figure 8.1 shows the classification of the aided communication systems.

Aided augmentative and alternative communication (AAC) systems vary from low-technology to *high-technology* systems. Most low-technology AAC systems do not require batteries or electricity to operate such as objects, symbols, communication boards and books, and written words (Baxter, Enderby, Evans, & Judge, 2012). However, low-technology AAC systems also encompass simple devices such as one button SGDs.

Object symbols can be used to represent real objects or activities. For example, an empty bottle of bubbles can be used to request that a teacher blow bubbles. Tangible symbols include two- or three-dimensional symbols (Rowland & Schweigert, 1989; Roche et al., 2014), while photographs of items consist of pictures intended to serve as symbols. Line drawings, such as picture communication symbols (PCS), are symbols that depict items, actions, or concepts (Mayer-Johnson, 2016). See Figure 5.4 in Chapter 5 for examples of tangible symbols, photographs, and line drawings. Furthermore, aided AAC includes communication boards (where symbols are stored on a single page or board and all symbols are visible

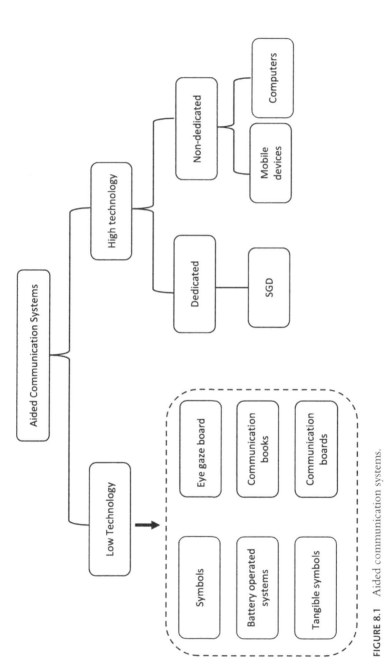

FIGURE 8.1 Aided communication systems.

Note. SGD = Speech generating device

at all times) and communication books (where symbols are stored in a book or notebook with symbols on multiple pages). Communication wallets consist of symbols stored in a wallet in photograph sleeves. See Figure 8.2 for examples of low-technology aided communication systems.

Given that the use of symbols is the primary component of using aided communication systems, it is important to determine the student's understanding and use of symbols. This includes evaluating the most appropriate size and placement of symbols, how many symbols the student should have in the AAC system, and how they should be organized. Furthermore, because symbols may range from

Communication book

Communication belt strip

Communication felt board

FIGURE 8.2   Examples of low–technology communication systems.

simple to complex, it is also necessary to assess the student's knowledge of the different levels of symbol iconicity. *Symbol iconicity* refers to how closely a picture, manual sign, gesture, or another symbol is connected to the attached message (Markham & Justice, 2004). There are three types of iconicity: (1) transparent, (2) translucent, and (3) opaque (Chompoobutr, Potibal, Boriboon, & Phantachat, 2013; Lloyd, Fuller, & Arvidson, 1997). Figure 8.3 illustrates the three types of iconicity.

(1) *Transparent symbol.* A highly guessable symbol given that it visually resembles its referent.
(2) *Translucent symbol.* A symbol that is less apparent than a transparent symbol because it typically requires additional information in order for the user to connect the symbol with its corresponding meaning.
(3) *Opaque symbol.* A symbol that is not readily obvious to the user even when additional information is provided. An opaque symbol does not resemble its referent. Typically, opaque symbols are arbitrary and tend to depict actions such as verbs and adverbs.

To assess a student's knowledge and use of symbols, the team could use specific *tools* such as the *Test of Aided Communication Symbol Performance* (TASP; Bruno, 2010) or use less formal methods. The TASP is designed to assess symbol size and number (i.e., most appropriate number of symbols to use in the AAC system), grammatical encoding (i.e., comprehension of verbs, nouns, adjectives, and location words), categorization (i.e., how a student organizes words), and syntactic performance (i.e., ability to use symbols to create novel sentences). If the AAC team conducts a non-commercial vocabulary assessment, Beukelman and Mirenda (2013) emphasize the use of a comprehensive approach. This approach includes five vocabulary assessment formats. Given that the vocabulary assessment

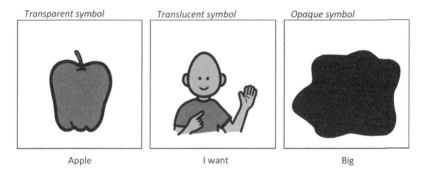

FIGURE 8.3 Symbol iconicity.

is knowledge-based, it is important for the AAC team to only use items and symbols of items the student is familiar with. This can be confirmed by obtaining input from family members, teachers, or others who are very familiar with the student's knowledge of items and activities. Beukelman and Mirenda recommend using at least ten functional items along with several types of symbols (e.g., line drawings, photographs, written words, tactile symbols, etc.) that correspond to the items. Each subsequent assessment format listed below evaluates more advanced symbol use than the previous format.

(1) *Functional use.* Determine if the student can use known items in a functional manner (i.e., can the student use the items as they were intended to be used?). For example, does the student use a toothbrush for brushing his or her teeth or a fork for eating? Depending on the student's physical capabilities and age, it may require the student to engage in pretend play or show knowledge by responding (through any means) to questions such as "Which one do you brush your teeth with? Or which one do you eat with?"

(2) *Receptive labeling.* Evaluate receptive labeling of symbols by asking the student "Show me the fork," "Point to the fork," or "Look at the fork." The directive should be aligned to whichever means of selection the student can perform. Also, the student should be presented with an array of two or more items or symbols.

(3) *Yes/no.* For students who can respond to yes/no questions, assess symbol identification by asking the student "Is this a toothbrush?" or "Is this a fork?"

(4) *Alternative visual-matching.* For students who cannot be assessed through receptive labeling and yes/no format, they can be evaluated by checking the student's ability to match an object to the symbol, or the reverse, to match a symbol to the corresponding object. The student should be provided with a single object/symbol and asked to match it from an array of objects/symbols. Matching can be completed through any direct selection method the student is able to perform.

(5) *Question-and-answer.* It is a good idea to determine if the student is able to use symbols to answer questions. The student should be asked questions that can be answered given an array of two or more symbols of the same type (e.g., objects, line drawings, photographs, etc.). This format differs from receptive labeling in that it does not ask the student to identify the items. Rather, the questions are more knowledge-based such as "What do you have to do before you go to bed?" Or "What did you play with during recess?"

(6) *Requesting.* A student's ability to spontaneously request preferred items is important and should be assessed. As with several other assessment formats, the AAC team provides the student with two or more symbols of preferred items within a naturalistic context (e.g., meal/snack time, play time, etc.). To

elicit spontaneous requesting, the environment should be set up to encourage communication. This could consist of placing the preferred items within view but out of reach, only providing a small portion of the item (e.g., one small sip of a beverage), or other using other sabotaging strategies described in Chapter 11. The teacher or other AAC team member should refrain from prompting the student by saying "Point to the picture of the item." Instead, the AAC team member should say "I don't understand what you want."

As part of the vocabulary assessment, an evaluation should be conducted to determine the most suitable symbol type and size for the student. The assessment described earlier emphasized the importance of trying various symbol types as not all types will be suitable for all students. In terms of symbol size, some students with visual impairments may benefit from using larger symbols. Likewise, students with fine motor limitations may also need larger symbols for easier grasping, pointing, or touching. The AAC evaluation team may want to refer to the TASP (Bruno, 2010) or other tools to help with this process.

The results of the vocabulary assessment along with a complete profile of the student's present level of academic achievement and functional performance (see Chapter 5) will allow the AAC team to make informed decisions about identifying an appropriate AAC system. The next step is to identify an AAC system that best meets the needs of the student. This process is known as feature matching (Abbott & McBride, 2014).

Aided Communication Feature Matching

The feature-matching process is time intensive given that it takes into account the student's present levels of functioning and matches them to the various features inherent in aided AAC systems. This typically requires the team to determine the most appropriate display of symbols in the AAC system, symbol size, its symbol arrangement, and the selection method. As with other assessments, determining which aided AAC system is most suitable for the student requires a comprehensive assessment that is conducted by experienced team members. However, the questionnaire in Figure 8.4 can be used as a screening tool to guide the evaluation team in determining if a low-technology aided AAC system is appropriate for the student with CCN. This low-technology feature-matching tool is designed to consider the student's motor and communication skills. While this tool is geared towards low-technology AAC systems, it is very possible that a high-technology AAC system may be recommended by the evaluation team if a low-tech system is insufficient to meet the short- and long-term needs of the student. If this is the case, the team will need to conduct a feature-matching assessment specific to high-technology systems (refer to Chapter 9).

Low Technology Feature Matching Screening Form

Student's name: _____   Low technology system: _____

Observer's name: _____   Date: _____

The *Low Technology Feature Matching Screening Form* provides a general outline of the student's motor and communicative behaviors as it pertains to low tech aided communication. It is highly recommended that a comprehensive assessment be conducted in collaboration with other team members, to determine a more accurate level of the student's ability to use aided communication forms.

Instructions. Complete the questions for each domain by checking Yes or No in the *Response* section. Begin with Q1. Record the total number of Yes and No in the *Results* section. Record any additional notes in the *Anecdotal Notes* section.

Representation				
Questions			YES	NO
Q1	What type of symbols will be used? ☐PCS ☐Minspeak ☐Symbolstix ☐Photographs ☐Clipart ☐Text		☐	☐
Q2	Will single key messages be used?		☐	☐
Q3	Will short phrase messages be used?		☐	☐
Q4	Will complete sentence messages be used?		☐	☐
Q5	Will the system display ☐words or ☐pictures or ☐both?		☐	☐
Q6	How many cells does the system display? # of cells_____			

Messages				
Questions			YES	NO
Q1	Does the system have speech output?		☐	☐
Q2	Will the system have an ☐adult or ☐peer voice? ☐Male ☐Female		☐	☐

Communication				
Questions			YES	NO
Q1	Does the student point to symbols to communicate?		☐	☐
Q2	Does the student grab symbols to communicate?		☐	☐
Q3	Does the student use vocalizations to communicate? Which one(s)_____		☐	☐
Q4	Does the student use his/her eyes to communicate?		☐	☐

Motor Control				
Questions			YES	NO
Q1	Does the student have hand control?		☐	☐
Q2	Does the student have body control?		☐	☐
Q3	Does the student have hand movement control?		☐	☐
Q4	Does the student have body movement control?		☐	☐
Q5	Does the student point?		☐	☐
Q6	Which hand does the student use? ☐Right ☐Left		☐	☐
Q7	Does the student have range of motion?		☐	☐
Q8	Does the student touch symbols? ☐.50" ☐1" ☐2" ☐___"		☐	☐
Q9	Does the student have the ability to walk?		☐	☐
Q10	Does the student have difficulties with balance?		☐	☐
Q11	Does the student use a wheelchair? ☐Manual ☐Power		☐	☐
Q12	Does the student have weight/size restrictions?		☐	☐

FIGURE 8.4   Low-technology feature-matching evaluation form.

(*Source:* AAC TechConnect, 2010)

Results			
Representation		Message	
NO	YES	NO	YES
/6	/6	/2	/2
Motor Control		Communication	
NO	YES	NO	YES
/12	/12	/4	/4
Anecdotal data.			

FIGURE 8.4   (Continued)

Symbol Selection

Based on the results of the vocabulary assessment, the AAC team should determine if the student could benefit from multiple types of symbols or is best served using one type. There are many commercially available symbol sets and systems in today's market. Examples include Blissymbolics® (Blissymbolics Communication International), DynaSyms® (Dynavox), Minspeak® (Semantic Compaction Systems; Prentke Romich Company), Picture Communication Symbols® (PCS; Boardmaker from Mayer-Johnson), Picture English® (Piclish; Language Symbols), Widgit Symbols® (Widget Software), among others. Symbols should not be selected simply based on convenience, but rather the student's needs and preferences. The AAC team should also consider the student's projected vocabulary growth and determine if the symbol system will allow for expansion. Even if the student is able to communicate with single symbols, it is possible that with time and training, the student will be able to combine symbols to communicate. Similarly, students who demonstrate the ability to communicate concrete concepts initially may later need a symbol system to communicate abstract concepts. Thus, it is important that the student's current and future needs are considered during the symbol selection process.

Display Arrangement

There are two main types of displays, static and dynamic. For low-technology systems, a *static display* contains graphic symbols that are displayed on a single page and do not require movement to be understood (Beukelman & Mirenda, 2013; Johnston, Reichle, Feeley, & Jones, 2012). A benefit of using a static display is that the cognitive requirements for the student are minimal as compared to using dynamic displays. The student does not have to navigate through multiple pages or folders to select a symbol. However, a drawback is that it takes up more space and, therefore, the vocabulary is limited. *Dynamic displays* require the user to navigate through different layers of the display in order to retrieve the graphic symbol. Low-technology systems only utilize static displays while high-technology systems can use either static or dynamic displays. Given that dynamic displays are relevant to high-technology systems, Chapter 9 contains specific information about the assessment considerations associated with dynamic displays.

The SLP or appropriate AAC specialist along with the special education teacher should determine how the student's abilities are impacted by the various displays and graphic symbol arrangement of the AAC system. In other words, the team should carefully consider how the display of an AAC system looks and how it is organized. This is important given that graphic symbol organization can greatly impact the student's ability to communicate effectively and efficiently (Wilkinson, O'Neill, & McIlvane, 2014). It is common practice for someone other than the student to determine how the symbols are arranged on the system display and how they are categorized. However, there is evidence to suggest that the student's world knowledge and experiences affect how the student cognitively organizes and processes information (Light & McNaughton, 2012). Thus, during the feature-matching process, the team should take into account this information and identify aided AAC systems that allow the symbols to be displayed and organized according to the student's ability to retrieve and process information efficiently. Similarly, Thistle and Wilkinson (2013) emphasized that different types of displays require different levels of memory processing. Thus, the working memory demand is also an important consideration during the feature-matching process particularly for students who have intellectual disabilities or impairments that affect memory processing. Not only is it important to consider the student's current abilities, but the team should plan for future changes. This may include changes that occur due to the student's learning growth or as a result of changes attributed to the student's disability (e.g., impairments that cause progressive neurological or intellectual deterioration of the student's abilities).

There are different types of displays typically seen in aided AAC systems. These include the following: (1) semantic-syntactic grid display, (2) clustered display, (3) distributed display, (4) taxonomic grid display, (5) activity grid display, (6) visual scene display, (7) hybrid display, and (8) pragmatic organization dynamic display. With the exception of visual scene display, the rest of these displays are typically arranged using a grid format with the symbols organized by rows and columns (Johnston et al., 2012). See Figure 8.5 for an example of the various types of displays. These examples display the symbols on a low-technology communication board. What is not shown are the different folders or pages that store the symbols when not in use.

(1) *Semantic-syntactic grid display.* Semantic-syntactic grid displays organize symbols based on the parts of speech (Beukelman & Mirenda, 2013; Drager, Light, Speltz, Fallon, & Jeffries, 2003). One variation is the use of the Fitzgerald Key. This typically includes color-coding and organizing symbols into who, what, when, where, and verbs (McDonald & Schultz, 1973). Color-coding can include using a colored background, a partially colored background, or

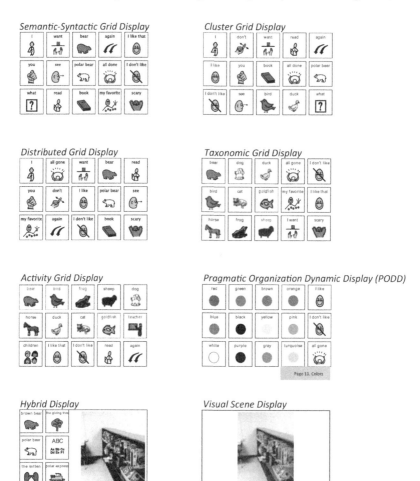

FIGURE 8.5   Examples of communication board grid displays.

using a colored border around each symbol. Semantic-syntactic displays are beneficial in that they are structured to encourage literacy concepts such as sentence formation (e.g., constructing sentences from left to right, and other basic concepts of print; Beukelman & Mirenda, 2013). Figure 8.6 provides three different guidelines for color-coding when using the semantic-syntactic grid display and Figure 8.7 illustrates four variations of a semantic-syntactic grid display.

(2) *Clustered display*. Another method of organizing symbols by color is called clustered display. Rather than organizing the symbol background color like in Fitzgerald Key, the clustered display categorizes symbols based on the internal color of the symbol (Wilkinson et al., 2014). For example, the internal color of a line drawing of a banana would be yellow. So all symbols with yellow as the internal color would be clustered together. According to Wilkinson, Carlin, and Thistle (2008), individuals who use clustered displays have faster selection speed than those who used distributed displays.

(3) *Distributed display*. Distributed displays do not use color for organizing the symbols. Rather, the symbols are dispersed throughout the display in a grid format without any specific sequence (Wilkinson et al., 2014).

(4) *Taxonomic grid display*. The taxonomic grid display organizes symbols by generic categories such as people, places, feelings, foods, and so forth (Drager et al., 2003; Petroi, Koul, &Corwin, 2014). This type of display may be advantageous in that it reduces the cognitive demands on the individual, particularly those with CCN due to brain injuries (Petroi et al., 2014).

(5) *Activity grid display*. Activity grid displays are also referred to as schematic grid layouts. They arrange the symbols into separate pages by events, activities, or routines (Drager et al., 2003; Gevarter et al., 2014). Because activity grid displays use activities and routines to guide the organization of symbols, it allows teacher, and practitioners to quickly create pages for a specific activity (Beukelman & Mirenda, 2013).

(6) *Visual scene display*. A visual scene display allows the individual to use photographs or line drawings of places or scenes as a strategy to incorporate context during communication interactions (Blackstone, 2005; Wilkinson, Light, & Drager, 2012). Rather than organizing the symbols using a grid layout, the symbols and their message are embedded schematically. For example, a student may have a visual scene display that depicts the student in a kitchen. The symbols needed to convey cooking a favorite dish are embedded throughout the scene where appropriate. This display may be advantageous in that it can be intuitive for the student, thus, aiding in potentially faster acquisition.

(7) *Hybrid display*. Displays that use hybrid formats may include the combination of visuals scenes along with one of the various grid layouts (Beukelmen & Mirenda, 2013; Gevarter et al., 2014). Once variation is having a split display in which one half contains the visual scene while the other half has a grid layout of symbols pertaining to the scene.

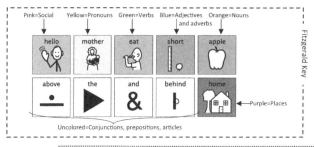

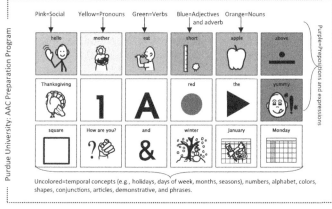

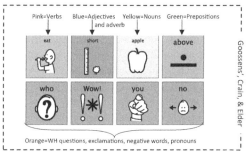

FIGURE 8.6   Color-coding suggested guidelines.

Tobii-Dynavox ©2017 Boardmaker. All rights reserved. (Used with permission.)

(*Sources:* Goossens', Crain, & Elder, 1992; Purdue University: AAC Preparation Program, 1994)

(8) *Pragmatic organization dynamic display. Pragmatic Organization Dynamic Display* (PODD; Porter, 2007) uses a variety of strategies to organize vocabulary with the intended focus of increasing functional communication. Because communicative efficiency is one of the goals of PODD, the student may have the same vocabulary symbols across pages to minimize symbol retrieval. A benefit is that the display is not geared towards using one organizational

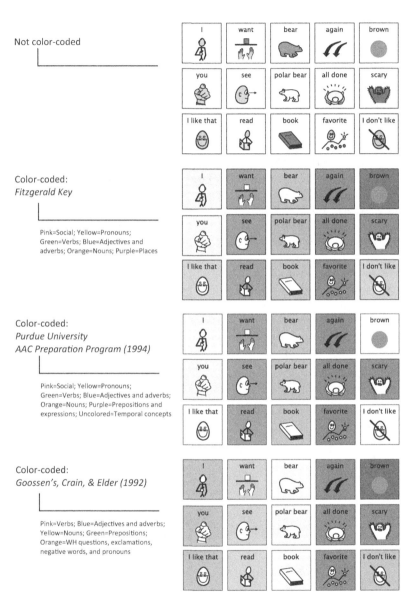

Not color-coded

Color-coded:
Fitzgerald Key

Pink=Social; Yellow=Pronouns;
Green=Verbs; Blue=Adjectives and
adverbs; Orange=Nouns; Purple=Places

Color-coded:
*Purdue University
AAC Preparation Program (1994)*

Pink=Social; Yellow=Pronouns;
Green=Verbs; Blue=Adjectives and adverbs;
Orange=Nouns; Purple=Prepositions and
expressions; Uncolored=Temporal concepts

Color-coded:
Goossen's, Crain, & Elder (1992)

Pink=Verbs; Blue=Adjectives and adverbs;
Yellow=Nouns; Green=Prepositions;
Orange=WH questions, exclamations,
negative words, and pronouns

FIGURE 8.7 Comparison of non–colored and color-coded communication displays.

Tobii-Dynavox ©2017 Boardmaker. All rights reserved. (Used with permission.)

(*Sources:* Goossens' et al., 1992; Purdue University: AAC Preparation Program, 1994)

method. Rather, PODD emphasizes individualization, access to a comprehensive number of vocabularies for the student and communication partner, and efficiency (Porter & Cafiero, 2009). A downside is that when the same symbols are placed in different pages of a communication book or another low-technology AAC system, it creates a bulky and cumbersome system.

Speech Output

All low-technology SGDs use digitized speech to emit the recorded message. *Digitized speech* entails the use of natural speech that has been digitally recorded and stored in the SGD (Schlosser, 2003). One example of a low-technology AAC system that uses digitized speech is the BIGmack® communicator. This device has the capacity to store a digitized recording of up to 2 minutes. Low-technology SGDs are advantageous in that they allow the teacher or caregiver to quickly and easily record messages to provide the student with a means to engage in a variety of activities. They are relatively inexpensive, very portable, and require little to no training to learn how to operate. On the contrary, because they only allow for a single, short message to be recorded, it limits what the student is able to communicate during a given activity. It does not allow the student opportunities to create novel messages, clarify, ask additional questions, or repair communication breakdowns. Thus, the team should consider using these simple SGDs in combination with other AAC systems such as a communication book if it is appropriate for the student. Figure 8.8 provides examples of some available low-technology speech-generating devices.

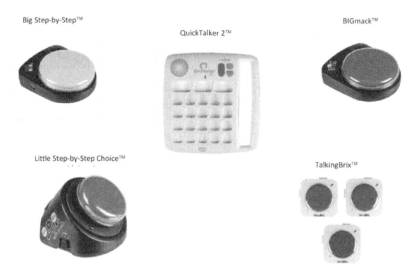

Big Step-by-Step™

QuickTalker 2™

BIGmack™

Little Step-by-Step Choice™

TalkingBrix™

FIGURE 8.8   Examples of low-technology speech-generating devices by Ablenet. (Reprinted with permission from Ablenet©.)

Selection Techniques

All aided AAC systems require the student to select the symbol in order to communicate with the communication partner. Selection techniques typically involve the use of direct or indirect selection. *Direct selection* requires the student to directly select the symbol with a hand/finger or an external apparatus, while *indirect selection* involves the use of intermediary steps to make a selection (Johnston et al., 2012). Given that different selection techniques involve varying levels of working memory demands, it is necessary to ensure the student is able to select the desired symbol(s) in the most efficient and effective method possible for that student. The working memory demands for each selection technique vary. For example, direct selection places the least amount of cognitive demand as compared to indirect selection methods such as scanning (Thistle & Wilkinson, 2013). Each scanning method varies in its pattern as well as its demands on the student's working memory (Thistle & Wilkinson, 2013). If the decision is made for the student to use scanning to access the AAC system, the team will need to consider which scanning selection method is most appropriate when taking into account the student's cognitive and sensory skills (refer to Chapter 5). For students who require the use of scanning selection methods, refer to Chapter 9 for information about *group, linear,* and *circular scanning.* All of these scanning patterns can occur in low- and high-tech AAC systems.

For low-technology systems, the scanning requires the use of a facilitator (McCarthy et al., 2006). This technique is known as *partner-assisted scanning.* The facilitator scans the symbols either by pointing or speaking, or if the student has significant visual and hearing impairments, the facilitator can present the symbols using tactile methods (Lloyd, Fuller, & Arvidson, 1997; Nevers, 2011). For visual scanning (i.e., pointing), the student requires adequate visual abilities to follow and recognize the symbols while the facilitator is pointing to each symbol. When auditory scanning (i.e., speaking) is used, the student should have sufficient hearing and comprehension skills to select the desired symbol as it is spoken by the facilitator. With tactile scanning (i.e., touching), the student needs to have adequate comprehension of what the symbols represent by feel as the facilitator guides the student to touch the tactile symbols. Partner-assisted scanning can also be done by combining two or more of these methods. Figure 8.9 shows an example of partner-assisted scanning.

Accessibility Apparatuses

Students who need external apparatuses to access aided AAC systems may need to use switches, keyboards, keyguards, trackballs, and wheelchair mounts. While none of these accessibility apparatuses are communication systems on their own, they are considered assistive technologies because they help the student access the aided AAC system. Figures 8.10 show examples of various accessibility apparatuses; see

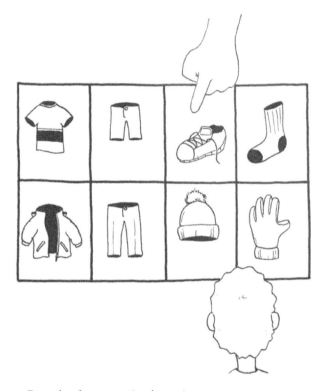

FIGURE 8.9 Example of partner-assisted scanning.

Figure 8.11 and 8.12 for examples of switches, and Figure 8.13 for examples of mounting systems.

Augmentative and Alternative Communication System Preferences

Although feature matching is critical to the successful utilization of the AAC system, another important factor is the student's preference of a specific system (van der Meer, Sigafoos, O'Reilly, & Lancioni, 2011). Considering a student's (and family's) preferences can mean the difference between complete buy-in into learning the system and system abandonment. In a review by van der Meer and colleagues (2011), they concluded that participants with developmental disabilities demonstrated preferences when they were taught to use two different AAC systems. Therefore, assessing preferences is important when identifying and selecting an appropriate AAC system for a student with CCN. However, it should be noted that preferences may change over time. Thus, it is equally important to reassess preferences in order to maximize system satisfaction over time. Although

Pillow Speaker

BigBlue VisionBoard

VisionBoard 2 - yellow

BigKeys LX Keyboard

BIGtrack Trackball

Rock Adapted Joystick

FIGURE 8.10 Examples of accessibility by Ablenet.
(Reprinted with permission from Ablenet©.)

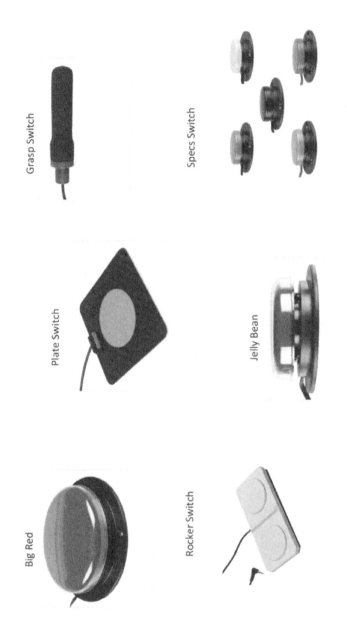

Grasp Switch

Specs Switch

Plate Switch

Jelly Bean

Big Red

Rocker Switch

FIGURE 8.11   Examples of switches by AbleNet©.
(Reprinted with permission.)

WobbleSwitch

Freedom Switch

FIGURE 8.12   Examples of switches by Prentke Romich Company©.
(Reprinted with permission.)

Table Top Suction Mount

Gooseneck Mounting System

Hover Mounting Systems

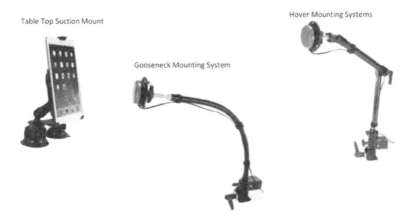

FIGURE 8.13   Examples of mounting systems by AbleNet©.
(Reprinted with permission.)

some students may have a difficult time learning at least one system, the team should operate on the principle that students are capable of learning multiple systems and choosing their preferred system. According to research conducted by Achmadi et al. (2014), students are more likely to be proficient in the system they prefer the most.

Trial Period

Once an aided AAC system has been selected and customized for the student, it is important to conduct a trial period. This allows the AAC team to determine if the AAC system is right for the student or if modifications or adaptations are needed. If the team recommends two systems, the trial period allows the student adequate time to try out both AAC systems to see which one is a better fit for the student. Similar to how most people will try on clothes, test-drive vehicles, and so forth, the student will need time to test the AAC systems. While there is no specific time for conducting the trial period, it is important that the trial is sufficiently long enough to allow the student to use the system with support from a knowledgeable SLP, teacher, and relevant practitioner. This is a critical step given that students with communication difficulties cannot be expected to immediately know how to use the AAC system. It is important to remind others that young children with typical development are immersed in a language-rich environment for a year or longer before it is expected that they will communicate an intelligible word (Kuhl, 2011). Thus, the trial period should be viewed as a period in which the student should be given the necessary training and support along with the AAC system.

Making decisions about the effectiveness of an AAC system requires that the AAC team take baseline data as a first step in the trial period. Baseline data will allow the AAC team to make informed decisions rather than relying on personal opinion. One straightforward strategy is to do a pre- and post-comparison of a participation inventory. This comparison will help determine if the student's participation in school tasks and activities has increased as a result of using the AAC system. Likewise, it can inform the AAC team if the AAC system has increased the student's social interactions and development of a greater social network (Beukelman & Mirenda, 2013).

Comparisons can also be made by reviewing the data gathered about the student's present level of performance and academic achievement (Chapter 5 and 6) and comparing it with the student's performance after using the AAC system. Specific communication skills pertinent to evaluate during the trial period include changes in requesting, commenting, responding, initiating, asking questions, and more. Another area that can be impacted as a result of using a functional communication system is a decrease in problem behaviors (Calculator, 1999). Students who do not have a reliable method of communicating in a functional manner can demonstrate problem behaviors as their way of communicating their wants, needs, and frustrations (Maag, 2017). Thus, when a student learns to use an AAC system to communicate for a variety of functions, it is expected to see a decrease in problem behaviors (Boesch & Wendt, 2009).

It is important to note that in order to answer questions about the student's performance with the AAC system, the system will need to be used in the student's natural environments. Otherwise, the barriers, communication partners, and communicative opportunities will most likely not be similar in the controlled environment when compared to the student's natural environments. Although low-technology AAC systems are usually created by the AAC team, each state has an assistive technology loan program. While most AAC systems available from the programs are classified as high-technology systems, the state-funded assistive technology programs can still be useful when a student is trying a low-technology AAC system. They usually provide training and other instructional supports to help facilitate the student's learning of the AAC system. Chapter 9 will provide a detailed overview of these programs and their services.

Key Points of Chapter 8

- Low-technology AAC systems consist of communication boards and books, written words, symbols, and other systems that do not require batteries or electricity to operate.
- Symbol assessments are key in selecting appropriate low-technology AAC systems.
- There are several vocabulary assessment formats including functional use, receptive labeling, yes/no, alternative visual-matching, question-and-answer, and requesting.
- Feature matching requires the AAC team to consider the student's overall current level of functioning and select an AAC system that best matches the student's needs.
- Several areas for consideration during the feature-matching process include symbol selection, display arrangement, selection techniques, and system preferences.
- A trial period is a critical component in identifying appropriate AAC systems.

Additional Resources

Augmentative Communication and Technology Services
www.acts-at.com/aac-at.php
Everyone Communicates: The Augmentative and Alternative Communication
    Resource
www.everyonecommunicates.org
Georgia Project for Assistive Technology
www.gpat.org
PrAACtical AAC
http://praacticalaac.org
Spectronics: Symbol Set Comparison
www.spectronics.com/au

References

Abbott, M. A., & McBride, D. (2014). AAC decision-making and mobile technology: Points to ponder. *Perspectives on Augmentative and Alternative Communication, 23*, 60–111. doi:10.1044/aac23.2104

Achmadi, D., Sigafoos, J., van der Meer, L., Sutherland, D., Lancioni, G. E., O'Reilly, M. F., . . . Marschilk, P. B. (2014). Acquisition, preference, and follow-up data on the use of three AAC options by four boys with developmental disability/delay. *Journal of Developmental and Physical Disabilities, 26*, 565–583. doi:10.1007/s10882-014-9379

Albis, J., & Reed, F. D., (2012). Modified stimulus presentation to teach simple discrimination within picture exchange communication system training. *Journal of Speech-Language Pathology and Applied Behavior Analysis, 5*, 42–46.

Baxter, S., Enderby, P., Evans, P., & Judge, S. (2012). Interventions using high-technology communication devices: A state of the art review. *Folia Phoniatrica et Logopaedica, 64*, 137–144. doi:10.1159/000338250

Beukelman, D. R., & Mirenda, P. M. (2013). *Augmentative and alternative communication: Supporting children and adults with complex communication needs* (4th ed.). Baltimore, MD: Paul H. Brookes.

Blackstone, S. (2005). What are visual scene displays? *RERC on Communication Enhancement, 1*(2), 1–6.

Boesch, M. C., & Wendt, O. (2009). Reducing self-injurious behaviors in individuals with autism: Benefits of functional communication training. *EBP Briefs, 4*(2), 1–13.

Bruno, J. (2010). *Test of aided communication symbol performance*. Pittsburgh, PA: Dynavox Mayer Johnson.

Calculator, S. N. (1999). AAC outcomes for children and youths with severe disabilities: When seeing is believing. *Augmentative and Alternative Communication, 15*, 4–12.

Chompoobutr, S., Potibal, P., Boriboon, M., & Phantachat, W. (2013). Perception and multimeaning analysis of graphic symbols for Thai picture-based communication system. *Disability and Rehabilitation: Assistive Technology, 8*, 102–107. doi:10.3109/17483107.2012.737531

Drager, K. D. R., Light, J. C., Speltz, J. C., Fallon, K. A., & Jeffries, L. Z. (2003). The performance of typically developing 2 ½ -year-olds on dynamic display AAC technologies with different system layouts and language organizations. *Journal of Speech, Language, and Hearing Research, 46*, 298–312. doi:10.1044/1092-4388(2003/024)

Gevarter, C., O'Reilly, M. F., Rojeski, L., Sammarco, N., Sigafoos, J., Lancioni, G. E., & Lang, R. (2014). Comparing acquisition of AAC-based mands in three young children with autism spectrum disorder using iPad application with different display and design elements. *Journal of Autism and Developmental Disorders, 44*, 2464–2474. doi:10.1007/s10803-014-2115-9

Johnston, S. S., Reichle, J., Feeley, K. M., & Jones, E. A. (2012). *AAC strategies for individuals with moderate to severe disabilities*. Baltimore, MD: Paul H. Brookes.

Kuhl, P. K. (2011). Early language learning and literacy: Neuroscience implications for education. *Mind Brain Education, 5*, 128–142. doi:10.1111/j.1751-228X.2011.01121.x

Light, J., & McNaughton, D. (2012). The changing face of augmentative and alternative communication: Past, present, and future challenges. *Augmentative and Alternative Communication, 28*, 197–204. doi:10.3109/07434618.2012.737024

Lloyd, L., Fuller, D., & Arvidson, H. (1997). *Augmentative and alternative communication: Handbook of principles and practices*. Needham Heights, MA: Allyn and Bacon.

Maag, J. W. (2017). *Behavior management: From theoretical implications to practical applications* (3rd ed.). Boston, MA: Cengage Learning.

Markham, P. T., & Justice, E. M. (2004) Sign language iconicity and its influence on the ability to describe the function of objects. *Journal of Communication Disorders, 37,* 535–546. doi:10.1016/j.jcomdis.2004.03.008

Mayer-Johnson. (2016). *PCS collections.* Retrieved from www.mayer-johnson.com/pcs-collections/

McCarthy, J., McCarthy, J., Light, J., Drager, K., McNaughton, D., Grodzicki, L., . . . Parkin, E. (2006). Redesigning scanning to reduce learning demands: The performance of typically developing 2-year-olds. *Augmentative and Alternative Communication, 22,* 269–283. doi:10.1080/00498250600718621

McDonald, E. T., & Schultz, A. R. (1973). Communication boards for cerebral-palsied children. *Journal of Speech and Hearing Disorders, 38,* 73–88. doi:10.1044/jshd.3801.73

Nevers, M. (2011). *Partner assisted scanning* [Webinar PowerPoint slides]. Retrieved from www.uvm.edu/~cdci/at/webinars/PAS_3_16_2011/files/PAS3_Slides_per_page.pdf

Petroi, D., Koul, R. K., & Corwin, M. (2014). Effect of number of graphic symbols, levels, and listening conditions on symbol identification and latency in persons with aphasia. *Augmentative and Alternative Communication, 30,* 40–54. doi:10.3109/07434618.2014.882984

Porter, G. (2007). *Pragmatic Organization Dynamic Display (PODD) communication books: Direct access templates.* Melbourne: Cerebral Palsy Education Centre.

Porter, G., & Cafiero, J. M. (2009). Pragmatic Organization Dynamic Display (PODD) communication books: A promising practice for individuals with autism spectrum disorders. *Perspectives on Augmentative and Alternative Communication, 18,* 121–129. doi:10.1044/aac18.4.121

Roche, L., Sigafoos, J., Lancioni, G. E., O'Reilly, M. F., Green, V. A., Sutherland, D., . . . Edrisinha, C. D. (2014). Tangible symbols as an AAC option for individuals with developmental disabilities: A systematic review of intervention studies. *Augmentative and Alternative Communication, 30,* 28–39. doi:10.3109/07434618.2013.878958

Rowland, C., & Schweigert, P. (1989). Tangible symbols: Symbolic communication for individuals with multisensory impairments. *Augmentative and Alternative Communication, 5,* 226–234, doi:10.1080/07434618912331275276

Schlosser, R. W. (2003). Roles of speech output in augmentative and alternative communication: A narrative review. *Augmentative and Alternative Communication, 19,* 5–27. doi:10.1080/0743461032000056450

Thistle, J. J., & Wilkinson, K. M. (2013). Working memory demands of aided augmentative and alternative communication for individuals with developmental disabilities. *Augmentative and Alternative Communication, 29,* 235–245. doi:10.3109/07434618.2013.815800

van der Meer, L., Sigafoos, J., O'Reilly, M. F., & Lancioni, G. E. (2011). Assessing preferences for AAC options in communication interventions for individuals with developmental disabilities: A review of the literature. *Research in Developmental Disabilities, 32,* 1422–1431. doi:10.1016/j.ridd.2011.02.003

Wilkinson, K., Carlin, M., & Thistle, J. (2008). The role of color cues in facilitating accurate and rapid location of aided symbols by children with and without Down Syndrome. *American Journal of Speech-Language Pathology, 17,* 179–193. doi:1058–0360/08/1702–0179

Wilkinson, K. M., Light, J., & Drager, K. (2012). Considerations for the composition of visual scene displays: Potential contributions of information from visual and cognitive sciences. *Augmentative and Alternative Communication, 28,* 137–147. doi:10.3109/07434618.2012.704522

Wilkinson, K. M., O'Neill, T., & McIlvane, W. J. (2014). Eye-tracking measures reveal how changes in the design of aided AAC displays influence the efficiency of locating symbols by school-age children without disabilities. *Journal of Speech, Language, and Hearing Research, 57*, 455–466. doi:10.1044/2013_JSLHR-L-12–0159

Williams, M., & Grove, N. (1989). Getting to grips with aided communication: An overview of the literature. *British Journal of Special Education, 16*, 63–68. doi:10.1111/j.1467–8578.1989.tb00781.x

9

DEFINING AND IDENTIFYING HIGH-TECHNOLOGY AIDED COMMUNICATION SYSTEMS

For students with complex communication needs (CCN) who have the need to use more sophisticated augmentative and alternative communication (AAC) systems with the option to use speech output, high-technology systems offer a greater range of features. High-technology, aided AAC systems include electronic or powered components. These devices include speech output, speech-generating, and the ability to store and retrieve messages (Baxter, Enderby, Evans, Judge, 2012; Ganz et al., 2017). Given the complexity of high-technology devices, they are further classified into dedicated and non-dedicated devices (e.g., mobile phones and tablets). See Figure 9.1 and Figure 9.2 for examples of high-technology aided communication systems.

Dedicated devices are systems whose sole purpose is to serve a communicative purpose. These dedicated devices do not have the capability to run software other than the device itself (Johnston, Reichle, Feeley, & Jones, 2012). The advantages of using a dedicated speech-generating devices (SGDs) are that most are designed for direct selection and/or scanning, have built-in speakers, switch ports, built-in shock absorption (especially important for wheelchair mounting), infrared (IR) environmental controls, technical support for both the hardware and software, and a minimum one-year device warranty (often with an option to extend the warranty; Abbott & McBride, 2014). However, high-technology dedicated devices have several cons associated with them. For instance, weight, size, cost, extra fees to allow internet access, and extra fees to unlock the features of Windows are downfalls of dedicated AAC devices. Dedicated devices are also generally much more expensive than non-dedicated high-technology devices (Abbott & McBride, 2014; Shane et al., 2012). These SGDs can cost as much as $7000 and typically have fewer functions than current alternatives to AAC devices (King, Brady, & Voreis, 2017).

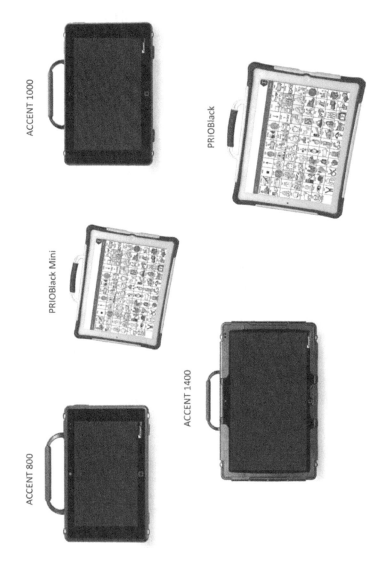

FIGURE 9.1 Examples of speech-generating devices by Prentke Romich Company©. (Reprinted with permission.)

Indi

T7

T15 with stand

T10

FIGURE 9.2 Examples of speech-generating devices by Tobii–Dynavox©. (Reprinted with permission.)

Non-dedicated systems are multipurpose which can also be used as a communicative modality. More recently, the field has witnessed the explosion of mobile technologies (e.g., touch screen phones and tablets such as the iPad) with a wide range of "apps" (i.e., software applications), including those intended to support communication (RERC on Communication Enhancement, 2011). The advent of mobile technologies has resulted in enhanced potential to meet the increased scope of communication needs for some individuals who require AAC (RERC, 2011).

There are numerous benefits to using non-dedicated systems. Foremost, given that mainstream society already uses computers, mobile phones, and tablets, there is an inherent social acceptance by society when individuals with CCN use non-dedicated systems as their AAC device. Because non-dedicated systems are widely available, the cost is relatively affordable, and they are simpler to program and use when compared to high-technology dedicated devices (Ganz et al., 2017). Thus, there is an increased adoption for AAC purposes, greater functionality and interconnectivity, and more extensive research on their use (McNaughton & Light, 2013). Mobile technologies, such as phones and tablets, are very portable due to their weight and size, and the user is able to freely access all the features and programs of the Windows, Android, or iOS interface (Abbott & McBride, 2014).

Although there are numerous positive aspects to using non-dedicated devices, they are not without any drawbacks. Beukelman and colleagues (2012) noted that the proliferation of mobile technologies has forced some individuals to make changes in their AAC technologies, not out of choice, but rather out of necessity when their technologies are no longer supported or when funding sources and school systems provide pressure to select cheaper, more commonly available technology. Many schools, as well as some families, are purchasing these systems based on popularity without assessing the students' motor, linguistic, cognitive, sensory, or environmental needs (Costello, Shane, & Caron, 2013). Although the use of small, highly portable technologies is a benefit to some individuals, access is a challenge for many with more severe physical and cognitive challenges (Chapple, 2011). Thus, it is important that AAC teams convey to the schools and families that one size does not fit all. Also, many of the applications marketed for AAC use do not have the empirical data to support their use. Thus, their benefits are unclear for students with CCN (McNaughton & Light, 2013). Because mobile technologies were not designed specifically for AAC use, accessories like speakers, protective cases, and switch interface devices may need to be added. Mobile technology devices typically lack the shock absorption needed if wheelchair mounting is being considered. They also have a limited warranty, which only pertains to the hardware (Abbott & McBride, 2014).

Despite these challenges, it does not mean that mobile technologies are not suitable for some students with AAC needs. On the contrary, mobile technologies provide a lot of flexibility for the student. According to Farrall (2016), there are over 250 AAC apps available on the market. There are many different types of AAC apps that serve various functions and use a variety of features to facilitate communication for students with CCN. Farrall, and others have organizations whose purpose is to disseminate information about AAC apps (www.janefarrall. com). Farrall categorizes the apps by symbol or picture, symbol and text based, and text based. Millar and McNeill from the Communication, Access, Literacy and Learning (CALL) Scotland research and development center developed an app wheel called *iPad Apps for Complex Communication Support Needs: Augmentative and Alternative Communication* (2016; www.callscotland.org.uk). They categorized AAC apps into seven functions: text-based AAC, symbol-based grid systems, hybrid app structures, basic systems, communication narratives, specific approaches, and skill building. Bradshaw (2013) outlined seven categories of AAC apps based on the former website AppsForAac.net: (1) *text to speech*, (2) symbols in grid-based system, (3) word predictor, (4) phrases, (5) eye pointing, (6) photo/visual story, and (7) picture exchange communication system. The website was originally created to complement SpeechBubble (http://speechbubble.org.uk/) which is a website that helps users compare AAC products, including 231 AAC apps.

Feature Matching: How to Determine What System will be Used

Feature matching is an important step in determining which AAC system best fits the needs of the student with CCN. Thus, a complete and accurate initial evaluation of the student's overall skills is important. Chapter 5 provides an overview of these critical skills the team must assess prior to selecting an AAC system.

Given that high-tech AAC systems have more features that are continually advancing as compared to low-tech systems, it makes selecting AAC systems more challenging for the AAC team. To adequately assess these systems, the team members must be aware of the features of new systems (Dietz, Quach, Lund, & McKelvey, 2012). Important features to consider during the AAC selection process include type of display, arrangement of the display, speech output, and selection techniques.

Symbol Selection

High-technology AAC systems are comprised almost exclusively of symbols to facilitate the student's communication. Thus, it is expected that symbol selection plays a critical component in the student's successful use of the SGD. Vocabulary on SGDs is represented using three forms of symbols: single meaning pictures, alphabet-based systems, and semantic compaction (Dodd, 2017). Depending on the vocabulary representation system, the *rate enhancement* features will vary. These features consist of encoding and prediction techniques (Beukelman & Mirenda, 2013). Encoding consists of using various shortcut techniques to speed symbol retrieval and message generation (Beukelman & Mirenda, 2013). These techniques can include the use of abbreviated spellings or letters (e.g., ORNJ = orange juice,

SHO = shower), number shortcuts (e.g., 2 = I, 3 = YOU), alphanumeric (e.g., PIC1 = picture, PIC2 = selfie, PIC3 = photography), and iconic (e.g., rainbow icon + heart icon = red). Prediction consists of the system user typing the first few letters of a word or message and the AAC system using these letters to bring up possible words or messages it believes the user is trying to generate (Trnka, McCaw, Yarrington, McCoy, & Pennington, 2009). Prediction can include the use of letters, words, or messages to increase the rate of communication.

Single meaning picture systems consist of each picture representing one word (Dodd, 2017). This type of AAC system can be relatively easy to learn, particularly if the symbols are transparent or translucent. Given the limited complexity of the system, it can be potentially useful for students with limited cognitive functioning or for beginning communicators. However, single meaning symbols systems may become cumbersome for advanced communicators who have larger vocabularies. Communicating with single meaning symbols may slow the retrieval process due to the large number of symbols and pages the student will need to navigate through. Figure 9.3 shows an example of Core First from Tobii-Dynavox®, which uses a variety of single meaning pictures as well as a keyboard to allow the student to type out messages.

Alphabet-based systems include spelling, word prediction, and letter codes that assist the student in generating messages. Students using alphabet-based systems need to have some ability to spell words in order to create accurate messages. Because spelling can be slow particularly for students with motor limitations or difficulties with cognitive processing, word prediction is frequently a feature in these systems (Trnka et al., 2009). With alphabet-based systems, students are able to create an endless number of messages and, with time and instruction, they can achieve automaticity. One downfall is that the initial learning process may be slower than with single meaning pictures. However, word prediction and automaticity speed the communication process as the student has opportunity to practice and become efficient. Figure 9.4 and 9.5 shows examples of the Compass Keyboard Core and Compass Gateway by Tobii-Dynavox®.

Semantic compaction is the only patented system and is based on multi-meaning icons. Minspeak® is classified as a semantic compaction system that uses encoding to represent a variety of words by using different symbol combinations (van der Merwe & Alant, 2004). This type of encoding system can be beneficial in developing the student's ability to use automaticity to quickly activate the symbols to generate the desired message. However, given the complexity of learning many symbol combinations, semantic compaction system may not be ideal for students with moderate to severe intellectual impairments. Similarly, the student will likely require some level of literacy skills such as the concept of verbs, adjectives, nouns, etc. Minspeak® symbols are available through the Unity language system which includes the *Language Acquisition through Motor Planning* (LAMP) Words for Life and CoreScanner systems (www.prentrom.com). Figure 9.6 shows an example of the Unity language system.

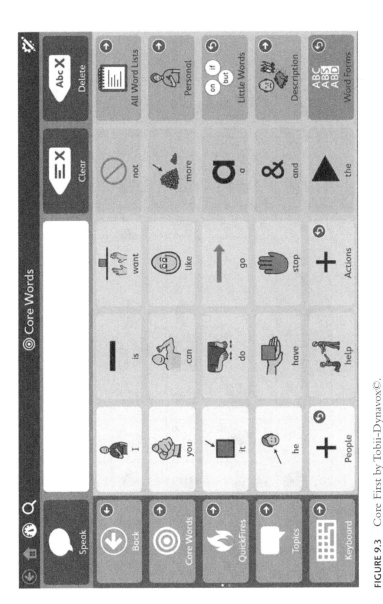

FIGURE 9.3 Core First by Tobii-Dynavox©.

(Reprinted with permission.)

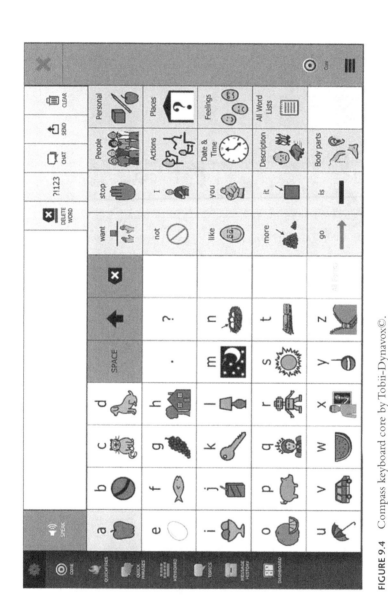

FIGURE 9.4 Compass keyboard core by Tobii-Dynavox©. (Reprinted with permission.)

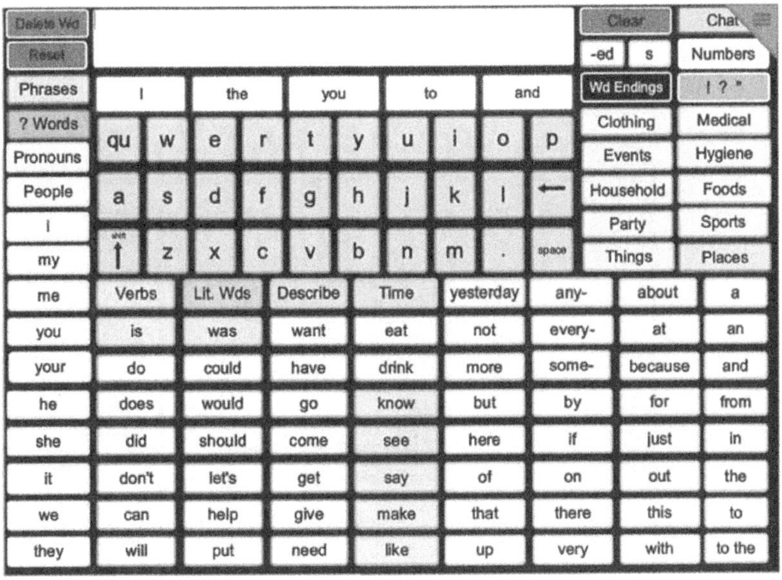

FIGURE 9.5   Compass Gateway by Tobii-Dynavox©.

(Reprinted with permission.)

Display Arrangement

Displays on high-technology AAC systems will use either static or dynamic displays. Static displays present the symbols in a stationary position and each symbol does not lead the student to additional symbols (see Chapter 8 for an in-depth description). For example, the QuickTalker SGD (AbleNet) uses a static display. On the other hand, in a dynamic display, the student is not able to view all of the symbols simultaneously (Johnston et al., 2012). Rather, when the student selects a symbol on the display, it brings up a new page with further symbol options. Although this type of display places a greater cognitive demand on the student (Quach & Beukelman, 2010), it allows for vocabulary growth. Aided systems such as the Accent or Prio SGDs (Prentke Romich Company) or the Indi and Tobii Dynavox T7 SGDs (TobiiDynavox) use dynamic displays. Some benefits of using a dynamic display are that additional symbols can be added and, in many cases, it allows the student to create novel messages for a variety of communicative needs. Given that static and dynamic displays offer different features, the AAC team will need to determine what type of display is most beneficial for the student.

Another component of the system's display is the symbol arrangement. The AAC team will need to decide how to best customize the symbol arrangement on the SGD to maximize the student's communicative efficiency. Refer to Chapter 8 for explanations of several types of displays for arranging the symbols. These

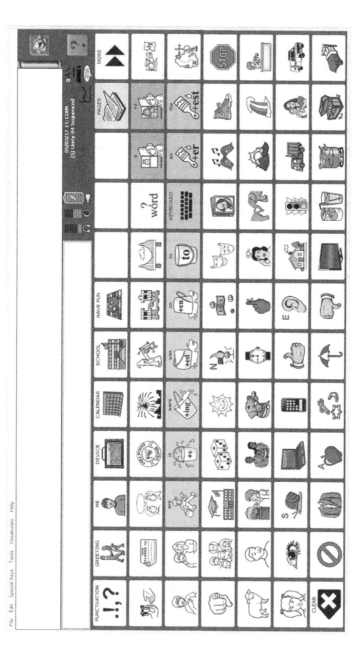

FIGURE 9.6 Unity by Prentke Romich Company©.

(Reprinted with permission.)

include semantic-syntactic grid display, clustered display, distributed display, taxonomic grid display, activity grid display, visual scene display, hybrid display, and pragmatic organization dynamic display.

According to Wilkinson and McIlvane (2013), the visual-perceptional attributes of the system display are important in how efficient the student is in locating symbols. A study with school-age children diagnosed with either Down Syndrome or autism spectrum disorder (ASD) was conducted in which the all of the participants were asked to locate symbols arranged in color-based clustered display and a distributed display on a computer. Data showed both participant groups were more accurate and faster in locating symbols with color-based clustering than with the distributed display. Thus, Wilkinson and McIlvane (2013) concluded that using a color-based clustered display was a preferred method of arranging symbols because it played to the strengths of the children's visual processing abilities.

However, this is not the only arrangement method that might be beneficial for some students with CCN. Visual scene displays (VSDs) appear to offer more benefits than various types of grid displays including color-based clustered displays (Light & McNaughton, 2012; Wilkinson, Light, & Drager, 2011). According to Light and McNaughton (2012), VSDs offer several advantages, including the following: (1) they utilize the human's natural tendency to quickly process visual information, (2) the additional visual information helps with recognition and object discrimination, (3) social interaction scenes serve as visual supports during communicative interactions, (4) they serve as a reminder of past events and experiences rather than relying on learned knowledge, (5) they use familiar context to teach language, and (6) the conceptual and visual information is represented similarly to real-world situations.

While various research supports the use of an array of displays, the goal is to select a display that encourages efficient symbol use while considering student preference. A specific display for organizing symbols may work well with one student but not with a different student. To facilitate this decision-making process, the AAC team may need to test two or more types of displays on the same device to determine which one the student uses more efficiently. Even beyond this initial testing, it is equally important to see which display yields the most usage across an extended period of time. Barton-Hulsey, Wegner, Brady, Bunce, and Sevcik (2017) found that for one child with mitochondrial disease and limited speech skills, performance with vocabulary comprehension was similar using a grid display and a VSD on an SGD. However, the child's usage of the grid display was significantly greater in the long run than with the VSD. Thus, assessment focused on identifying an appropriate display is essential in the communicative competence of students with AAC needs.

Keyboards are another element to consider that focuses on letter symbol arrangement. Although low-tech alphabet boards exist on the market, keyboards are typically associated with a number of high-technology AAC devices. However, not all of the keyboards are arranged in the same manner. The ABC keyboard organizes the keys in alphabetical order while the QWERTY keyboard does not. Yet, the QWERTY keyboard is the most widely used and is the default arrangement in computers, tablets, smartphones, and other mobile technologies (Helling & Minga, 2014). In some devices, the keyboard is accessed directly on the screen, while in other devices, it is an external component of the device. Devices that have screen-based keyboards sometimes have the option to use the standard QWERTY letter arrangement or change it to the ABC keyboard format. Keyguards are available for students who are unable to accurately activate individual keys on a screen. Figure 9.7 shows a variety of keyboards and keyguards.

Speech Output

One of the advantages of using a high-tech system over other systems is that most devices have speech output capabilities. They use digitized speech, synthesized speech, or a combination of both types. Digitized speech is simply recorded speech that has been digitally stored in the device. When the button or icon is activated, the recorded speech is emitted. Depending on the capability of the SGD, some SGDs will allow for longer recordings of messages to be stored while others will only store a short recording per symbol.

Synthesized speech is artificially produced based on phonemes using a mathematical algorithm (Beukelman & Mirenda, 2013). More sophisticated SGDs have the capability to use synthesized speech. In the past, synthesized speech sounded robotic. However, with advances in technology, some SGDs can produce synthesized speech that approximates natural speech production. SGDs that

ACCENT 800 with keyguards

ACCENT 1400 with keyguards

FIGURE 9.7 Examples of speech-generating devices with keyguards from Prentke Romich Company©.

(Reprinted with permission.)

use synthesized speech are advantageous in that is does not require someone to program each symbol with the appropriate spoken referent. Instead, the algorithm inherent in the device is automatically generated when a symbol is activated. One potential disadvantage is that some SGDs may not allow for voice customization. Thus, if the only option of the device is to emit synthesized speech that has masculine qualities to it, a female student may find the voice unappealing. Similarly, synthesized speech software is known to mispronounce names and other words. These issues may lead the student to hesitate using the SGD if he or she believes peers may view his or her spoken communication in a negative light.

Although the AAC team will need to consider the nuances of speech output in devices, having speech capabilities in a device allows the student to communicate with a greater range of communicative partners because it uses a modality that is already familiar to others. Additionally, if the communication partner has a visual impairment or has little to no literacy skills, the speech output continues to provide a communicative method that is understood without needing special assistance. Similar to when people use natural speech, the student who uses speech output via the device is able to communicate from a distance and reduce the demands of gaining someone's attention (Beukelman & Mirenda, 2013). Despite the numerous advantages of speech output capabilities, it may still be difficult to be understood in loud environments or when the communicative partner has a hearing impairment.

Selection Techniques

There are two types of selection techniques, direct and indirect. Direct selection is the most direct form, hence the name. The student directly selects the symbol or button on the device via a finger, hand, head pointer, joystick, or mouse (Johnston et al., 2012). Direct selection places less demand on the student's working memory (Thistle & Wilkinson, 2013) so for many students without significant motor limitations, it is best to use this selection method. On the other hand, indirect selection requires the student to take additional steps to select a symbol icon on the device. This extra step makes it more cumbersome for the student (Johnston et al., 2012). *Scanning* is classified as an indirect selection technique and can be accessed through visual or auditory methods. It is also more cognitively demanding than direct selection methods (Wagner & Jackson, 2006).

Scanning involves four main types of patterns: (1) group–item scanning is when the student selects a large group of symbols first, and then the group continues to get smaller until the desired symbol is selected; (2) in linear scanning, the items are arranged in rows and columns and the student scans one row or column at a time; (3) with circular scanning, the items are arranged in a circle and are scanned clockwise; and (4) in row–column scanning, items are scanned row by row until the desired row is reach, and then the student scans each symbol within the column until the desired symbol is identified Lloyd, Fuller, & Arvidson, 1997; McCarthy et al., 2006). See Figure 9.8 for an illustration of block scanning, Figure 9.9

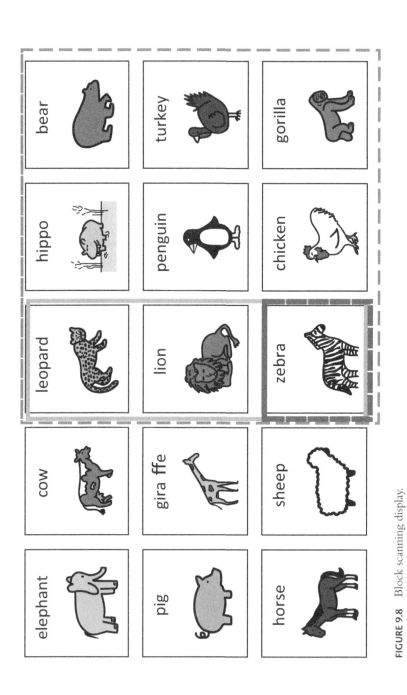

FIGURE 9.8 Block scanning display.

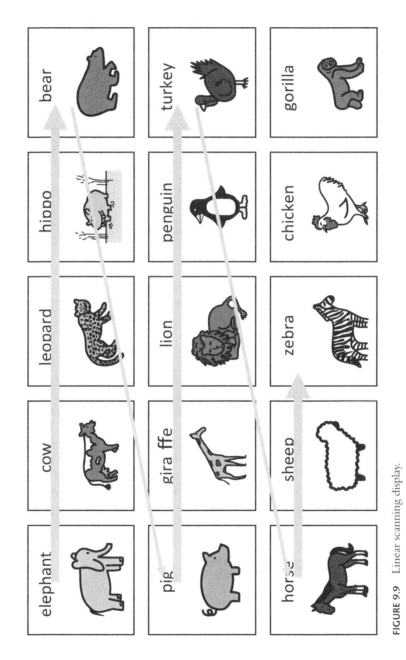

FIGURE 9.9 Linear scanning display.

Tobii-Dynavox ©2017 Boardmaker. All rights reserved. (Used with permission.)

for an illustration of linear scanning, Figure 9.10 for an illustration of row–column scanning, and Figure 9.11 for an illustration of circular scanning.

To access high-technology AAC devices, the student will need an external apparatus such as a switch to select the desired symbol via scanning (see Chapter 8 for examples) or an eye gaze recognition system. The eye gaze recognition system such as the NuEye® Tracking System (www.prentrom.com) is suitable for students with extensive physical limitations who are unable to use switches or other selection methods to activate their AAC devices (see Figure 9.12 and 9.13 for examples of eye gaze systems). Given that students with AAC needs have a range of motor, sensory, and cognitive abilities, the AAC team will need to identify a suitable selection method that allows the student to efficiently use the AAC system. If the student's capabilities are not considered, there is a risk of slowing the speed in which the student is able to select symbols. It could also increase the number of errors the student makes when selecting a symbol on the system display. These issues create obstacles in the student's path to achieving communicative competence.

Preference

Part of conducting the feature-matching process is to utilize a person-centered planning approach. This entails considering the student's preferences as well as the communication partner's (Brady et al., 2016). Therefore, deciding on an AAC system is a delicate balance between several important areas including what the student needs, the projected growth, the system features, and the student's (and family's) preferences. The student's preference for a specific high-tech device is key in encouraging and maintaining student motivation to learn and use the device (Lorah, Parnell, Whitby, & Hantual, 2014). According to Lorah and colleagues (2014), considering the student's preferences for a device is "recognition of the child's rights of autonomy and self-determination" (p. 3801). Another facet of conducting a person-centered assessment is the selection of an AAC system that is minimally intrusive and stigmatizing. While some students and their families may not see this as an issue, other students may reject certain AAC systems based on specific features that may be viewed as stigmatizing. Therefore, student and family input is paramount to minimize potential system abandonment.

Conducting an Ongoing Assessment

High-technology SGDs have multiple features which requires the AAC team to consider the student's present level of performance and correspond it to the features of the SGD. Due to the complex nature of this process and the needs of the student, it is important for team members with specialized training to provide input relevant their area. For example, the physical therapist should provide guidance when considering the access methods as it will require fine or gross motor

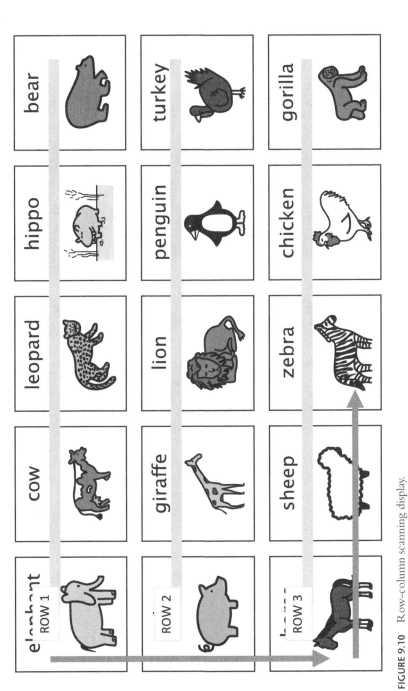

FIGURE 9.10 Row–column scanning display.

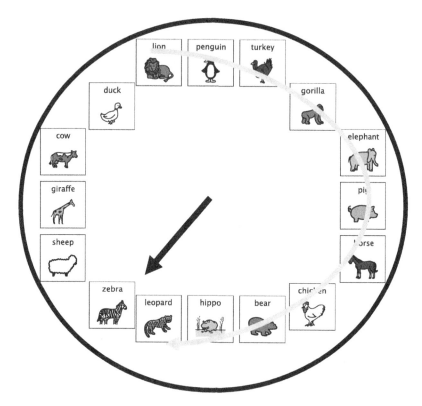

FIGURE 9.11 Circular scanning display.

Tobii-Dynavox ©2017 Boardmaker. All rights reserved. (Used with permission.)

skills. The vision specialist should provide input pertaining to visual skills and the audiologist or other hearing specialist should assist with the auditory features of the device as well as the hearing capabilities of the student.

Figure 9.14 displays the *Accessibility and Scanning Screening Form*. This is a screening questionnaire that can be used by the AAC team to evaluate the access and scanning capabilities of high-technology AAC devices. It is not intended to be used in isolation; rather, it can be part of a more comprehensive assessment. This screening tool can also be adapted for low-technology AAC systems. The section on access methods is aimed at determining how the student may potentially access an AAC system. Thus, when the AAC team is identifying an appropriate AAC system, they can consider if the AAC system under consideration has the features to allow the student to access it based on his or her motor abilities. Similarly, the scanning options section of the screening tool is designed to determine if the student's visual and hearing abilities allow the student to access the system via scanning selection methods.

ACCENT 1000 with Nueye®

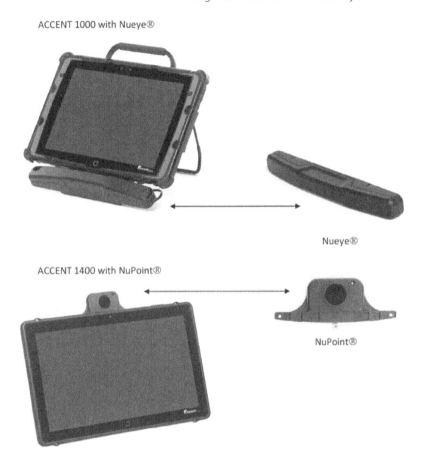

Nueye®

ACCENT 1400 with NuPoint®

NuPoint®

FIGURE 9.12   Examples of speech-generating devices with eye gaze systems by Prentke Romich© Company.

(Reprinted with permission.)

If the AAC team is considering the use of a non-dedicated tablet, it is important to also evaluate the apps. *The AAC App Features Screening Form* in Figure 9.15 is designed to help the AAC team systematically assess the components of AAC apps and can be useful when comparing various apps. This rubric has three main categories for evaluation. The representation section asks the evaluator to assess the app based on how symbols are represented in the device, how they are organized, how they are activated, the size and number of symbols, and other symbol representation aspects. The messages section is primarily focused on evaluating how symbols are used to create messages and how they are emitted to the communication partner. In the motor control section, the main focus is to determine

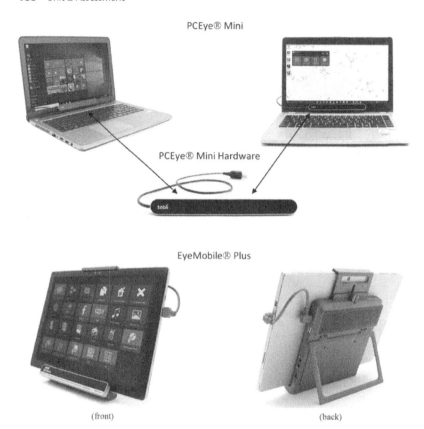

PCEye® Mini

PCEye® Mini Hardware

EyeMobile® Plus

(front)   (back)

FIGURE 9.13 Examples of speech–generating devices with eye gaze systems by Tobii-Dynavox©.

(Reprinted with permission.)

what motor requirements the student will need to demonstrate in order to use the app. The student's motor and sensory capabilities were previously discussed in Chapter 5. This assessment information is relevant because it encompasses fine motor skills necessary for accessing the device and activating the symbols, hearing and vision skills for interpreting the auditory and visual feedback of the device, and gross motor skills for device placement and positioning. Brady and colleagues (2016) emphasized the importance of addressing these motor and sensory skills during the assessment process to ensure the student's communication skills were representative of the student's actual capabilities.

These types of evaluation tools are important given that most of the apps available on the market have not been empirically validated to assess their effectiveness in increasing the communicative competence of individuals with AAC needs.

Accessibility and Scanning Screening Form

Student's name: _____   Observer's name: _____   Date: _____

The *Accessibilty and Scanning Screening Form* questionnaire provides general guidelines for access methods and scanning options for aided devices. It is highly recommended that a comprehensive assessment be conducted in collaboration with other team members to determine a more accurate level of the student's ability to use aided communication forms.

Instructions. Complete the questions for each of the domains by checking Yes or No in the *Response* section. Begin with Q1. Record the total number of Yes and No in the *Results* section. Record any additional notes in the *Anecdotal Notes* section.

Access Methods		
Instructions. Begin with Q1. If the student cannot use direct selection, do not complete this section and move to the Scanning Options section of this form. Select the method(s) of access most appropriate for the student.		

Questions	Response	
	YES	NO
Q1 Does the student use his/her hand for direct selection? ☐Right ☐Left	☐	☐
Q2 How does the student direct select? ☐ Finger ☐ Joystick ☐ Mouse ☐ Knuckle ☐ Pointer ☐ Trackball		
Q3 Does the student use their head for direct selection? ☐ Head pointer ☐ Head switch ☐ Head mouse	☐	☐
Q4 Does the student use any body part for direct selection? Which body part? _____	☐	☐

Scanning Options		
Instructions. Complete the questions addressed in Scanning Options by checking Yes or No in the Response section. For Q3, select the appropriate symbol size the student can visually use. If a size is not listed, write the appropriate size in the space provided. After completing the questions, select the type(s) of scanning most appropriate for the student when accessing their device.		

Questions	Response	
	YES	NO
Q1 Does the student wear glasses?	☐	☐
Q2 Does the student use a hearing aid?	☐	☐
Q3 Does the student have the ability to scan? ☐ Linear ☐ Row/Column ☐ Group ☐ Step ☐ Inverse ☐ Auto	☐	☐
Q4 Does the student have the ability to visually scan?	☐	☐
Q5 Does the student have the visual ability to use symbols?	☐	☐
☐.25" ☐.50" ☐1" ☐2" ☐_____"		
Q6 Does the student have the ability to auditorily scan?	☐	☐

Results			
Access Method		Scanning Options	
NO	YES	NO	YES
/4	/4	/6	/6

Type of System		
☐ Dedicated communication system ☐ Non-dedicated communication system ☐ APP		

Type of Scanning		Scanning Feedback
☐ Linear ☐ Row/Column		☐ Visual feedback
☐ Group ☐ Inverse		☐ Auditory feedback
☐ Step ☐ Auto		

Anecdotal notes.

FIGURE 9.14 Accessibility and scanning screening form.

(*Source:* AAC TechConnect, 2013)

Therefore, it is up to the AAC team to use an evaluation mechanism to determine if the features of an app will likely meet the needs of the student. Currently there are three tools available online intended to evaluate and compare AAC apps include the *Rubric for Evaluating the Language of Apps for AAC* (RELAAACs; Parker & Zangari, 2012), the *Features of Augmentative and Alternative Communication Applications Checklist* (Marfilius & Fonner, 2012), and the *Feature Matching Communication Applications* (Caron, 2011). While these app rubrics and checklists are not intended to be used in isolation, they can be valuable when used in combination with the expert opinion of the AAC team and the input and preferences of the student and family.

Trial Period

When the AAC team is deciding what high-technology AAC system will be most appropriate for the student, the team should conduct a trial period. Given that not all high-technology AAC systems are readily owned by school districts, the AAC team may consider obtaining a device via a loan program. Fortunately, some manufacturers will loan a device so the AAC team can conduct an assessment and to give the student a brief period to try out the device prior to making a purchase. In some cases, the device may need to be tested out on a longer-term basis. In these situations, the manufacturer may offer a device rental option. However, if the manufacturer does not have a loan or rental program, the devices may be borrowed through the state's assistive technology (AT) loan program (Abbott & McBride, 2014; Dietz et al., 2012), which is part of the Association of Assistive Technology Act Programs. Table 9.1 provides a list of each state's AT program. These programs loan out devices at no cost to the consumer given that the programs are funded by Assistive Technology Act.

In addition to these AT loan programs, teachers and parents can also download "lite" versions of apps for iPads to try out with their students. These lite versions of apps offer less features than the full version. For example, some lite versions do not allow you to customize options and may have less core vocabulary to choose from (Abbott & McBride, 2014; Costello et al., 2013). Thus, Costello and colleagues (2013) stressed the importance of not relying on the lite version as the permanent app for the student because of the limited features.

Teachers and therapists must also consider trying out several different types of access methods for their students. This allows the AAC team to determine the student's preferences between the different methods, such as direct access, eye tracking, or a track ball (Dietz et al., 2012). As part of this evaluation, the team should also identify how efficient the student is in using these access methods. If limitations or difficulties are noted, it is important to determine if additional time is needed to learn the system or if changes to the system or instruction are warranted.

AAC App Features Screening Form

Student's name: _____   App's name: _____

Evaluator's name: _____   Date: _____

The *AAC App Feature Screening Form* provides general considerations for the evaluation of a communication app. It is highly recommended that a comprehensive assessment be conducted of the app using available rubrics and checklist.

Instructions. Complete the questions for each domain by checking Yes or No in the *Response* section. Begin with Q1. Record the total number of Yes and No in the *Results* section. Record any additional notes in the *Anecdotal notes* section.

Representation		
Questions	Response	
	YES	NO
Q1 Does the app represent words?	☐	☐
Q2 How does the app represent words? ☐Photographs ☐Pictures ☐Pictures with words ☐Letters ☐Words	☐	☐
Q3 Does the app allow for upload of photographs?	☐	☐
Q4 What type of symbols does the app use? ☐PCS ☐Minspeak ☐Symbolstix ☐Photographs ☐Clipart ☐Text		
Q5 Does the app represent language? If yes, how? ☐Visual scene displays ☐Phrase based ☐Pictures with single meanings ☐Alphabet	☐	☐
Q6 Does it use single key messages?	☐	☐
Q7 Does it use icons with short hit sequences to form words? #of words_____	☐	☐
Q8 Does the app use a sequence of symbols to form a single word or phrase?	☐	☐
Q9 Does the app use language representation features? ☐Routine phrases ☐Predictive sentences	☐ ☐	☐ ☐
Q10 Does the app use grammar?	☐	☐
Q11 Does the app display ☐words or ☐pictures?	☐	☐
Q12 Does the app highlight each word as it is spoken?	☐	☐
Q13 How many keys does the app display? # of keys_____		
Q14 What is the size of the screen display? ☐Small ☐Medium ☐Large		

Messages		
Questions	Response	
	Yes	No
Q1 What features does the app use for messages? ☐Pre-made vocabulary ☐Prediction		
Q2 Does the app organize language?	☐	☐
Q3 How does the app organize language? ☐Categorically ☐Situation-based		
Q4 Does the app have spoken output?	☐	☐
Q5 What features does the app use for output? ☐Synthesized speech ☐Digitized speech ☐Multiple languages		
Q6 When does the app speak? ☐Each word ☐Each sentence ☐On demand		
Q7 Does the app use different gender voices? ☐Male ☐Female	☐	☐
Q8 Does the app use child voices?	☐	☐

FIGURE 9.15   AAC app features screening form.

(*Source:* AAC TechConnect, 2013)

Motor Control			
Questions		Response	
		Yes	No
Q1	What type of display does the device use? ☐Static ☐Dynamic		
Q2	What features does the app have for navigation? ☐Linked buttons ☐Lists ☐Next/back buttons ☐Other:_____		
Q3	Who is allowed to make page changes? ☐Facilitator ☐User		
Q4	How many pages does the app allow? # of pages_____		
Q5	Does the app use a keyboard?	☐	☐
Q6	What kind of keyboard does the app use? ☐QWERTY ☐ABC ☐Frequency of use		

Results					
Representation		Messages		Motor Control	
NO	YES	NO	YES	NO	YES
/14	/14	/8	/8	/6	/6
Anecdotal data.					

FIGURE 9.15 (Continued)

TABLE 9.1 Assistive Technology Programs by State.

State	Program
Alabama	STAR, Alabama's Assistive Technology Resource
Alaska	Alaska Assistive Technology Program
American Samoa	American Samoa Assistive Technology Service
Arizona	Arizona Technology Access Program
Arkansas	Arkansas Increasing Capabilities Access Network
California	Ability Tools
Colorado	Assistive Technology Partners
Connecticut	Connecticut Assistive Technology Program
Delaware	Delaware Assistive Technology Initiative
District of Columbia	Assistive Technology Program for the District of Columbia
Florida	Florida Alliance for Assistive Services and Technology
Georgia	Tools for Life, Georgia's Assistive Technology Act Program
Hawaii	Assistive Technology Resource Centers of Hawaii
Idaho	Idaho Assistive Technology Program
Illinois	Illinois Assistive Technology Program
Indiana	Indiana Assistive Technology Act Project
Iowa	Iowa Program for Assistive Technology
Kansas	Assistive Technology for Kansas Program
Kentucky	Kentucky Assistive Technology Service Network

State	Program
Louisiana	Louisiana Assistive Technology Access Network
Maine	Maine Consumer Information and Technology Training Exchange
Maryland	Maryland Technology Assistance Program
Massachusetts	Massachusetts Maximizing Assistive Technology in Consumers' Hands
Michigan	Michigan Assistive Technology Project
Minnesota	Minnesota STAR Program
Mississippi	Mississippi Project START
Missouri	Missouri Assistive Technology
Montana	Montana Assistive Technology Program
Nebraska	Nebraska Assistive Technology Partnership
Nevada	Nevada Assistive Technology Collaborative
New Hampshire	Assistive Technology in New Hampshire
New Jersey	Richard West Assistive Technology Advocacy Center of DRNJ
New Mexico	New Mexico Technology Assistance Program
New York	NYS TRAID Program NYS Justice Center
North Carolina	North Carolina Assistive Technology Program
North Dakota	North Dakota Assistive
Ohio	Assistive Technology of OHIO
Oklahoma	Oklahoma ABLE Tech
Oregon	Oregon's Statewide Assistive Technology Program
Pennsylvania	Pennsylvania's Initiative on Assistive Technology
Rhode Island	Rhode Island Assistive Technology Access Partnership
South Carolina	South Carolina Assistive Technology Program
South Dakota	South Dakota Assistive Technology Program
Tennessee	Tennessee Technology Access Program
Texas	Texas Technology Access Program
Utah	Utah Assistive Technology Program
Vermont	Vermont Assistive Technology Program
Virginia	Virginia Assistive Technology System
Washington	Washington Assistive Technology Act Program
West Virginia	West Virginia University Center for Excellence in Disabilities
Wisconsin	Wisconsin Assistive Technology Program
Wyoming	Wyoming Assistive Technology Resources
Northern Mariana Islands	Commonwealth of Northern Mariana Islands Assistive Technology
Guam	Guam System for Assistive Technology
Puerto Rico	Puerto Rico Assistive Technology Program
U.S. Virgin Islands	U.S. Virgin Islands Technology Related Assistance for Individuals with Disabilities

(*Source*: Association of Assistive Technology Act Programs, 2016)

The guiding principle should not be to make a decision immediately after the student is given access to the device, rather, it should be to give the student sufficient opportunities to use the tailored device with appropriate instructional support so that adoption decisions are accurately made. The trial period is not one week or one month long. Instead, it is dependent upon the student's capabilities. For some students, the trial period will be shorter than for other students. But, the intent for all device adoption decisions is to consider the students' current and projected skills, their personal and families' preferences, and their communicative competence with the AAC device when compared to not having it. Finally, the trial period is simply one step in the overall AAC assessment and adoption process. Similar to students with typical communicative development, students with CCN will also change with time. Changes may occur for a number of reasons, including developmental impairments, communication partners, environments, interests, and general academic and developmental growth. Therefore, ongoing assessment and reevaluation of AAC needs is critical for optimal communicative progression.

Key Points

- High-technology devices are power operated and have speech-generating capabilities.
- The sole purposed of dedicated AAC devices is to serve a communicative function.
- Non-dedicated devices can perform functions other than communication.
- During the feature-matching process, the AAC team must consider the system display, arrangement of icons, speech output, selection techniques, and a student's preference.
- The trial period is crucial before adopting an AAC system for students.

Resources

Ablenet
www.ablenetinc.com
Attainment Company
www.attainmentcompany.com
CALL Scotland: iPad Apps for Complex Communication Support Needs
www.callscotland.org.uk
Jane Farrall Consulting: Literacy, AAC & Assistive Technology
www.janefarrall.com
National Assistive Technology Act Technical Assistance and Training (AT3) Center
www.at3center.net
Prentke Romich Company
www.prentrom.com
Tobii Dynavox
www.dynavoxtech.com

References

AAC TechConnect. (2013). *The person: Skills and features to consider for assistive technology.* Retrieved from https://atspedresources.wikispaces.com/file/view/Person%20AT%20 consideration.pdf/596117582/Person%20AT%20consideration.pdf

Abbott, M. A., & McBride, D. (2014). AAC decision-making and mobile technology: Points to ponder. *Perspectives on Augmentative and Alternative Communication, 23,* 104–111. doi:10.1044/aac23.2.104

Association of Assistive Technology Act Programs. (2016). Retrieved from www.ataporg.org

Barton-Hulsey, A., Wegner, J., Brady, N. C., Bunce, B. H., & Sevcik, R. A. (2017). Comparing the effects of speech-generating device display organization on symbol comprehension and use by three children with developmental delays. *American Journal of Speech-Language Pathology, 28,* 227–240.

Baxter, S., Enderby, P., Evans, P., & Judge, S. (2012). Barriers and facilitators to the use of high-technology augmentative and alternative communication devices: A systematic review and qualitative synthesis. *International Journal of Language and Communication Disorders, 47,* 115–129. doi:10.1111/j.1460–6984.2011.00090.x

Beukelman, D. R., Blackstone, S., Caves, K., DeRuyter, F., Fried-Oken, M., Higginbotham, J., . . . Williams, M. (2012). *2012 State of the science conference in AAC: AAC-RERC final report—communication enhancement for people with disabilities in the 21st century* [AAC-RERC Spread the Word]. Baltimore, MD: Paul H. Brookes.

Beukelman, D. R., & Mirenda, P. (2013). *Augmentative and alternative communication: Supporting children and adults with complex communication needs* (4th ed.). Baltimore, MD: Paul H. Brookes.

Bradshaw, J. (2013). The use of augmentative and alternative communication apps for the iPad, iPod and iPhone: An overview of recent developments. *Tizard Learning Disability Review, 18,* 31–37. doi:10.1108/13595471311295996

Brady, N. C., Bruce, S., Goldman, A., Erickson, K., Mineo, B., Ogletree, B. T., . . . Wilkinson, K. (2016). Communication services and supports for individuals with severe disabilities: Guidance for assessment and intervention. *American Journal on Intellectual and Developmental Disabilities, 121,* 121–138. doi:10.1352/ 1944–7558–121.2.121

Caron, J. (2011). *Feature matching communication applications.* Retrieved from https://aac-ucf. unm.edu/common/brochures/aac-apps-list.pdf

Chapple, D. (2011). The evolution of augmentative communication and the importance of alternate access. *Perspectives on Augmentative and Alternative Communication, 20,* 34–37. doi:10.1044/aac20.1.34

Costello, J. M., Shane, H. C., & Caron, J. (2013). *AAC, mobile devices, and apps: Growing pains with evidence based practice.* Retrieved from www.childrenshospital.org/clinicalservices/ Site2016/mainpageS2016P20.html, 1–8.

Dietz, A., Quach, W., Lund, S. K., & McKelvey, M. (2012). AAC assessment and clinical-decision making: The impact of experience. *Augmentative and Alternative Communication, 28,* 148–159. doi:10.3109/07434618.2012.704521

Dodd, J. L. (2017). *Augmentative and alternative communication intervention: An intensive, immersive, socially based service delivery model.* San Diego, CA: Plural Publishing.

Farrall, J. (2016). *AAC apps lists.* Retrieved from www.janefarrall.com/aac-apps-lists/

Ganz, J. B., Morin, K. L., Foster, M. J., Vannest, K. J., Tosun, D. G., Gregori, E. V., & Gerow, S. L. (2017). High-technology augmentative and alternative communication for individuals with intellectual and developmental disabilities and complex communication needs:

A meta-analysis. *Augmentative and Alternative Communication, 33*, 224–238. doi:10.1080 /07434618.2017.1373855

Helling, C. R., & Minga, J. (2014). Developing an effective framework for the augmentative and alternative communication evaluation process. *Perspectives on Augmentative and Alternative Communication, 23*, 91–98. doi:10.1044/aac23.2.91

Johnston, S. S., Reichle, J., Feeley, K. M., & Jones, E. A. (2012). *AAC strategies for individuals with moderate to severe disabilities.* Baltimore, MD: Paul H. Brookes.

King, A. M., Brady, K. W., & Voreis, G. (2017). "It's a blessing and a curse": Perspectives on tablet use in children with autism spectrum disorder. *Autism and Developmental Language Impairments, 2*, 1–12. doi:10.1177/2396941516683183

Light, J., & McNaughton, D. (2012). The changing face of augmentative and alternative communication: Past, present, and future challenges. *Augmentative and Alternative Communication, 28*, 197–204. doi:10.3109/07434618.2012.737024

Lloyd, L. L., Fuller, D. R., & Arvidson, H. H. (1997). *Augmentative and alternative communication: A handbook of principles and practices.* Boston, MA: Allyn and Bacon.

Lorah, E. R., Parnell, A., Whitby, P. S., & Hantual, D. (2014). A systematic review of tablet computers and portable media players as speech generating devices for individuals with autism spectrum disorder. *Journal of Autism and Developmental Disorders, 45*, 3792–3804. doi:10.1007/s10803-014-2314-4

Marfilius, S., & Fonner, K. (2012). *Feature matching checklists.* Retrieved from www.spectron ics.com.au/conference/2012/pdfs/handouts/kelly-fonner/Feature_Match_Check-lists_JAN2012.pdf

McCarthy, J., McCarthy, J., Light, J., Drager, K., McNaughton, D., Grodzicki, L., . . . Parkin, E. (2006). Re-designing scanning to reduce learning demands: The performance of typically developing 2-year olds. *Augmentative and Alternative Communication, 22*, 269–283. doi:10.1080/00498250600718621

McNaughton, D., & Light, J. (2013). The iPad and mobile technology revolution: Benefits and challenges for individuals who require augmentative and alternative communication. *Augmentative and Alternative Communication, 29*, 107–116. doi:10.3109/07434618 .2013.784930

Millar, S., & McNeill, G. (2017). *iPad apps for complex communication support needs: Augmentative and alternative communication.* Retrieved from www.callscotland.org.uk/common-assets/cm-files/posters/ipad-apps-for-complex-communication-support-needs.pdf

Parker, R., & Zangari, C. (2012). *Rubric for evaluating the language of apps for AAC: RELAAACs.* Retrieved from https://coe.uoregon.edu/cds/files/2016/09/AAC-App-Rubric-for-Language.pdf

Quach, W., & Beukelman, D. (2010). Facilitating children's learning of dynamic-display AAC devices: The effect of two instructional methods on the performance of 6- and 7-year-olds with typical development using a dual-screen prototype. *Augmentative and Alternative Communication, 26*, 1–11. doi:10.3109/07434610903561068

RERC on Communication Enhancement. (2011). *Mobile devices and communication apps: An AAC-RERC White paper.* Retrieved from http://aac-rerc.psu.edu/index.php/pages/show/id/46

Shane, H. C., Laubscher, E. H., Schlosser, R. W., Flynn, S., Sorce, J. F., & Abramson, J. (2012). Applying technology to visually support language and communication in individuals with autism spectrum disorders. *Journal of Autism and Developmental Disorders, 42*, 1228–1235. doi:10.1007/s10803-011-1304-z

Thistle, J. J., & Wilkinson, K. M. (2013). Working memory demands of aided augmentative and alternative communication for individuals with developmental disabilities.

Augmentative and Alternative Communication, 29, 235–245. doi:10.3109/07434618.201 3.815800

Trnka, K., McCaw, J., Yarrington, D., McCoy, K. F., & Pennington, C. (2009). User interaction with word prediction: The effects of prediction quality. *ACM Transactions on Accessible Computing, 1*(3), 1–34. doi:10.1145/1497302.1497307

van der Merwe, E., & Alant, E. (2004). Associations with Minspeak icons. *Journal of Communication Disorders, 37*, 255–274. doi:10.1016/j.jcomdis.2003.10.002

Wagner, B. T., & Jackson, H. M. (2006). Developing memory capacity resources of typical children retrieving picture communication symbols using direct selection and visual linear scanning with fixed communication displays. *Journal of Speech-Language-Hearing Research, 49*, 113–126. doi:10.1044/1092–4388(2006/009

Wilkinson, K. M., Light, J., & Drager, K. (2011). Considerations for the composition of visual scene displays: Potential contributions of information from visual and cognitive sciences. *Augmentative and Alternative Communication, 28*, 137–147. doi:10.3109/07434 618.2012.704522

Wilkinson, K. M., & McIlvane, W. J. (2013). Perceptual factors influence visual search for meaningful symbols in individuals with intellectual disabilities and Down syndrome or autism spectrum disorders. *American Journal on Intellectual and Developmental Disabilities, 118*, 353–364. doi:10/1352/1944–7558–118.5.353

UNIT 3

Goal Setting and Implementation Practices

10
WRITING EFFECTIVE COMMUNICATION GOALS

When considering embedding communication skills in the student's Individualized Educational Program (IEP), the IEP team will need to focus on ensuring individualized and systematic instructional supports, while holding the team members accountable for its implementation (Lynch & Adams, 2008). This chapter will outline an effective process in identifying and setting instructional goals for students with complex communication needs (CCN). It will offer a structure for IEP teams to use to ensure that goals are set accurately, and that they are written in an observable and measurable manner.

As a legal document, the IEP outlines the student's current skills, the areas of needs, and the supports needed to successfully meet the school requirements. According to IDEA (2004), there are seven components that must be included in the IEP. These include the following: (1) present level of academic achievement and functional performance (PLAAFP); (2) measurable annual goals with short-term objectives; (3) a description of how the student's progress will be recorded towards meeting the annual goals; (4) a statement on special education and related services; (5) to what extent the student will participate in general education; (6) a statement on accommodations and modifications for classroom activities and assessments (school and state); and (7) the date, frequency, and duration of services.

Some questions have been raised about the development process and quality of IEPs (Blackwell & Rosetti, 2014), IEPs' individualization (Castro, Pinto, & Simeonsson, 2014; Ruble, McGrew, Dalrymple, & Jung, 2010), and the influence of the school environment on IEPs (Castro et al., 2014; Sanches-Ferreira, Lopes-dos-Santos, Alves, Santos, & Silveira-Maia, 2013). To safeguard the quality and the process, the individualization of these documents should be maintained and the components of the IEP should be objectively outlined to ensure accurate measures of the student's progress (Hauser, 2017). This will also promote accountability from all team members (Alberto & Troutman, 2017) and ensure ongoing and effective evaluation of the program.

Embedding Augmentative and Alternative Communication into the IEP

The purpose of implementing augmentative and alternative communication (AAC) strategies and using AAC systems is to address the communication needs of students who are unable to functionally communicate through conventional methods such as spoken language (Beukelman & Mirenda, 2013; Brady et al., 2016; Downing, 2000). This impacts school settings directly as the law "requires schools to use assistive technology devices and services to maximize accessibility for children with disabilities" (Wright, Wright, & O'Connor, 2010, p. 74). This law is particularly important for students with CCN because they can benefit from assistive technology (AT) devices. With the increased use of classroom technologies, the outlook of the IEP needs to change to effectively and accurately support students with CCN. IEP teams should consider how to accommodate the student's needs through the use of AT. The law mandates that students with CCN will be provided the supports and services needed to develop into independent communicators (Brady et al., 2016; Light & McNaughton, 2013).

Evidence supports the notion that AAC services and strategies are critical and effective in supporting students with CCN (Beukelman & Mirenda, 2013; Light & McNaughton, 2015; Millar, Light, & Schlosser, 2006; Schlosser & Raghavendra, 2004). AAC systems and strategies can increase a student's independence (McNaughton & Bryen, 2007; Smith, 2015), self-determination (Kleinert, Harrison, Fisher, & Kleinert, 2010), educational performance (Kleinert et al., 2015; Wehmeyer, Smith, Palmer, & Davies, 2004), and active participation across environments and activities (Jones & Hinesmon-Matthews, 2014). Although AAC strategies can meaningfully impact the communication repertoire of students with CCN, it is a challenging task to identify creative ways to embed communication skills and AAC strategies and services into the IEP (Klang et al., 2016; Rowland, Quinn, & Steiner, 2014; Sanches-Ferreira et al., 2013). The goal in embedding AAC into the IEP is to ensure the student's communicative needs are being met, and that team members are held accountable for providing the student with communicative opportunities.

Individualizing IEPs is a critical task to provide effective instruction (Bateman & Linden, 2012; Twachtman-Cullen & Twachtman-Bassett, 2011). As a result, IEP teams need to identify and outline the overarching goals being set for the student (e.g., independence, educational performance, active participation). The *Augmentative and Alternative Communication IEP Goal Setting Framework* (see Figure 10.1) provides teams with a structure that supports effective IEP development. This framework is based on the notion that three main components need to be addressed to best support students with CCN. The main focus of this framework

Augmentative and Alternative Communication IEP Goal Setting Framework

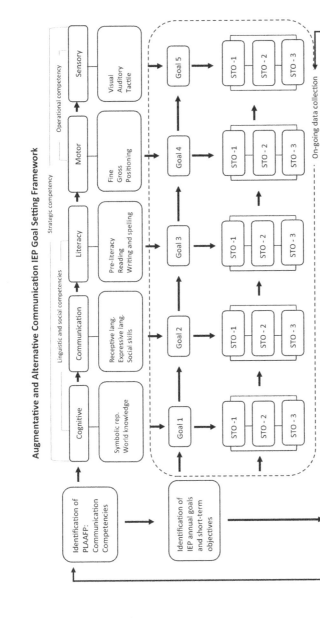

FIGURE 10.1 Communication skills goal setting.

(*Sources:* Capizzi, 2008; Light, 1989; The Dynamic AAC Goals Grid 2, 2014)

Note. IEP = Individualized Educational Program; Lang. = language; PLAAFP = Present Level of Academic Achievement and Functional Performance; Rep. = representation; STO = short-term objectives.

is to outline the student's skills and team plans based on the student's current communication competencies (see Light, 1989 and Chapter 2 for more details).

Teams should use the framework to individualize the planning for students with CCN. Yet, to effectively embed AAC systems and services into the IEP, teams will need to go beyond just instructional planning. To successfully embed AAC into the IEP, teams should include information related to the student's communication competencies and the AAC system into the three main parts of the IEP, this includes:

(1) Present level of academic achievement and functional performance.
(2) Measurable and meaningful IEP goals and objectives.
(3) Service identification and provision.

Figure 10.2 illustrates the process in embedding AAC into the IEP. The intent is to follow and maintain a clear, systematic process in writing the IEP to support the student's communication needs and to ensure accountability of all team members in this process.

Present Level of Academic Achievement and Functional Performance

Prior to creating language and communication goals and an educational program to help the student achieve those goals, the IEP team needs to identify the

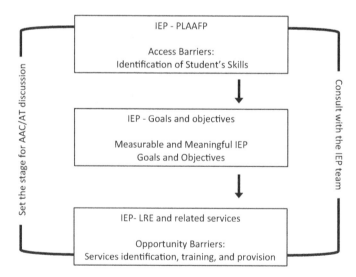

FIGURE 10.2 Consideration for embedding augmentative and alterntaive communication into the IEP.

Note. PLAAFP = present level of academic achieverment and functional performance.

student's communication strengths and areas of needs. The identification of the PLAAFP is a critical part of an effective IEP, as it provides current information on the student's performance (Bateman & Linden, 2012; Christle & Yell, 2010).

A dynamic assessment should be conducted prior to considering AAC systems and services. The goal of this assessment should be for the IEP team to gather baseline data on the student's current abilities (see Chapter 5 for detailed information). The IEP team will need to determine the student's current skills in five main areas when considering the evaluation of access barriers:

(1) *Cognitive skills.* For example, does the student have limited cognitive skills that prevent him or her from learning more advanced AAC systems or will the student have difficulty identifying when a communication breakdown occurs?

(2) *Communication skills.* For example, does the student currently have an effective means of communication?

(3) *Literacy skills.* For example, does the student have the reading skills necessary to identify text on an AAC system or does the student have sufficient writing skills to compose a message?

(4) *Physical and motor skills.* For example, does the student have any motor limitations that may prevent him or her from adequately activating an AAC system or accessing all of the physical components of a system?

(5) *Sensory skills (visual and auditory).* For example, does the student have hearing or vision problems that limit his or her ability to use an AAC system?

By having a better understanding of the student's skills in these areas, IEP teams will be able to assess the needs specific to the student's settings, staff members, and the student to eliminate any potential barriers. This will also help team members identify areas of potential training needs to better support the student (see Figure 10.3 for an illustration of these five main assessment components).

Another key step in identifying present levels is for IEP teams to determine the student's current level of communication, that is, if the student is a non-symbolic or symbolic communicator (Ogletree & Pierce, 2010; see Chapter 5 for details on levels of communication). In addition, the IEP team will need to evaluate the student's communicative competency skills (see Chapter 2 for detailed information on communication competencies and Chapter 5 for a description of assessment considerations). The communication competencies can help outline the student's baseline levels and can help the IEP team identify potential goals that will fill in gaps in the areas of communication competencies where they exist (Gilette, 2009). A useful resource for IEP teams to gather baseline information on the student's performance is the Dynamic AAC Goals Grid 2 (DAGG-2) developed by Dynavox and Dynamic Therapy Associates of Kennesaw Georgia (2014; www.mydynavox.com/resources/aacgoalwriting). The DAGG-2 offers a systematic way to evaluate the communication skills of a student with CCN. More specifically, the DAGG-2 assesses skills that are directly linked to the use of AAC. The DAGG-2 strives to ensure that all levels

FIGURE 10.3 Augmentative and alternative communication related present level of performance to be emdedded in the IEP.

of communicative competencies are considered and that the student's strengths and areas of needs can be identified and analyzed. For example, the purpose of the *Ability Level Continuum* on the DAGG-2 is to identify the student's current baseline or present level of communication performance. No matter the tool(s) used for this purpose, the goal should be to gather objective baseline information that will help identify the student's areas of needs, so that the student's abilities can be described in detail in the PLAAFP. Figure 10.4 offers an example to document and summarize the student's PLAAFP based on Light's (1989) communication competencies (see Chapter 2 for more information on the communication competencies).

Measurable and Meaningful IEP Goals and Objectives

Based on the information gathered in the PLAAFP, the IEP team will need to outline goals and objectives that are directly linked to the student's PLAAFP.

Communication Competency Present Level of Performance Form

Student's name: _____   Completed by: _____   Date: _____

Instructions. Under each AAC related domain, select the *communication competencies* being addressed. Under the *Source of Information,* indicate how the data were obtained (e.g., ongoing observational data, testing). Under the *Skill* section, indicate the specific skill being addressed. Under the *Present Level of Performance* section, provide an objective and detailed description of the skill and the student's current level of functioning (provide examples). Under the heading of *Criterion,* indicate the student's current level of ability in an objective manner (e.g., 3/5 trials, 60%).

Domains	Comm. Competencies				Source of information	Skill	Present level of performance	Criterion
	Linguistic	Operational	Social	Strategic				
Cognitive	☐	☐	☐	☐				
	☐	☐	☐	☐				
	☐	☐	☐	☐				
Communication	☐	☐	☐	☐				
	☐	☐	☐	☐				
	☐	☐	☐	☐				
Literacy	☐	☐	☐	☐				
	☐	☐	☐	☐				
	☐	☐	☐	☐				
Motor	☐	☐	☐	☐				
	☐	☐	☐	☐				
	☐	☐	☐	☐				
Sensory	☐	☐	☐	☐				
	☐	☐	☐	☐				
	☐	☐	☐	☐				

FIGURE 10.4   Communication competency present level of performance form.

Note. Comm. = Communication

Communication skills that are linked to the communicative competencies, but can also support the student across academic areas, tasks, skills, settings (including home), and communication partners should be prioritized. It is the IEP team's responsibility to determine the skills to be addressed based on each communication competency and the student's PLAAFP. Beyond the PLAAFP, The DAGG-2 (Dynavox, 2014) can also be used to as a resource to identify, guide, and set *annual goals* and objectives. The DAGG-2 offers systematic *Goal Setting Sheets* that are divided into the four communication competencies. These goal setting sheets outline and describe developmental skill under each competency. Additionally, the DAGG-2 offers an *AAC Goal Worksheet* that can help IEP teams to set annual goals and objectives for students with CCN. Beyond the use of the DAGG-2, the IEP team can generate a form to draft and outline annual IEP goals and objectives under each communication competency. Figure 10.5 provides an example of a *Communication Competency IEP Goals and Objectives Form* and Figure 10.6 provides a completed example of the *Communication Competency IEP Goals and Objectives Form*. This form can be used across team members so that specific skills are being considered that may directly or indirectly support skills for successful use of AAC.

Communication Competency IEP Goals and Objectives Form

Student's name: _____   Completed by: _____   Date: _____

Communication Competencies		**IEP Goals and Objectives**
	Linguistic	Goal-
		1.
		2.
		3.
	Operational	Goal-
		1.
		2.
		3.
	Social	Goal-
		1.
		2.
		3.
	Strategic	Goal-
		1.
		2.
		3.

FIGURE 10.5 Communication competency IEP goals and objectives form.

Note. Objectives are outlined below each communication competency goal.

Communication Competency IEP Goals and Objectives Form

Student's name: _Cora Bayle_   Completed by: _Mrs. Rogers_   Date: _08/15/17_

Communication Competencies		IEP Goals and Objectives
	Linguistic	Cora will receptively (by touching when requested) and expressively (by providing it to the communication partner) identify 40 words (e.g., daily activity, routines, and reinforcers) using graphic symbols for 3 consecutive data days by May 2018.
		1. During classroom routines, Cora will receptively identify 20 symbol representations with 100% accuracy for 3 consecutive data collection days as measured by teacher created data collection sheets by November 2017.
		2. During classroom routines, Cora will receptively identify 30 symbol representations for 3 consecutive data collection days as measured by teacher created data collection sheets by January 2018.
		3. During classroom routines, Cora will receptively identify 40 symbol representations for 3 consecutive data collection days as measured by teacher created data collection sheets by March 2018.
		4. During classroom routines, Cora will request an item or action using symbol representations in 100% of the opportunities for 3 consecutive data collection days as measured by teacher created data collection sheets by May 2018.
	Operational	Cora will make choices out of a field of 4 graphic symbols in 80% of opportunities by May 2018.
		1. During classroom routines, Cora will make a choice out of a field of 2 symbol representations in 80% of the opportunities for 3 consecutive data collection days as measured by teacher created data collection sheets by December 2017.
		2. During classroom routines, Cora will make a choice out of a field of 3 symbol representations in 80% of the opportunities for 3 consecutive data collection days as measured by teacher created data collection sheets by February 2018.
		3. During classroom routines, Cora will make a choice out of field of 4 symbol representations in 80% of the opportunities for 3 consecutive data collection days as measured by teacher created data collection sheets by May 2018.
	Social	Cora will greet a peer and adult in 100% of the given opportunities using her communication device by May 2018.
		1. When entering the classroom, Cora will greet a peer (e.g., "Hi Sally") using her communication device in 80% of the opportunities for 3 consecutive data collection days as measured by teacher created data collection sheets by May 2018.
		2. When entering the classroom, Cora will greet an adult (e.g., "Hi Mrs. Rogers") using her communication device in 80% of the opportunities for 3 consecutive data collection days as measured by teacher created data collection sheets by May 2018.
		3. During morning circle, Cora will greet peers (e.g., Hi) using her communication device in 80% of the opportunities for 3 consecutive data collection days as measured by teacher created data collection sheets by May 2018.
		4. When leaving the classroom, Cora will express a farewell (e.g., Bye) to an adult using her communication device in 80% of the opportunities for 3 consecutive data collection days as measured by teacher created data collection sheets by May 2018.
	Strategic	Cora will initiate a communication interaction with an adult by expressing wants or needs using symbolic representations on her communication device in 80% of the given opportunities by May 2018.
		1. During one-on-one activities, Cora will initiate a communicative interaction with an adult by selecting a graphic symbol on her communication device 80% of the opportunities for 3 consecutive data collection days as measured by teacher created data collection sheets by May 2018.
		2. During classroom routines, Cora will request an item by selecting a graphic symbol on her communication device in 80% of the opportunities for 3 consecutive data collection days as measured by teacher created data collection sheets by May 2018.
		3. During classroom routines, Cora will request an action by selecting a graphic symbol on her communication device in 80% of the opportunities for 3 consecutive data collection days as measured by teacher created data collection sheets by May 2018.

FIGURE 10.6 Example of completed communication competency IEP goals and objectives form.

Note. Objectives are outlined below each communication competency goal.

To productively integrate the AAC system into IEP goals and objectives, the IEP team should ensure that the student's communication needs are being addressed across multiple settings, individuals, and tasks (Light & McNaughton, 2013). This is critical as it has been suggested that students with CCN are passive learners and often do not actively participate in classroom activities (Bunning, Smith, Kennedy, & Greenham, 2013; Chung, Carter, & Sisco, 2012; Karvonen, Wakeman, Browder, Rogers, & Flowers, 2011). When writing goals and objectives for a student with CCN, determination of what the student is expected to accomplish during the specified timeframe is paramount. The identification of these skills and the expectations being set by the IEP team should be a reflection of the student's present level data.

The purpose of annual IEP goals is to enable the student to learn skills that are necessary to become independent and meet the expectations being set by the student's various environments. Annual IEP goals are expected to guide the instruction, making them a fundamental component in the IEP (Bornman & Murphy, 2006; Poppes, Vlasklamp, de Geeter, & Nakken, 2002). Each annual IEP goal should be written as a general statement that focuses on an area of need. The goals should be challenging, yet reasonable and feasible to accomplish within a year (i.e., by the next annual IEP meeting). Annual IEP goals should be observable and measurable and, at a minimum, should be comprised of four components: (1) the student, (2) the behavior or skill, (3) the *criteria*, and (4) the timeline. Short-term objectives, on the other hand, are smaller steps the student will achieve to reach the annual goal. They can be set as developmental milestones or unique steps to achieve a task. Short-term objectives can serve as a measurement to monitor the student's progress in each stepping stone. Short-term objectives, at a minimum, should include seven components: (1) a condition, (2) the student, (3) the behavior or skill, (4) the criteria, (5) consistency of the skill, (6) a timeline, and (7) a method to measure the student's progress. When writing short-term objectives, an essential consideration is supporting and outlining skill generalization (i.e., across people, places, and materials). Figure 10.7 provides an outline of the key factors in writing accurate, effective, measurable, and observable annual IEP goals and objectives. It also provides examples of the various components.

Identifying the *skills* to be addressed and how these skills can be broken into smaller steps (i.e., short-term objectives) can be challenging. The purpose of Figure 10.8 is to provide a starting point in the identification of potential skills under each communication competency. AAC-related goals and objectives are not different from other annual IEP goals or short-term objectives. The focus of AAC-related goals should be on language and communication development, which has a direct impact on academic skills (e.g., Mirenda, 2014), participation (e.g., Granlund, 2013; Light & McNaughton, 2014; van der Meer, Sigafoos, O'Reilly, & Lancioni, 2011), independence (e.g., Light & McNaughton, 2015; van der Meer et al., 2011), and social skills (e.g., Light & McNaughton, 2014; Therrien, Light, &

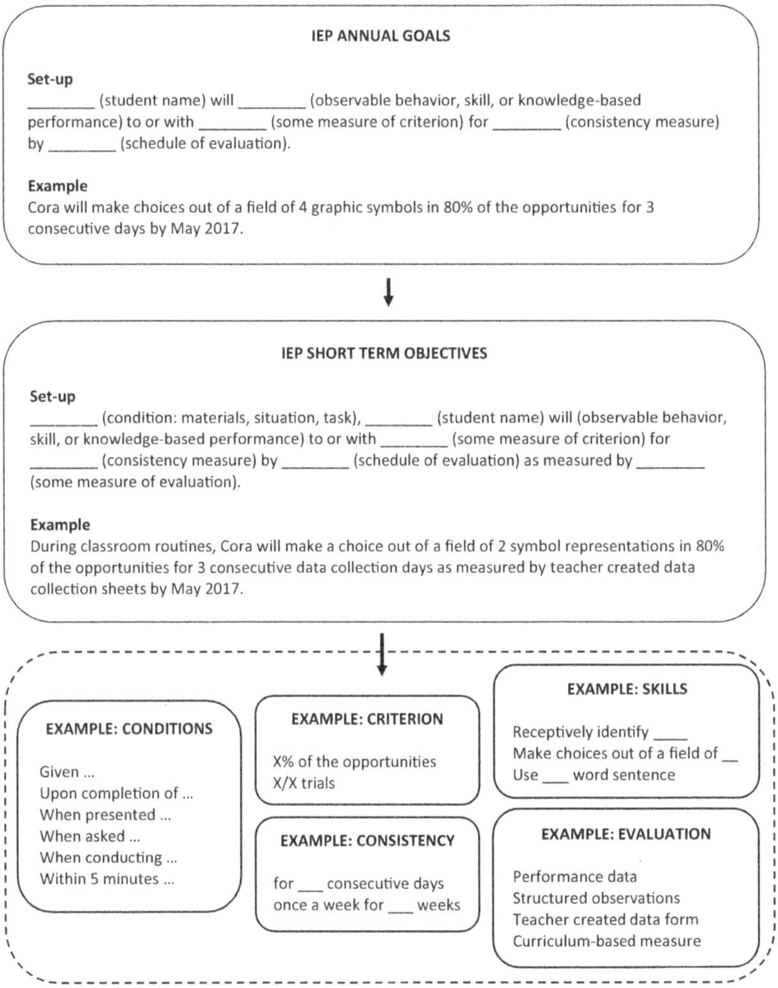

IEP ANNUAL GOALS

Set-up

_____ (student name) will _____ (observable behavior, skill, or knowledge-based performance) to or with _____ (some measure of criterion) for _____ (consistency measure) by _____ (schedule of evaluation).

Example

Cora will make choices out of a field of 4 graphic symbols in 80% of the opportunities for 3 consecutive days by May 2017.

IEP SHORT TERM OBJECTIVES

Set-up

_____ (condition: materials, situation, task), _____ (student name) will (observable behavior, skill, or knowledge-based performance) to or with _____ (some measure of criterion) for _____ (consistency measure) by _____ (schedule of evaluation) as measured by _____ (some measure of evaluation).

Example

During classroom routines, Cora will make a choice out of a field of 2 symbol representations in 80% of the opportunities for 3 consecutive data collection days as measured by teacher created data collection sheets by May 2017.

EXAMPLE: CONDITIONS

Given ...
Upon completion of ...
When presented ...
When asked ...
When conducting ...
Within 5 minutes ...

EXAMPLE: CRITERION

X% of the opportunities
X/X trials

EXAMPLE: CONSISTENCY

for ___ consecutive days
once a week for ___ weeks

EXAMPLE: SKILLS

Receptively identify ____
Make choices out of a field of __
Use ___ word sentence

EXAMPLE: EVALUATION

Performance data
Structured observations
Teacher created data form
Curriculum-based measure

FIGURE 10.7   Writing observable and measurable annual goals and short-term objectives.

Pope, 2016). In essence, annual IEP goals should be thought of as integrated goals that can be embedded across various activities and materials, rather than isolated goals (see Figure 10.9 for an example of an isolated versus an integrated goal for a student with CCN). Beyond this, data on annual IEP goals and short-term objectives should be collected on an ongoing basis and results should be recorded (see "Progress Monitoring" section for more details) and graphed (see Figure 10.10 for an example of baseline and intervention data on "requesting") to make data-driven instructional decisions.

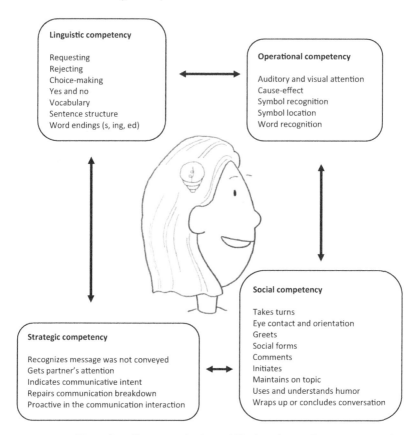

FIGURE 10.8 Example of communication skills based on the communication competencies.

Services Identification and Provision

Identification of opportunity barriers is a challenging and time-consuming process. However, it is a necessary one (see Chapter 4 for more details on opportunity barriers). Identifying opportunity barriers is important, as they are essential in determining the training needs of family members and all service providers. Opportunity barriers cannot be eliminated simply by providing an AAC system or intervention to the student (Beukelman & Mirenda, 2013). Instead, opportunity barriers will require a thoughtful action plan for the IEP team to address.

The provision of related services to a student with CCN is dependent on the type and amount of support the student will need and who the classroom staff are (i.e., special education teacher, general education teacher, paraeducators). Related services providers, such as an occupational therapist (OT), speech-language pathologist (SLP), or AT and AAC consultant will have valuable input on

The student: Cora   The skill: Initiate conversation

Isolated annual IEP goal

Cora will initiate conversation in 100% of given opportunities for three consecutive days by May 2018.

Integrated annual IEP goal ⟶ Academic skills

Cora will ask for clarification (e.g., what are we doing?) using her communication device during classroom activities in 80% of given opportunities for three consecutive days by May 2018.

Integrated annual IEP goal ⟶ Social skills

Cora will greet peers (e.g., Hi, how are you today?) using her communication device during morning group meeting in 80% of given opportunities for three consecutive days by May 2018.

Integrated annual IEP goal ⟶ Participation

Cora will ask for a turn or indicate she has a comment to make using her communication device during classroom activities and games in 80% of given opportunities for three consecutive days by May 2018.

FIGURE 10.9 Example of isolated and integrated annual IEP goals.

Adapted from *Augmentative and alternative communication: A handbook of principles and practices*, by L. L. Lloyd, D. R. Fuller, and H. H. Arvidson (1997), Needham Heights, MA: Allyn and Bacon, p. 239.

the student's assessment, instruction, and implementation of the IEP. Identification of the appropriate related services and supports needed can be challenging for the IEP team, as the team may struggle to embed the student's AT and AAC needs into the IEP (Bausch, Ault, Evmenova, & Behrmann, 2008; Zabala et al., 2000). When assistive technology (including AAC systems) are necessary for a student to receive an appropriate education, "the law requires assistive technology services,

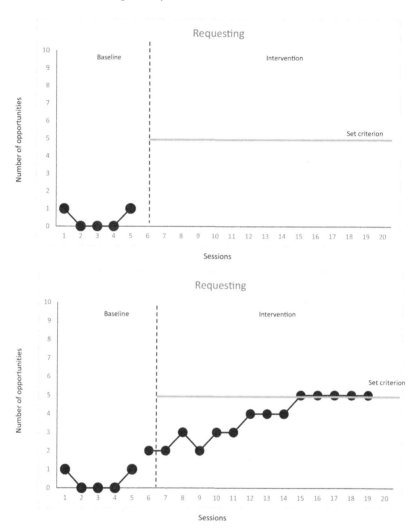

FIGURE 10.10 Example graph of establishing criteria for mastery and data collecting on student's performance.

including training of the teachers, child, and family" to be written into a student's IEP (Wright et al., 2010, p. 78).

Based on the Individuals with Disabilities Education Act (IDEA, 2004), related services are designed to enable the student with special needs to be supported in their educational environment. If the student qualifies for related services, these must be written into the student's IEP (Wright et al., 2010). As part of this process, the team must determine the type of services the student will need, direct, or consult.

Consultation services are often selected when support or training is needed for school personnel. Consultation services are designed to provide school personnel with the knowledge and skills needed to accurately and effectively support students and help reach the set annual goals and objectives. Effective communication and documentation of the consultation services (and training) is critical as families may request consulting reports from the service providers (Wright et al., 2010). These reports should include, but are not limited to, the following: what consultation services took place, when it took place, with whom they took place, and what was discussed or targeted during the consultation. On the other hand, if it is determined that the student will benefit from direct related services, not only will school personnel and families receive support and training, but the student with CCN will also receive individualized and direct support. This means that the related service provider will need to set goals for the student and will be held accountable for the student's progress towards those goals.

Because of the difference in service provision, thoughtful discussion and evaluation should be the premises in determining what will be most beneficial for the student. The key is to identify related services that will help the student achieve the set goals. There are two main questions to guide this process: (1) how much support does the student need in each particular domain (e.g., motor-occupational or physical therapist) to meet the set goals? and (2) how much training is needed for all those who will be involved in the student's education? The main goal is to effectively and accurately support students with CCN and to train school personnel in the most effective and efficient way to help the student achieve the goals and objectives included in the IEP.

Integrating the AAC System into the IEP

To identify an appropriate AAC system, the IEP team should have a conversation about the appropriateness of specific AAC services and AT devices for the student (Light & McNaughton, 2013; Zabala, 2005). The system should be selected following a systematic, yet dynamic feature-matching assessment to determine the most effective system (see Chapters 7, 8, and 9 for more details on the possibilities and assessment process). According to Beukelman and Mirenda (2013), in the process of identifying a communication system, the team will need to administer a number of thoughtfully selected criterion-referenced assessments. The team will also need to conduct observations of the student across various tasks and settings that will help answer relevant questions about the student's current skill level. Questions about the student's abilities and areas of need can be used to explore AT options for the student. These questions may include but are not limited to these:

(1) Does the student understand symbolic representation (e.g., line drawings)?
(2) Can the student read (e.g., decode and understand words)?
(3) Does the student have the motor abilities needed to select using his or her hands?

(4) What body part can the student use independently and consistently?
(5) Does the student use low technology consistently and effectively?
(6) Has the student ever used any type of high-technology systems to communicate?
(7) Have the tools used been useful for the purposes of communication? Why or why not?

The purpose of posing these questions should be to guide the team in identifying the most appropriate means for the student to select, to represent, and to transmit messages. See Chapters 8 and 9 for more detail information on each of these components.

By using a feature-matching approach to answer these (and any other) questions, the team will be able to identify an appropriate unaided and aided (low- and high-technology) AAC system. One possible way to conduct a trial of these systems is by contacting the state Assistive Technology Center. Students with CCN are supported by the Assistive Technology Act (2004). The purpose of the Assistive Technology Act, also known as the "Tech Act," is to support states by improving the access to AT systems and devices for individuals with special needs. This act also provides states with funds to support three major programs: (1) AT reutilization programs, (2) AT demonstration programs, and (3) alternative financing and device loan programs (Assistive Technology Public Law, 2004; Mittler, 2007). Similarly to the state programs, companies that sell dedicated communication systems also have loaner programs. These loaner programs can be very beneficial to IEP teams, as systems can be used with the student for a trial period to see if the system is beneficial for the student. Because the length of time it takes for a student to learn a new skill may vary, extended trial periods of at least one month may be beneficial to obtain sufficient data to determine if the system is the most effective and appropriate for the student (Lund, Quach, Weissling, McKelvey, & Dietz, 2017). By gathering data on the student's response to instruction using the device and the student's ability to use the device, teams can make data-driven decisions prior to committing to any given system.

After the AAC system has been identified, any equipment or other devices should be embedded into the IEP by identifying goals where the skill being addressed will require the student to use the AAC system. Another possibility is to create conditions (e.g., communication partners, settings, topics, materials) that may require the student to use the system when writing the annual IEP goals. The IEP team will need to ensure the AAC system is included in the accommodations and modifications section of the IEP as well. In doing so, the student will have the opportunity to have access to the system in a more systematic manner, as team members will be accountable for providing such opportunities. In turn, the student will have the opportunity to generalize the skills being addressed and expectations being set (Jones & Hinesmon-Matthews, 2014; Pretti-Frontczak & Bricker, 2000) and increase self-determination skills and independence while using the system (Kleinert et al., 2010). Figure 10.11 provides a sample data

Communication System Data Collection Form

Student's name: _____   Completed by: _____   Week: _____

Instructions. The purpose of the *Communication System Data Collection Form* is to collect systematic data on the student's use of a specific communication system. This data collection form should be use for a week. To complete the data collection form, indicate under the *System* heading the communication system being used and also select the specific information of that system (i.e., unaided, aided, low technology, and high technology). For each day of data collection, indicate the date, time in which data is being collected, the setting, and task or communication partner. Collect five trials or opportunities of data of the student's use of the system during the interaction. Check the level of support needed for each trial and then calculate the total number of correct responses. Use the anecdotal notes for any additional information that may be relevant to the student's performance.

Comm. System: _____   ☐ Unaided   ☐ Aided   ☐ Low tech.   ☐ High tech.

Comm. Partner: _____   Setting: _____   Activity/Task: _____

Levels of support	Date:	Time:					Date:	Time:					Date:	Time:					Date:	Time:					Date:	Time:				
	Trials						Trials						Trials						Trials						Trials					
	1	2	3	4	5		1	2	3	4	5		1	2	3	4	5		1	2	3	4	5		1	2	3	4	5	
Independent	☐	☐	☐	☐	☐		☐	☐	☐	☐	☐		☐	☐	☐	☐	☐		☐	☐	☐	☐	☐		☐	☐	☐	☐	☐	
Verbal prompt	☐	☐	☐	☐	☐		☐	☐	☐	☐	☐		☐	☐	☐	☐	☐		☐	☐	☐	☐	☐		☐	☐	☐	☐	☐	
Gestural prompt	☐	☐	☐	☐	☐		☐	☐	☐	☐	☐		☐	☐	☐	☐	☐		☐	☐	☐	☐	☐		☐	☐	☐	☐	☐	
Partial physical	☐	☐	☐	☐	☐		☐	☐	☐	☐	☐		☐	☐	☐	☐	☐		☐	☐	☐	☐	☐		☐	☐	☐	☐	☐	
Full physical	☐	☐	☐	☐	☐		☐	☐	☐	☐	☐		☐	☐	☐	☐	☐		☐	☐	☐	☐	☐		☐	☐	☐	☐	☐	
DN participate	☐	☐	☐	☐	☐		☐	☐	☐	☐	☐		☐	☐	☐	☐	☐		☐	☐	☐	☐	☐		☐	☐	☐	☐	☐	
TOTAL																															

Anecdotal notes.

Weekly Total

FIGURE 10.11 Communication system data collection form.

Note. Comm. = communication; DN = does not; Tech. = technology.

collection form to better understand how the student uses communication systems. This form can be completed across systems so a comparison of systems can be conducted.

Progress Monitoring

Recording student progress and outcomes is critical to determine if the student is meeting the expectations that have been set (i.e., goals and objectives). It is the IEP team's responsibility to specify how data will be collected to monitor the student's progress towards the goals and objectives (Twachtman-Cullen & Twachtman-Bassett, 2011). Unfortunately, conventional assessment methods (e.g., administration of formal assessment tools) may not always provide a holistic representation of the student's strengths, limitations, and preferences (Beukelman & Mirenda, 2013). Scheduled classroom observations are necessary to evaluate students with CCN who may not necessarily be candidates for formal assessment processes (Deveney, Hoffman, & Cress, 2012). These should be daily documentations of the student's skills across people, environments, materials, and times of day (Chung & Douglas, 2014). Information gained from systematic and structured observations of the student's skills (and behaviors) and anecdotal notes can provide important information related to the student's access and opportunity barriers as well (Beukelman & Mirenda, 2013).

Monitoring the student's progress on his or her annual IEP goals will greatly depend on the specific goal, the student, and the setting (Alberto & Troutman, 2017; Feeley & Jones, 2012). Beyond data collection on annual IEP goals and short-term objectives, a particular consideration for students with CCN is that data should be collected across AAC systems if the student is using different systems on a trial basis (Parette, Peterson-Karlan, Wojcik, & Bardi, 2007). This process will help with the identification of the most effective AAC system for the student. To obtain accurate data the student has to be provided with sufficient time to explore the device, understand the structure of the system, and the vocabulary within the system. The goal is to determine whether the AAC system is effectively enhancing student performance (Parette et al., 2007).

Before conducting an intervention on an annual IEP goal, baseline data will need to be collected to better understand the students present level of performance (Cooper, Heron, & Heward, 2007). Baseline data should illustrate a stable pattern of response (minimum of five data points). That is, neither upward or downward trends, before intervention begins (Cooper et al., 2007; Gast & Ledford, 2014). Likewise, with intervention data, the goal should be to obtain consistency in the data. If the data is not showing positive intervention trends, as predicted, change the intervention will be needed (Cooper et al., 2007; Gast & Ledford, 2014). This process is essential in making data-driven instructional decisions (Hauser, 2017; Rowland et al., 2014). To accomplish this, teams will need to create effective data collection systems that will allow them to objectively and systematically evaluate student's process. Figure 10.12 outlines ten key steps to progress monitor a student's outcomes.

10 Steps for Progress Monitoring

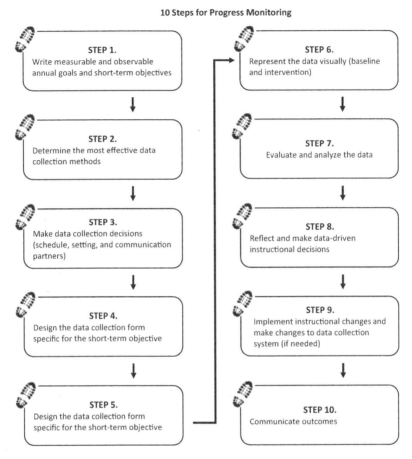

STEP 1.
Write measurable and observable annual goals and short-term objectives

STEP 2.
Determine the most effective data collection methods

STEP 3.
Make data collection decisions (schedule, setting, and communication partners)

STEP 4.
Design the data collection form specific for the short-term objective

STEP 5.
Design the data collection form specific for the short-term objective

STEP 6.
Represent the data visually (baseline and intervention)

STEP 7.
Evaluate and analyze the data

STEP 8.
Reflect and make data-driven instructional decisions

STEP 9.
Implement instructional changes and make changes to data collection system (if needed)

STEP 10.
Communicate outcomes

FIGURE 10.12 Ten steps for progress monitoring.

Each of these steps illustrates the importance of writing accurate and feasible annual IEP goals and short-term objectives. In order to effectively collect data, a data collection system will need to be designed based on the goals being set, and it will need to match these to the most appropriate data collection methods. There are five main data collection methods to be considered: (1) *duration recording*, (2) event or frequency recording, (3) *latency recording*, and (4) *time sampling* (Alberto & Troutman, 2017; Feeley & Jones, 2012; see Table 10.1).

Duration Recording

One way to measure student progress is through duration. The purpose of this measure is to determine how long a behavior occurs (Alberto & Troutman, 2017; Cooper et al., 2007). This is the best measurement tool to use when the increase

TABLE 10.1 Recording Methods During Data Collection

Recording Method	Description	Example of Behaviors or Skills
Event	Number of times a behavior or skill occurs (reported as total number of occurrences). The behavior or skill must be brief and discrete.	Requesting Choice making Pointing
Interval (partial and whole)	Approximate number of times (reported as percentage of occurrences). To record continuous and high frequency behaviors or skills. *Partial*—behavior or skill occurs during any portion of the interval. *Whole*—behavior or skill occurs during the entire duration of an interval.	On/off-task behavior Commenting Requesting Eye gazing
Time Sampling	Approximate number of times (reported as percentage of occurrences). To observe over longer periods of time. To record frequent or long duration behaviors or skills.	On/off-task behavior Commenting Requesting Eye gazing
Duration	Length of response (reported as total duration of each occurrence). To record low frequency behaviors or skills that last several seconds or minutes. Must have clear beginning to the end.	Tantrum Crying Eye gazing
Latency	Length between request and the start of the task performance (reported as total duration of each occurrence). To record how long it takes to perform a task, skill, behavior, once requested.	Asked to point to a symbol Asked to activate an icon Asked to start a task

or decrease of time length is important to a goal. Behaviors and skills being measured should have clear beginning and end; that is, the behavior or skill need to last for a least several seconds or minutes (e.g., social interaction; Alberto & Troutman, 2017; Cooper et al., 2007; Feeley & Jones, 2012). This is a challenging data collection method to embed during instruction as the recorder will need to use a clock or stop watch to determine the beginning and end of the behavior or skill being observed. Duration can be reported using the raw data across multiple sessions or trials, or as an average of the times observed. To report an average using duration, the total duration should be divided by the total occurrences of the behavior or skill. Figure 10.13 provides an example of a data collection form to evaluate the student's progress using duration as the method of data collection.

Duration Data Collection Form

Student's name: Completed by: Date:

Behavior (or skill):   Behavior (or skill) definition:

Instructions. To use the *Duration Data Collection Form,* indicate under the *behavior* what is being observed and provide an objective, observable, and measurable definition under *Behavior definition.* Select if the data collection form will be used to observe the setting or communication partner, and the communication systems being used. Under the setting or *communication partner,* indicate the specific being observed (e.g., peers, reading center). Under the *Duration* heading indicate the beginning and end time. Under *Occurrence,* select if the behavior was observed before the stimulus, during the stimulus, or after. Under *total time,* indicate how long the student engaged in the behavior/skill. Use the *Anecdotal notes* section for any additional information that may be relevant to the student's performance (e.g., student not feeling well).

☐ Setting   Communication system:
☐ Communication partner

Date	Setting or communication partner	Duration		Occurrences			Total Time
		Begin	End	Before	During	After	
		:	:	☐	☐	☐	:
		:	:	☐	☐	☐	:
		:	:	☐	☐	☐	:
		:	:	☐	☐	☐	:
		:	:	☐	☐	☐	:
		:	:	☐	☐	☐	:
		:	:	☐	☐	☐	:
		:	:	☐	☐	☐	:
		:	:	☐	☐	☐	:
		:	:	☐	☐	☐	:
Anecdotal notes.							

FIGURE 10.13 Duration data collection form.

Event Recording

Event or frequency measurements evaluate the number of times a behavior occurs during a set period of time. This method of data collection should be used when the behavior or skill is discrete and brief (e.g., requesting); that is, when there is a discrete, clear start and end of the skill or behavior (Alberto & Troutman, 2017; Feeley & Jones, 2012). Data can be reported using raw data or total numbers, averages, rates, or percentage. When calculating the average of the behavior or skill, the total number of times the behavior or skill occurs is divided by the total number of observations. To calculate the rate of behavior, the total number of times the behavior occurred will then be divided by the length of time the behavior was observed. To calculate the percentage of the behavior or skill, divide the number of behavior occurrences over the number of presented opportunities and multiply it by 100. Figure 10.14, 10.15, and 10.16 provide examples data collection forms using *event recording* as the method of data collection. Figure 10.14 is a skill-based data collection form, Figure 10.15 is an example of levels of performance data collection form.

Latency Recording

Latency records the length of time it takes for a student to respond to a given stimulus, prompt, or request. Latency recording is useful when tracking goals that focus on increasing or decreasing the amount of time it takes to elicit a response from a student once requested (e.g., responding to a question, time to formulate a message using a set number of symbols, requesting a break; Alberto & Troutman, 2017; Feeley & Jones, 2012). An advantage of latency is that it can be reported either using raw data or an average. The raw data would show the latency across opportunities, whereas the averages would report the total latency period of all occurrences divided by the total number of occurrences. Figure 10.16 provides an example of a data collection form to evaluate the student using latency as the method of data collection.

Time Sampling

Time sampling records approximate occurrences of a behavior or skill by identifying a time period (e.g., 5 minutes, half hour, 1 hour) and dividing it into equal intervals. Typically, these intervals are divided into seconds (e.g., 5 seconds, 10 seconds, 30 seconds; Cooper et al., 2007). Time sampling should be used for behaviors that occur frequently or for long periods of time (e.g. transporting one's device, orienting to a speaker; Alberto & Troutman, 2017; Cooper et al., 2007).

This method of data collection can be partial interval recording, whole interval recording, or momentary time sampling. During *partial interval recording*, the behavior or skill is recorded if it occurs at any point during the selected time

Event Recording Data Collection Form

Student's name: _____ Completed by: _____ Week: _____

Skills: _____ Criterion: _____ Comm. System: _____

Instructions. The purpose of the *Skill-based Data Collection Form* is to collect systematic data on the student's progress on a sole skill. This data collection form can be used for a week. To complete the data collection form, indicate under the *Skill* heading the skill being addressed and, under the *Criterion* heading, indicate the set mastery level for the student. For each day of data collection, indicate the date, the time in which data is being collected, and the setting. Provide five trials or opportunities for the student to complete the skill being addressed. Check the level of support needed for each trial and then calculate the total number of correct responses. Use the anecdotal notes section for any additional information that may be relevant to the student's performance (e.g., student not feeling well).

Levels of support	Date: ___ Time: ___ Setting: ___ Trials					Date: ___ Time: ___ Setting: ___ Trials					Date: ___ Time: ___ Setting: ___ Trials					Date: ___ Time: ___ Setting: ___ Trials					Date: ___ Time: ___ Setting: ___ Trials				
	1	2	3	4	5	1	2	3	4	5	1	2	3	4	5	1	2	3	4	5	1	2	3	4	5
Independent	☐	☐	☐	☐	☐	☐	☐	☐	☐	☐	☐	☐	☐	☐	☐	☐	☐	☐	☐	☐	☐	☐	☐	☐	☐
Verbal prompt	☐	☐	☐	☐	☐	☐	☐	☐	☐	☐	☐	☐	☐	☐	☐	☐	☐	☐	☐	☐	☐	☐	☐	☐	☐
Gestural prompt	☐	☐	☐	☐	☐	☐	☐	☐	☐	☐	☐	☐	☐	☐	☐	☐	☐	☐	☐	☐	☐	☐	☐	☐	☐
Partial physical	☐	☐	☐	☐	☐	☐	☐	☐	☐	☐	☐	☐	☐	☐	☐	☐	☐	☐	☐	☐	☐	☐	☐	☐	☐
Full physical	☐	☐	☐	☐	☐	☐	☐	☐	☐	☐	☐	☐	☐	☐	☐	☐	☐	☐	☐	☐	☐	☐	☐	☐	☐
DN participate	☐	☐	☐	☐	☐	☐	☐	☐	☐	☐	☐	☐	☐	☐	☐	☐	☐	☐	☐	☐	☐	☐	☐	☐	☐
TOTAL																									

Anecdotal notes.

Weekly Total

FIGURE 10.14 Event recording data collection form.

Note. DN = does not.

Levels of Support Data Collection Form

Student's name: _____   Completed by: _____

Skill: _____   Criterion: _____   Week: _____

Instructions. On the *Levels of Performance Data Collection Form*, indicate under the *Skill* heading, indicate the skill being addressed and, in the *Criterion* heading, indicate the mastery level for the student. Provide five trials or opportunities for the student to complete the skill being addressed. Select the level of support needed for each trial and then calculate the total number of correct responses based on the level of support.

Date: _____ Time: _____ Setting: _____

Levels of support	Trials									
	1	2	3	4	5	6	7	8	9	10
Independent	☐	☐	☐	☐	☐	☐	☐	☐	☐	☐
Verbal prompt	☐	☐	☐	☐	☐	☐	☐	☐	☐	☐
Gestural prompt	☐	☐	☐	☐	☐	☐	☐	☐	☐	☐
Visual prompt	☐	☐	☐	☐	☐	☐	☐	☐	☐	☐
Model prompt	☐	☐	☐	☐	☐	☐	☐	☐	☐	☐
Partial physical	☐	☐	☐	☐	☐	☐	☐	☐	☐	☐
Full physical	☐	☐	☐	☐	☐	☐	☐	☐	☐	☐
DN participate	☐	☐	☐	☐	☐	☐	☐	☐	☐	☐

Date: _____ Time: _____ Setting: _____

Levels of support	Trials									
	1	2	3	4	5	6	7	8	9	10
Independent	☐	☐	☐	☐	☐	☐	☐	☐	☐	☐
Verbal prompt	☐	☐	☐	☐	☐	☐	☐	☐	☐	☐
Gestural prompt	☐	☐	☐	☐	☐	☐	☐	☐	☐	☐
Visual prompt	☐	☐	☐	☐	☐	☐	☐	☐	☐	☐
Model prompt	☐	☐	☐	☐	☐	☐	☐	☐	☐	☐
Partial physical	☐	☐	☐	☐	☐	☐	☐	☐	☐	☐
Full physical	☐	☐	☐	☐	☐	☐	☐	☐	☐	☐
DN participate	☐	☐	☐	☐	☐	☐	☐	☐	☐	☐

Date: _____ Time: _____ Setting: _____

Levels of support	Trials									
	1	2	3	4	5	6	7	8	9	10
Independent	☐	☐	☐	☐	☐	☐	☐	☐	☐	☐
Verbal prompt	☐	☐	☐	☐	☐	☐	☐	☐	☐	☐
Gestural prompt	☐	☐	☐	☐	☐	☐	☐	☐	☐	☐
Visual prompt	☐	☐	☐	☐	☐	☐	☐	☐	☐	☐
Model prompt	☐	☐	☐	☐	☐	☐	☐	☐	☐	☐
Partial physical	☐	☐	☐	☐	☐	☐	☐	☐	☐	☐
Full physical	☐	☐	☐	☐	☐	☐	☐	☐	☐	☐
DN participate	☐	☐	☐	☐	☐	☐	☐	☐	☐	☐

Date: _____ Time: _____ Setting: _____

Levels of support	Trials									
	1	2	3	4	5	6	7	8	9	10
Independent	☐	☐	☐	☐	☐	☐	☐	☐	☐	☐
Verbal prompt	☐	☐	☐	☐	☐	☐	☐	☐	☐	☐
Gestural prompt	☐	☐	☐	☐	☐	☐	☐	☐	☐	☐
Visual prompt	☐	☐	☐	☐	☐	☐	☐	☐	☐	☐
Model prompt	☐	☐	☐	☐	☐	☐	☐	☐	☐	☐
Partial physical	☐	☐	☐	☐	☐	☐	☐	☐	☐	☐
Full physical	☐	☐	☐	☐	☐	☐	☐	☐	☐	☐
DN participate	☐	☐	☐	☐	☐	☐	☐	☐	☐	☐

Date: _____ Time: _____ Setting: _____

Levels of support	Trials									
	1	2	3	4	5	6	7	8	9	10
Independent	☐	☐	☐	☐	☐	☐	☐	☐	☐	☐
Verbal prompt	☐	☐	☐	☐	☐	☐	☐	☐	☐	☐
Gestural prompt	☐	☐	☐	☐	☐	☐	☐	☐	☐	☐
Visual prompt	☐	☐	☐	☐	☐	☐	☐	☐	☐	☐
Model prompt	☐	☐	☐	☐	☐	☐	☐	☐	☐	☐
Partial physical	☐	☐	☐	☐	☐	☐	☐	☐	☐	☐
Full physical	☐	☐	☐	☐	☐	☐	☐	☐	☐	☐
DN participate	☐	☐	☐	☐	☐	☐	☐	☐	☐	☐

TOTAL

Levels of support	Days of the Week				
	M	T	W	TR	F
Independent					
Verbal prompt					
Gestural prompt					
Visual prompt					
Model prompt					
Partial physical					
Full physical					
DN participate					

FIGURE 10.15 Levels of support data collection form.

Note. DN = does not.

interval (Cooper et al., 2007; Feeley & Jones, 2012). On the other hand, in *whole interval recording*, the behavior or skill is recorded only if it occurs during the entire time interval (Cooper et al., 2007; Feeley & Jones, 2012). In *momentary time sampling*, the behavior is only recorded if it is occurring the moment the interval ends. To record data using this method of data collection, the data collection form should track the occurrence and non-occurrence of the behavior or skill (e.g., using a checkmark for occurrences and nothing for non-occurrences). When

Latency Data Collection Form

Student's name: _____ Completed by: _____ Date: _____

Behavior (or skill): _____ Behavior (or skill) definition: _____

Instructions. To use the *Latency Data Collection Form*, indicate under the *behavior* what is being observed and provide an objective, observable, and measurable definition under *Behavior definition*. Select if the data collection form will be used to observe the setting or communication partner, and the communication systems being used. Under the *setting or communication partner*, indicate the specific being observed (e.g., peers, reading center). Under the *Prompt* heading indicate the directive, task, behavior, or skill being requested to be completed. Under *Latency*, indicate when the prompt was provided (time of prompt) and when the student initiated a behavior, response, or skill (time of response). Under the *total latency* indicate the time between the prompt and response. Use the *Anecdotal notes* section for any additional information that may be relevant to the student's performance (e.g., student not feeling well).

☐ Setting Communication system:
☐ Communication partner _____

| Date | Prompt | Latency | | Total latency |
		Time of prompt	Time of response	
		:	:	:
		:	:	:
		:	:	:
		:	:	:
		:	:	:
		:	:	:
		:	:	:
		:	:	:
		:	:	:
		:	:	:
Anecdotal notes.				

FIGURE 10.16 Latency data collection form.

using time sampling, it is important to record the time of day when the recording began and ended (Alberto & Troutman, 2017). A disadvantage of time sampling is that the data may be more difficult to analyze as this method may overstate or understate the number of occurrences (Alberto & Troutman, 2017). This type of recording would be most useful for recording behaviors or skills in which the student will be using a communication system during a set time (Feeley & Jones, 2012). Figure 10.17 provides an example of a data collection form to evaluate the student using *interval recording* as the method of data collection.

Interval Recoding Data Collection Form

Student's name: Completed by: Date:

_____   _____   _____

InstructionsTo use the _Interval Recording_ _Data Collection Form,_ indicate under the _behavior_ what is being observed and provide an objective, observable, and measurable definition under _Behavior Definition._ Also indicate the communication partner, setting, type of interval (partial or whole), length of interval and observation, and the communication systems being used. Under the Intervals, indicate by using tally marks the number of times the behavior occur. Indicate the total number of tallies at under the _Total_ heading and the _Percentage_ heading to determine the percentage of time engaged in the behavior or skill (total/10 x 100). Use the anecdotal notes section for any additional information that may be relevant to the student's performance (e.g., student not feeling well).

Note. For _partial interval_ the student needs to engage in the target behavior for any length of time. As long as it is seen one time, it is recorded in the interval in which it was seen. For _whole-interval_ the student has to engage in the behavior for the entire interval in order for it to be counted as an occurrence. Intervals are currently set at 10 seconds. The dotted line is to record 5 second intervals

Behavior (or skill):   Behavior (or skill) definition:

_____

☐ Partial-interval   _____

                                        _____

☐ Whole-interval   Length of observation: Length of interval:

Setting: Communication system: Communication partner:

_____   _____   _____

		Intervals									Total	%
	1	2	3	4	5	6	7	8	9	10		
Date:												
Time:												
	1	2	3	4	5	6	7	8	9	10		
Date:												
Time:												
	1	2	3	4	5	6	7	8	9	10		
Date:												
Time:												
	1	2	3	4	5	6	7	8	9	10		
Date:												
Time:												
	1	2	3	4	5	6	7	8	9	10		
Date:												
Time:												

Anecdotal notes.

FIGURE 10.17 Interval recording data collection form.

IEP Team Questionnaire for Embedding
Augmentative and Alternative Communication into the IEP

Student: _____   Date: _____

Team members: _____

_____

The purpose of this form is to provide IEP teams with general guidelines in embedding AAC into the IEP. The goal is to support the student effectively and to accurately identify the services needed.

Instructions. IEP teams will answer *Yes* or *No* to the questions listed below. If *Yes* is selected for Questions 1-7, the IEP team may continue to the remaining questions (Questions 8-20). Questions 8-20 outline the steps to effectively embed AAC into the IEP. If *No* is answered to any of the questions under the *Pre-IEP Meeting Questions* (Q 1-7), the IEP team will need to address this *prior* to embedding AAC in the IEP (Q 8-20).

Pre-IEP Meeting Questions		Responses	
		YES	NO
Q1.	Is AAC needed to increase, maintain, or improve the student's communication (verbal or written)?	☐	☐
Q2.	Is AAC needed to increase, maintain, or improve the student's participation in classroom activities?	☐	☐
Q3.	Have the purpose and rationale of AAC strategies and services been discussed with the parents?	☐	☐
Q4.	Has the family been provided with information on AAC strategies and services?	☐	☐
Q5.	Do all IEP team members understand the purpose of using AAC practices (systems and strategies)?	☐	☐
Q6.	Have opportunity barriers been identified and discussed?	☐	☐
Q7.	Has a plan of action been outlined to decrease opportunity barriers?	☐	☐

Embedding AAC into the IEP Questions		Sections in the IEP	Responses	
			YES	NO
Q8.	Are the student's *current* communication skills outlined in the PLAAFP within the IEP (based on each level of communication competencies)?	PLAAEP	☐	☐
Q9.	Are the student's access barriers outlined in the PLAAFP within the IEP (i.e., cognitive, communication, literacy, motor, and sensory domain)?		☐	☐
Q10.	Are there goals and objectives in the IEP related to increasing the student's participation?	G&O	☐	☐
Q11.	Are there goals and objectives in the IEP that relate to enhancing the student's communication skills?		☐	☐
Q12.	Are there goals and objectives in the IEP that relate to enhancing the student's independence?		☐	☐
Q13.	Has an appropriate AAC or AT system been identified for the student? If the team answered yes, is the system: ☐ Unaided ☐ Aided: Low tech. ☐ Aided: High tech.	A&M	☐	☐
Q14.	Have the appropriate AAC strategies been identified for the student?		☐	☐
Q15.	Have the needs for AAC and AT related accommodations and modifications been discussed (e.g., written output)?		☐	☐
Q16.	Have the needs for AAC and AT related accommodations and modifications been documented in the IEP?		☐	☐
Q17.	Have AAC services been discussed?	RS	☐	☐
Q18.	Have AAC services been documented in the IEP?		☐	☐
Q19.	Have AAC training needs been discussed?		☐	☐
Q20.	Have AAC training needs been documented in the IEP?		☐	☐

FIGURE 10.18 IEP team questionnaire for embedding augmentative and alternative communication into the IEP.

Note. AAC = augmentative and alternative communication; A&M = accomodations and modifications; AT = assistive technology; G&O = goals and objectives; PLAAF = present level of academic achievement and functional performance; RS = related services; Tech. = technology.

It is important for teachers to have knowledge about the student's background and communication skills in order to work with the team to identify targeted areas for in-depth evaluation and for instructional considerations. The process of embedding AAC into the student's IEP is a challenging task, but it is a critical step in supporting, planning for, and advocating for students with CCN. To ensure the needs of students with CCN are met, IEP teams will need to continuously evaluate how the system is being implemented into the student's daily activities and the opportunities being given to the student. Furthermore, ongoing evaluation of the student's communication competencies is critical to ensure that the IEP is accurate and meets the needs of the student (Chung & Douglas, 2014). To better support and safeguard the student's IEP process, the team will need to systematically consider the student's needs (Rowland et al., 2014). One way to do so is for teams to create a checklist of questions that can guide this process. For example, the *IEP Team Questionnaire for Embedding Augmentative and Alternative Communication into the IEP* (see Figure 10.18) provides a questionnaire IEP teams can complete to ensure that all components that need to be addressed in the process are being evaluated, discussed, and embedded accurately in the student's IEP.

Key Points of Chapter 10

- Outlining the student's current communication, overall participation, and independence skills in the IEP is essential for the development of an individualized, accurate, and effective IEP.
- The student's PLAAFP sets the foundation for the IEP.
- The *AAC IEP Goal Setting Framework* helps set the stage to effectively evaluate a student with CCN's progress.
- There are five main considerations for embedding AAC into the IEP: (1) assessing the student's present level of academic achievement and functional performance, (2) setting goals, (3) identifying the system, (4) identifying opportunity barriers and services, and (5) progress monitoring.
- IEP goals and objectives for the student with CCN should be focused on the four communication competencies.
- IEP goals and objectives should be feasible, observable and measurable.
- Both access and opportunity barriers can significantly impede implementation of accurate and effective practices and instructional programs.
- There are five main data collection methods to be considered: (1) duration recording, (2) event or frequency recording, (3) latency, and (4) time sampling.
- IEP teams are responsible in collecting data to monitor the student's progress towards the annual IEP goals and short-term objectives.
- Data should be collected on student's performance on the use of different AAC systems to accurately determine the most suitable system for the student.

Additional Resources

The Dynamic AAC Goals Grid 2 (DAGG-2): www.mydynavox.com/Con
tent/resources/slp-app/Goals-Goals-Goals/the-dynamic-aac-goals-grid-
2-dagg-2.pdf

The IRIS Center

https://iris.peabody.vanderbilt.edu

National Professional Development Center on Autism Spectrum Disorders
http://autismpdc.fpg.unc.edu

References

Alberto, P., & Troutman, A. C. (2017). *Applied behavior: Analysis for teachers*. Boston, MA:
Pearson.

Assistive Technology Act, 29 U.S.C. § 3001 (2004).

Bateman, B. D., & Linden, M. A. (2012). *Better IEPs: How to develop legally correct and educa-
tionally useful programs* (5th ed.). Verona, WS: Attainment Company.

Bausch, M. E., Ault, M. J., Evmenova, A. S., & Behrmann, M. M. (2008). Going beyond
AT devices: Are AT services being considered? *Journal of Special Education Technology, 23*,
1–16. doi:10.1177/016264340802300201

Beukelman, D. R., & Mirenda, P. M. (2013). *Augmentative and alternative communication:
Supporting children and adults with complex communication needs* (4th ed.). Baltimore, MD:
Paul H. Brookes.

Blackwell, W. H., & Rosetti, Z. S. (2014). The development of individualized education
programs: Where have we been and where should we go? *SAGE Open, 4*. doi:10.1177/
2158244014530411

Bornman, J., & Murphy, J. (2006). Using the ICF in goal setting: Clinical supplication using
Talking Mats. *Disability and Rehabilitation: Assistive Technology, 1*, 145–154. doi:10.1080/
17483100612331392745

Brady, N. C., Bruce, S., Goldman, A., Erickson, K., Mineo, B., Ogletree, B. T.,. . Wilkinson,
K. (2016). Communication services and supports for individuals with severe disabilities:
Guidance for assessment and intervention. *American Journal on Intellectual and Develop-
mental Disabilities, 121*, 121–138. doi:10.1352/1944–7558–121.2.121

Bunning, K., Smith, C., Kennedy, P., & Greenham, C. (2013). Examination of the communication interface between students with severe to profound and multiple intellectual
disability and educational staff during structured teaching sessions. *Journal of Intellectual
Disability Research, 57*, 39–52. doi:10.1111/j.1365–2788.2011.01513.x

Capizzi, A. M. (2008). From assessment to annual goal: Engaging a decision-
making process in writing measurable IEPs. *Teaching Exceptional Children, 41*, 18–25.
doi:10.1177/004005990804100102

Castro, S., Pinto, A., & Simeonsson, R. J. (2014). Content analysis of Portuguese individualized education programmes for young children with autism using the ICF-CY framework. *European Early Childhood Education Research Journal, 22*, 91–104. doi:10.1080/13
50293x.2012.704303

Christle, C. A., & Yell, M. L. (2010). Individualized education programs: Legal requirements
and research findings. *Exceptionality, 18*, 109–123. doi:10.1080/09362835.2010.491740

Chung, Y.-C., Carter, E. W., & Sisco, L. G. (2012). Social interactions of students with disabilities who use argumentative and alternative communication in inclusive classrooms.

American Journal of Intellectual and Developmental Disabilities, 117, 349–367. doi:10.1352/ 1944–7558–117.5.349

Chung,Y.-C., & Douglas, K. H. (2014). Communicative competence inventory for students who use augmentative and alternative communication: A team approach. *TEACHING Exceptional Children, 47,* 56–68. doi:10.1177/0040059914534620

Cooper, J. O., Heron, T. E., & Heward, W. L. (2007). *Applied behavior analysis* (2nd ed.). New York City, NY: Pearson.

Deveney, S. L., Hoffman, L., & Cress, C. J. (2012). Communication-based assessment of developmental age for young children with developmental disabilities. *Journal of Speech Language, and Hearing Research, 55,* 695–709. doi:10.1044/1092–4388(2011/10–0148)

Downing, J. E. (2000). Augmentative communication devices: A critical aspect of assistive technology. *Journal of Special Education Technology, 15,* 35–38.

DynaVox Mayer-Johnson. (2014). *The dynamic AAC goal grid 2.* Retrieved from www. mydynavox.com/Content/resources/slp-app/Goals-Goals-Goals/the-dynamic-aac-goals-grid-2-dagg-2.pdf

Feeley, K. M., & Jones, E. A. (2012). Monitoring learner performance. In S. S. Johnston, J. Reichle, K. M. Feeley, & E. A. Jones (Eds.), *AAC strategies for individuals with moderate to severe disabilities* (pp. 183–204). Baltimore, MD: Paul H. Brookes.

Gast, D. L., & Ledford, J. R. (2014). *Single case research methodology: Applications in special education and behavioral sciences* (2nd ed.). New York, NY: Routledge.

Gilette,Y. (2009) Integrating assistive technology with augmentative communication. In G. Soto & C. Zangari (Eds.), *Practically speaking: Language, literacy, & academic development for students with AAC needs* (pp. 265–285). Baltimore, MD: Paul H. Brookes.

Granlund, M. (2013). Participation—challenges in conceptualization, measurement and intervention. *Child: Care, Health and Development, 39,* 470–473. doi:10.1111/cch.12080

Hauser, M. D. (2017). The essential and interrelated components of evidenced-based IEPs: A user's guide. *TEACHING Exceptional Children, 49,* 420–428. doi:10.1177/ 0040059916688327

Individuals with Disabilities Education Act, 20 U.S.C. § 1400 (2004).

Jones, V. L., & Hinesmon-Matthews, L. J. (2014). Effective assistive technology consideration and implications for diverse students. *Computers in the Schools: Interdisciplinary Journal of Practice, Theory, and Applied Research, 31,* 220–232. doi:10.1080/07380569.2014.932682

Karvonen, M., Wakeman, S. Y., Browder, D. M., Rogers, M. A. S., & Flowers, C. (2011). *Academic curriculum for students with significant cognitive disabilities: Special education teacher perspectives a decade after IDEA 1997.* Retrieved from ERIC database (ED521407).

Klang, N., Rowland, C., Fried-Oken, M., Steiner, S., Granlund, M., & Adolfsson, M. (2016). The content of goals in individual educational programs for students with complex communication needs. *Augmentative and Alternative Communication, 32,* 41–48. doi:10.3 109/07434618.2015.1134654

Kleinert, J. O., Harrison, E. M., Fisher, T. L., & Kleinert, H. L. (2010). "I can" and "I did:" Self-advocacy for young students with developmental disabilities. *TEACHING Exceptional Children, 43,* 16–26. doi:10.1177/004005991004300202

Kleinert, H., Towles-Reeves, E., Quenemoen, R., Thurlow, M., Fluegge, L., Weseman, L., & Kerbel, A. (2015). Where students with the most significant cognitive disabilities are taught: Implications for general curriculum access. *Exceptional Children, 81,* 312–328. doi:10.1177/0014402914563697

Light, J. (1989). Toward a definition of communicative competence for individuals using augmentative and alternative communication systems. *Augmentative and Alternative Communication, 5,* 137–144. doi:10.1080/07434618912331275126

Light, J., & McNaughton, D. (2013). Putting people first: Re-thinking the role of technology in augmentative and alternative communication intervention. *Augmentative and Alternative Communication, 29*, 299–309. doi:10.3109/07434618.2013.848935

Light, J., & McNaughton, D. (2014). Communicative competence for individuals who require augmentative and alternative communication: A new definition for a new era of communication? *Augmentative and Alternative Communication, 30*, 1–18. doi:10.3109 /07434618.2014.885080

Light, J., & McNaughton, D. (2015). Designing AAC Research and intervention to improve outcomes for individuals with complex communication needs. *Augmentative and Alternative Communication, 31*, 85–96. doi:10.3109/07434618.2015.1036458

Lund, S. K., Quach, W., Weissling, K., McKelvey, M., & Dietz, A. (2017). Assessment with children who need Augmentative and Alternative Communication (AAC): Clinical decisions of AAC specialists. *Language, Speech, and Hearing Services in Schools, 48*, 56–68. doi:10.1044/2016_LSHSS-15–0086

Lynch, S., & Adams, P. (2008). Developing standards-based individualized education program objectives for students with significant needs. *TEACHING Exceptional Children, 40*, 36–39. doi:10.1177/004005990804000303

McNaughton, D., & Bryen, D. N. (2007). AAC technologies to enhance participation and access to meaningful societal roles for adolescents and adults with developmental disabilities who require AAC. *Augmentative and Alternative Communication, 23*, 217–229. doi:10.1080/07434610701573856

Millar, D. C., Light, J. C., & Schlosser, R. W. (2006). The impact of augmentative and alternative communication intervention on the speech production of individuals with developmental disabilities: A research review. *Journal of Speech, Language, and Hearing Research, 49*, 248–264. doi:10.1044/1092–4388(2006/021)

Mirenda, P. (2014). Revisiting the mosaic of supports required for including people with severe intellectual or developmental disabilities in their communities. *Augmentative and Alternative Communication, 30*, 19–27. doi:10.3109/07434618.2013.875590

Mittler, J. (2007). Assistive technology and IDEA. In C. Warger (Ed.), *Technology integration: Providing access to the curriculum for students with disabilities.* Arlington, VA: Technology and Media Division (TAM).

Ogletree, B. T., & Pierce, H. K. (2010). AAC for individuals with severe intellectual disabilities: Ideas for nonsymbolic communicators. *Journal of Developmental and Physical Disabilities, 22*, 273–287. doi:10.1007/s10882-009-9177-1

Parette, H. P., Peterson-Karlan, G. R., Wojcik, B. W., & Bardi, N. (2007). Monitor that progress! Interpreting data trends for assistive technology decision making. *TEACHING Exceptional Children, 40*, 22–29. doi:10.1177/004005990704000103

Poppes, P., Vlasklamp, C., de Geeter, K. I., & Nakken, H. (2002). The importance of setting goals: The effect of instruction and training on the technical and intrinsic quality of goals. *European Journal of Special Needs Education, 17*, 241–250. doi:10.1080/08856250210162149

Pretti-Frontczak, K., & Bricker, D. (2000). Enhancing the quality of Individualized Education Plan (IEP) goals and objectives. *Journal of Early Intervention, 23*, 92–105. doi:10.1177/ 105381510002300204

Rowland, C. M., Quinn, E. D., & Steiner, S. A. M. (2014). Crafting high-quality IEPs for children with complex communication needs. *Communication Disorders Quarterly, 37*, 53–62. doi:10.1177/1525740114551632

Ruble, L. A., McGrew, J., Dalrymple, N., & Jung, L. A. (2010) Examining the quality of IEPs for young children with autism. *Journal of Autism and Developmental Disorders, 40*, 1459–1470. doi:10.1007/s10803-010-1003-1

Sanches-Ferreira, M., Lopes-dos-Santos, P., Alves, S., Santos, M., & Salveira-Maia, M. (2013). How individualised are the individualised education programmes (IEPs): An analysis of the contents and quality of the IEPs goals. *European Journal of Special Needs Education, 28*, 507–520. doi:10.1080/08856257.2013.830435

Schlosser, R. W., & Raghavendra, P. (2004). Evidence-based practice in augmentative and alternative communication. *Augmentative and Alternative Communication, 20*, 1–21. doi:1 0.1080/07434610310001621083

Smith, M. M. (2015). Adolescence and AAC: Intervention challenges and possible solutions. *Communication Disorders Quarterly, 36*, 112–118. doi:10.1177/1525740114539001

Therrien, M. C. S., Light, J., & Pope, L. (2016). Systematic review of the effects of interventions to promote peer interactions for children who use aided AAC. *Augmentative and Alternative Communication, 32*, 81–93. doi:10.3109/07434618.2016.1146331

Twachtman-Cullen, D., & Twachtman-Bassett, J. (2011). *The IEP from A to Z: How to create meaningful and measurable goals and objectives* (2nd ed.). San Francisco, CA: Jossey-Bass.

van der Meer, L., Sigafoos, J., O'Reilly, M. F., & Lancioni, G. E. (2011). Assessing preferences for AAC options in communication interventions for individuals with developmental disabilities: A review of the literature. *Research in Developmental Disabilities, 32*, 1422–1431. doi:10.1016/j.ridd.2011.02.003

Wehmeyer, M. L., Smith, S. J., Palmer, S. B., & Davies, D. K. (2004). Technology use by students with intellectual disabilities: An overview. *Journal of Special Education Technology, 19*, 7–21. doi:10.1177/016264340401900402

Wright, P. W. D., Wright, P. D., & O'Connor, S. W. (2010). *All about IEPs*. Hartfield, VA: Harbor House Law Press.

Zabala, J. (2005). Ready, SETT, go! Getting started with the SETT framework. *Closing the Gap, 23*, 1–3.

Zabala, J., Blunt, M., Carl, D., Davis, S., Deterding, C., Foss, T., . . . Reed, P. (2000). Quality indicators for assistive technology services in school settings. *Journal of Special Education Technology, 15*, 25–36. doi:10.1177/016264340001500403

11

IMPLEMENTING EFFECTIVE INSTRUCTIONAL PRACTICES

Communication occurs throughout the day. When planning and implementing augmentative and alternative communication (AAC) instruction, practices that can be easily embedded throughout the day and that can reinforce the goals being set are key in the success of its implementation. This chapter will describe evidence-based instructional strategies that have been recommended as effective practices for students with complex communication needs (CCN; e.g., Browder, Wood, Thompson, & Ribuffo, 2014; Gervarter et al., 2013). To set the ground for instruction and to meet the unique needs of students with CCN, Lloyd et al. (1997) suggested 14 AAC instructional principles. These principles are grounded in the belief that AAC instruction should:

(1) Be based on the premises that everyone can communicate.
(2) Keep the student with CCN as the main focus.
(3) Not be delayed or denied AAC instruction or services based on prerequisite skills.
(4) Focus on current and future skills.
(5) Not replace student's communicative behaviors that are functional.
(6) Occur concurrently with ongoing process monitoring.
(7) Be based on a team approach.
(8) Be guided by observable, measurable, and feasible goals and short-term objectives.
(9) Occur within natural settings.
(10) Plan for decreasing and eliminating opportunity and access barriers.
(11) Focus on what skill will be taught and how the skill will be taught.
(12) Be based on data-driven instructional reflection and planning.
(13) Result in positive changes and outcomes for the student with CCN.
(14) Be linked to the Law of Parsimony.

These AAC instructional principles suggest that the team not only has the responsibility to select *what* will be taught, but also *how* it will be taught and *when* will it be taught. Figure 11.1 illustrates the 14 AAC instructional principles to be used during planning and instruction. The philosophy behind this is that all components and characteristics of the planning and instruction will have an impact on the student's outcome (see Lloyd et al., 1997 for more information).

When planning for instruction for students with CCN, the challenge often faced is how to embed the communication systems into classroom activities and routines. The goal should be to decrease any barriers that may influence the integration of the communication system into the student's life. Personal factors such as knowledge and skills of the system, expectations, and personal preferences of both the students with CCN and the communication partner(s) may impact whether the AAC system is used (Smith & Connolly, 2008). As a result, it is the team's responsibility to consider these factors and the specific features of the communication system. For example, the team should consider the student's accessibility to the appropriate vocabulary, the reliability of the system, the capabilities of speech output, and anything that may have a direct impact on the student's communicative attempts (Smith & Connolly, 2008). These are essential considerations in the development of effective instructional plans and the integration of the communication system. To support the integration of the system, three main steps should be followed to ensure effective instructional programming.

Step 1. A preference assessment should be conducted to determine reinforcers. This will support the instruction by providing engaging communication opportunities and maintain the student's motivation to participate in instruction (McDonald, Battaglia, & Keane, 2015).

Step 2. The most suitable methods of instruction should be determined to better meet the needs of the student and the skills being addressed (Light & McNaughton, 2013).

Step 3. Instructional strategies that will enhance the instruction should be determined to better support the student (Browder et al., 2014; Gervarter et al., 2013).

Embedding these steps is crucial in the instruction of students with CCN. It has been reported that, in general, special education teachers initiate communication with students with special needs on average 1.62 times per minute (Brady, Herynk, & Fleming, 2010). Unfortunately, it has also been indicated that in a typical school day, teachers provide models of the use of the communication systems only two or three times per day (Barker, Akaba, Brady, & Thiemann-Bourque, 2013) and, on average, students with CCN communicate five to six times per day using their communication system (Barker et al., 2013). This clearly demonstrates the various challenges faced in the classroom setting and the need for changes to the instruction and opportunities being provided to these students. For students with CCN to be competent communicators, real-life opportunities to interact,

AAC Instructional Principles

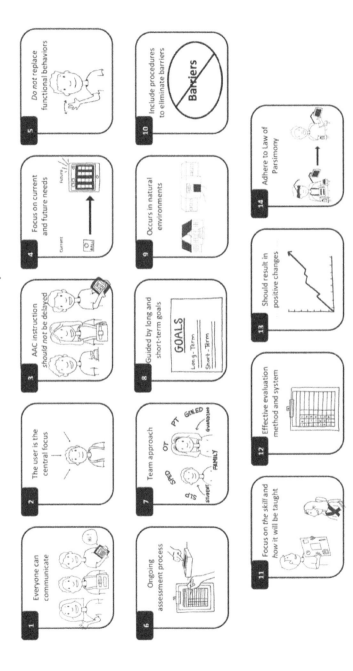

FIGURE 11.1 AAC instructional principles.

(*Source:* Lloyd et al., 1997)

communicate, participate, and socialize will be an essential part of the instruction. The instructional strategies that have been effective in teaching students with CCN are grounded in the educational and psychological field (Lloyd et al., 1997). From the merging of these fields, several evidence-based practices (EBP) have been recommended for students with CCN, including (see Table 11.1 for a summary):

(1) Identification and use of reinforcers.
(2) Aided language stimulation.
(3) Environmental arrangements.
(4) Picture exchange communication system.
(5) Prompting strategies.
(6) Peer-mediated instruction.

TABLE 11.1 Instructional Strategies

Strategy	Description or Purpose	Steps of Implementation	Online Resources
Reinforcers	To determine preferences to support engagement and motivation.	(1) Identification of reinforcers (2) Choice-based assessment (3) Reinforcer assessment	Autism Internet Modules Evidence-based instructional practices The IRIS Center
Aided language stimulation (ALS)	A communication strategy often used to model and encourage functional communication within communication interactions.	(1) Identification of skills and activities (2) Generate of interactive scripts (3) Design picture symbols and overlays (4) Provision of the communication system (5) Intervention aimed at training spontaneous, interactive communication	AAC Institute PrAACtical AAC
Environmental arrangements	Physical, communication, and social changes that are made to a setting to facilitate communication and social interactions.	*Arranging the setting* (1) Physical structure (2) Scheduling (3) Work system (4) Routine (5) Visual structure *Non-directive teaching* (1) Novelty (2) Visible but unreachable	Evidence-based instructional practices TEACCH

Strategy	Description or Purpose	Steps of Implementation	Online Resources
		Arranging the task Non–directive teaching (1) Forgetfulness (2) Violation of expectations (3) Piece by piece (4) Lack of assistance (5) Interruption or delay	
Picture exchange communication system (PECS)	An instructional program that teaches students to place symbol or symbols on a sentence strip to communicate with the communication partner.	(1) How to communicate (2) Distance and persistence (3) Picture discrimination (4) Sentence structure (5) Responsive requesting (6) Commenting	Pyramid Educational Consultants
Prompting	Prompting is a strategy to systematically assist or support students to learn and use new skills.	*Procedures* (1) Least-to-most (2) Most-to-least (3) Simultaneous (4) Graduated guidance (5) Delayed *Types* (1) Verbal prompts (2) Gestural prompts (3) Visual prompts (4) Model prompts (5) Partial physical prompts (6) Full physical prompts	Autism Internet Modules Evidence-based instructional practices The IRIS Center
Peer-mediated instruction (PMI)	Peer-mediated instructional is a strategy where the peer is taught how to interact and to communicate with students with CCN		Autism Internet Modules The IRIS Center

Identification and Use of Reinforcers

To increase student motivation during instructional activities and decrease the frequency of undesirable behaviors, *reinforcers* can be used to support the student's engagement. The use of reinforcement during instruction is a well-documented procedure (e.g., Call, Trosclair-Lasserre, Findley, Reavis, & Shillingsburg, 2012; Da Fonte et al., 2016). A *preference assessment* determines the preference of the frequency with which one selects a stimulus (e.g., games, food, praise, toys, or tangible items) from an array of options (Tullis et al., 2011). It is assumed that the stimulus selected most frequently is the most preferred compared to the other options (Stafford, Alberto, Fredrick, Heflin, & Heller, 2002). The end goal is for the identified stimulus to then be used to motivate the student to communicate or interact using his or her current communication repertoire.

An important component in this process is to effectively identify these stimuli by accurately assessing the student. Da Fonte and colleagues (2016) discussed a three-step framework to identify reinforcers by using (1) a preference inventory checklist, (2) a choice-based assessment, and (3) a reinforcer assessment (see Da Fonte et al., 2016 for details on the cómplete process). See Figure 11.2 for a reinforcer assessment form that follows the three-step framework. The goal of conducting this three-step assessment process is to accurately identify stimuli that are motivating to the student (see Figure 11.3 for a preference identification checklist to identify stimuli that can be used during assessment and instruction). The goal is to create favorable conditions to motivate the student to interaction and to elicit communicative attempts from the student.

A preference assessment should be considered the first step in any instructional program. This will allow a better understanding of the student's interests which, in turn, will set the stage for successful communicative interaction and increase the probability that a student will be interested in communicating and engaging in instructional activities. Figures 11.4 and 11.5 illustrate two examples of instructional supports where the student can be provided with an opportunity to work for his or her chosen reinforcers. Figure 11.4 offers an example of a first-then board (see Loring & Hamilton, n.d. for more details) and Figure 11.5 provides an example of a token reward system (see Matson & Boisjoli, 2009 for additional information).

Aided Language Stimulation

Aided language stimulation is a communication strategy that is grounded in modeling to encourage functional communication. It is a multi-sensory approach to receptive language learning (i.e., "hear it" and "see it"). A main characteristic of aided language stimulation is that it requires planning, as the environment must be set up so that the materials and activities are readily available to better support the communicative interaction (Goosens', 1989; Goossens', Crain, & Elder,

3-Step Preference and Reinforcer Assessment Form

Student name: Completed by: Date:

_____ _____ _____

Instructions: Complete each step in its entirety before moving to the next step. The results from Step 1 will inform the preferences to assess in Step 2 and the results from Step 2 will inform Step 3 of the top reinforcers to assess. Individual instructions for each step are found below.

Step 1-List items in which the student shows interest and check the box of the category of the item. It is crucial that multiple people in relation to the student complete the _Preference Inventory_ to gather information about preferred items across multiple environments and people. Be sure to identify the person who is providing the information.

Step 2- In the preference section, write items that were identified as highly motivating from the Step 1. The number assigned to the items must remain throughout Step 2. To record the student's response, circle the item selected under the response column. Circle _NS_ if no selection was made. Calculate the results using the formula: (number of times the item was selected/4) * 100 = %. List the percentages highest to lowest for the top 5 in the _Percentages_ section and the corresponding item in the _Rank Order_ section.

Step 3- In the _Preference 1_ section, list the 1st ranked item and in _Preference 2_ list the 2nd ranked item found in Step 2. Present the items to the student immediately after the completion of a task or task steps. In the response section, mark _Y_ for yes the student completed or performed the task or _N_ for no the student did not complete or perform the task after the item was offered. A total of five trials must be completed for each preference.

STEP 1: Preference Inventory			
Category	Items selected by...		
	Parents	Teacher	☐ Staff ☐ Related Services
Activity ☐			
Edibles ☐			
Sensory ☐			
Social ☐			
Tangible ☐			
Notes			

FIGURE 11.2 Reinforcer assessment.

Adapted from "_A 3-step reinforce identification framework: A step-by-step process_," by M. A. Da Fonte, M. C. Boesch, M. E. Edwards-Boyer, M. W. Restrepo, B. P. Bennett, & G. P. Diamond, 2016, _Education and Treatment of Children, 39_, 398–409.

1992). Aided language stimulation seeks to develop the ability to comprehend and communicate using picture symbols (Dada & Alant, 2009; Jonsson, Kristoffers-son, Ferm, & Thunberg, 2011) and communication system proficiency (Bruno & Trembath, 2006).

STEP 2: Choice-Based Assessment							
Preferences	Trials	Choices	Response			Results	
1.	1	1 and 3	1	3	NS	Percentages	Rank Order
	2	5 and 2	5	2	NS	1=	1st
2.	3	3 and 4	3	4	NS		
3.	4	5 and 1	5	1	NS	2=	2nd
	5	2 and 3	2	3	NS		
4.	6	1 and 2	1	2	NS	3=	3rd
	7	4 and 5	4	5	NS		
5.	8	2 and 4	2	4	NS	4=	4th
	9	3 and 5	3	5	NS		
	10	4 and 1	4	1	NS	5=	5th
Notes							

STEP 3: Reinforcer Assessment							
Preference 1 (rank 1st)	Trials	Response		Preference 2 (rank 2nd)	Trials	Response	
		Y	N			Y	N
	1	☐	☐		1	☐	☐
	2	☐	☐		2	☐	☐
	3	☐	☐		3	☐	☐
	4	☐	☐		4	☐	☐
	5	☐	☐		5	☐	☐
Notes							

FIGURE 11.2   (Continued)

The goal of aided language stimulation is to expose students with CCN with the same language structures and modalities they will be using to communicate. The philosophy behind this is that students with CCN are required to communicate using aided language modalities, even when the communication partner models and responds verbally (unaided). Figure 11.6 illustrates the premises of aided language stimulation by outlining the differences in exposure and learning processes of peers who are typically developing and those of students with CCN. These are based on the fact that students with CCN are often not provided the models necessary to be competent communicators. Therefore, the intent of aided language stimulation is for the communication partner to use and model the

Preference Identification Checklist

Student's name: _____   Completed by: _____   Date: _____

Instructions: Complete the *Preference Identification Checklist* by selecting items and activities that seem *motivating and interesting to the student.* It is highly suggested that at least three items from each category be identified for further evaluation. The *anecdotal notes* should be used to provide specific information on the item or activity being selected (e.g., brand, type, name).

Note. It is highly recommended that multiple people complete the *Preference Identification Checklist* in order to gather information on preferences across setting and individuals.

Activities			
☐ Books	☐ Movie	☐ Play cards	☐ Other _____
☐ Computer	☐ Mobile device	☐ Magazine	☐ Other _____
☐ Dance	☐ Play game	☐ Walk	☐ Other _____
Edibles			
☐ Candy	☐ Chocolate	☐ Drink	☐ Other _____
☐ Cereal	☐ Cookies	☐ Gummies	☐ Other _____
☐ Chips	☐ Crackers	☐ Pretzels	☐ Other _____
Sensory			
☐ Bouncing	☐ Lotion	☐ Run	☐ Other _____
☐ Brushing	☐ Music	☐ Shaving cream	☐ Other _____
☐ Jump	☐ Rocking	☐ Swing	☐ Other _____
Social			
☐ Adult attention	☐ High 5s	☐ Smile	☐ Other _____
☐ Alone time	☐ Peer attention	☐ Thumbs up	☐ Other _____
☐ Fits bump	☐ Praise	☐ Social time	☐ Other _____
Tangibles			
☐ Blanket	☐ Money	☐ Stickers	☐ Other _____
☐ Coins/token	☐ Stamps	☐ Stuffed animal	☐ Other _____
☐ Fidget	☐ Stars	☐ Toy	☐ Other _____
Anecdotal notes.			

FIGURE 11.3   Preference identification checklist.

communication systems being used by the student with CCN. That is, the communication partner points to picture symbols (e.g., photographs, line drawings) that represent words or messages being communicated (e.g., "more juice"), while simultaneously stating the words. The purpose is for the student to observe how the communication partner is communicating and imitate what the adult has modeled (Bruno & Trembath, 2006; Jonsson et al., 2011).

When implementing aided language stimulation, the context for instruction should be based on providing students with CCN with highly motivating activities and materials and with frequently occurring communicative opportunities during known routines (Beck, Stoner, & Dennis, 2009; Goossens' et al., 1992).

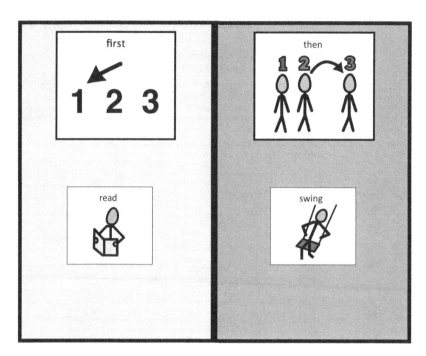

FIGURE 11.4 Example of first-then board.

FIGURE 11.5 Example of a token reward system.

Language Input and Output: Typically Developing Versus Users of AAC

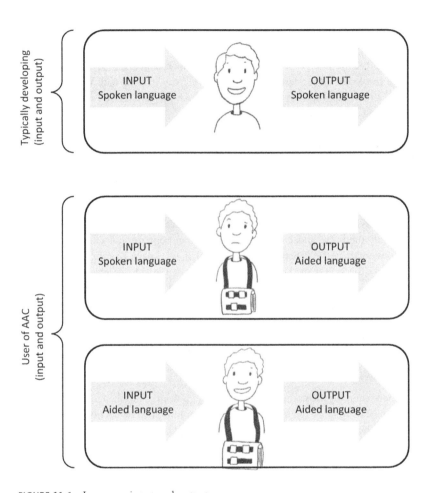

FIGURE 11.6 Language input and output.

Adapted from "*Pragmatic Organization Dynamic Display (PODD) communication books: Direct access templates* (A4/A5 paper version)," by G. Porter, 2007, Melbourne: Cerebral Palsy Education Centre.

Beyond this, there are five phases to plan for the implementation of aided language stimulation that have been suggested in the literature. These include the following:

(1) Identifying and prioritizing skills and activities (activity-based curriculum).
(2) Generating interactive scripts.

(3) Designing and creating picture symbols and overlays.
(4) Identifying, providing, and making accessible the communication system.
(5) Providing intervention aimed at training spontaneous, interactive communication.

For successful aided language stimulation implementation, the adult should be sure to obtain the student's attention, provide the student with motivating, age- and activity-appropriate vocabulary and symbols, and model, respond, and be engaging during the interaction.

Environmental Arrangements

Environmental arrangements refer to aspects of the classroom setting (or any other environment) and materials that are set up to facilitate communication and social interactions and increase task engagement. In other words, environmental arrangement is when the placement of furniture, materials, task, and activities are purposefully thought out and changed to promote appropriate and effective behaviors (Goossens et al., 1992; Schreibman et al., 2015). The goal is that these arrangements become the center of the instruction as they can lead to increased communicative and social interactions with peers and adults (Chung, Carter, & Sisco, 2012; McMillan & Renzaglia, 2014). To set up the environment for effective communicative interaction, there are two main steps: arranging the setting and arranging the task. Figure 11.7 illustrates the key considerations of environmental arrangements.

Arranging the Setting

When arranging the setting, several components need to be taken into account to set the stage to enhance the frequency of the communicative interactions and opportunities. The *Treatment and Education of Autism and Communication Related Handicapped Children* (TEACCH; see www.teacch.com for more details on this program) is an example of a program that considers environmental arrangements as their key component. TEACCH is based on an array of instructional principles and strategies that are grounded on visual information processing, social communication, attention, and executive function (Mesibov & Shea, 2010; Virues-Ortega, Julio, & Pastor-Barriuso, 2013). The goal of TEACCH is to provide students with special needs, specifically students with autism spectrum disorder, with a setting that is organized and structured in a specific manner to better support their needs. Within TEACCH, there are five principles (Mesibov & Shea, 2010; Virues-Ortega et al., 2013):

(1) *Physical structure.* The physical structure refers to the layout or classroom (home or community) set-up. That is, there are clearly defined boundaries within the setting to separate the different parts of the room (e.g., work stations, break area, transition areas).

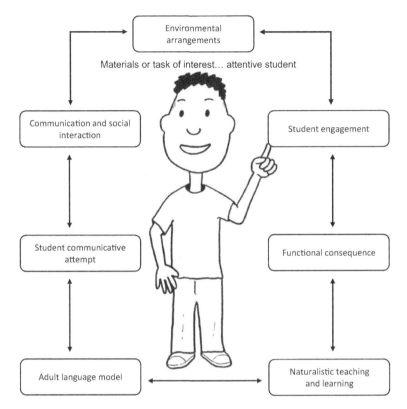

FIGURE 11.7 Environmental arrangements.

(2) *Scheduling.* Scheduling refers to the student's schedule or task to be accomplished during the day and during a specific task. That is, *what* the student is supposed to do and *when* the student is supposed to do it.

(3) *Work systems.* The work system refers to the task(s) the student is to complete. That is, it offers a beginning and an end to a task by clearly outlining *how much* is supposed to be accomplished, and *what happens* after the activity is completed. The goal of work systems is to teach the student to work independently.

(4) *Routine.* The routine refers to having a set time for the student to check the schedule and follow the set work system.

(5) *Visual structure.* The visual structure refers to visual cues provided throughout the setting with the purpose of guiding the student with the classroom organization, clarify the task(s) to be completed, provide a clear structure of the expectations of the task(s) and activities, and provide an understanding of what is expected of the student. The use of visual structure is also one that sets the stage for the other classroom structure principles.

The goal is to provide students with a structure to decrease any necessary receptive and expressive language, sequential memory, and transition barriers and to promote meaningful engagement in activities (Mesibov & Shea, 2010; Virues-Ortega et al., 2013).

Using Visual Supports

Visual supports, more specifically, the use of *visual schedules*, are an environmental arrangement strategy used to increase communication and participation opportunities through the predictability and structure of classroom routines, transitions, and activities (Spriggs, Mims, van Dijk, & Knight, 2017). The goal of visual supports is to assist students by making language and information more concrete through the use of objects, photographs, words, or line drawings (Jaime & Knowlton, 2007). Evidence supports the use of visual schedules in the classroom (e.g., Banda & Grimmett, 2008). In fact, it has been suggested that the use of visual schedules can increase students' social interactions (e.g., Machalicek et al., 2009), increase engagement in classroom activities and routines (e.g., Spriggs, Gast, & Ayers, 2007), increase transitions across and within activities (e.g., Pierce, Spriggs, Gast, & Luscre, 2013), and decrease challenging behaviors (e.g., Lequia, Machalicek, & Rispoli, 2012).

Visual supports, therefore, are a simple, inexpensive, natural, and non-intrusive way to increase students' independence and decrease dependence on adults for prompting in the classroom and in community-based settings. Visual schedules can closely resemble the day planners and digital calendars that their typical peers use every day (Spriggs et al., 2007; Spriggs, van Dijk, & Mims, 2015). There are three types of visual schedules: (1) individualized visual schedules or personal schedules; (2) visual schedules within an activity or a task analysis; and (3) classroom-wide daily schedules (e.g., calendar). Figure 11.8 offers an example of the three types of visual schedules.

Beyond these, there are two non-directive teaching strategies that can be considered when arranging the setting. The goal in embedding these non-directive teaching strategies is to provide students with communicative opportunities in their natural environment and within routine activities. These strategies include the following:

(1) *Novelty.* Novelty, or something new, refers to when the adult sets something unknown in the environment. The purpose is to offer a natural opportunity for students to ask questions, comment, and interact socially.

(2) *Visible but unreachable.* Visible but unreachable, also known as "out of reach," refers to when the adult sets preferred or needed materials out of reach of the student. The purpose is to create opportunities for the students to get the adult's attention, request the item, and engage or comment on the items needed. Items placed visibly but out of reach should be needed for an activity or should be used as novelty items.

Individualized visual schedule

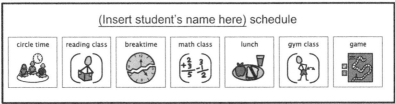

Visual schedule within an activity

Classroom-wide daily schedules

FIGURE 11.8 Examples of visual schedules.

Table 11.2 outlines non-directive teaching strategies used in naturalistic teaching and provides examples for implementation.

Arranging the Task

The goal of arranging the task is to increase communication, participation, and engagement during instructional activities. To do so, naturalistic teaching should be considered as it occurs in the natural context across the day (Alzrayer, Banda, & Koul, 2014). This offers the student with CCN a familiar context and fosters maintenance and generalization of the skills (Brady et al., 2016), while at the same time creating ground for more complex skills.

Evidence supports the notion that when students with CCN are provided with appropriate models within naturalistic contexts, they make observable gains in expressive language (Lane, Lieberman-Betz, & Gast, 2016) and receptive language skills (Drager, Light, & McNaughton, 2010), and become more active

TABLE 11.2 Non-directive Naturalistic Teaching Strategies

Strategy	Purpose	Examples
Forgetfulness	When the adult purposefully leaves out a necessary material to complete an activity with the goal of the student recognizing the need for an item and requesting it.	During art, the teacher tells the student to cut the paper but does not give the student scissors.
Interruption or delay	When the adult interrupts or delays a step in the activity.	The teacher stands in front of the soap dispenser while the student is washing his or her hands.
Lack of assistance	When the adult sets the task or activity where the student will not be able to complete the task independently.	During a cooking activity, the class is making peanut butter and jelly sandwiches. The teacher asks the student to open the jar of peanut butter knowing the student will need help to do so.
Novelty	When the adult sets something unknown in the environment.	The teacher sets a new fish tank in the classroom before the students arrive.
Piece-by-piece	When the adult purposefully only provides one piece of the needed materials at a time to complete an activity.	The teacher gives one cotton ball at a time during an art project so that the student has to ask for more.
Violation of expectations	When the adult omits a step in a task or changes an activity.	During circle time, the teachers skips the student's favorite song so that the student has to request it.
Visible but unreachable	When the adult sets preferred or needed materials out of reach of the student.	During snack, the teacher sets the student's snacks out of reach (but within sight) so the student has to ask for his or her snack.

participants in daily routines (Nunes, 2008; Nunes & Hanline, 2007). To better support students reaching these outcomes, there are five non-directive teaching strategies that can be implemented when arranging the task (see Table 11.2 for a summary on all the non-directive teaching strategies). As in arranging the setting, the goal in the implementation of these five non-directive teaching strategies is to provide the student with CCN with communicative opportunities that will enhance their overall skill development, maintenance, and generalization. Five non-directive teaching strategies that can be used in arranging the task include the following:

(1) *Forgetfulness.* Forgetfulness, also known as "omission," is when the adult withholds materials. The purpose is to offer a natural opportunity for the student to request the materials needed to complete the task. That is, in forgetfulness, the adult purposefully leaves out a necessary material to complete an activity with the goal of the student recognizing the need for an item and requesting it.
(2) *Violation of expectations.* Violation of expectations, or changes in the activity or routine, is when the adult omits a step in a task or changes an activity. The purpose is to offer a natural opportunity for students to recognize the changes, ask questions, comment about the changes or what is needed, and interact socially with peers and adults.
(3) *Piece by piece.* Piece by piece or withholding materials refers to when the adult purposefully only provides one piece at a time of the needed materials to complete an activity. The purpose is for the student to recognize that materials are missing or needed, and then have to request these in order to complete the task. In this case, materials can be withheld through omission (forgetfulness), placing pieces out of reach (visible but, unreachable), or providing materials in an inaccessible format (lack of assistance).
(4) *Lack of assistance.* Lack of assistance refers to when the adult sets the task or activity where the student will not be able to complete the task independently. The purpose is to offer a natural opportunity for students to ask for help and comment.
(5) *Interruption or delay.* Interruption or delay refers to when the adult interrupts or delays a step in a task or activity. The purpose is to offer a natural opportunity for students to request for more, comment, or interact socially.

To successfully embed and implement environmental arrangements, scripted routines are needed. *Scripted routines* are detailed procedures or pre-established steps that are embedded in everyday activities (Martinez-Santiago, Diaz-Galiano, Ureña-Lopez, & Mitkov, 2015). The purpose of these is for the student to learn the scripted routines so that the student can anticipate and predict the expectation within the activity. To support this, students will need to be taught the routine so that they can acknowledge when something is missing and make a request or comment. Students should also be provided with and allowed to have ownership in the materials to be used and the task to be completed. Providing students with choices will help increase opportunities for communication and self-determination skills (e.g., Strafford et al., 2002; Wehmeyer & Palmer, 2003). Choice-making is an interaction that involves two communication partners, in which one communication partner is the initiator (the one who offers the choices) and the other communication partner is the respondent (the one who makes a selection).

Picture Exchange Communication System

Picture Exchange Communication System (PECS) is an instructional program that uses a behavioral approach (Bondy & Frost, 1994; Frost & Bondy, 2002). The goal of PECS is to teach functional communication skills to students with CCN (Bondy & Frost, 1994; Frost & Bondy, 2002; Ganz, Simpson, & Lund, 2012). In PECS, the student is taught to place symbols on a sentence strip to communicate with the communication partner. That is, the student is taught to become an initiator in the communication interaction by exchanging a picture symbol for a desired object (McDonald et al., 2015). A main component in PECS is to teach students to gain the communication partner's attention prior to the communication interaction (Bondy & Frost, 1994; Carr & Felce, 2007; Ganz et al., 2012). To accomplish this, PECS breaks down the instruction into six phases:

> *Phase 1: How to Communicate.* In phase one, the student is taught to exchange a single symbol for items or activities that are highly motivating.
>
> *Phase 2: Distance and Persistence.* In phase two, still using a single picture, the student is taught take the symbol to the communication partner. The goal of this phase is for the student to learn to generalize the skill learned in different places, with different communication partners, and across distances.
>
> *Phase 3: Picture Discrimination.* In phase three, the student is taught to select (make a choice) from a field of two or more symbols to ask for a reinforcing item or activity. In this phase, the student begins to use a communication book.
>
> *Phase 4: Sentence Structure.* In phase four, the student is taught to communicate using short sentences (two to three symbols). The use of a sentence strip is added into this phase where the student will use a "I want" symbol, followed by a symbol of the student selection.
>
> *Phase 5: Responsive Requesting.* In phase five, the student is taught to respond to questions using their communication symbols. For example: "What do you want?"
>
> *Phase 6: Commenting.* In phase six, the student is taught to comment in response to a question from their communication partner using their communication symbols. This is when students begin to learn how to complete sentences with given statements such as: "I see" and "I feel" (among others).

A starting point in the use of PECS is for highly motivating and desirable reinforcers to be identified *prior* to its implementation. Picture symbols should then be created for all identified reinforcers. After these have been created, the adult can systematically begin the instruction following the six phases of PECS. Throughout this process both reinforcement and prompting strategies will be used to support the student's learning of communicative skills (Bondy & Frost, 1994; Frost & Bondy, 2002).

To implement PECS in the classroom, four planning and instructional considerations should be taken into account (see Frost & Bondy, 2002 for more details):

(1) *The environment.* The environment is key in the generalization of communication skills. In the early phases of PECS, the environment should be consistent and structured. The communication partner will need to plan to provide the student with communicative opportunities across environments.

(2) *The communication partners and supports.* In early phases of PECS, two adults are required to conduct the instruction. One adult will serve as the communication partner, while the other will serve as the prompter. The communication partner and the prompter should rotate to ensure generalization of the skills being taught. In later phases of PECS, the student should be provided with opportunities to communicate with various communication partners (peers and adults).

(3) *The communication system.* In the early phases of PECS, only one picture symbol should be used at a time. In early phases, a communication book is only used for the purpose of storing the picture symbols. As the student learns to receptively (and expressively) identify the picture symbols, these will be added to the communication book. The goal is to increase the student's communicative repertoire (vocabulary) to a point where the student can communicate using sentences (using a sentence strip).

(4) *Progress monitoring.* As with any other instructional strategy, data collection is essential. It is important to collect data on each phase to make data-driven decisions on the student's progress and to fade the level of prompting being provided. In PECS, it is recommended that the student reached 80% or greater proficiency for a minimum of three days before moving on to the next phase.

The overall goal is to teach the student to initiate the communicative interaction by successfully and independently making requests. After the student has achieved this, other communicative functions such as labeling, commenting, and questioning can be taught. These, in turn, will require the student to make longer communicative interactions (sentences).

Prompting Strategies

Prompting, also known as "errorless learning," is an essential instructional strategy to systematically assist or support students to learn and use new skills (Kurt & Tekin-Iftar, 2008; Mueller, Palkovic, & Maynard, 2007). Prompts are generally provided *prior to* or *as* the student attempts the skill. Prompting provides the student with the support needed to reduce incorrect responds as the student acquires new skills.

Prompting can be used with discrete, single or short duration skills, and with chained skills (e.g., Laarhover, Chandler, McNamara, & Zurita, 2010). To effectively provide prompts, there are three general steps to consider prior to implementation: (1) determine the type of prompt hierarchy to use; (2) decide how to transfer the stimulus control; and (3) implement and fade the prompting. The purpose of a prompt hierarchy is to outline the fading of the prompting, where the last level of the hierarchy is the controlling prompt (Alberto & Troutman, 2013). A *controlling prompt* is a prompt (e.g., verbal, visual, gestural, partial, or full physical) that provides the student with the least amount of support necessary to successfully achieve the skill (Alberto & Troutman, 2013).

There are several prompting procedures, including the following: (1) least-to-most or most-to-least prompting; (2) simultaneous prompting; (3) graduated guidance; and (4) delayed prompting. Within these procedures, there are also different types of prompts that are based on the level of support needed. These include verbal, gestural, visual, model, partial physical, and full physical prompting. To avoid prompt dependency, prompts should be faded as soon as the student can complete the skill and the least intrusive prompts should be considered (Allen & Cowan, 2008).

Least-to-Most and Most-to-Least Prompting

Least-to-most and most-to-least prompting are opposite hierarchies that outline the levels of support needed by the student. Least-to-most provides the student the opportunity to complete the task independently prior to providing any supports (van der Meer et al., 2013; Neitzel & Wolery, 2009b; Xin & Leonard, 2015). On the other hand, most-to-least prompting is when a student needs a high level of supports. This type of prompting hierarchy is often used when teaching a new skill (Alberto & Troutman, 2013; Xin & Leonard, 2015). The goal is that after the skill is learned, the amount of support is systematically faded to lower levels of prompting.

There are six types of prompts that can be embedded within a prompt hierarchy (Alberto & Troutman, 2013; see Figure 11.9 for a list of the types of prompting and examples of each). The selection and implementation of a prompt hierarchy should be based on the student's abilities and needs. The six types of prompting include these:

(1) *Verbal prompts.* Verbal prompts are any verbal support provided to the student, beyond the initial directive or instruction, to help the student complete the task. Verbal prompts can vary in intrusiveness based on the directive (e.g., explicit direction versus an indirect direction or hint).

(2) *Gestural prompts.* Gestural prompts refer to when the adult provides a gesture to guide the student on *what, when,* or *how* to complete a task. Gesture prompts should be direct and provide the student with sufficient information on the expectation of the demand.

(3) *Visual prompts.* Visual prompts refer to when the adult provides the student with a visual support that is exclusively used to provide a visual guide to

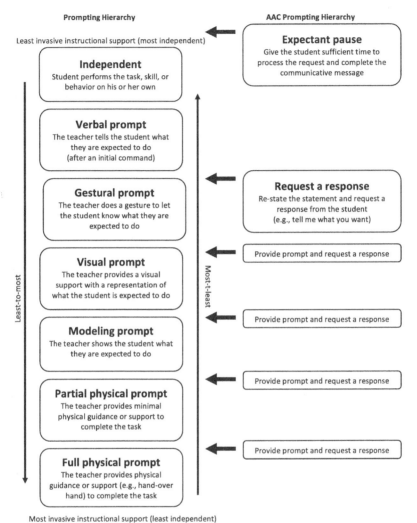

FIGURE 11.9 Prompting hierarchies.

(*Sources:* Positive AACtion, 2010; Xin & Leonard, 2015; YAACK, 1999)

complete a task. Visual prompts may include checklists, pictures symbols, schedules, or written instructions.

(4) *Model prompts.* Model prompts refer to when the adult demonstrates how to complete a task. Model prompts can vary in intrusiveness based on how much of the task is being modeled for the student (e.g., partial task or a step versus the complete task). Often, this type of prompt is only used if verbal, gestural, or visual prompts are not sufficient.

(5) *Partial physical prompts.* Partial physical prompt is when the adult provides physical assistance (minimal support) to the student in order for the student to complete the demand.

(6) *Full physical prompts.* Full physical prompt is when the adult leads a student through the task by providing full physical guidance. Full physical prompts are often used when the student is learning a new skill. The purpose is to support the student's learning of the specific motor planning behaviors to complete the task. This type of prompting (and partial physical) are also used when less restrictive prompting does not fully support the student's needs.

Simultaneous Prompting

Simultaneous prompting refers to the presentation of a directive followed by a controlling prompt (Morse & Schuster, 2004). That is, the student is provided with the least instructive prompt (i.e., the same type of prompting throughout the instruction) after a zero-second delay. This instructional strategy is often used with both discrete (e.g., single responses—requesting; Birkan, 2005) and chained skills (e.g., sequenced responses—participating in a communicative and social interaction; Maciag, Schuster, Collins, & Cooper, 2000). A unique characteristic of simultaneous prompting is that it includes two types of instructional sessions, a teaching session and a probe session (Akmanoglu, Kurt, & Kapan, 2015; Neitzel & Wolery, 2009c). In the instructional session, the task direction and the controlling prompt are delivered simultaneously. Later, in the probe sessions, the task direction is delivered without the use of any prompts. The probe sessions are used to determine whether the student is learning the skill and if fading of the prompting can occur (Alberto & Troutman, 2013).

Graduated Guidance

Graduated guidance is a strategy that uses physical guidance and fading to support the student in achieving a skill. It is based on providing the student with physical prompting to teach a skill. Graduated guidance should be used with chained skills, specifically with skills that include a physical task (e.g., morning routine). The goal is to provide the student with the controlling prompt (i.e., physical support) and then gradually remove the prompt during the instruction (Alberto & Troutman, 2013; Neitzel & Wolery, 2009a). That is, the adult changes and decreases the intensity of the prompt being provided to the student in a systematic manner (e.g., from full physical to partial physical), until the student is able to complete the task independently.

Delayed Prompting

Time delay is response-prompting procedure that focuses on systematically fading the use of prompts during instructional activities so that the student can complete the task independently (Neitzel & Wolery, 2009d). Time delay also helps prevent student's dependence on prompting (Alberto & Troutman, 2013). This is critical as dependence on adult prompting will limit the student's ability to maintain and generalize the skills learned. Progressive and constant time delay are two types of delayed prompting. In *progressive time delay*, the adult provides the directive and the controlling prompt that will guarantee the desired response simultaneously (Neitzel & Wolery, 2009d). *Constant time delay*, on the other hand, is when the time between providing the directive and the prompt remains the same (Browder et al., 2014; Neitzel & Wolery, 2009d). In both cases, the controlling prompt is the least intrusive prompt. Over time, gradually and systematically, the time between the directive and the controlling prompt will increase.

Mand-Model

Mand-model is another instructional strategy that can be easily embedded to teach communication skills, specifically requesting skills (Nigam, Schlosser, & Lloyd, 2006) and enhancing overall communication skills (Arroyo, Goldfarb, Cahill, & Schoepflin, 2010). For students with CCN, mand-model has been suggested to be an effective instructional strategy to support teaching of a new skill (Schaefer-Whitby, Lorah, Love, & Lawless, 2016). A key to the successful implementation of mand-model is for the adult to set the environment (environmental arrangements) considering what the student may want, be interested in, or motivated by. Then, when the student initiates or directs his or her attention to the item, the adult can provide the mand-modeling procedures. Figure 11.10 outlines the procedures of mand-model and offers an example of adult directives. Just as with any initial communication training, it is crucial that all initiations and requests from the student be acknowledged and honored. This will support positive and reinforcing interactions between the student and the communication partner, as well as skill generalization (Schaefer-Whitby et al., 2016).

Peer-Mediated Instruction

Peer-mediated instruction is a strategy where the communication partner (in this case the peer) is taught how to interact and to communicate with students with CCN (Kent-Walsh, Murza, Malani, & Binger, 2015; Trottier, Kamp, & Mirenda, 2011). The goal of peer-mediated instruction is for the student with CCN to have increased the social interaction opportunities within the setting. Training peers to be responsive communication partners of students with CCN can lead to social and communicative gains (Chung & Carter, 2013; Kent-Walsh et al., 2015; Thiemann-Bourque, 2012). Explicit environmental arrangements can facilitate and promote these social interactions among the student with CCN and his or her peers (Chung et al., 2012). By implementing grouping strategies, such as pairing or small groups of students, using peer-initiation training or a buddy approach, or social networking strategies, students will have opportunities to engage with

Mand- Model Procedure

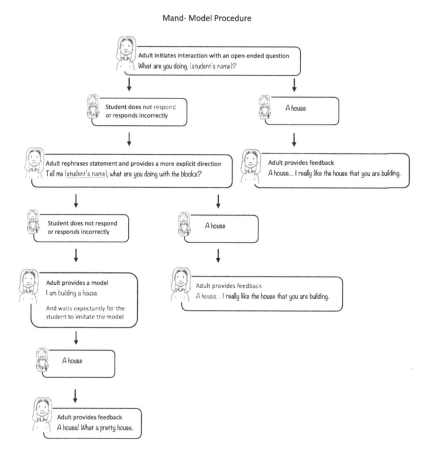

FIGURE 11.10   Mand–model procedures.

same age peers which, in turn, will enhance their communicative and social skills (Chung et al., 2012; Kent-Walsh et al., 2015).

Long-term instructional programs for students with CCN need to include relevant aspects of the student's interests, lives, environments, and communication partners (Sherlock, 2011). For successful AAC instructional planning and implementation, training is needed not only for the peers, but for all communication partners (Kent-Walsh et al., 2015). Trained communication partners will increase the success and accuracy of communication exchanges (King & Fahsl, 2012). Taking a perspective where only one instructional strategy is being considered for implementation may not be the most effective approach. In fact, it has been suggested that merging and blending different instructional strategies that aim to build and enhance the communication skill of students with CCN is the most effective approach (Brady et al., 2016). The goal should be to support students with CCN by providing:

(1) A language rich environment where motivating items can support the instruction of various language skills (identification and use of reinforcers).
(2) An environment that is set up to support the specific needs of the student (environmental arrangements).
(3) Systematic instruction in various communication skills (PECS).
(4) Expectations that are clearly outlined and modeled (aided language stimulation and prompting).
(5) Training to all communication partners (peer-mediated instruction).

By considering all these supports and providing student's with CCN an individualized communication system that meets the student's communicative needs, students with CCN will be able to develop and enhance their social and communication skills.

Key Points of Chapter 11

- Identification and use of reinforcers should be the starting point for any instructional program.
- Reinforcers should be evaluated on an ongoing basis as students' interests will change.
- Aided language stimulation is an instructional strategy that encourages functional communication through the use of modeling.
- Environmental arrangement is an instructional strategy that considers how to set up the student's environment and tasks to provide opportunities for communicative interactions.
- Arranging the setting considers the use of visual supports and two non-directive teaching strategies (novelty and visible but unreachable) to encourage communicative interactions.
- Arranging the task considers how the task will be adapted for the student to increase engagement, communication, and motivation to participate.
- In arranging the task, five non-directive teaching strategies can be considered. These include forgetfulness, interruption or delay, lack of assistance, piece by piece, and violation of expectations.
- Picture exchange communication system (PECS) is an instructional strategy that teaches students to share with a communication partner a symbol or a sentence strip to communicate.
- Picture exchange communication system (PECS) is composed of six instructional phases.
- Prompting is also known as errorless learning.

- Prompting is an instructional strategy to systematically assist or support students to learn and use new skills.
- There are a variety of prompting procedures including least-to-most, most-to least, simultaneous prompting, graduated guidance, and delayed prompting.
- There are several types of prompting, including verbal, gestural, visual, model, partial physical, and full physical.
- Peer-mediated instruction is a strategy used to train peers to be effective communication partners to students with CCN.
- Instruction of students with CCN is not one strategy fits all. It should be a blending of different intervention strategies to enhance the communication skill of students with CCN.

Additional Resources

AAC Institute
https://aacinstitute.org
Autism Internet Modules
www.autisminternetmodules.org
PrAACtical AAC
http://praacticalaac.org
Tasks Galore
www.tasksgalore.com
The IRIS Center
https://iris.peabody.vanderbilt.edu
Treatment and Education of Autistic and Communication related handicapped Children
www.teacch.com
Vanderbilt Kennedy Center: Evidence-Based Instructional Practices
http://vkc.mc.vanderbilt.edu/ebip/

References

Akmanoglu, N., Kurt, O., & Kapan, A. (2015). Comparison of simultaneous prompting and constant time delay procedures in teaching children with autism the responses to questions about personal information. *Educational Sciences: Theory and Practice, 15*, 723–737. doi:10.12738/estp.2015.3.2654

Alberto, P. A., & Troutman, A. C. (2013). *Applied behavior analysis for teachers* (9th ed.). Upper Saddle River, NJ: Pearson.

Allen, K. D., & Cowan, R. J. (2008). Naturalistic teaching procedures. In J. K. Luiselli, D. C. Russo, W. P. Christian W. P., & S. M. Wilczynski (Eds.), *Effective practices for children with autism*. New York, NY: Oxford University Press.

Alzrayer, N., Banda, D. R., & Koul, R. K. (2014). Use of iPad/iPods with individuals with autism and other developmental disabilities: A meta-analysis of communication interventions. *Review Journal of Autism and Developmental Disorders, 1*, 179–191. doi:10.1007/s40489-014-0018-5

Arroyo, C. G., Goldfarb, R., Cahill, D., & Schoepflin, J. (2010). AAC interventions: Case study of in-utero stroke. *The Journal of Speech and Language Pathology—Applied Behavior Analysis, 5*, 32–47. doi:http://dx.doi.org/10.1037/h0100260

Banda, D. R., & Grimmett, E. (2008). Enhancing social and transition behaviors of person with autism through activity schedules: A review. *Education and Training on Developmental Disabilities, 43*, 324–333. doi:www.jstor.org/stable/23879794

Barker, R. M., Akaba, S., Brady, N. C., & Thiemann-Bourque, K. (2013). Support for AAC use in preschool, and growth in language skills for young children with developmental disabilities. *Augmentative and Alternative Communication, 29*, 334–346. doi:10.3109/074 34618.2013.848933

Beck, A. R., Stoner, J. B., & Dennis, M. L. (2009). An investigation of aided language stimulation: Does it increase AAC use with adults with developmental disabilities and complex communication needs? *Augmentative and Alternative Communication, 25*, 42–54. doi:10.1080/07434610802131059

Birkan, B. (2005). Using simultaneous prompting for teaching various discrete task to students with mental retardation. *Education and Training in Developmental Disabilities, 40*, 68–79. doi:www.jstor.org/stable/23879773

Bondy, A., & Frost, L. (1994). The picture exchange communication system. *Focus on Autism and Other Developmental Disabilities, 9*, 3–19. doi:10.1177/108835769400900301

Brady, N. C., Bruce, S., Goldman, A., Erickson, K., Mineo, B., Ogletree, B. T.,. . Wilkinson, K. (2016). Communication services and supports for individuals with severe disabilities: Guidance for assessment and intervention. *American Journal on Intellectual and Developmental Disabilities, 121*, 121–138. doi:10.1352/1944–7558–121.2.121

Brady, N. C., Herynk, J. W., & Fleming, K. (2010). Communication input matters: Lesson from prelinguistic children learning to use AAC in preschool environments. *Early Childhood Services, 4*, 141–154.

Browder, D. M., Wood, L., Thompson, J., & Ribuffo, C. (2014). *Evidence-based practices for students with severe disabilities* (Document No. IC-3). Retrieved from University of Florida, Collaboration for Effective Educator, Development, Accountability, and Reform Center website http://ceedar.education.ufl.edu/tools/innovation-configurations/

Bruno, J., & Trembath, D. (2006). Use of aided language stimulation to improve syntactic performance during a weeklong intervention program. *Augmentative and Alternative Communication, 22*, 300–313. doi:10.1080/07434620600768318

Call, N. A., Trosclair-Lasserre, N. M., Findley, A. J., Reavis, A. R., & Shillingsburg, M. A. (2012). Correspondence between single versus daily preference assessment outcomes and reinforce efficacy under progressive-ratio schedules. *Journal of Applied Behavior Analysis, 45*, 763–777. doi:10.1901/jaba.2012.45–763

Carr, D., & Felce, J. (2007). The effects of PECS teaching to phase III on the communicative interactions between children with autism and their teachers. *Journal of Autism and Developmental Disorders, 37*, 724–737. doi:10.1007/s10803-006-0203-1

Chung, Y-C., & Carter, E. W. (2013). Promoting peer interactions in inclusive classrooms for students who use speech-generating devices. *Research and Practices for Person with Severe Disabilities, 38*, 94–109. doi:10.2511/027494813807714492

Chung, Y-C., Carter, E. W., & Sisco, L. G. (2012). Social interactions of students with disabilities who use augmentative and alternative communication in inclusive classrooms. *American Journal on Intellectual and Developmental Disabilities, 117*, 349–367. doi:10.1352/1944–7558–117.5.349

Da Fonte, M. A., Boesch, M. C., Edwards-Bowyer, M. E., Restrepo, M. W., Bennett, B. P., & Diamond, G. P. (2016). A three-step reinforce identification framework: A step-by-step process. *Education and Treatment of Children, 39*, 389–410. doi:10.1353/etc.2016.0017

Dada, S., & Alant, E. (2009). The effect of aided language stimulation on vocabulary acquisition in children with little or no functional speech. *American Journal of Speech-Language Pathology, 18*, 50–64. doi:10.1044/1058–0360

Drager, K., Light, J., & McNaughton, D. (2010). Effects of AAC interventions on communication and language for young children with complex communication needs. *Journal of Pediatric Rehabilitation Medicine, 3*, 303–310. doi:10.3233/PRM-2010–0141.

Frost, L., & Bondy, A. (2002). *The picture exchange communication system training manual* (2nd ed.). Cherry Hill, NJ: Pyramid Educational Consultants.

Ganz, J. B., Simpson, R. L., & Lund, E. M. (2012). The Picture Exchange Communication System (PECS): A promising method for improving communication skills of learners with autism spectrum disorders. *Education and Training in Autism and Developmental Disabilities, 47*, 176–186,

Gervarter, C., O'Reilly, M. F., Rojeski, L., Sammarco, N., Lang, R., Lancioni, G. E., & Sigafoos, J. (2013). Comparing communication systems for individuals with developmental disabilities: A review of single-case research studies. *Research in Developmental Disabilities, 34*, 4415–4432. doi:10.1016/j.ridd.2013.09.017

Goossens', C. (1989). Aided communication intervention before assessment. *Augmentative and Alternative Communication, 5*, 14–26.

Goossens', C., Crain, S., & Elder, P. (1992). *Engineering the preschool environment for interactive symbolic communication: 18 months to 5 years developmentally*. Birmingham, AL: Southeast Augmentative Communication Conference Publications Clinician Series.

Jaime, K., & Knowlton, E. (2007). Visual supports for students with behavior and cognitive challenges. *Intervention in School and Clinic, 42*, 259–270.

Jonsson, A., Kristofferson, L., Ferm, U., & Thunberg, G. (2011). The ComAlong communication boards: Parents' use and experiences of aided language stimulation. *Augmentative and Alternative Communication, 27*, 103–116. doi:10.3109/07434618.2011.580780

Kent-Walsh, J., Murza, K. A., Malani, M. D., & Binger, C. (2015). Effects of communication partner instruction on the communication of individuals using AAC: A meta-analysis. *Augmentative and Alternative Communication, 31*, 271–284. doi:10.3109/07434618.2015.1052153

King, A., & Fahsl, A. (2012). Supporting social competence in children who use augmentative and alternative communication. *TEACHING Exceptional Children, 45*, 42–49.

Kurt, O., & Tekin-İftar, E. (2008). A comparison of constant time delay and simultaneous prompting within embedded instruction on teaching leisure skills to children with autism. *Topics in Early Childhood Special Education, 28*, 53–64. doi:10.1177/0271121408316046

Laarhover, T., Chandler, L. K., McNamara, A., & Zurita, L. M. (2010). A comparison of three prompting procedures: Evaluating the effectiveness of photos, AAC, or video-based prompting for teaching cooking skills to your children with developmental disabilities. *Assistive Technology and Autism Spectrum Disorders: Research-Based Practices and Innovation in the Field*, 1–18.

Lane, J. D., Lieberman-Betz, R., & Gast, D. L. (2016). An analysis of naturalistic interventions for increasing spontaneous expressive language in children with autism spectrum disorder. *The Journal of Special Education, 50*, 49–61. doi:10.1177/0022466915614837

Lequia, J., Machalicek, W., & Rispoli, M. J. (2012). Effects of activity schedules on challenging behaviors exhibited with autism spectrum disorders: A systematic review. *Research in Autism Spectrum Disorders, 6*, 480–492. doi:10.1016/j.rasd.2011.07.008

Light, J., & McNaughton, D. (2013). Putting people first: Re-thinking the role of technology in augmentative and alternative communication intervention. *Augmentative and Alternative Communication, 29*, 299–309. doi:10.3109/07434618.2013.848935

Lloyd, L. L., Fuller, D., & Arvidson, H. (1997). *Augmentative and alternative communication: A handbook of principles and practices.* Needham Heights, MA: Allyn and Bacon.

Loring, W., & Hamilton, M. (n.d.). *Visual supports and autism spectrum disorders.* Retrieved November 28, 2017, from www.autismspeaks.org/docs/sciencedocs/atn/visual_supports.pdf

Machalicek, W., Shogren, K., Lang, R., Rispoli, M., O'Reilly, M. F., Hetlinger Franco, J., & Sigafoos, J. (2009). Increasing play and decreasing the challenging behaviors of children with autism during recess with activity schedules and task correspondence training. *Research in Autism Spectrum Disorders, 3,* 547–555. doi:10.1016/j.rasd.2008.11.003

Maciag, K. G., Schuster, J. W., Collins, B. C., & Cooper, J. T. (2000). Training adults with moderate and severe mental retardation in vocational skills using a simultaneous prompting procedure. *Education and Training in Mental Retardation and Developmental Disabilities, 35,* 306–316.

Martinez-Santiago, F., Diaz-Galiano, M. C., Ureña -Lopez, L. A., & Mitkov, R. (2015). A semantic grammar for beginning communicators. *Knowledge-Based Systems, 86,* 158–172. doi:https://doi.org/10.1016/j.knosys.2015.06.002

Matson, J. L., & Boisjoli, J. A. (2009). The token economy for children with intellectual disabilities and/or autism: A review. *Research in Developmental Disabilities, 30,* 240–248. doi:10.1016/j.ridd.2008.04.001

McDonald, M. E., Battaglia, D., & Keane, M. (2015). Using fixed interval-based prompting to increase a student's initiation of the picture exchange communication system. *Behavior Development Bulletin, 20,* 265–275. doi:10.1037/h0101315

McMillan, J. M., & Renzaglia, A. (2014). Supporting speech generating device use in the classroom. Part two: Student communication outcomes. *Journal of Special Education Technology, 29,* 49–61

Mesibov, G. B., & Shea, V. (2010). The TEACCH Program in the era of evidence-based practice. *Journal of Autism and Developmental Disorders, 40,* 570–579. doi:10.1007/s10803-009-0901-6

Morse, T. E., & Schuster, J. W. (2004). Simultaneous prompting: A review of the literature. *Education and Training in Developmental Disabilities, 39,* 153–168.

Mueller, M. M., Palkovic, C. M., & Maynard, C. S. (2007). Errorless learning: Review and practical application for teaching children with pervasive developmental disorders. *Psychology in the Schools, 44,* 691–700. doi:10.1002/pits.20258

Neitzel, J., & Wolery, M. (2009a). *Steps for implementation: Graduated guidance.* Chapel Hill, NC: National Professional Development Center on Autism Spectrum Disorders, Frank Porter Graham Child Development Institute, The University of North Carolina.

Neitzel, J., & Wolery, M. (2009b). *Steps for implementation: Least-to-most prompts.* Chapel Hill, NC: National Professional Development Center on Autism Spectrum Disorders, Frank Porter Graham Child Development Institute, The University of North Carolina.

Neitzel, J., & Wolery, M. (2009c). *Steps for implementation: Simultaneous prompting.* Chapel Hill, NC: National Professional Development Center on Autism Spectrum Disorders, Frank Porter Graham Child Development Institute, The University of North Carolina.

Neitzel, J., & Wolery, M. (2009d). *Steps for implementation: Time delay.* Chapel Hill, NC: The National Professional Development Center on Autism Spectrum Disorders, Frank Porter Graham Child Development Institute, The University of North Carolina.

Nigam, R., Schlosser, R. W., & Lloyd, L. L. (2006). Concomitant use of the matrix strategy and the mand-model procedure in teaching graphic symbol combinations. *Augmentative and Alternative Communication, 22,* 160–177. doi:10.1080/07434610600650052

Nunes, D. R. (2008). AAC interventions for autism: A research summary. *International Journal of Special Education, 23,* 17–26.

Nunes, D. R., & Hanline, M. F. (2007). Enhancing the alternative and augmentative communication through a parent-implemented naturalistic intervention. *International Journal of Disability, Development, and Education, 54*, 177–197. doi:10.1080/10349120701330495

Pierce, J. M., Spriggs, A. D., Gast, D. L., & Luscre, D. (2013). Effects of visual activity schedules on independent classroom transitions for students with autism. *International Journal of Disability, Development, and Education, 60*, 253–269. doi:10.1080/1034912X.2013.812191

Porter, G. (2007). *Pragmatic Organization Dynamic Display (PODD) communication books: Direct access templates* (A4/A5 paper version). Melbourne: Cerebral Palsy Education Centre.

Positive AACtion. (2010). *Information kit for AAC teams: Prompting techniques to support AAC use.* Retrieved November 28, 2017, from www.rockybay.org.au/wp-content/uploads/2013/04/6.4-Prompting-Techniques-to-Support-AAC-Use.pdf

Schaefer-Whitby, P. J., Lorah, E. R., Love, J., & Lawless, H. (2016). Enhancing communication and language development. In D. Zager, D. F., Cihak, & A. Stone-MacDonald (Eds)., *Autism spectrum disorders: Identification, education, and treatment.* New York, NY: Routledge.

Schreibman, L., Dawson, G., Stahmer, A. C., Landa, R., Rogers, S. J., McGee, G. G., . . . Halladay, A. (2015). Naturalistic developmental behavioral interventions: Empirically validated treatments for autism spectrum disorder. *Journal of Autism and Developmental Disorders, 45*, 2411–2428. doi:10.1007/s10803-015-2407-8

Sherlock, C. (2011). Becoming reading to use a voice output communication aid. *Journal of Assistive Technologies, 5*, 233–241. doi:10.1108/17549451111190632

Smith, M. M., & Connolly, I. (2008). Roles of aided communication: Perspectives of adults who use AAC. *Disability and Rehabilitation: Assistive Technology, 3*, 260–273. doi:10.1080/17483100802338499

Spriggs, A. D., Gast, D. L., & Ayers, K. M. (2007). Using picture activity schedule books to increase on-schedule and on-task behaviors. *Education and Training in Developmental Disabilities, 42*, 209–223.

Spriggs, A. D., Mims, P. J., van Dijk, W., & Kinght, V. F. (2017). Examination of the evidence base for using visual activity schedules with students with intellectual disability. *The Journal of Special Education, 51*, 14–26. doi:10.1177/0022466916658483

Spriggs, A. D., van Dijk, W., & Mims, P. J. (2015). How to implement visual activity schedules for students with disabilities. *DADD Online Journal, 2*, 21–34.

Stafford, A., Alberto, P., Fredrick, L., Heflin, J., & Heller, K. (2002). Preference variability and the instruction of choice making with students with severe intellectual disabilities. *Education and Training in Mental Retardation and Developmental Disorders, 37*, 70–88.

Thiemann-Bourque, K. (2012). Peer-mediated AAC instruction for young children with autism and other developmental disabilities. *Perspectives in Augmentative and Alternative Communication, 21*, 159–166. doi:10.1044/aac21.4.159

Trottier, N., Kamp, L., & Mirenda, P. (2011). Effects of peer-mediated instruction to teach use of speech-generating devices to students with autism in social game routines. *Augmentative and Alternative Communication, 27*, 26–39. doi:10.3109/07434618.2010.546810

Tullis, C. A., Cannella-Malone, H. I., Basbigill, A. R., Yeager, A., Fleming, C. V., Payne, D., & Wu, P-F. (2011). Review of the choice and preference assessment literature for individuals with severe to profound disabilities. *Education and Training in Autism and Developmental Disabilities, 46*, 576–595.

van der Meer, L., Kagohara, D., Roche, L., Sutherland, D., Balandin, S., Green, V. A., O'Reilly, M. F., Lancioni, G. E., Marschik, P. B., & Sigafoos, J. (2013). Teaching multi-step requesting and social communication to two children with autism spectrum disorders with three AAC options. *Augmentative and Alternative Communication, 29*, 222–234. doi:10.3109/07434618.2013.815801

Virues-Ortega, J., Julio, F. M., & Pastor-Barriuso, R. (2013). The TEACCH program for children and adults with autism: A meta-analysis of intervention studies. *Clinical Psychology Review, 33*, 940–953. doi:10.1016/j.cpr.2013.07.005

Wehmeyer, M. L., & Palmer, S. B. (2003). Adult outcomes for students with cognitive disabilities three-years after high school: The impact of self-determination. *Education and Training in Developmental Disabilities, 38*, 131–144.

Xin, J. F., & Leonard, D. A. (2015). Using iPads to teach communication skills of students with autism. *Journal of Autism and Developmental Disorders, 45*(12), 4154–4164. doi:10.1007/s10803-014-2266-8

YAACK. (1999). *Prompting and prompt-free strategies.* Retrieved December 28, 2017, from http://aac.unl.edu/yaack/d3.html#d3b3

12

IMPLEMENTING AUGMENTATIVE AND ALTERNATIVE COMMUNICATION ACROSS SETTINGS

During the implementation process of an educational program, there are a number of aspects to consider. One of these aspects is the implementation of the augmentative and alternative communication (AAC) system across multiple settings (i.e., activities and environments). This aspect includes the implementation of supports and strategies so the student is able to functionally use the AAC system across communication partners and settings. This chapter discusses ways to implement and integrate AAC strategies and systems across settings. Given the multifaceted process of assisting the student to learn and use the AAC system across settings, this chapter uses the SETT framework to address the critical components important in creating a solid foundation for the student.

The SETT Model

The *SETT model* (and acronym) is a framework that sets up collaboration between the Student, the Environments, the Tasks, and the Tools for the implementation of AAC systems and strategies (Zabala, 2005). This model focuses on using a student-centered, decision-making process that factors in the student's environments, tasks, and tools (Da Fonte & Boesch, 2016). Although these four areas are discussed as separate components, they should not be considered as compartmentalized areas. Rather, they are interconnected and should be considered as such. Figure 12.1 illustrates the SETT Model and it outlines key questions and considerations.

By taking a student-centered approach to planning, there is a greater likelihood that there will be numerous opportunities to practice using the AAC system across settings. Teachers and other related service providers charged with providing supports should consider using a variety of techniques to gather information about the student's daily routines throughout the school day. The following sections will

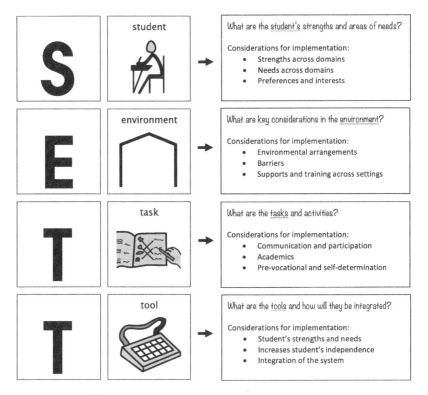

	student	What are the student's strengths and areas of needs? Considerations for implementation: • Strengths across domains • Needs across domains • Preferences and interests
S		
E	environment	What are key considerations in the environment? Considerations for implementation: • Environmental arrangements • Barriers • Supports and training across settings
T	task	What are the tasks and activities? Considerations for implementation: • Communication and participation • Academics • Pre-vocational and self-determination
T	tool	What are the tools and how will they be integrated? Considerations for implementation: • Student's strengths and needs • Increases student's independence • Integration of the system

FIGURE 12.1 SETT model.

(*Source:* Zabala, 2005) Tobii-Dynavox ©2017 Boardmaker. All rights reserved. (Used with permission.)

discuss techniques for gathering information along with guidelines for integrating the AAC system to facilitate the student's communicative competence.

Student

Given that the SETT framework is a student-centered approach, an appropriate starting point is to consider (1) the student's present levels of performance, which includes the student's strengths and needs across various domains (Chapters 5 and 6); (2) the student's preferences and interests; and (3) the long-term goals and short-term objectives to increase the student's communicative independence (see Chapter 10). This information is the foundation for creating an appropriate intervention program for the student.

The focus of instructional AAC planning should center on the student. To ensure adherence to student-centered approach, all of the student's communication partners must recognize this approach. Otherwise, it would jeopardize the rights of the student to have an instructional program that is individualized and gives the student the opportunity to obtain communicative competence (Norburn, Levin, Morgan, & Harding, 2016). Given that the overarching, long-term goal is to facilitate the student's communicative competence across multiple environments and with a variety of communication partners, the teachers and other service providers should develop a plan for how to ensure that the goals and objectives discussed in Chapter 10 are implemented. For students with AAC needs, many of the goals and objectives involve the student demonstrating a systematic and functional means of communication and vocabulary in the form of symbols and icons on the AAC system. Chapter 6 it discussed the importance of assessing the student's phonological and phonemic awareness. This information is important to create an intervention plan that focuses on developing long-term literacy skills. Likewise, individualized vocabulary directly impacts the student's ability to effectively communicate and engage in long-term learning (Weiser, 2013). While the student develops these skills, the communication partner may need some support to be able to acknowledge and better understand the student's communicative attempts. In this case, the communication partners may need a *communication dictionary* to better support these interactions (see Figure 12.2 for an example of a communication dictionary).

Vocabulary Selection

The AAC team has the critical task of determining what vocabulary should be reflected in the student's AAC system. Based on a comprehensive vocabulary assessment, the vocabulary should mirror the student's communicative needs, cultural background, and personal preferences when possible (Anderson, Balandin, & Stancliffe, 2016). Yet, creating a set of vocabulary that reflects these aspects is sometimes difficult to do. Teachers may struggle with determining if the vocabulary is appropriate for the student. It is not uncommon to find AAC systems that reflect only nouns. Yet, this is not aligned to the typical trajectory of how peers without disabilities learn and use vocabulary throughout the day (Trembath, Balandin, & Togher, 2007). The vocabulary should be functional and meaningful, which includes vocabulary that is adequate, relevant, and as diverse as possible for the student (Wilkinson & Hennig, 2007). When students are able to communicate for a variety of purposes such as requesting, commenting, rejecting, answering questions, and more, it allows the students to not only have their needs and wants met, but also to form and maintain relationships (Blackstone & Hunt-Berg, 2012; Brady et al., 2016; Light, Parsons, & Drager, 2002). Thus, a good starting point is to consider core vocabulary.

Core Vocabulary

There are commonalities across the vocabularies of individuals without disabilities. These vocabulary words are known as *core vocabulary* because they have universal application by people and are frequently used words which provide a grammatical

Communication Dictionary

Student's name: Observer's name: Date:

Instructions:
- In the left column, describe the communication modality used by the student.
- In the right column, describe the meaning of that modality as it pertains to the student communicative attempt.
- Example: Left Column: When I...stick my tongue out; Right Column: I am trying to communicate *no*.
- Add any additional notes or suggestions for response in the Additional Notes section below.

Note. All student communicative attempts should be acknowledged. Communication partner(s) should respond accordantly to the student's communicative attempt.

Communication modality: When I...	Meaning: I am trying to communicate...
Additional notes	

FIGURE 12.2   Communication dictionary.

(*Sources:* Beukelman & Mirenda, 2013; Siegel & Cress, 2002; Siegel & Wetherby, 2000)

structure within a message (Banajee, DiCarlo, & Stricklin, 2003; Lloyd, Fuller, & Arvidson, 1997). In a recent study by Deckers, Zaalen, Van Balkom, and Verhoeven (2017), they found that children with Down Syndrome and intellectual disabilities had a similar core vocabulary as their peers without disabilities.

Core vocabulary is critical for students who use AAC (McCarthy, Schwarz, & Ashworth, 2017). It is practical and should be part of an AAC system when possible, given their wide application regardless of the context in which they are used. Beukelman and Mirenda (2013) stated that finding core vocabulary lists for students who use AAC systems should be based on three potential sources: (1) the vocabulary-use patterns of others with a successful history of using their AAC systems, (2) the individual's own pattern of vocabulary use, and (3) the vocabulary of speakers or writers who communicate within similar contexts.

Based on multiple studies focused on identifying core vocabulary, there are numerous lists that show the top core vocabulary of individuals across age ranges. Banajee and colleagues (2003) found that the most commonly used words for preschool age children without disabilities were *I, no, yes/yeah, want, it, that, my, you,* and *more.* Wood, Appleget, and Hart (2016) assessed the core vocabulary words that children used in writing personal narratives in order to support the implementation of AAC systems used in literacy instruction. They found that 70% of the total words used included 191 different words that comprised of content and function words. Boenisch and Soto (2015) also evaluated the core vocabulary of typically developing children and found that 80% of their vocabulary included 200 words.

Core vocabulary should be easily accessible to students regardless of which AAC system they are using. The vocabulary is necessary to allow students to adequately interact with the world around them (McCarthy et al., 2017). For students with severe intellectual disabilities and AAC needs who may not have the capacity to learn and use a large vocabulary, it is paramount that core vocabularies are taught. Core vocabulary allows the student to communicate a larger number of messages than if relying solely on fringe vocabulary. Similarly, when students only have a limited number of symbols within their AAC system, it makes sense to include vocabulary that will maximize their communicative abilities (Snodgrass, Stoner, & Angell, 2013). Figure 12.3 displays the various functions of the core vocabulary (Deckers et al., 2017).

Fringe Vocabulary

Although core vocabulary lists are a great starting point, they do not contain all of the vocabulary needed for a student to communicate effectively across different situations. Thus, the AAC team will need to consider adding fringe vocabulary. *Fringe vocabulary* consists of words that are unique to the student based on his or her needs, interests, and situations (Lloyd et al., 1997). Although fringe vocabulary is not always similar across students, it is important to incorporate it into the student's AAC system. This allows the student to express things that are of interest and value to the student such as activities, locations, and people (Beukelman & Mirenda, 2013; Deckers et al., 2017; Dodd & Gorey, 2014; Lloyd et al., 1997; Peterson, 2017).

To create an individualized list of fringe vocabulary, the teacher or speech-language pathologist (SLP) may need to seek input from people who are familiar with the student and his or her interests. This may include asking parents, siblings, peers, and other educators. Some students with CCN may be able to provide information about their personal interests and vocabulary needs. However, this depends on the

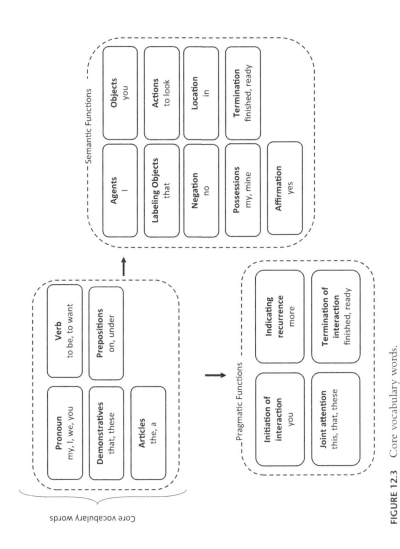

FIGURE 12.3 Core vocabulary words.

(*Sources*: Deckers et al., 2017)

student's age and current language and cognitive skills (Beukelman & Mirenda, 2013). Another method is to use environmental and ecological inventories (Lloyd et al., 1997; see Figure 12.4 for an example of an *Ecological Inventory Screening Form*). This is explicitly discussed in the "Environment" section. In essence, caution should be taken

Ecological Inventory Screening Form

Student's name:	Setting:	Date: _____
_____	_____	Time: _____
Observer's name:	Task:	☐ New task
_____	_____	☐ Routine task

Instructions: Complete the *Ecological Inventory Screening Form* by indicating the setting, task, date, time, and if it is a new or routine task. Under the *Analysis of Communication Interaction*, indicate the student's communication modality, the communicative functions used, the appropriateness of the communication, and the vocabulary used. Under the heading *Ecological Analysis*, indicate the domain, the environment, and sub-environment where the task will be completed. Under the *Skills* heading, indicate the steps needed to complete the task or activity and, under the *Levels of Participation*, indicate the level of support needed. Under the Analysis headings (communication and ecological) identify barriers, supports needed, and plan for instruction

Analysis of Communication Interaction		
Comm. modality: _____	Comm. functions: ☐ Request ☐ Reject ☐ Comments ☐ Initiates ☐ Greets ☐ Answer questions	
Appropriate of comm.: ☐ Yes ☐ No	Vocabulary used: _____ _____ _____	

Ecological Analysis		
Domain: _____	Environment: _____	Sub-environment: _____

Skills		IND	VP	GP	VIP	MP	PPP	FPP	DNP
		\multicolumn{8}{Levels of Participation}							
1									
2									
3									
4									
5									

Analysis and Plan

FIGURE 12.4 Ecological inventory screening form.

(*Sources:* Reichle, York, & Sigafoos, 1991)

Note. Comm. = communication; DNP = does not participate; FPP = full physical prompt; GP = gestural prompt; IND = independent; MP = model prompt; PPP = partial physical prompt; VP = verbal prompt; VIP = visual prompt.

to ensure the student's AAC system is not comprised solely on core or fringe vocabulary. Rather, a combination of both types of vocabularies may best serve the student as it allows for a more comprehensive range of communicative purposes.

Sight Words

There are several word lists that contain sight words that are the most frequently found in children's literature or are difficult to decode phonetically (January, Lovelace, Foster, & Ardoin, 2017). The premise of *sight words* is that if a person knows these words, then it makes it easier to focus on learning other words when reading (Ring, Barefoot, Avrit, Brown, & Black, 2012). The website www.sightwords.com provides a variety of instructional resources about three primary sets of sight words, the Dolch Sight Words, the Fry Sight Words, and the Top 150 Written Words. The Dolch Sight Words list is not only the oldest but also the most used (Sightwords, 2018). It is named after the developer, Dr. Edward Dolch, who created the list by taking the most commonly used words in children's books. There are 315 words, 95 of which are frequently used nouns. Because the Dolch list was originally created in the 1930/40s, Dr. Edward Fry revised it to include the top 1,000 commonly founds words in grades 3–9 reading material. It is estimated that a child can successfully read about 90% of the content found in various reading material if the students knows the words in the Fry Sight Words list. The Top 150 Written Words list is comprised of commonly used words based on the Word Frequency Book. Many nonnative English language learners use this word list to help them in learning English (Sightwords, 2018).

There are numerous vocabulary words to choose from based on the core, fringe, and sight word lists. Thus, it is important to focus on the student's needs when deciding which words to incorporate into the student's AAC system. Figures 12.5 and 12.6 provide a form that teachers can use to identify potential vocabulary that is specific to the student based on parts of speech (Figure 12.5) and core and fringe vocabulary (Figure 12.6). When determining how to approach vocabulary instruction, teachers should consider using a preference assessment (Snodgrass et al., 2013). Teaching vocabulary can be dependent on the student's interest. Therefore, the preference assessment helps identify the student's preferences on activities, items, and interests. Then, a subset of the vocabulary should reflect these preferences. Chapter 11 explains how to conduct this process. Regardless of how vocabulary instruction is approached, it is important to give students ample opportunities to practice using the vocabulary. Research shows explicit instruction and repeated exposure are fundamental to long-term learning (Weiser, 2013).

Environment

Given that the purpose of fitting a student with an AAC system is to assist the student in communicating within a variety of environments, an important area to consider is the student's environments. In the SETT framework, the environment

Parts of Speech Vocabulary Selection Observation Form

Student's name: Observer's name: Date:

Activity: Setting:

Instructions. To complete this form, identify the activity being observed and the setting. Under *Parts of Speech*, list the vocabulary words to be considered for the communication system for each heading. Include any additional comments or notes under the *Anecdotal notes* heading.

Part of Speech		
Pronouns	Nouns	Adjectives
Verbs	Adverbs	Interjections
Prepositions	Conjunctions	Miscellaneous
Anecdotal notes.		

FIGURE 12.5   Parts of speech vocabulary selection observation form.

is defined as any location in which the student is expected to use the AAC system (Zabala, 2005). While there are many things within the environment which may affect the student's ability to functionally use the AAC system, at a minimum, data should be gathered about the environmental arrangement, the supports needed by the student in each environment, and the roles of the student's communication partners (Erdem, 2017). This information can be gathered through an *ecological*

Core and Fringe Vocabulary Selection Observation Form

Student's name: _____ Observer's name: _____ Date: _____

Activity: _____ Setting: _____

Instructions. To complete this form, identify the activity being observed and the setting. Under *Core*, list the vocabulary words to be considered for the communication system that may be used across activities, domains, settings, and communication partners. Under *Fringe*, list the vocabulary words to be considered for the communication system that are specific to the activity. Include any additional comments or notes under the *Anecdotal notes* heading.

Core

Fringe

Anecdotal notes.

FIGURE 12.6 Core and fringe vocabulary selection observation form.

inventory, an information-gathering technique with a long history of usage. Sobsey (1987) described the ecological inventory as using four procedures:

(1) determining the most relevant and functional current and future environments (commonly grouped into domestic, leisure, community, and vocational domains), (2) identifying relevant subenvironments within those

environments, (3) identifying activities that typically occur in those subenvironments, [and] (4) determining the skills or functions required to participate in those activities.

(p. 5)

Environmental Arrangements

Once there is sufficient data about the student's environments, the next step is to arrange the environments in the manner that is most conducive for the student to learn and use the AAC system (Zabala, 2005). For students with significant and/or multiple disabilities, the AAC team may need to significantly engineer the environment in order to allow the student the best opportunity to succeed (Calculator & Black, 2009). Below are a few questions that should be considered regarding each environment (Brady et al., 2016):

(1) *Clutter.* Is the student able to move around the area without bumping into things? Is there an area to place the AAC system so that the student is able to efficiently access it? Is the work or activity area free of clutter and other potential distractors?

(2) *Environmental distractions.* Is the physical space arranged in a way to minimize distractions? Are any of the displays on the wall or around the room interfering with the student's attention?

(3) *Familiarity.* Are the environment and activities familiar to the student? Does the student appear to enjoy engaging in the activities or interacting with the individuals in the setting?

(4) *Lighting.* Are the lights too bright or too dim? Do the lights cause a glare on the AAC system, which may interfere with the student's ability to view the icons, on an SGD, or the pictures on the communication board?

(5) *Physical arrangement.* How is the furniture arranged? Where are people seated? Does it impede the student's ability to see or hear others? Can the student be seen and heard adequately?

(6) *Sound levels.* Is it too noisy? Can the student adequately hear the teacher or peers when necessary? Does the speech-generating device (SGD) require a volume adjustment?

(7) *Temperature.* Is it too hot or too cold in the setting? Is the temperature of the room interfering with the student's learning?

(8) *Training support.* Is there at least one person in the environment who is skilled in supporting the student with the AAC system (Stoner et al., 2010)?

(9) *Visual supports.* Are there visual supports within the environment? Are the visual supports adequate for their intended purpose?

All of these environmental considerations are important given that a student's rate of communicative success with others depends on the factors associated within the environment (Da Fonte & Boesch, 2016; Rowland et al., 2012). Thus, if any environmental barriers are evident, the AAC team may need to modify its location or physical structures (Beukelman & Mirenda, 2013). Otherwise, there is a greater likelihood that the student will abandon the AAC system if environmental supports are not adequate (Zabala, 2005).

Classroom

Students will spend a significant amount of time in school from the time they enter preschool or kindergarten to when they exit their secondary school placement. Thus, it is not surprising that most of the planning consideration is geared towards the classroom setting. However, planning for student instruction should also consist of training the teachers and support staff and peers to support the student's AAC use.

Kent-Walsh and McNaughton (2005) adapted an instructional model by Ellis, Deshler, Lenz, Schumaker, and Clark (1991) to create a comprehensive intervention to train communication partners. The eight stages consisted of these: (1) pretest and commitment to instructional program, (2) strategy description, (3) strategy demonstration, (4) verbal practice of strategy steps, (5) controlled practice and feedback, (6) advanced practice and feedback, (7) post-test and commitment to long-term strategy use, and (8) generalization of targeted strategy use. This training can be used to teach special education teachers to model the use of the AAC system when possible, and train others to also model for the student (Blackstone, 2008). Training should also consist of instructing teachers and other support staff to encourage communicative interactions between the student with AAC needs and his or her peers (Chung, Carter, & Sisco, 2012). Teacher training is important given that the teacher will need to address and troubleshoot as needed when any difficulties emerge in the classroom setting (Stoner et al., 2010).

Although Chapter 11 discusses a number of intervention techniques appropriate for teaching students to communicate, it is important to mention several practices that are critical to the student's communicative success in the classroom environment. Foremost, because AAC systems are usually underutilized (Kleinert et al., 2015), a concentrated effort should be made to ensure the student's AAC system is accessible at all points in time (Chung et al., 2012). This includes making sure the symbols or icons are available in the AAC system. If the student uses a high-tech AAC system, it should be fully charged and operational. The teacher should encourage the use of the AAC system by creating opportunities for the student to communicate across activities, people, and settings. Goossens, Crain, and Elder (1994) emphasized that AAC systems should be incorporated during 80% of the daily classroom activities for preschool children.

Goossens' et al. (1994) identified six phases to facilitate the use of AAC in the classroom setting:

(1) *Phase 1* was to prioritize classroom activities that can incorporate AAC use.
(2) *Phase 2* was to determine whether the student needed additional words or sentences in order to communicate during the specific activity.
(3) *Phase 3* was to identify the appropriate selection technique and system display for the given activities.
(4) *Phase 4* was to determine what display was needed for each activity and select the symbols and displays required to participate in the activity.
(5) *Phase 5* was to ensure the student had supplemental symbols.
(6) *Phase 6* was to make the displays and symbols readily accessible to the student and facilitator so that they are ready for communicative interactions.

Figures 12.7–12.9 provide examples of various environmental arrangements that take into account the phases recommended by Goossens' et al.

Home

When it comes to providing AAC support for students, there is a greater emphasis on the school setting. Yet, students who have AAC needs typically spend more time in the home setting than in other environments. This highlights the importance of the AAC team also providing adequate training and support in the home environment. It should include training the parents or other caregivers, siblings, and other family members who interact with the student on a daily basis. Alant, Champion, and Peabody (2012) reported that training and collaboration for home and school personnel was beneficial in addressing challenges that emerged during AAC instruction in both environments. Furthermore, when the family's input is sought (Bailey, Parette, Stoner, Angell, & Carroll, 2006) and when AAC training is provided to family members, there is a decreased risk of AAC system abandonment (Anderson et al., 2016). Specifically, training needs to be individualized for the family based on the type of AAC system the student uses. For low-tech AAC systems, less training may be needed than when a student has a SGD requiring customization and programming. Critical training skills for families may include learning how to add, modify, or delete vocabulary, how to customize the speech output settings (including alternative pronunciations; Anderson et al., 2016), and how to program the system in the family's native language if needed (Wilkinson & Hennig, 2007).

Fortunately, training leads to the family's increased confidence in their ability to troubleshoot at home when needed (Mandak, O'Neill, Light, & Fosco, 2017). Most importantly, training support in the home environment helps the student become more proficient in using the AAC system because additional communicative opportunities are provided in various environments (Alant et al., 2012). The training supports should not be restricted to a one-time event. Rather, continuous support and collaboration

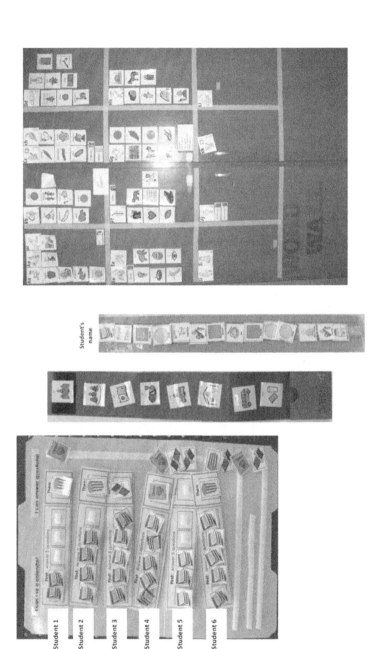

FIGURE 12.7 Examples of visual supports.

FIGURE 12.8 Examples of classroom rules and reinforcers.

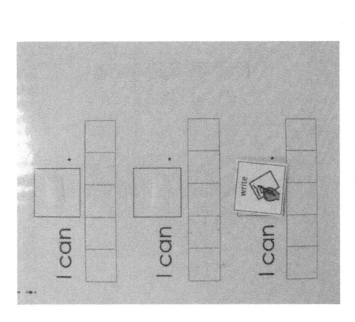

FIGURE 12.9 Examples of "I can" statements.

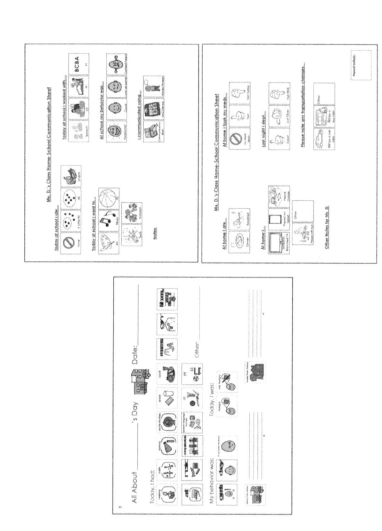

FIGURE 12.10 Examples of school–home communication.

between the home and school environments is important for greater impact (Bailey et al., 2006). Figures 12.10 provide examples of systems for communicating with parents about the student's performance at school. Communication systems such as these are useful in maintaining daily communication with the student's family.

Community

The school and home settings are two areas in which the student should be supported in using the AAC system. A third setting is in the community. The community setting is comprised of multiple locations the student will visit. These locations may include the work setting, grocery stores, movie theaters, restaurants, shopping malls, parks, recreational centers, government centers, and other venues. As with the other two settings, the supports and services should also focus on encouraging the student to communicate across a variety of people and situations. In order for this communication to occur, the use of the AAC system should be modeled during real-life situations (Ballin, Balandin, Stancliffe, & Togher, 2011). Even if the student is able to successfully use his or her AAC system in one situation, the student may not be able to do the same in a different setting. Also, being able to utilize his or her AAC system will enhance a student's sense of belonging in the community (Calculator & Black, 2009). Thus, part of the instructional plan should include training the student in various situations and environments to increase the probability of the student generalizing the skill. Chapter 11 describes a number of different instructional techniques that are appropriate for teaching students with complex communication needs (CCN) to use their AAC systems.

Tasks

In addition to ensuring the AAC system can be utilized across all environments, the AAC team will need to develop a plan to teach the student to use the AAC system across all *tasks* and activities that occur throughout the student's day. When considering Light's communication competencies (1989; Light & McNaughton, 2014), the teacher, SLP, and others responsible for teaching the student should determine how to teach the student so that he or she is linguistically, operationally, socially, and strategically competent with the AAC system during all tasks and activities. By supporting the student to be successful within each competency domain, it brings the student closer to functionally communicating under various instructional and non-instructional situations.

Academics Skills

It is recommended that special education teachers and other related service providers encourage student participation during academic tasks and activities. Participation typically entails communicating in some capacity during math, literacy, and prevocational learning activities. Because these activities will require different communication skills that are context and student specific, it is useful to first conduct a task analysis for each activity selected for instruction. A task analysis is helpful in determining what activities occur during the student's day and what the expectations are for completing the specific tasks (Snodgrass, Meadan, Ostrosky, & Cheung, 2017; see Figure 12.11 for an example *Task Analysis Observation Form*). The *Activity Participation Inventory Form* in Figure 12.12 is not only useful in identifying the steps of activities and tasks, but it also allows the teacher to determine the extent to which the student is participating (i.e., the number and type of prompts required to participate in the task) as compared to the student's peers.

Literacy

Students who require the use of AAC frequently do not get the same experiences at home as their peers without AAC needs (Rosa-Lugo & Kent-Walsh, 2008). It is not uncommon for their parents to have low expectations about their child's literacy development (Cox, Clark, Skoning, Wegner, & Muwana, 2015). As a result, reading at home is often limited for students with CCN. Shared storybook reading is important for literacy development (Rosa-Lugo & Kent-Walsh, 2008) as is integrating the AAC system into shared reading activities (Cox et al., 2015). Given these outcomes, teachers and families should provide ample opportunities to engage in literacy activities as well as provide support for using the AAC system during these activities (Rosa-Lugo & Kent-Walsh, 2008).

Phonological and phonemic awareness are critical in acquiring reading skills (National Institute of Child Health and Human Development—NICHHD, 2000). Specific skills include letter-sound correspondence, decoding, fluency, word recognition, and word comprehension, among others skills (NICHHD, 2000). Thus, it is important to address these skills through literacy interventions. A study by Benedek-Wood, McNaughton, and Light (2016) showed that young children with autism and limited speech were able to successfully learn letter-sound correspondence after intervention. If the student with CCN needs to acquire letter-sound correspondence, it is recommended that instruction begin with the letters most frequently used such as a, *m*, *t*, and *s* (Carnine, Silbert, Kame'enui, & Tarver, 2010). It is also best if the instruction is done separately for letters that sound similar (e.g., *t* and *d*) and look similar (e.g., *m* and *n*) (Carnine et al., 2010; Light & McNaughton, 2009).

Fluency in reading can be difficult for students with disabilities. However, with appropriate instruction, it is possible for students to gain reading fluency. Bradford, Shippen, Alberto, Houchins, and Flores (2006) were able to teach decoding skills to students with moderate intellectual impairments. The students achieved fluency through the acquisition of letter-sound correspondence, sounding out words, sound blending, decoding irregularly spelled words, sentence reading, and 2nd grade level short passage reading.

Task Analysis Observation Form

Student's name: _____ Setting: _____ Activity: _____

Observer's name: _____ Date: _____ Time: _____

Instructions: Complete the *Task Analysis Observation Form* by selecting the setting, activity, date, and time. Under the *Steps* heading, indicate the steps needed to complete the task or activity and, under the *Levels of Participation*, check the prompting level the student needs to complete the task. Under the heading *Instructional Factors*, indicate the grouping within the activity, how the student accesses the materials or task being presented, and any additional specific environmental considerations.

STEPS	IND	VP	GP	VIP	MP	PPP	FPP	DNP
								LEVELS OF PARTICIPATION
1	☐	☐	☐	☐	☐	☐	☐	☐
2	☐	☐	☐	☐	☐	☐	☐	☐
3	☐	☐	☐	☐	☐	☐	☐	☐
4	☐	☐	☐	☐	☐	☐	☐	☐
5	☐	☐	☐	☐	☐	☐	☐	☐
6	☐	☐	☐	☐	☐	☐	☐	☐
7	☐	☐	☐	☐	☐	☐	☐	☐
8	☐	☐	☐	☐	☐	☐	☐	☐
9	☐	☐	☐	☐	☐	☐	☐	☐
10	☐	☐	☐	☐	☐	☐	☐	☐

Instructional Factors

Grouping

☐ Large group ☐ Small group ☐ Centers ☐ One-on-one ☐ Independent work

Access

☐ Original format

☐ Accommodations ➜ ☐ Timing ☐ Format ☐ Presentation

☐ Modifications ➜ ☐ Level ☐ Content ☐ Performance criteria

☐ Adaptations ➜ ☐ Materials ☐ Set-up ☐ Device/system

Other: _____ _____

Environment

☐ Lighting ☐ Acoustic ☐ Scent ☐ Positioning ☐ Time of the day

FIGURE 12.11 Task analysis observation form.

Adapted from "*Choosing outcomes and accommodations for children* (3rd ed.)," by M. F. Giangreco, M. F., C. J. Cloninger, and V. S. Iverson, 2011, Paul H. Brookes.

Note. DNP = does not participate; FPP = full physical prompt; GP = gestural prompt; IND = independent; MP = model prompt; PPP = partial physical prompt; VP = verbal prompt; VIP = visual prompt.

Although students with CCN may have difficulty in decoding, research shows that, with intervention, they can successfully learn to decode words. Ahlgrim-Delzell, Browder, and Wood (2014) implemented a treatment package consisting of time delay, prompting procedures, and a speech-generating device to evaluate its effects on several phonics skills (e.g., phoneme identification, phoneme blending, and phoneme blending with picture referents) of students with intellectual and speech impairments. Data indicated skill acquisition for all of the participants. In terms of decoding, the participants were able to decode common words as well as words related to the stories used in the study. In another study led by Ahlgrim-Delzell (Ahlgrim-Delzell et al., 2016), participants with developmental disabilities

Activity Participation Screening Inventory

Student's name: _____ Setting: _____ Date: _____

Time: _____

Observer's name: _____ Task: _____ ☐ New task

☐ Routine task

Instructions: Complete the *Activity Participation Screening Inventory* by selecting setting, task, date, and time. During the observation of the student (S), select a target peer (P) to whom the student will be compared during the task. Under the *Task* heading, indicate the steps needed to complete the task or activity. Under the *Levels of Participation*, indicate the student's and peer's level of support needs (prompting level) to complete the task. Under the heading *Discrepancy*, indicate if there is any discrepancy between the two students.

Task		IND	VP	GP	VIP	MP	PPP	FPP	DNP	YES	NO
		Levels of Participation								Discrepancy	
1	S	☐	☐	☐	☐	☐	☐	☐	☐	☐	☐
	P	☐	☐	☐	☐	☐	☐	☐	☐		
2	S	☐	☐	☐	☐	☐	☐	☐	☐	☐	☐
	P	☐	☐	☐	☐	☐	☐	☐	☐		
3	S	☐	☐	☐	☐	☐	☐	☐	☐	☐	☐
	P	☐	☐	☐	☐	☐	☐	☐	☐		
4	S	☐	☐	☐	☐	☐	☐	☐	☐	☐	☐
	P	☐	☐	☐	☐	☐	☐	☐	☐		
5	S	☐	☐	☐	☐	☐	☐	☐	☐	☐	☐
	P	☐	☐	☐	☐	☐	☐	☐	☐		
6	S	☐	☐	☐	☐	☐	☐	☐	☐	☐	☐
	P	☐	☐	☐	☐	☐	☐	☐	☐		
7	S	☐	☐	☐	☐	☐	☐	☐	☐	☐	☐
	P	☐	☐	☐	☐	☐	☐	☐	☐		
8	S	☐	☐	☐	☐	☐	☐	☐	☐	☐	☐
	P	☐	☐	☐	☐	☐	☐	☐	☐		
9	S	☐	☐	☐	☐	☐	☐	☐	☐	☐	☐
	P	☐	☐	☐	☐	☐	☐	☐	☐		
10	S	☐	☐	☐	☐	☐	☐	☐	☐	☐	☐
	P	☐	☐	☐	☐	☐	☐	☐	☐		

FIGURE 12.12   Activity participation inventory form.

(*Sources:* Blackstien-Adler, 2003; Beukelman & Mirenda, 2013)

Note. DNP = does not participate; FPP = full physical prompt; GP = gestural prompt; IND = independent; MP = model prompt; PPP = partial physical prompt; VP = verbal prompt; VIP = visual prompt.

and no functional speech were taught a variety of skills such as segmenting, decoding, sight word recognition, and comprehension of short passages. These skills were taught via a phonics-based reading curriculum (treatment group) or sight word instruction (control group). For participants in the treatment group, the decoding skills resulted in a large effect. These results show that students with CCN can learn decoding skills when provided with the appropriate instructional program.

Furthermore, instruction should focus on providing students with repeated practice in reading text and paired reading in addition to developing decoding skills and text comprehension (Light & McNaughton, 2013). The ability to comprehend text requires a multitude of skills by the student. Foremost, it requires the student to understand the word by sight. Although this may sound like a simple task, it requires decoding skills as well as the ability to retrieve the meaning of the text within the context of the passage while also linking it to personal knowledge (Beukelman & Mirenda, 2013). Figure 12.13 shows an example of a reading activity in which the student requires text comprehension. Although the activity includes picture symbols, the student also needs to derive meaning from the embedded text.

For teachers looking to adopt comprehensive literacy curricula specific to students with severe disabilities, the *MEville to WEville Early Literacy and Communication Program* (AbleNet, 2013; ablenetinc.com) is designed for this population. The curriculum is aligned to the Common Core and other widely used standards. The MEville to WEville program focuses on emergent literacy and communication skills given the unique needs of students with CCN and severe disabilities. This curriculum is also unique in that it is designed to incorporate AAC systems. It comes prepackaged with several communication devices, device overlays, and switches (see Figure 12.14). Another research-based literacy curriculum is the *Early Literacy Skills Builder* (Browder, Gibbs, Ahlgrim-Delzell, Courtade, & Lee, 2016; www.attainmentcompany.com). For students with AAC needs, it can be combined with the *Early Literacy Communication Package* (Attainment, 2016). This communication package includes a communication device and device overlays. The curriculum is also aligned to the Common Core and other state and national standards for students in grades K–5.

During literacy instruction, teachers will also need to ensure that a student's AAC system is set up to facilitate shared stories (Lee, 2012). Other teaching strategies to encourage literacy learning for students with AAC needs include scaffolding, direct instruction, and shared book reading. Additionally, teachers are highly encouraged to adapt literacy-based activities in order to include students who use AAC (Machalicek et al., 2009). Figures 12.15 through 12.17 show various adapted books and expanding instructional activities.

Math Skills

Engaging in math activities is not typically viewed as a communication activity, particularly for students who use AAC systems. However, math skills are important in helping the student become independent in many areas of daily living. Math concepts such as number identification, basic number operations, and problem solving can be useful during shopping activities, meal preparation, and participating in other daily life activities. For students with AAC systems, engaging in any of these activities will likely require the students to access their AAC systems. There are several commercially available math curricula. One curriculum

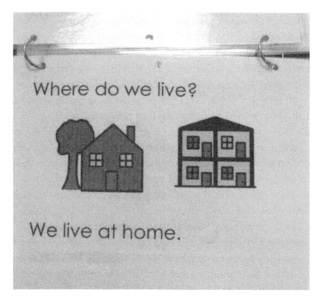

FIGURE 12.13   Example of text comprehension.

designed to teach math to students with severe developmental disabilities, including AAC needs, is Equals Mathematics by AbleNet (www.ablenetinc.com). It is a comprehensive, K–12 grade standards-based program with some research to show its effectiveness (AbleNet, 2016). The curriculum covers content from pre-readiness math skills (e.g., cause-effect, attention, everyday patterns), numbers, math operations, and measurement, to more advanced skills such as algebra and geometry. It also integrates problem solving within the context of school, home, and community settings (AbleNet, 2017; see Figure 12.18). Figure 12.19 shows examples of visual supports for math skill instruction.

Teacher's Guide with
over 200 lessons

45 printed vocabulary cards

3 elementary and 3 secondary
themed books to support
vocabulary and lessons

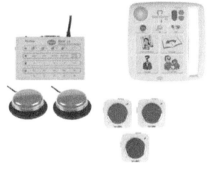

Assistive Technology Kit with QuickTalker 7
and printed overlay, TalkingBrix, and Hitch 2.0
computer switch interface with
2 Jelly Bean switches

Online Members Only Portal
available 24/7 with access to
additonal resources

FIGURE 12.14 Meville to Weville Literacy Curriculum.

(Reprinted with permission from Ablenet®.)

Prevocational Skills

A major component of educating students with severe disabilities and AAC needs
is teaching prevocational skills to increase functional daily living skills. Prevocational skills can include a variety of areas such as self-help skills, recreation/leisure
skills, choice-making skills, safety skills, and following instructions and rules. For
many students without disabilities, learning these prevocational skills occurs without a lot of dedicated time devoted to only prevocational skills. These skills are
learned in naturalistic situations and by observing others. Yet, the same learning
process does not occur for students with severe disabilities who often have AAC
needs. Instead, teachers and family members should provide specific prevocational
skills training across multiple environments, activities, and tasks. Otherwise, students with severe disabilities will have difficulty generalizing these skills if training
only occurs in one setting or if the opportunities to practice these skills are spo-
radic (Maag, 2018). As part of the prevocational skills training, special education

Answering 'wh' questions (Diamond, 2016)

Our community (Diamond, 2016)

FIGURE 12.15 Examples of teacher-created storybooks.

Brown bear, brown bear, what do you see?
(Martin & Carle, 1967)

The cat and the hat
(Dr. Seuss, 1957)

Chicka chicka boom boom
(Martin & Archambault, 1989)

FIGURE 12.16 Examples of teacher-adapted commercially available storybooks.

Froggy goes to school
(London, 1996)

Brown bear, brown bear, what do you see?
(Martin & Carle, 1967)

FIGURE 12.17 Examples of storybook interaction activities.

Equals Mathematics

Equals PreK

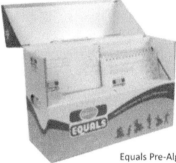

Equals Pre-Algebra and Pre-Geometry

FIGURE 12.18 *Equals Math Curriculum.*
(Reprinted with permission from Ablenet©.)

teachers should focus on supporting the use of the student's AAC system. This provides additional opportunities for the student to communicate. Many prevocational skills can be incorporated into other academic teaching or they can be embedded into daily routine activities. Figures 12.20 through 12.23 provide examples of classroom supports that can be used to encourage concept learning and prevocational skills such as independent work tasks and work stations, song and book choice-making, and leisure centers.

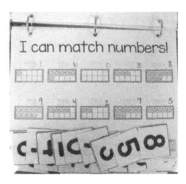

FIGURE 12.19   Examples of math concepts visual support activities.

Tools

The final component of the SETT framework involves the tools to assist the student in gaining communicative competence with the AAC system. Zabala (2005) stressed that the tools not only include the technologies such as the AAC systems, but also the strategies and services. Although it may be tempting to see which tools are already in place and then branch out from there, it is best to identify the student's needs first and then decide what tools and services are necessary to address the needs.

Identifying an AAC system is not a quick process. A comprehensive assessment involves a thorough evaluation of the student's present level of performance as well as personal preferences among other things. The selection of the AAC system is one of the last components of the selection process. The focus of the AAC team should be to determine which features the student needs from an AAC system instead of trying to identify specific devices or systems (Bonnet, 2015). While there are a lot of AAC system features to consider, listed below are a few features the AAC team should evaluate:

(1) *System display.* Can the student see the system sufficiently to use it? Is the display adequate for different environments? Is the system big or small enough?
(2) *Symbol organization.* What type of symbol organization is most suitable for the student? Can the symbols in the system be arranged in this manner?

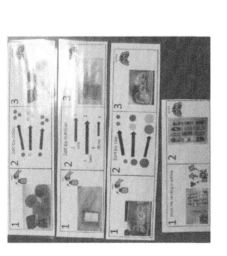

Student's name

FIGURE 12.20 Examples of work stations and task analyses.

Tobii–Dynavox ©2017 Boardmaker. All rights reserved. (Used with permission.) Representations from G. Diamond and C. Douthwaite classrooms and classroom materials (used with permission).

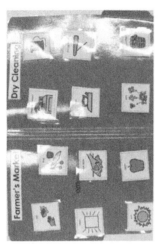

FIGURE 12.21 Examples of adapted activities.

FIGURE 12.22 Examples of concept learning activities.

Tobii-Dynavox ©2017 Boardmaker. All rights reserved. (Used with permission.) Representations from G. Diamond and C. Douthwaite classrooms and classroom materials (used with permission).

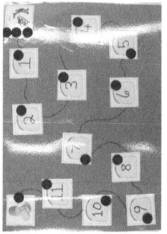
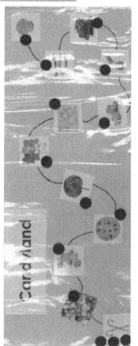

FIGURE 12.23 Examples of adapted games.

(3) *Vocabulary.* How many symbols can the system hold? Is it sufficient for the needs of the student? Can the vocabulary be customized? Is it relatively easy for the teacher or family to add, delete, or customize the symbols?

(4) *Symbol size.* What size of symbols does the student need? Can the symbols be customized to the specifications needed?

(5) *Speech capabilities.* Does the student need speech output? Is the volume sufficient for the student and communication partners to hear? Does the system allow for programming in other languages?

(6) *Portability.* How heavy is the system? Can the student transport it independently? Are there options to make the system more portable (e.g., backpack, wheelchair mount, system stands)?

(7) *Accessibility.* Can the student use direct selection with the system? If not, can it be accessed via switches, eye gaze system, etc.? Does the student need additional apparatuses to access this system (e.g., keyguard or a case with a handle)? Does the system require the use of a facilitator?

(8) *Internet capability.* Does the student need internet capability for accessing specific online software or programs?

After identifying a suitable AAC system for the student as described in Chapters 7, 8, and 9, the services for teaching the student to use the system should be identified. Services can include the training for the student on using the AAC system as well as training the communication partners (e.g., peers, teachers, and family members) how to model the use of the AAC system, how to engage in communicative exchanges, how to respond to the student and, in general, how to support the student to communicate successfully. This training is important given that a student's willingness to use the AAC system is higher when it is novel to the student. Thus, after some time, the student may need additional support to encourage continued AAC use (Stoner et al., 2010). Furthermore, the student's ability to communicate across settings increases when AAC training is provided in naturalistic environments and situations (Brady et al., 2016). Refer to the previous sections ("Student," "Environment," and "Tasks") for additional information about training needs.

The final step in the process is to monitor the student's progress to determine if the AAC system and intervention supports are increasing the student's communication skills. Progress monitoring is not a one-day or one-week process. Instead, it should be a continuous and ongoing process given that the student's abilities and needs will likely change with time. If the student is not making progress towards his or her goals and objectives, it is important to determine why progress is not occurring. The AAC team will need to examine if changes to the AAC system are warranted or if the AAC services and supports need to be revisited.

Overall, the goal of the SETT framework is to provide students with CCN the optimal opportunity to become successful communicators. To accomplish this goal, it requires the AAC team to address the student's needs by developing a comprehensive plan. This plan begins with identifying the student's needs using a transdisciplinary team approach and concludes with ongoing progress monitoring to ensure that the student's needs are continuing to be best addressed with the current educational program. When a student is able to communicate independently with multiple communication partners across environments and situations, it gives the student a sense of independence and belonging (Calculator & Black, 2009); helps facilitate interpersonal relationships with family, peers, and others (Dodd, Schaefer, & Rothbart, 2015); and encourages inclusion in the community (Brady et al., 2016).

Key Points for Chapter 12

- The SETT model stands for "Student, Environment, Tasks, and Tools" and is a framework used for implementation of AAC intervention.
- "Student" means that the intervention will be student-centered or individualized.
- "Environment" means that the AAC system will be implemented across all environments the student will be in, including the classroom, home, and in the community.
- "Tasks" means that the AAC system will be utilized for all activities in which the student will participate.
- "Tools" include the AAC system itself and all of the intervention components necessary for implementation.

Additional Resources

Assistive Technology
www.assistedtechnology.weebly.com
National Institute for Literacy: What Content-Areas Teachers Should Know About Adolescent Literacy
https://lincs.ed.gov/publications/pdf/adolescent_literacy07.pdf
Read Write Think
www.readwritethink.org
The Meadows Center for Preventing Educational Risk
www.meadowscenter.org
Sharing the SETT Framework
www.joyzabala.com

References

Ahlgrim-Delzell, L., Browder, D., & Wood, L. (2014). Effects of systematic instruction and an augmentative communication device on phonics skills acquisition for students with moderate intellectual disability who are nonverbal. *Education and Training in Autism and Developmental Disabilities, 49*, 517–532.

Ahlgrim-Delzell, L., Browder, D., Wood, L., Stranger, C., Preston, A., & Kemp-Inman, A. (2016). Systematic instruction of phonics skills using an iPad for students with developmental disabilities who are AAC users. *The Journal of Special Education, 50,* 86–97. doi:10.1177/002466915622140

Alant, E., Champion, A., & Peabody, E. C. (2012). Exploring interagency collaboration in AAC intervention. *Communication Disorders Quarterly, 34,* 172–183. doi:10.1177/1525740112455432

Anderson, K. L., Balandin, S., & Stancliffe, R. J. (2016). "It's got to be more than that." Parents and speech-language pathologists discuss training content for families with a new speech generating device. *Disability and Rehabilitation: Assistive Technology, 11,* 375–384. doi:10.3109/17483107.2014.967314

Bailey, R. L., Parette, H. P., Stoner, J. B., Angell, M. E., & Carroll, K. (2006). Family members' perceptions of augmentative and alternative communication device use. *Language, Speech, and Hearing Services in Schools, 37,* 50. doi:10.1044/0161–1461(2006/006)

Ballin, L., Balandin, S., Stancliffe, R. J., & Togher, L. (2011). Speech-language pathologists' views on mentoring by people who use speech generating devices. *International Journal of Speech-Language Pathology, 13,* 446–457. doi:10.3109/17549507.2011.522254

Banajee, M., DiCarlo, C., & Stricklin, S. (2003). Core vocabulary determination for toddlers. *Augmentative and Alternative Communication, 19,* 67–73. doi:10.1080/074346103000112034

Benedek-Wood, E., McNaughton, D., & Light, J. (2016). Instruction in letter-sound correspondences for children with autism and limited speech. *Topics in Early Childhood Special Education, 36,* 43–54. doi:10.1177/0271121415593497

Beukelman, D. R., & Mirenda, P. (2013). *Augmentative and alternative communication: Supporting children and adults with complex communication needs* (4th ed.). Baltimore, MD: Paul H. Brookes.

Blackstone, S. (2008). AAC in today's classrooms. *Augmentative Communication News, 20*(4), Retrieved from www.augcominc.com/newsletters/index.cfm/newsletter_50.pdf

Blackstone, S., & Hunt-Berg, M. (2012). *Social networks: A communication inventory of individuals with complex communication needs and their communication partners* (4th ed.). Baltimore, MD: Paul H. Brookes.

Boenisch, J., & Soto, G. (2015). The oral core vocabulary of typically developing English-speaking school-aged children: Implications for AAC practice. *Augmentative and Alternative Communication, 31,* 77–84. doi:10.3109/07434618.2014.1001521

Bonnet, L. K. (2015). SETTing up successful AAC use. *ASHA Leader, 20,* 34–36. doi:10.1044/leader.scm.20072015.34

Bradford, S., Shippen, M. E., Alberto, P., Houchins, D. E., & Flores, M. (2006). Using systematic instruction to teach decoding skills to middle school students with moderate intellectual disabilities. *Education and Training in Developmental Disabilities, 414,* 333–343.

Brady, N. C., Bruce, S., Goldman, A., Erickson, K., Mineo, B., Ogletree, B. T., ... Wilkinson, K. (2016). Communication services and supports for individuals with severe disabilities: Guidance for assessment and intervention. *American Journal of Intellectual and Developmental Disabilities, 121,* 121–138. doi:10.1352/1944–7558–121.2.121

Browder, D., Gibbs, S., Ahlgrim-Delzell, L., Courtade, G., & Lee, A. (2016). *Early literacy skills builder.* Verona, WI: Attainment.

Calculator, S. N., & Black, T. (2009). Validation of an inventory of best practices in the provision of augmentative and alternative communication services to students with severe disabilities in general education classrooms. *American Journal of Speech- Language Pathology, 18,* 329–342. doi:10.1044/1058–0360(2009/08–0065)

Carnine, D. W., Silbert, J., Kame'enui, E. J., & Tarver, S. G. (2010). *Direct instruction reading* (5th ed.). Upper Saddle River, NJ: Prentice Hall.

Chung, Y-C., Carter, E. W., & Sisco, L. G. (2012). A systematic review of interventions to increase peer interactions for students with complex communication challenges. *Research and Practice for Persons with Severe Disabilities, 37,* 271–287. doi:10.2511/027494813805327304

Cox, A. S., Clark, D. M., Skoning, S. N., Wegner, T. M., & Muwana, F. C. (2015). The effects of home-based literacy activities on the communication of students with severe speech and motor impairments. *Exceptionality Education International, 25,* 33–54.

Da Fonte, M. A., & Boesch, M. C. (2016). Recommended augmentative and alternative communication competencies for special education teachers. *Journal of International Special Needs Education, 19,* 47–58. doi:10.9782/2159–4341–19.2.47

Deckers, S. R. J. M., Zaalen, Y. V., Van Balkom, H. V., & Verhoeven, L. (2017). Core vocabulary of young children with Down syndrome. *Augmentative and Alternative Communication, 33,* 77–86. doi:10.1080/07434618.2017.1293730

Dodd, J. L., & Gorey, M. (2014). AAC intervention as an immersion model. *Communication Disorders Quarterly, 35,* 103–107. doi:10.1177/1525740113504242

Dodd, J., Schaefer, A., & Rothbart, A. (2015). Conducting an augmentative and alternative communication assessment as a school-based speech-language pathologist: A collaborative experience. *Perspectives on School-Based Issues, 16,* 105.

Ellis, E., Deshler, D., Lenz, B., Schumaker, J., & Clark, F. (1991). An instructional model for teaching learning strategies. *Focus on Exceptional Children, 23*(6), 1–24.

Erdem, R. (2017). Students with special educational needs and assistive technologies: A literature review. *The Turkish Online Journal of Educational Technology, 16,* 128–146.

Goossens, C., Crain, S., & Elder, P. (1994). *Communication displays for engineered preschool environments: Book I.* Solana Beach, CA: Mayer-Johnson.

January, S. A., Lovelace, M. E., Foster, T. E., & Ardoin, S. P. (2017). A comparison of two flashcard interventions for teaching sight words to early readers. *Journal of Behavioral Education, 26,* 151–168. doi:10.1007/s10864-016-9263-2

Kent-Walsh, J., & McNaughton, D. (2005). Communication partner instruction in AAC: Present practices and future directions. *Augmentative and Alternative Communication, 21,* 195–204. doi:10.1080/07434610400006646

Kleinert, H., Towles-Reeves, E., Quenemoen, R., Thurlow, M., Fluegge, L., Weseman, L., & Kerbel, A. (2015). Where students with the most significant cognitive disabilities are taught: Implications for general curriculum access. *Exceptional Children, 81,* 312–328. doi:10.1177/0014402914563697

Lee, C. D. (2012). *Teaching students with severe and multiple disabilities: The implementation of shared stories.* (Doctoral dissertation). Retrieved from http://acumen.lib.ua.edu/u0015/0000001/0001069/u0015_0000001_0001069.pdf

Light, J. C., & McNaughton, D. B. (2009). Addressing the literacy demands of the curriculum for conventional and more advanced readers and writers who require AAC. In C. Zangari & G. Soto (Eds.), *Practically speaking: Language, literacy, and academic development for students with AAC needs* (pp. 217–246). Baltimore, MD: Paul H. Brookes.

Light, J. C., & McNaughton, D. B. (2013). Literacy intervention for individuals with complex communication needs. In D. Beukelman & P. Mirenda (Eds.), *Augmentative and alternative communication: Supporting children and adults with complex communication needs* (pp. 309–351). Baltimore, MD: Paul H. Brookes.

Light, J. C., & McNaughton, D. B. (2014). Communicative competence for individuals who require augmentative and alternative communication: A new definition for a new era of communication? *Augmentative and Alternative Communication, 30*, 1–18. doi:10.3109/07434618.2014.885080

Light, J. C., Parsons, A. R., & Drager, K. (2002). "There's more to life than cookies": Developing interactions for social closeness with beginning communicators who use AAC. In J. Reichle, D. R. Beukelman, & J. C. Light (Eds.), *Exemplary practices for beginning communicators* (pp. 187–218). Baltimore, MD: Paul H. Brookes.

Lloyd, L., Fuller, D., & Arvidson, H. (1997). *Augmentative and alternative communication: Handbook of principles and practices.* Needham Heights, MA: Allyn and Bacon.

Maag, J. W. (2018). *Behavior management: From theoretical implications to practical applications* (3rd ed.). Boston, MA: Cengage Learning.

Machalicek, W., Sanford, A., Lang, R., Rispoli, M., Molfenter, N., & Mbeseha, M. K. (2009). Literacy interventions for students with physical and developmental disabilities who use aided AAC devices: A systematic review. *Journal of Developmental and Physical Disabilities, 22*, 219–240. doi:10.1007/s10882-009-9175-3

Mandak, K., O'Neill, T., Light, J., & Fosco, G. M. (2017). Bridging the gap from values to actions: A family systems framework for family-centered AAC services. *Augmentative and Alternative Communication, 33*, 32–41. doi:10.1080/07434618.2016.1271453

McCarthy, J. H., Schwarz, I., & Ashworth, M. (2017). The availability and accessibility of basic concept vocabulary in AAC software: A preliminary study. *Augmentative and Alternative Communication, 33*, 131–138. doi:10.1080/07434618.2017.1332685

National Institute of Child Health and Human Development. (2000). *Report of the national reading panel: Teaching children to read: An evidence-based assessment of the scientific research literature on reading and its implications for reading instruction—Reports of the subgroups* (NIH Publication No. 00–4754). Washington, DC: U.S. Government Printing Office.

Norburn, K., Levin, A., Morgan, S., & Harding, C. (2016). A survey of augmentative and alternative communication used in an inner city special school. *British Journal of Special Education, 43*, 289–306. doi:10.1111/1467–8578.12142

Peterson, H. (2017). *The success of an aided language stimulation training video for communication partners working with children with autism spectrum disorders* (Honors research project). University of Akron, Ohio.

Reichle, J., York, J., & Sigafoos, J. (1991). *Implementing augmentative and alternative communication: Strategies for learners with severe disabilities.* Baltimore, MD: Paul H. Brooks.

Ring, J. J., Barefoot, L. C., Avrit, K. J., Brown, S. A., & Black, J. L. (2012). Reading fluency instruction for students at risk for reading failure. *Remedial and Special Education, 34*, 102–112. doi:10.1177/0741932511435175

Rosa-Lugo, L. I., & Kent-Walsh, J. (2008). Effects of parent instruction on communicative turns of Latino children using augmentative and alternative communication during storybook reading. *Communication Disorders Quarterly, 30*, 49–61. doi:10.1177/1525740108320353

Rowland, C., Fried-Oken, M., Steiner, S. A. M., Lollar, D., Phelps, R., Simeonsson, R. J., & Granlund, M. (2012). Developing the ICF-CY for AAC profile and code set for children who rely on AAC. *Augmentative and Alternative Communication, 28*, 21–32. doi:10.3109/07434618.2012.654510

Siegel, E., & Wetherby, A. (2000). Nonsymbolic communication. In M. Snell & F. Brown (Eds.), *Instruction of students with severe disabilities* (5th ed., pp. 409–451). Columbus, OH: Merrill.

Siegel, E. B., & Cress, C. J. (2002). Overview of the emergence of early AAC behaviors: Progression from communicative to symbolic skills. In J. Reichle, D. Beukelman, & J. Light (Eds.), *Implementing an augmentative communication system: Exemplary strategies for beginning communicators* (pp. 219–272). Baltimore, MD: Paul H. Brookes.

Sightwords. (2018). *Overview of sight words.* Retrieved from www.sightwords.com/sightwords/

Snodgrass, M. R., Meadan, H., Ostrosky, M. M., & Cheung, W. C. (2017). One step at a time: Using task analysis to teach skills. *Early Childhood Education Journal, 45,* 855–862. doi:10.1007/s10643-017-0838-x

Snodgrass, M. R., Stoner, J. B., & Angell, M. E. (2013). Teaching conceptually referenced core vocabulary for initial augmentative and alternative communication. *Augmentative and Alternative Communication, 29,* 322–333. doi:10.3109/07434618.2013.848932

Sobsey, D. (1987). *Ecological inventory exemplars.* Edmonton, Canada: University of Alberta.

Stoner, J. B., Angell, M. E., & Bailey, R. L. (2010). Implementing augmentative and alternative communication in inclusive educational settings: A case study. *Augmentative and Alternative Communication, 26,* 122–135. doi:10.3109/07434618.2010.481092

Trembath, D., Balandin, S., & Togher, L. (2007). Vocabulary selection for Australian children who use augmentative and alternative communication. *Journal of Intellectual and Developmental Disability, 32,* 291–301. doi:10.1080/13668250701689298

Weiser, B. L. (2013). Ameliorating reading disabilities early: Examining an effective encoding and decoding prevention instruction model. *Learning Disability Quarterly, 36,* 161–177. doi:10.1177/0731948712450017

Wilkinson, K. M., & Hennig, S. (2007). The state of research and practice in augmentative and alternative communication for children with developmental/intellectual disabilities. *Mental Retardation and Developmental Disabilities Research Reviews, 13,* 58–69. doi:10.1002/mrdd.20133

Wood, C., Appleget, A., & Hart, S. (2016). Core vocabulary in written personal narratives of school-age children. *Augmentative and Alternative Communication, 32,* 199–207. doi:10.1080/07434618.2016.1216596

Zabala, J. S. (2005). Ready, SETT, go! Getting started with the SETT framework. *Closing the Gap, 23,* 1–3.

GLOSSARY

AAC expert. An individual who is a researcher, university personnel, or administrator who trains pre-service professionals, acts as a leader, and develops programs and policies about AAC.

AAC facilitator. An individual who provides support to an individual who uses AAC with new or unfamiliar people.

AAC finder. An individual who identifies a communication need of an individual that is currently unmet and who may benefit from the use of AAC system.

AAC specialist. An individual who can conduct assessments and provide direct instruction in AAC strategies, as well as serve as consultant to outline or implement AAC services.

Access barriers. The individuals' limitations to gather information from their environment in order to develop more abstract skills due to their cognitive, communicative, literacy, motoric, and sensory skills.

Activity grid display. A display in which symbols are organized into separate pages by events, activities, or routines.

Aided communication. Forms of communication (e.g., pictures symbols, devices) used outside of the individual's body to communicate.

Aided communication systems. Communication systems that require the use of specific tools or equipment such as low and high technology. These can include, but are not limited to, picture symbols and speech-generating devices.

Aided language stimulation. A multi-sensory instructional strategy that is based on adult model to encourage the development of functional communication skills from the student.

Alphabet-based systems. Systems that include spelling, word prediction, and letter codes that assist the student in generating messages.

Annual goals. Describes a measurable and observable skill that has been set based on the student's current educational and functional performance. The components of an annual goal include the following: measurable and observable behavior or skill, mastery level, consistency, and timeframe to be attained.

Attitude barriers. A type of opportunity barrier. Attitude barriers are imposed by the communication partner on the student with CCN, based on the communication partner's feelings and beliefs towards the student with CCN.

Circular scanning. A scanning technique in which the items are arranged in a circle and are scanned clockwise.

Clustered display. A display that organizes symbols based on the internal color of the symbol.

Cognitive skills. Refers to the individual's ability to respond to stimuli in his or her environment. This includes skills such as having awareness to stimuli, communicative intent, memory for learning, understanding of symbolic representation, and word knowledge.

Collaboration. When a group of individuals (e.g., general educators, special educators, related service providers, families, among others) work together to create a comprehensive education experience for the student.

Communication. The process of sharing information among two or more people with the purpose of social closeness.

Communication Bill of Rights. Fifteen communicative rights of all individuals, including those with severe disabilities.

Communication competence. The ability to communicate effectively by understanding *who* you are communicating with, *how* you will communicate, *what* you are communicating, and *when* you are communicating. This includes linguistic, operational, social, and strategic competencies (see each competency for definition).

Communication dictionary. A document that outlines and describes the student's current communicative behaviors to provide unfamiliar communication partners with a clear description of the individual's communication attempts.

Communication disorder. An impairment of the speech and/or language systems.

Communication partner. The individual with whom the person is trying to communicate.

Complex communication needs (CCN). A broad term used to describe someone who is unable to communicate in a functional manner (e.g., using verbal, written communication).

Comprehension. The ability to understand the message being communicated by a speaker during a communicative interaction.

Condition. Any given materials, setting, people, or situation which is presented in which the goal will be completed.

Constant time delay. The pre-determined time period between a directive and the delivery of a prompt that remains the same throughout the instruction.

Consultation. When a specialist is asked to provide opinions and shares information of how to improve outcomes based on his or her own experience and expertise.

Content. Domain of language that refers to the words a speaker uses and their meaning (e.g., semantics, lexicon).

Controlling prompts. The least intrusive prompt or amount of support needed from the student to successfully complete a skill or task.

Conventional gestures. Gestures that are specific to an object, person, or event in a specific context and may be culturally bound.

Core vocabulary. Vocabulary that is utilized most frequently by a range of speakers.

Criteria. The level set on the annual goal or objectives (short-term or lesson) to which the student must perform the set skill in order to show mastery.

Dedicated devices. Devices whose sole purpose is to serve a communicative function.

Deictic gestures. Gestures that are content specific. These gestures are used to call attention to an object or event (e.g., pointing to a ball on the playground).

Dictation. An adult reads a word(s) aloud and the student writes it using the AAC system or a writing utensil.

Digitized speech. Natural speech that has been digitally recorded and stored in an SGD.

Direct selection. Any selection technique in which an individual selects a symbol with no intermediate steps (e.g., using a hand/finger, eye gaze, etc.).

Distributed display. A display in which symbols are placed in a grid format and dispersed without any specific sequence.

Duration recording. Measuring the length of time a behavior or skill occurs.

Dynamic display. Displays that span across multiple pages that require the user to navigate between the pages when selecting symbols.

Ecological inventory. Gathering information about the student's environment in order to evaluate what communication partners, activities, and barriers that may exist in each environment.

Environment. All of the settings in which the device will be used.

Environmental arrangements. The placement of furniture, materials, task, and activities that have been purposefully changed to promote and facilitate communication, social interactions, motivation, and task engagement.

Event recording. Measures the number of occurrences of a behavior or skill during in a selected period of time.

Expressive communication. Words and messages (e.g., use of symbols) communicated through either verbal or nonverbal communication to a communication partner (e.g., ability to request).

Expressive language. Refers to language "output"; describes an individual's ability to generate or produce ideas to be communicated through gestures, facial expressions, vocalizations, words, phrases, or sentences.

Eye gaze. Intentional movement of the eyes towards a joint item or symbol to communicate a desired action, object, or activity to the communicative partner.

Feature matching. Determining what AAC system will best fit the needs of a student with CCN by evaluating the skills required to operate each AAC system and what skills the student possesses.

Fine motor skills. Describes small movements made by fingers, hands, tongue, feet, or toes (e.g., pinching, cutting, writing).

Fluency. Refers to an individual's ability to decode and comprehend text with consistency, speed, and accuracy.

Form. Domain of language that refers to the structure of words, sentences, and sounds that convey meaning (e.g., syntax, phonology, and morphology).

Forms of communication (forms). Refers to the type or style of a communication behavior (e.g., gestures versus facial expressions versus vocalizations).

Formulation. The process of pulling your thoughts together before you communicate. Through pulling the thoughts together, they become organized and are ready to be communicated.

Fringe vocabulary. Vocabulary words that are unique to the individual student and are based on his or her needs, interests, and situations.

Full physical prompts. Physical guidance that leads a student through the task.

Functions of communication (function). Refers to motivation of communication form (e.g., to accept, comment, agree, disagree, or reject).

Gestural prompts. Gestures to guide the student on what, when, or how to complete a task.

Gestures. A physical communicative attempt that signifies some idea, meaning, or desire (e.g., dancing to let the communication partner know that you want to listen to music).

Graduated guidance. The use of physical prompt (or guidance) that is used with chained skills and is then faded to support a student's ability to learn how to complete a task independently.

Gross motor skills. Describes the large movements made by the body (e.g., kicking, running, crawling, jumping).

Group scanning. A scanning technique in which the student selects a group of symbols first and then symbols are presented one at a time.

High technology. Systems that include electronic or powered components, including voice output, speech-generating; they can store and retrieve messages.

Hybrid display. A display that includes the combination of visual scenes and one of the grid layouts.

Iconic gestures. Gestures that are specific to an object, person, or event in a specific context and can be understood across cultures.

Iconicity. How closely a symbol (e.g., line drawings, manual sign, photograph) represents the point of reference.

Indirect selection. Any selection technique in which an individual utilizes intermediate steps in making a selection, such as scanning through symbols.

Individualized educational program. Written document created by a team to outline a student's current level of performance, areas of strengths and needs, annual goals and short-term objectives, and other supports need for a student to be successful in the educational environment.

Intelligibility. The ability of a communication attempt to be understood and to convey a message.

Intentional communication. Term describing the communicative skills and cognitive ability to purposefully make a plan to communicate a message and the ability to execute.

Intentional communicators. The ability of an individual to communicate purposefully with a communication partner.

Interdisciplinary team. A team of specialists from multiple areas of expertise that share information with other specialists, but only perform tasks related specifically to their area of expertise when working with a student.

Interval recording. Measures approximate occurrences of behavior by identifying a time period and dividing it into equal intervals, typically in seconds.

Knowledge barriers. A type of opportunity barrier. Knowledge barriers are imposed by the communication partner on the student with CCN based on the communication partner's lack of understanding of the characteristics of students with CCN, AAC strategies, and AAC systems.

Language. A system of conventional spoken or written symbols (e.g., manual sign, words) used by people within a shared community to express thoughts (e.g., wants and needs) and feelings.

Latency recording. Measures the length of time it takes for a student to respond to a given stimulus, prompt, or request.

Letter–sound correspondence. The ability to know that a sound is represented by a letter and that a letter represents a sound.

Lexicon. A term used for vocabulary.

Linear scanning. A scanning technique in which items are arranged in rows and columns and the student scans one row/column at a time.

Linguistic competence. The understanding of the language spoken in one's environment, as well as the language being represented by the communication system (receptively and expressively).

Literacy. The ability to read and write.

Literacy skills. Describes an individual's ability to navigate written language across five components: phonemic awareness, phonics, vocabulary, fluency, and text comprehension (see each component for individual definitions).

Low technology. Communication technology that does not require any electricity or batteries to operate (e.g., objects, graphic symbols, communication boards, communication books, written words).

Manual sign. Using one's hands to communicate, to supplement, or aid spoken language with predefined communicative parameters. The most commonly used form of manual sign is American Sign Language.

Model prompts. A demonstration of how to complete a task.

Momentary time sampling. When a behavior is recorded at the end of a time interval.

Morphology. The organization of words (e.g., adding /ed/ to *walk* to form *walked*).

Motor complexity. The individual's ability to produce manual signs that require directional movement, contact between hands, and proximity to the user's body.

Multidisciplinary team. A team of specialists from multiple areas of expertise who independently provide instruction when working with a student, with no sharing of goal setting and implementation among specialist when working with a student.

Non-dedicated devices. Devices that are multipurpose and can serve functions other than communication.

Non-symbolic communication. Describes communication efforts that are pre-intentional and related to awareness of the environment; communication at the non-symbolic level has no linguistic code attached to messages being conveyed; communication partners are often left to determine the meaning of what is being conveyed.

Nonverbal communication. A communicative means to express a message that does not include language (e.g., body movement, facial expressions, touch, space, and distance).

Opaque symbol. A symbol that is not connected to its referent in any way and requires training to decode.

Operational competence. Possessing the knowledge and skills needed to use, understand, and operate all modes of communication effectively (aided and unaided).

Opportunity barriers. Barriers imposed on the student with CCN by the environment; that is, by the communication partners and overall structures within a setting. There are five different types of opportunity barriers.

Partial interval recording. A type of interval recording that tracks behavior if it occurs at any point during the pre-determined interval.

Partial physical prompts. A physical assistance or support that helps the student complete a task.

Partner-assisted scanning. A form of scanning in which the facilitator scans symbols by pointing or speaking (or using tactile methods) and the student selects the desired symbol.

Phoneme blending. Blending the individual phonemes in a word to decode a word. For example, the sounds /k/, /a/, and /t/ blend to form the word "cat."

Phoneme segmentation. Identifying the individual phonemes in a word. For example, the word "cat" can be segmented into the phonemes /k/, /a/, and /t/.

Phonemic awareness. The ability to hear and manipulate the individual sounds within words.

Phonics. Refers to an individual's ability to recognize phonemes in the written form.

Phonological awareness. Refers to the individual's ability to hear and distinguish individual sounds in oral speech and language.

Phonology. Combining sounds to form syllables and words (e.g., /m/ and /ay/ to create *may*).

Picture exchange communication system (PECS). An instructional program that uses a behavioral approach to teach functional communication skills to students by exchanging a symbol and placing symbols on a sentence strip.

Policy barriers. A type of opportunity barrier. Policy barriers are imposed by the communication partner on the student with CCN based on policies that may impact the student (overall outcomes), the services being provided, and the potential systems to be used.

Practice barriers. A type of opportunity barrier. Practice barriers are imposed by the communication partner on the student with CCN based on procedures and practices that are not policies, yet, are common practices within the setting.

Pragmatic organization dynamic display. A display in which vocabulary is organized into pages by category or topic. The student may have the same vocabulary across multiple pages. The purpose of this display is to focus on social language in multiple environments.

Pragmatics. The way that language is used to enhance how the message will be transmitted to a communication partner within a social context. *How* we communicate.

Pre-intentional communicators. The communicative and cognitive developmental stage where the individual is dependent on the communication partner to interpret the communicative behavior.

Preference assessment. The evaluation and analysis of the student's preference based on the frequency with which the student selects a stimulus from an array of options.

Present level of academic achievement and functional performance. An in-depth data-driven objective description of how a student is performing across areas. It also describes how the disability may have an effect on the student's education and participation.

Progressive time delay. The pre-determined time period between the directive and the controlling prompt that will gradually change, guaranteeing a response from the student.

Prompting. An errorless learning instructional strategy to systematically support prior to or as the student attempts to complete a skill.

Rate enhancement. Increasing how quickly a student can communicate by utilizing word prediction, recently used lists, and storing commonly used phrases.

Reception. The ability to receive a message that is being communicated by the speaker during communication.

Receptive communication. The understanding or comprehension of messages and words that have been expressed by a communication partner (e.g., following directions).

Receptive language. Refers to language "input"; describes an individual's ability to receive and interpret ideas being communicated from another's gestures, facial expressions, vocalizations, words, phrases, or sentences.

Reinforcers. An incentive provided to a student after the student has complied with a directive or completed a task with the intention that will support the student learning and the likelihood of the student completing the task.

Representational gestures. Used to communicate an action, object, event, or person and has a specific meaning.

Scanning. A type of indirect selection.

Scripted routines. Detailed procedures or pre-established steps that are embedded in everyday activities.

Self-determination. Demonstrating the ability to make own choices, identify own needs, problem-solve, and to seek the means needed to achieve goals.

Semantic compaction. A patented system based on multi-meaning icons. It uses encoding to increase the number of vocabulary each symbol and symbol combination represents.

Semantics. The consideration of language and its meaning. The *content* of language.

Semantic-syntactic grid display. A display that organizes symbols based on the parts of speech.

Sensory skills. Describes an individual's ability to perceive his or her surroundings or environment; refers to visual, tactile, auditory, gustatory, olfactory, or proprioceptive awareness.

SETT model. A student-centered framework that sets up collaboration between the student, the environment, the task, and the tools that go into setting up implementation of AAC systems and strategies.

Short-term objectives. Benchmarks or milestones to meet the annual goal. Short-term objectives help to plan for generalization of the skill being addressed in the annual goal. The components of a short-term objective include the following: condition, measurable and observable behavior or skill, mastery level, consistency, how it will be measured, and timeframe to be obtained on a smaller scale

Sight word. A sight word is a word that a student should be able to read automatically without decoding it. Sight words are often words seen frequently in text and some may not be decodable using phonetic rules.

Simultaneous prompting. A strategy used with both discrete and chained skills that is based on providing a directive, followed by the least intrusive prompt, after zero-time delay.

Skill. A measurable and observable behavior that is targeted in an annual goal or short-term objective.

Skill barriers. A type of opportunity barrier. Skill barriers are imposed by the communication partner on the student with CCN based on the lack of skills of the communication partner with regard to AAC strategies and AAC systems.

Social competence. The knowledge and skills needed to effectively communicate or interact socially with the communication partner (e.g., initiating, maintaining, terminating). This includes the ability to know when, where, to whom, and how to communicate.

Social relational competence. Essential skills for the development of interpersonal relationships.

Sociolinguistic skills. Pragmatic functions used during a communicative interaction (e.g., requesting, protest).

Sound blending. The ability to blend phonemes or sounds.

Speech. Voluntary neuromuscular behavior that allows humans to express language, or the spoken output of language.

Speech-generating devices. AAC devices that use digitized speech, synthesized speech, or a combination of both in order to relay messages.

Static display. Displays in which the symbols are located on a single page that does not change.

Strategic competence. The knowledge and skills needed to demonstrate coping strategies used to make up for a communicative limitation. This can include overcoming environmental, communicative, and disability related barriers.

Student. AAC implementation is student-centered and takes the individual into consideration.

Symbol. Anything that represents an idea, word, action, or object other than the referent itself.

Symbolic communication. Describes an intentional communication exchange that includes a linguistic code.

Symbol iconicity. How closely a picture, manual sign, gesture, or another symbol is connected to the attached message.

Syntax.   The manner in which sentences are structured.

Synthesized speech.   Artificially produced speech based on phonemes using a mathematical algorithm.

Tasks.   All of the activities that occur in each of the environments in which the device will be used.

Taxonomic grid display.   A display in which symbols are organized into generic categories such as people, places, feelings, foods, etc.

Text to speech.   Apps that allow a user to input text and convert it into spoken communication.

Time delay.   A pre-determined time used to support students after a directive has been provided which helps to systematically fade the use of prompts during instructional activities.

Time sampling.   A type of interval recording that tracks behavior only if it occurs at the end of the selected interval.

Tool.   All of the tools and interventions required to train a student on the AAC system.

Transdisciplinary team.   A team of specialists from multiple areas of expertise that share information and provide training among team members. This team sets holistic goals to enhance and reinforce team identified target skills/behaviors.

Translucent symbol.   A symbol whose referent can be determined when given additional information.

Transmission.   The mechanics of relaying a message.

Transparent symbol.   A symbol that is easily guessable and closely resembles its referent.

Unaided communication systems.   Communication systems that do not require additional tools or equipment beyond one's body. That is, messages are expressed through facial expressions, gestures, and manual signs.

Use.   Domain of language that refers to how a person uses language to functionally meet his or her wants and needs (e.g., pragmatics).

Verbal prompts.   A verbal support to help the student complete the task, beyond the initial directive.

Visual prompts.   The use of visual support that is exclusively provided as visual guide to complete a task.

Visual schedule.   A schedule or a task analysis that is represented with objects, photographs, or line drawings.

Visual scene display.   A display that organizes symbols within a photograph or drawing of a place or scene.

Visual supports.   An inexpensive, non-intrusive, natural means to provide students with a visual with the purpose of making language and information more concrete through the use of objects, photographs, words, or line drawings.

Vocabulary. Refers to the language represented within the AAC system of the individual on the basis of age, social interests, expressed gender, or environment.

Vocabulary selection. Deciding what words should be included in the student's AAC system.

Vocalizations. Speech production, which may be voluntary or involuntary, made by individuals who may not have the linguistic competency to communicate. Vocalizations can take the form of grunts, word approximations, and utterances.

Whole interval recording. A type of interval recording that records behavior only if it occurs throughout the entire pre-determined interval.

Word prediction. Guessing the next word in a sentence based on what has already been selected; a method for rate enhancement.

INDEX

Note: Page numbers in *italic* indicate a figure and page numbers in **bold** indicate a table on the corresponding page.

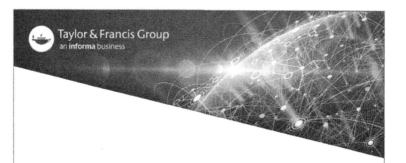

Made in United States
North Haven, CT
05 September 2023

41181917R00183